THE LION OF RORA

AN ONI PRESS PUBLICATION

THE LION OF RORA

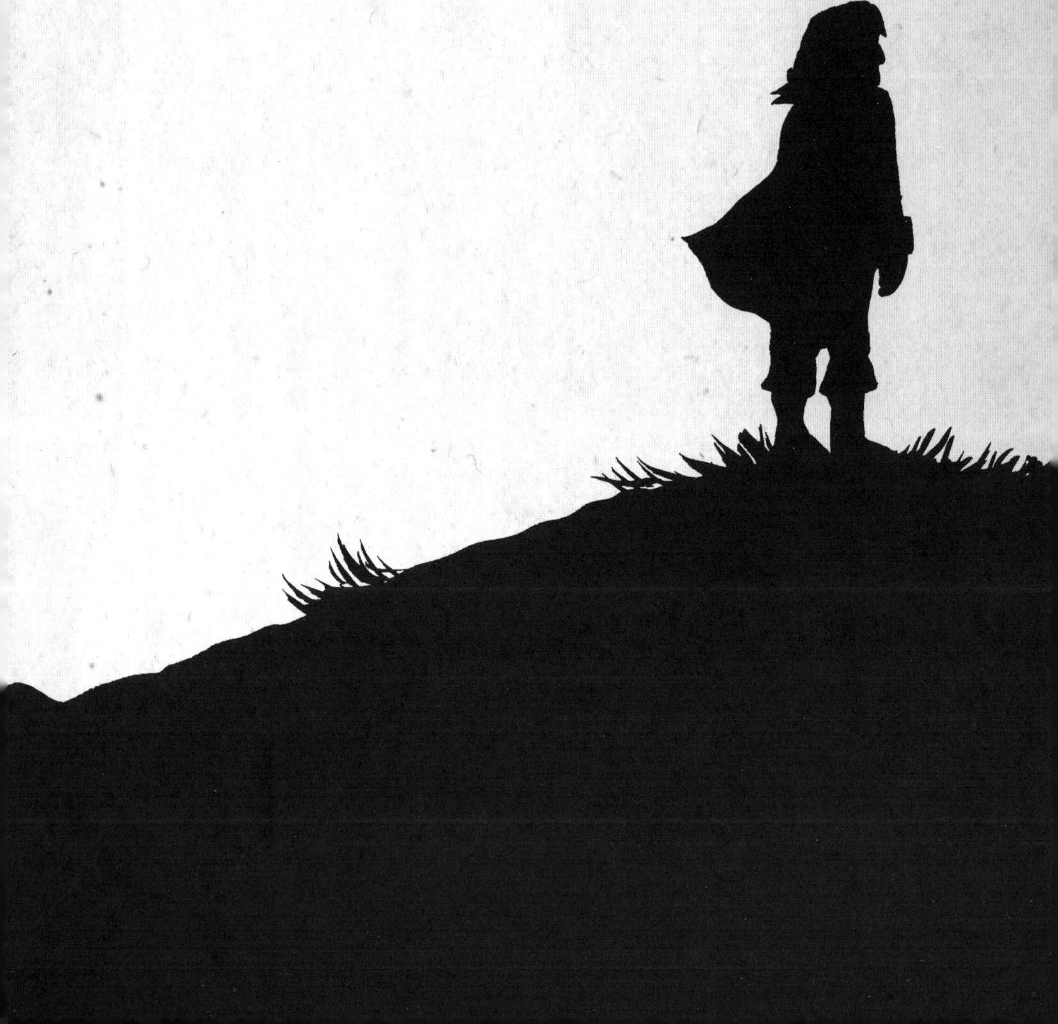

WRITTEN BY

CHRISTOS GAGE

RUTH FLETCHER GAGE

ILLUSTRATED BY

JACKIE LEWIS

LETTERED BY

JENNY VY TRAN

EDITED BY

JAMES LUCAS JONES

BOOK DESIGN BY

HILARY THOMPSON

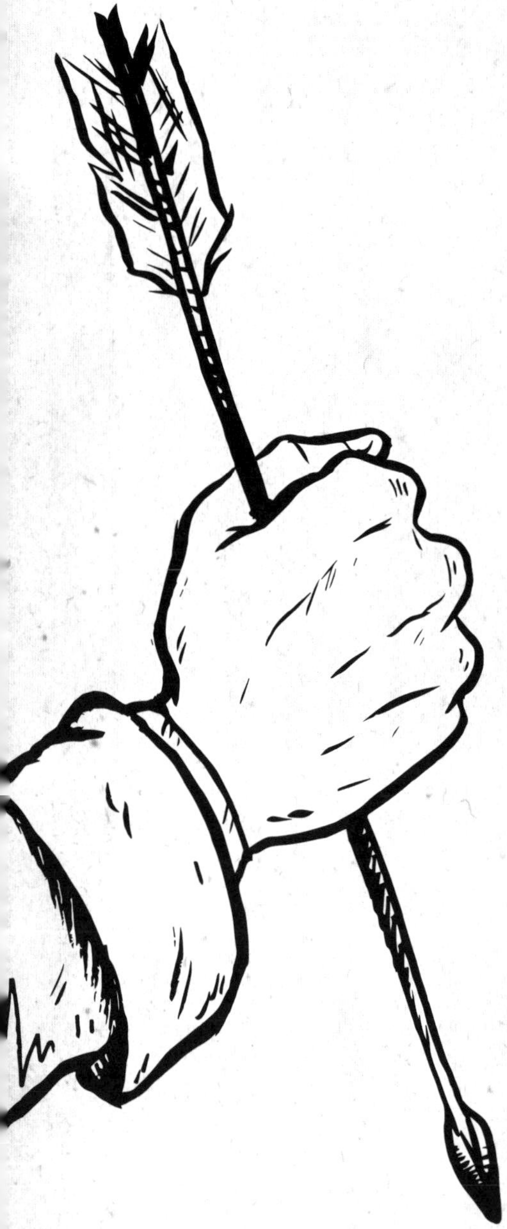

PUBLISHED BY ONI PRESS, INC.

JOE NOZEMACK, PUBLISHER

JAMES LUCAS JONES, EDITOR IN CHIEF

CHEYENNE ALLOTT, DIRECTOR OF SALES

FRED RECKLING, DIRECTOR OF PUBLICITY

TROY LOOK, PRODUCTION MANAGER

HILARY THOMPSON, GRAPHIC DESIGNER

JARED JONES, PRODUCTION ASSISTANT

CHARLIE CHU, SENIOR EDITOR

ROBIN HERRERA, EDITOR

ARI YARWOOD, ASSOCIATE EDITOR

BRAD ROOKS, INVENTORY COORDINATOR

JUNG LEE, OFFICE ASSISTANT

ONIPRESS.COM
FACEBOOK.COM/ONIPRESS
TWITTER.COM/ONIPRESS
ONIPRESS.TUMBLR.COM
INSTAGRAM.COM/ONIPRESS

FIRST EDITION: AUGUST 2015

ISBN 978-1-62010-248-0
EISBN 978-1-62010-249-7

PRINTED IN CHINA.

LIBRARY OF CONGRESS CONTROL NUMBER: 2015931033

1 2 3 4 5 6 7 8 9 10

For my mother, Rheta Micol Robinson, whose dedication to Waldensian history made this book possible.

RUTH

—

For Ruth. I love you.

CHRISTOS

—

For everyone who ever taught me to stand up for myself.

JACKIE

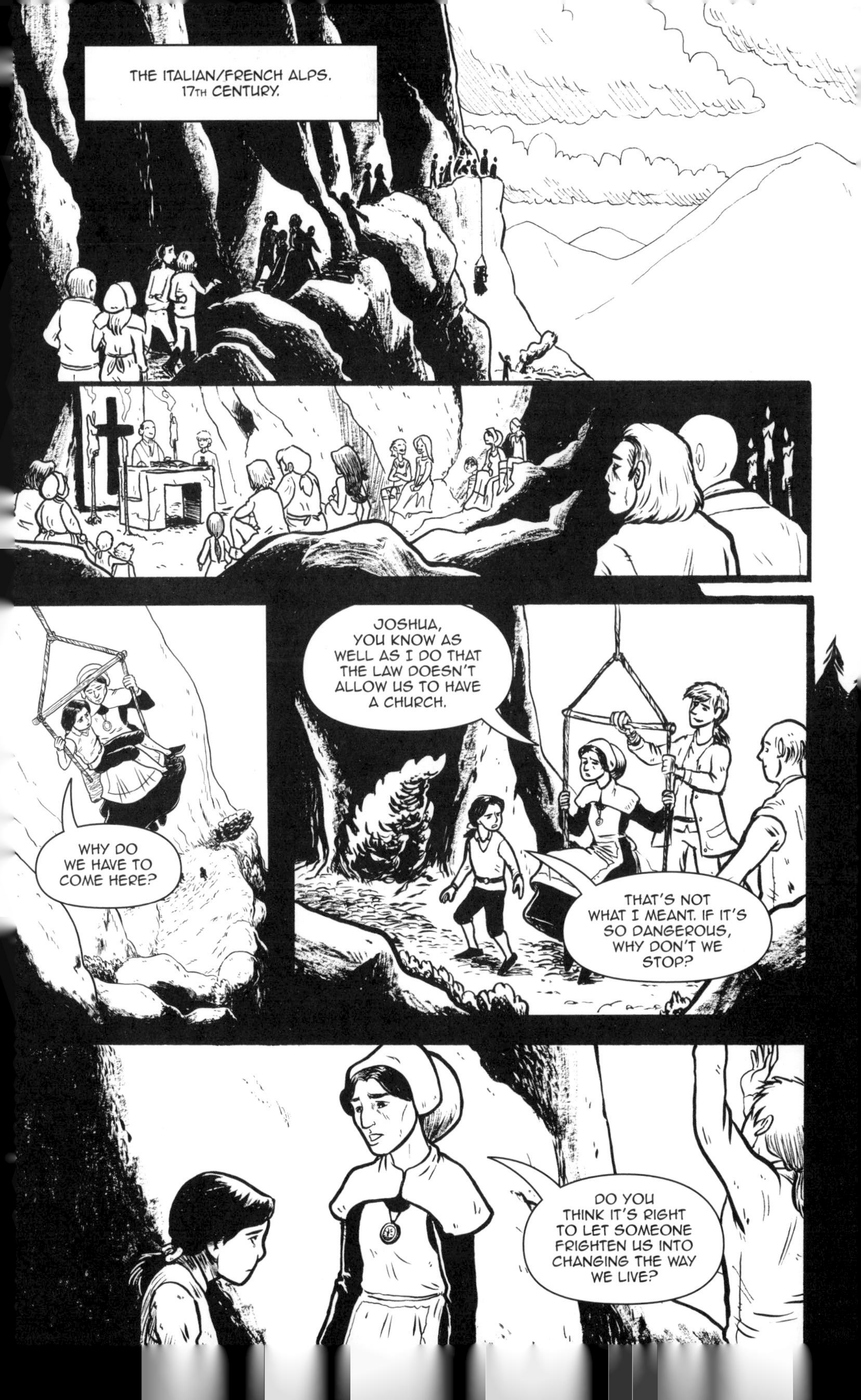
THE ITALIAN/FRENCH ALPS. 17TH CENTURY.
WHY DO WE HAVE TO COME HERE?
JOSHUA, YOU KNOW AS WELL AS I DO THAT THE LAW DOESN'T ALLOW US TO HAVE A CHURCH.
THAT'S NOT WHAT I MEANT. IF IT'S SO DANGEROUS, WHY DON'T WE STOP?
DO YOU THINK IT'S RIGHT TO LET SOMEONE FRIGHTEN US INTO CHANGING THE WAY WE LIVE?

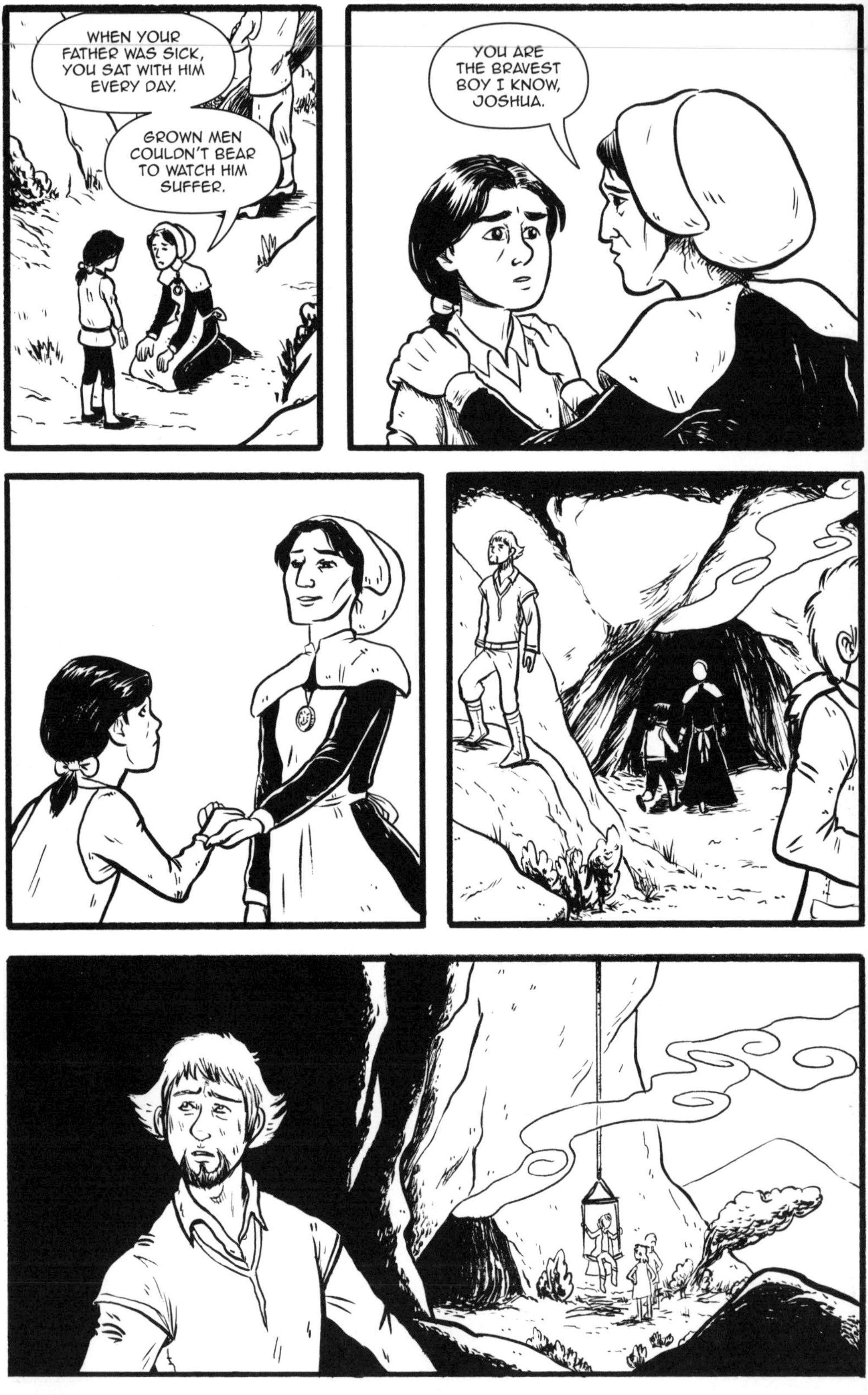
WHEN YOUR FATHER WAS SICK, YOU SAT WITH HIM EVERY DAY.
GROWN MEN COULDN'T BEAR TO WATCH HIM SUFFER.
YOU ARE THE BRAVEST BOY I KNOW, JOSHUA.

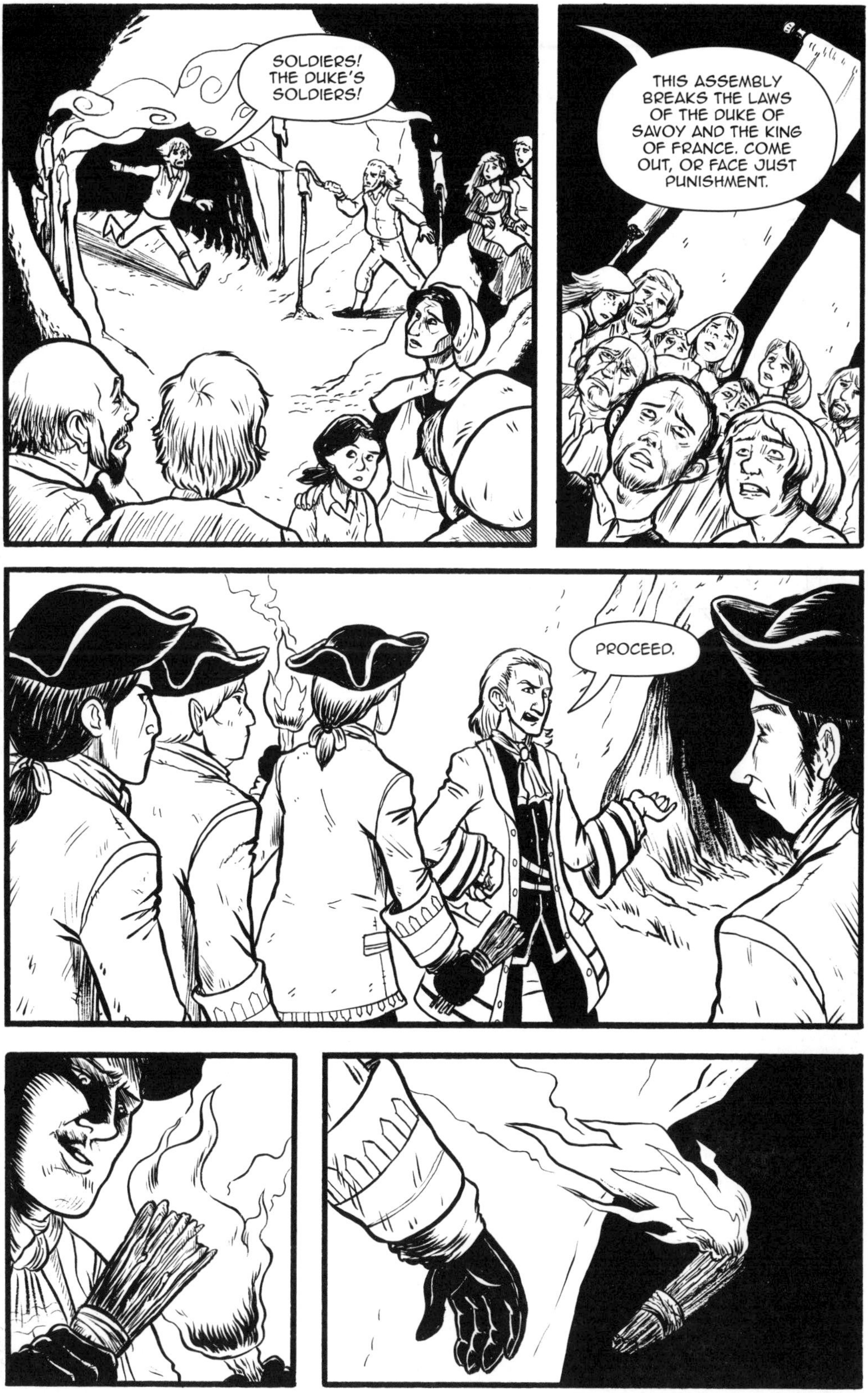
SOLDIERS! THE DUKE'S SOLDIERS!
THIS ASSEMBLY BREAKS THE LAWS OF THE DUKE OF SAVOY AND THE KING OF FRANCE. COME OUT, OR FACE JUST PUNISHMENT.
PROCEED.

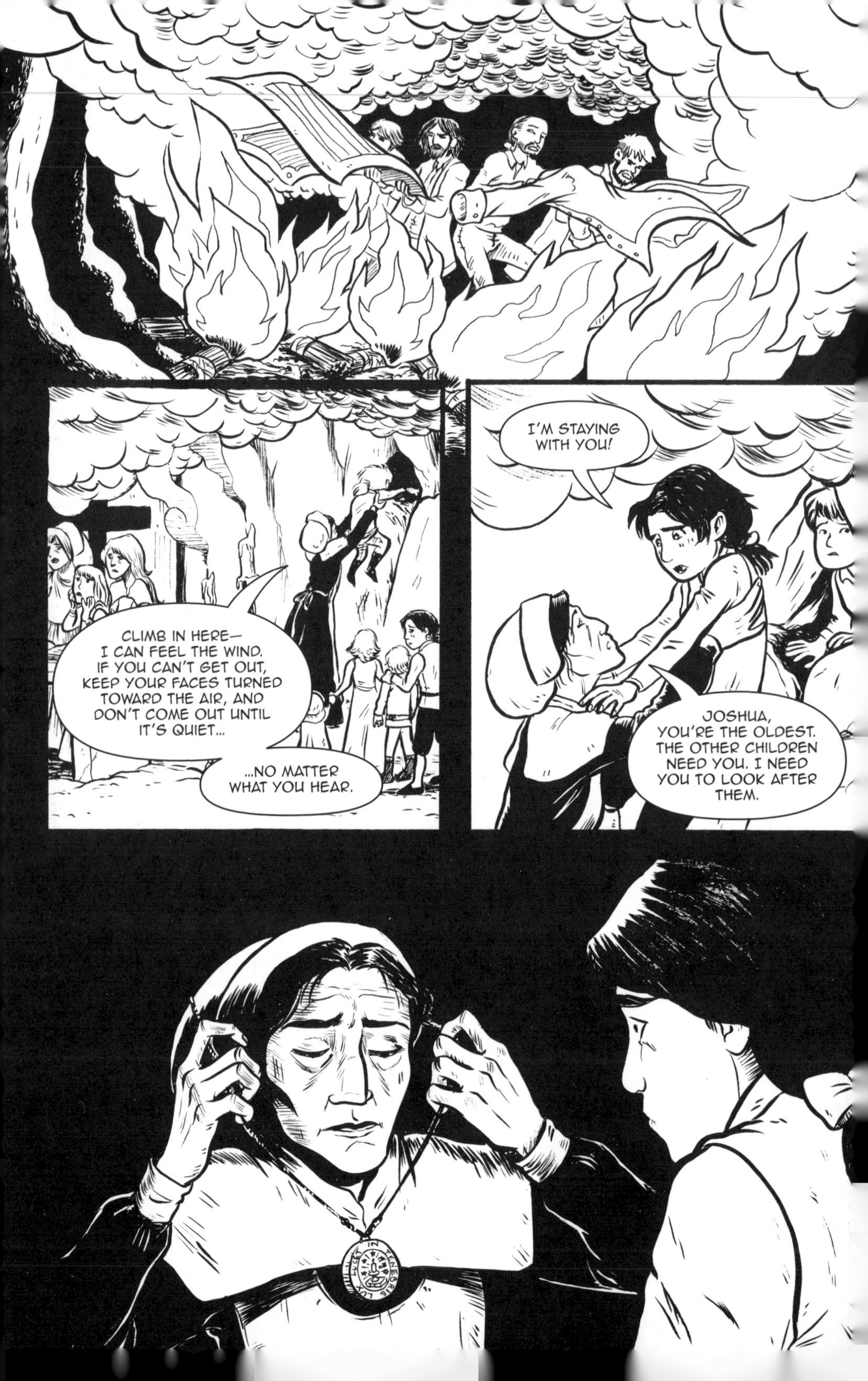
CLIMB IN HERE— I CAN FEEL THE WIND. IF YOU CAN'T GET OUT, KEEP YOUR FACES TURNED TOWARD THE AIR, AND DON'T COME OUT UNTIL IT'S QUIET...
...NO MATTER WHAT YOU HEAR.
I'M STAYING WITH YOU!
JOSHUA, YOU'RE THE OLDEST. THE OTHER CHILDREN NEED YOU. I NEED YOU TO LOOK AFTER THEM.

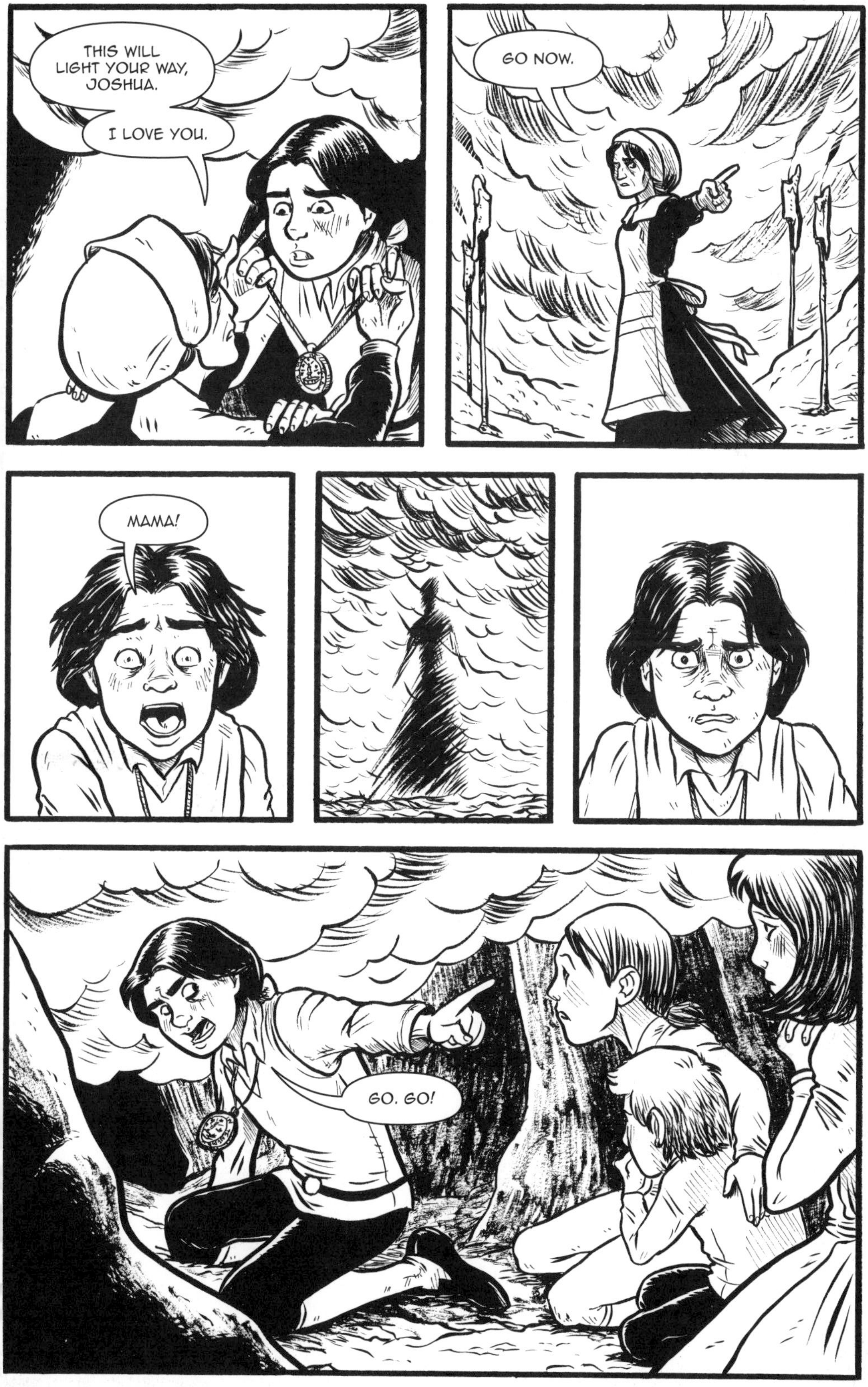
THIS WILL LIGHT YOUR WAY, JOSHUA.
I LOVE YOU.
GO NOW.
MAMA!
GO. GO!

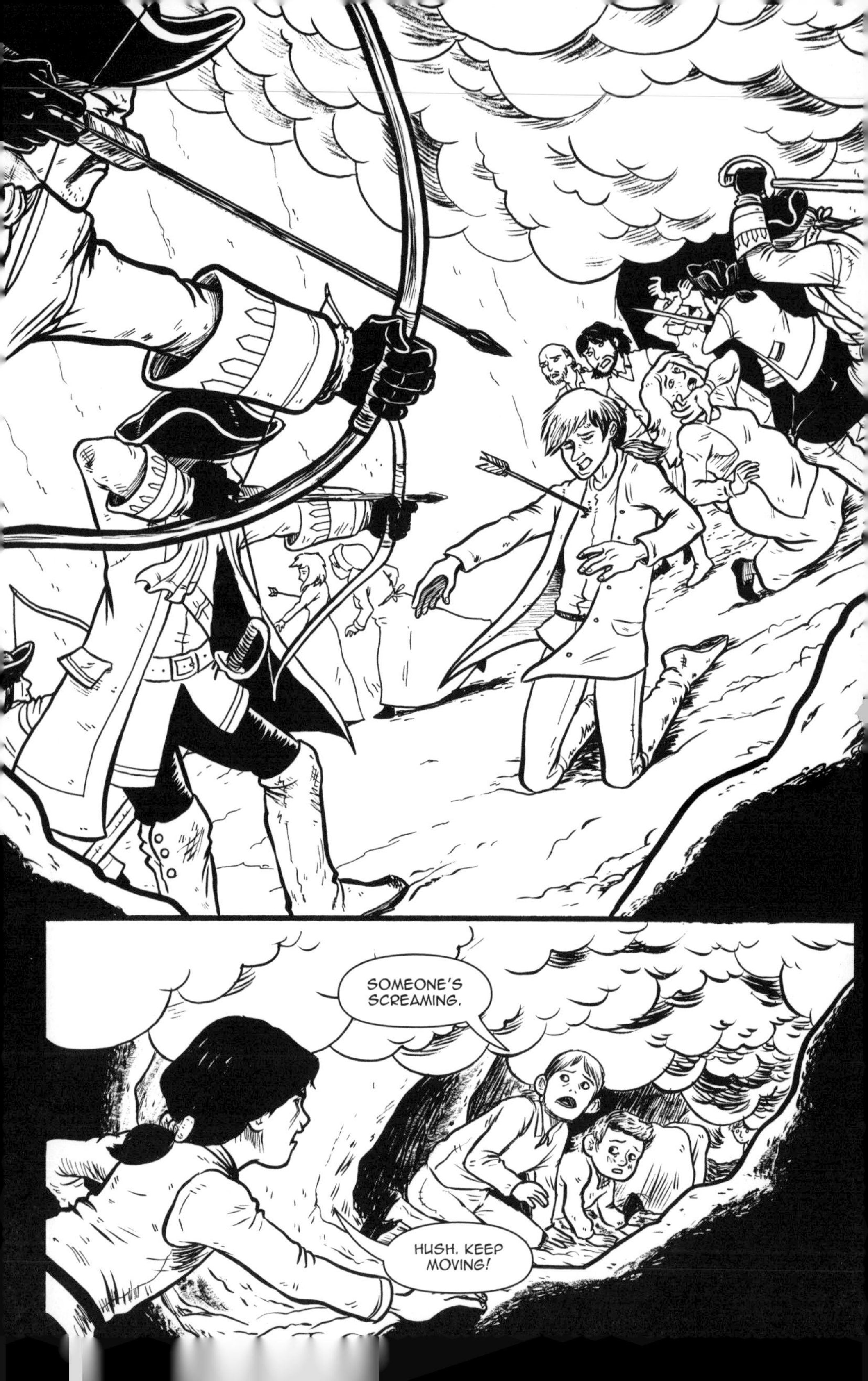
SOMEONE'S SCREAMING.
HUSH. KEEP MOVING!

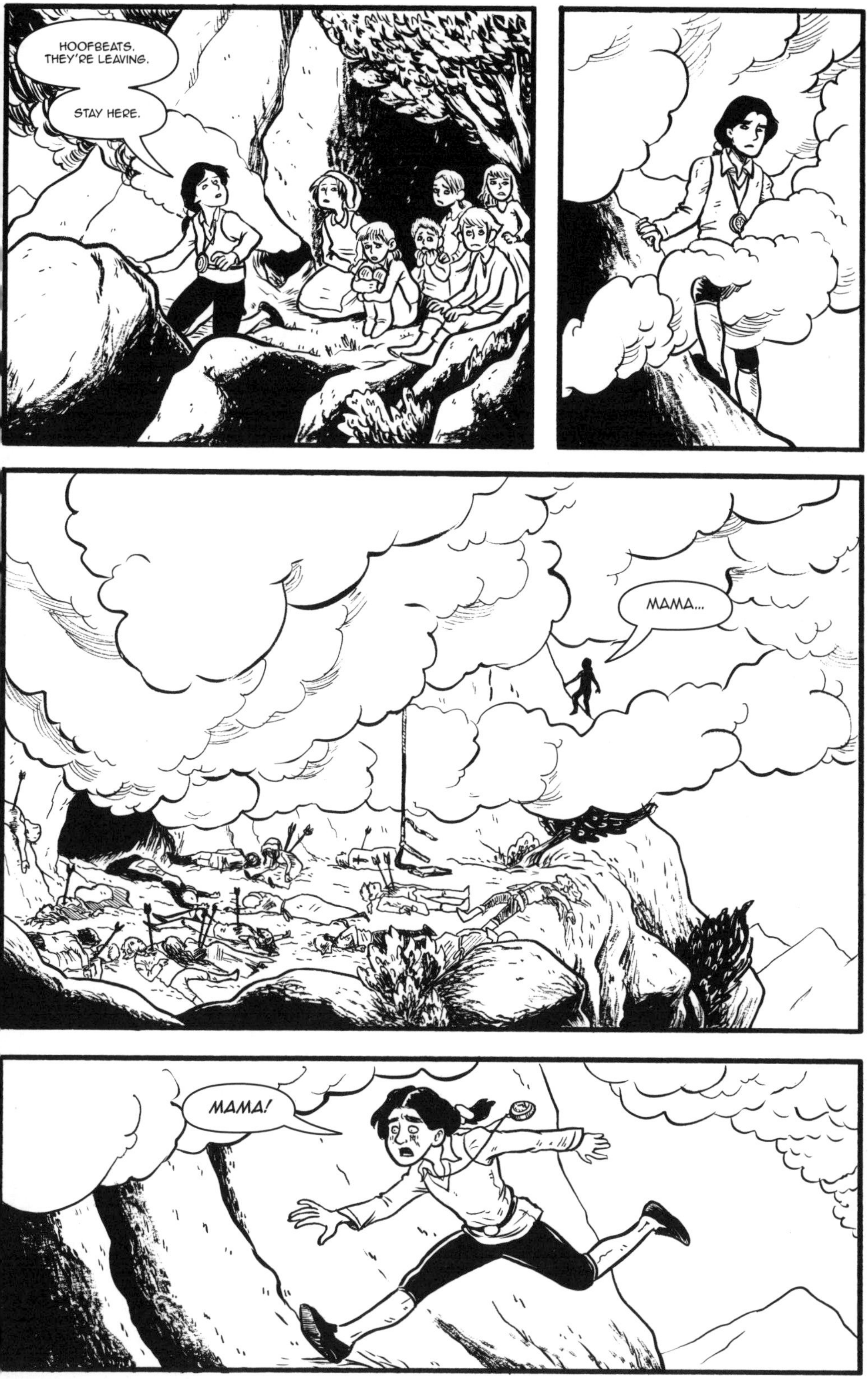
HOOFBEATS. THEY'RE LEAVING.
STAY HERE.
MAMA...
MAMA!

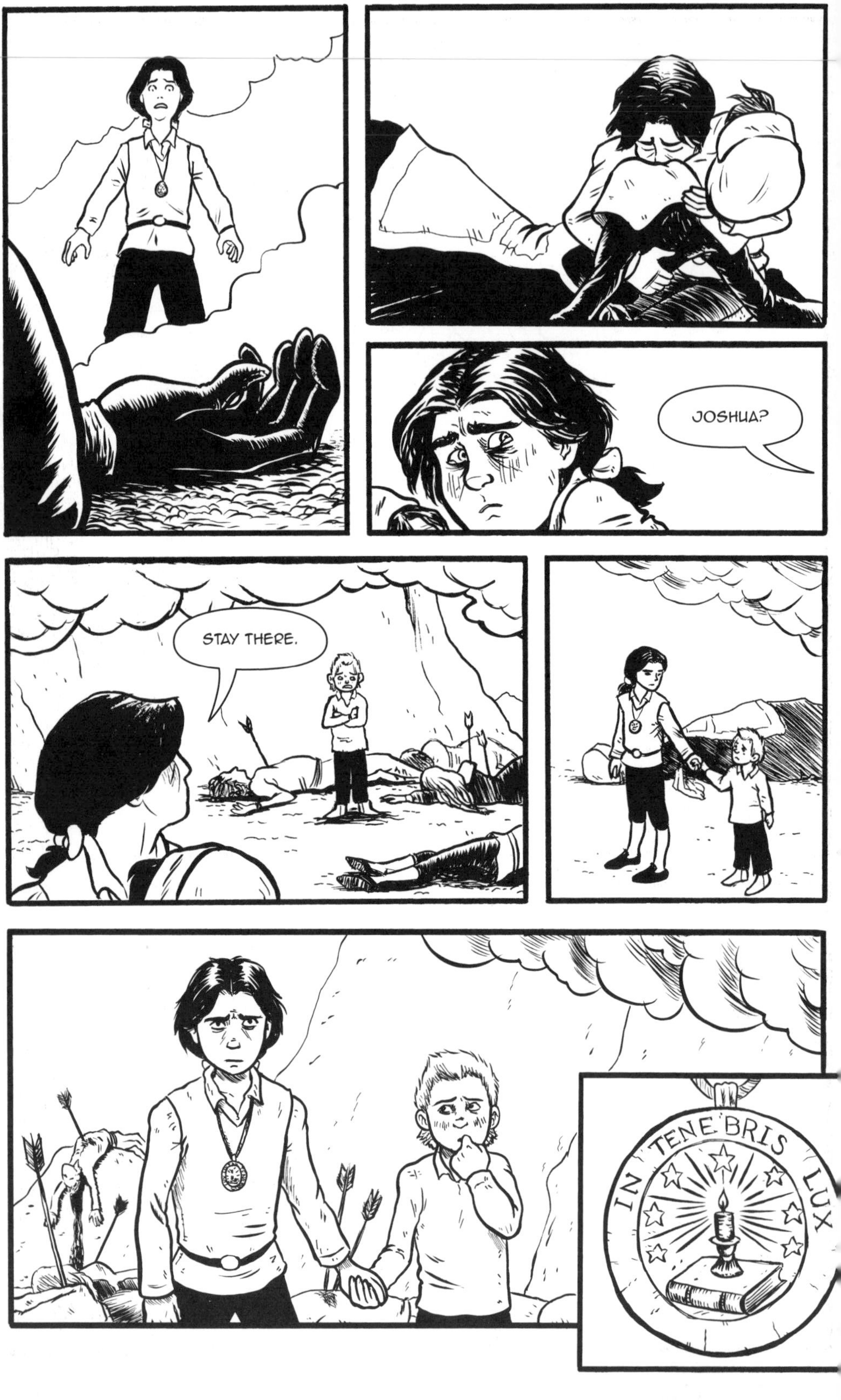
JOSHUA?
STAY THERE.
IN TENEBRIS LUX

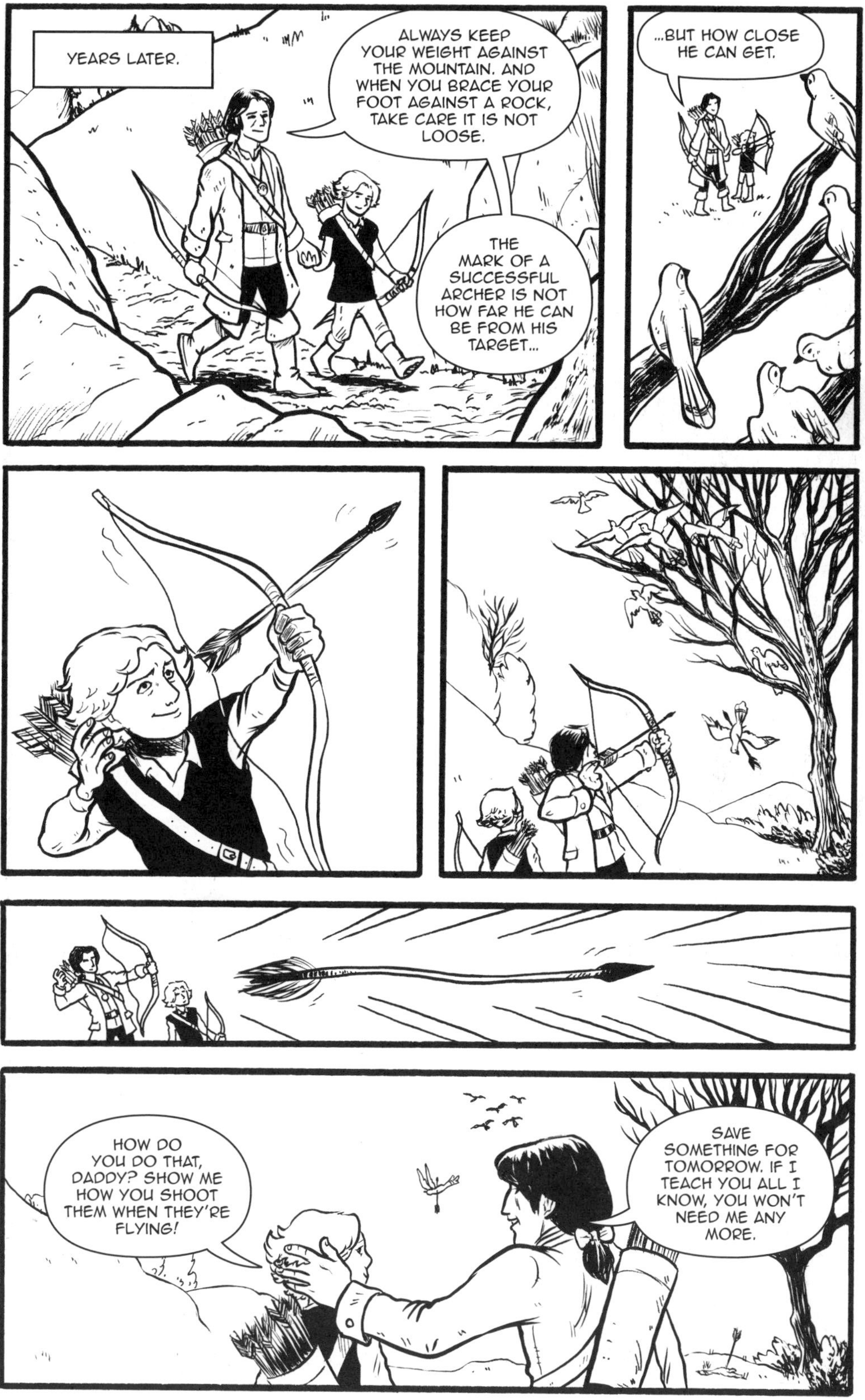
YEARS LATER.
ALWAYS KEEP YOUR WEIGHT AGAINST THE MOUNTAIN. AND WHEN YOU BRACE YOUR FOOT AGAINST A ROCK, TAKE CARE IT IS NOT LOOSE.
THE MARK OF A SUCCESSFUL ARCHER IS NOT HOW FAR HE CAN BE FROM HIS TARGET...
...BUT HOW CLOSE HE CAN GET.
HOW DO YOU DO THAT, DADDY? SHOW ME HOW YOU SHOOT THEM WHEN THEY'RE FLYING!
SAVE SOMETHING FOR TOMORROW. IF I TEACH YOU ALL I KNOW, YOU WON'T NEED ME ANY MORE.

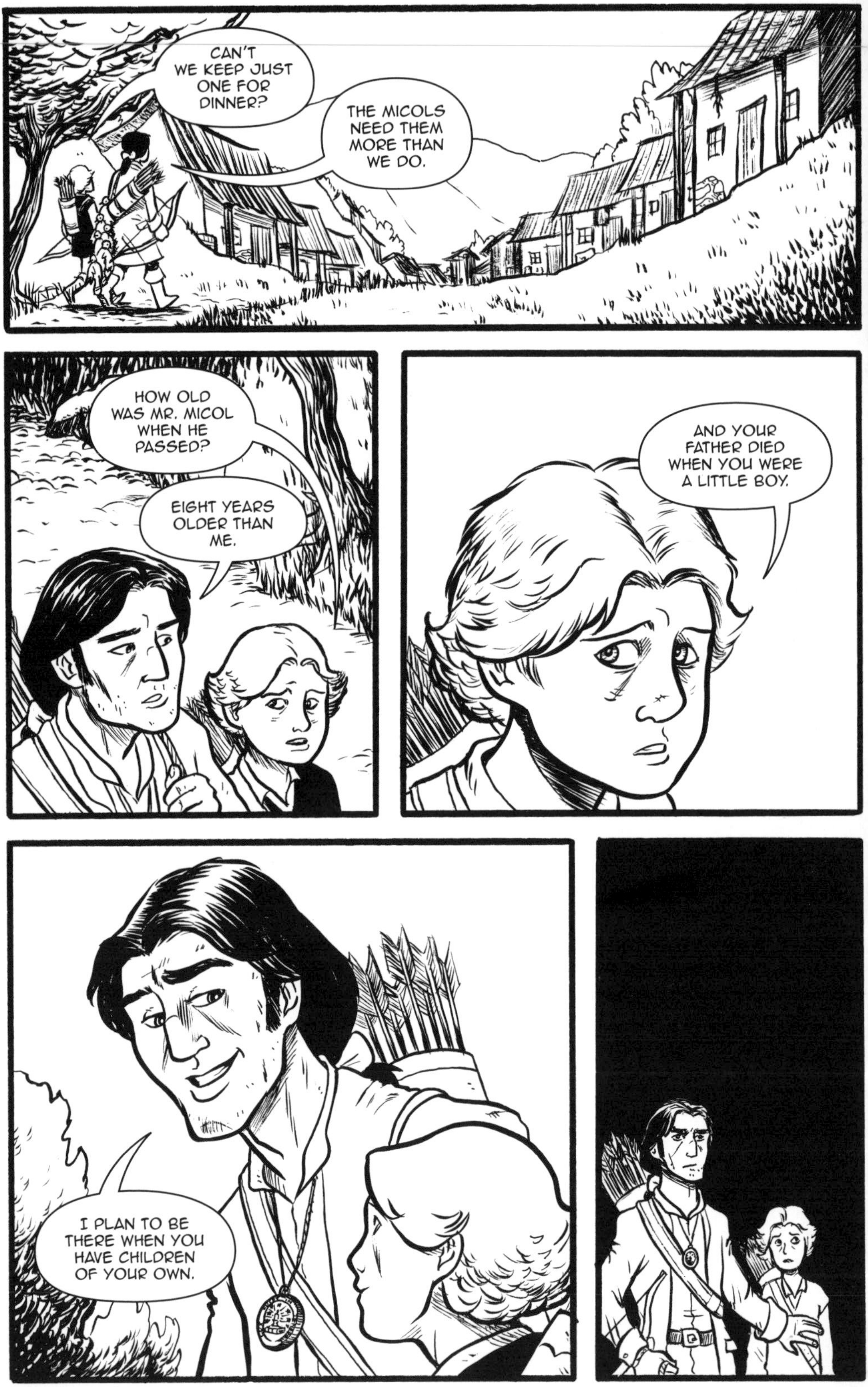
CAN'T WE KEEP JUST ONE FOR DINNER?
THE MICOLS NEED THEM MORE THAN WE DO.
HOW OLD WAS MR. MICOL WHEN HE PASSED?
EIGHT YEARS OLDER THAN ME.
AND YOUR FATHER DIED WHEN YOU WERE A LITTLE BOY.
I PLAN TO BE THERE WHEN YOU HAVE CHILDREN OF YOUR OWN.

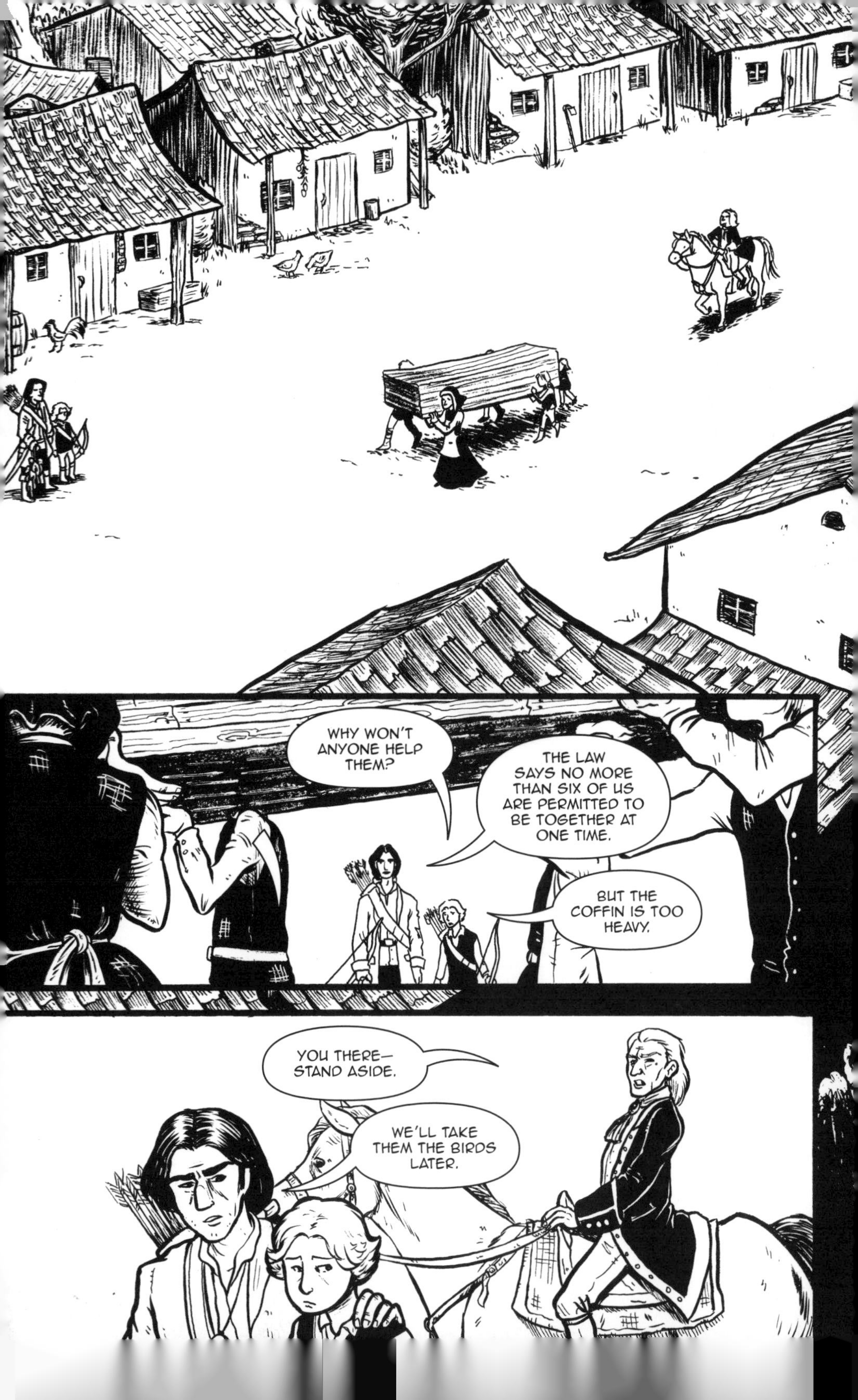
WHY WON'T ANYONE HELP THEM?
THE LAW SAYS NO MORE THAN SIX OF US ARE PERMITTED TO BE TOGETHER AT ONE TIME.
BUT THE COFFIN IS TOO HEAVY.
YOU THERE— STAND ASIDE.
WE'LL TAKE THEM THE BIRDS LATER.

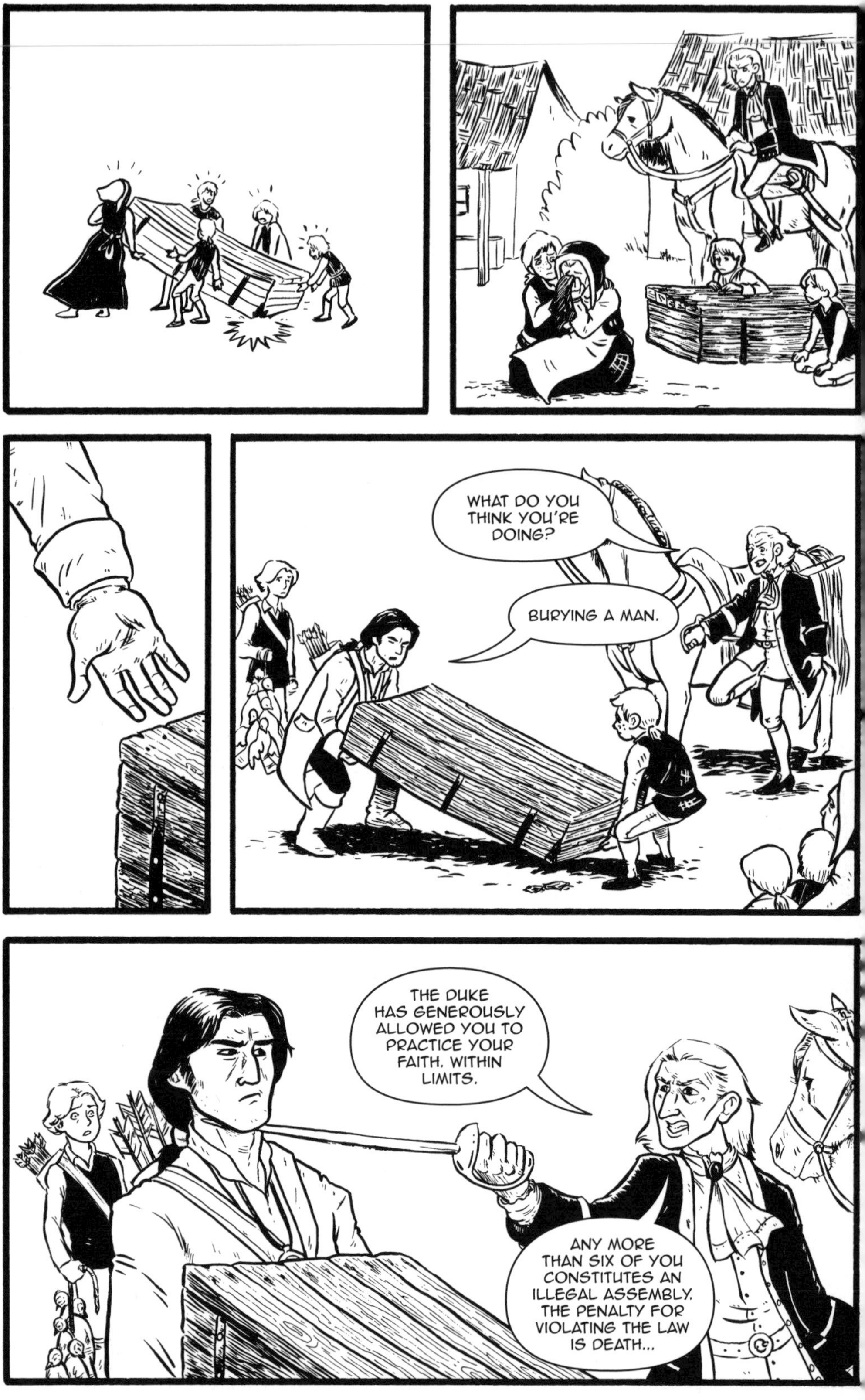
WHAT DO YOU THINK YOU'RE DOING?
BURYING A MAN.
THE DUKE HAS GENEROUSLY ALLOWED YOU TO PRACTICE YOUR FAITH. WITHIN LIMITS.
ANY MORE THAN SIX OF YOU CONSTITUTES AN ILLEGAL ASSEMBLY. THE PENALTY FOR VIOLATING THE LAW IS DEATH...

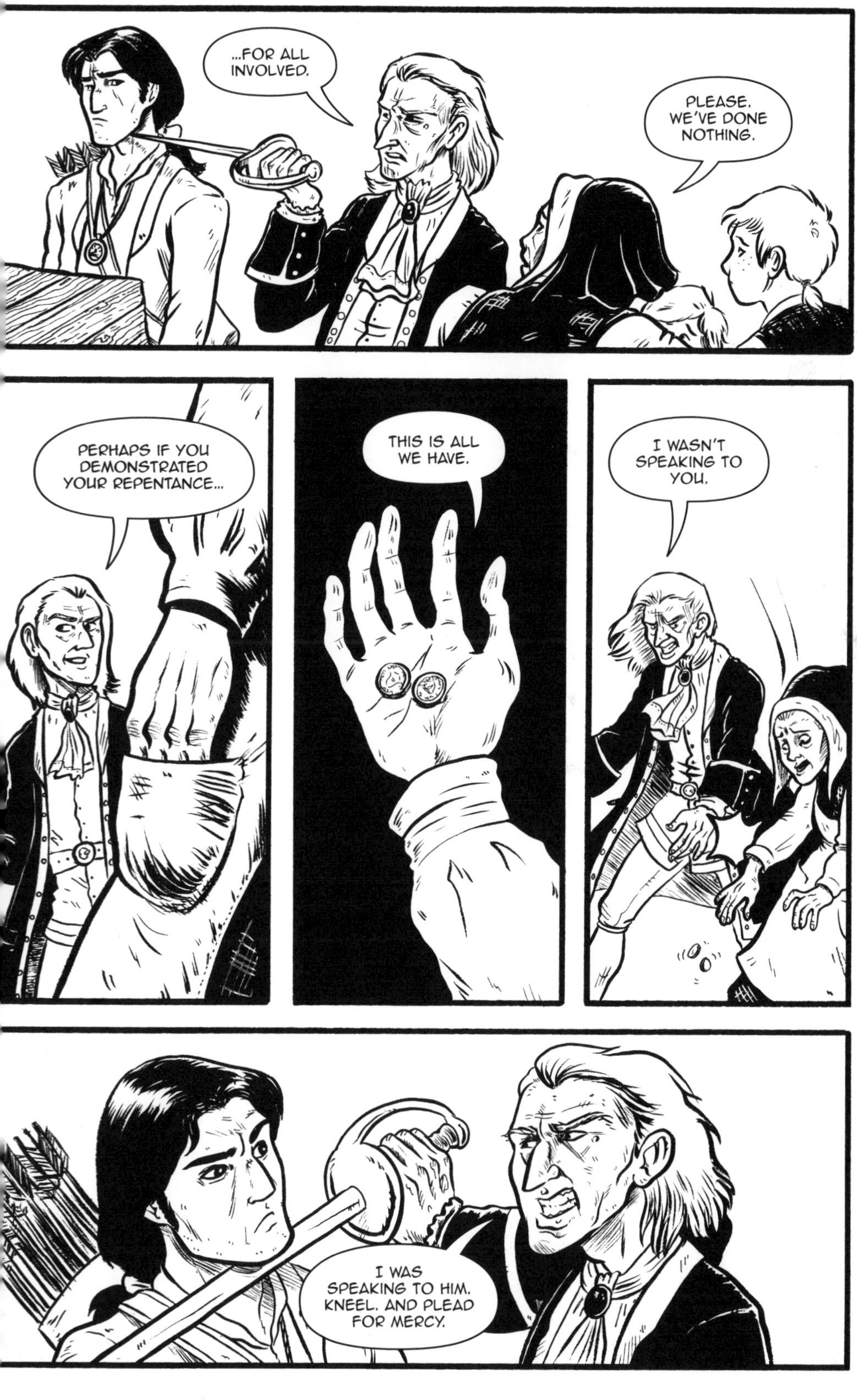
...FOR ALL INVOLVED.
PLEASE. WE'VE DONE NOTHING.
PERHAPS IF YOU DEMONSTRATED YOUR REPENTANCE...
THIS IS ALL WE HAVE.
I WASN'T SPEAKING TO YOU.
I WAS SPEAKING TO HIM. KNEEL. AND PLEAD FOR MERCY.

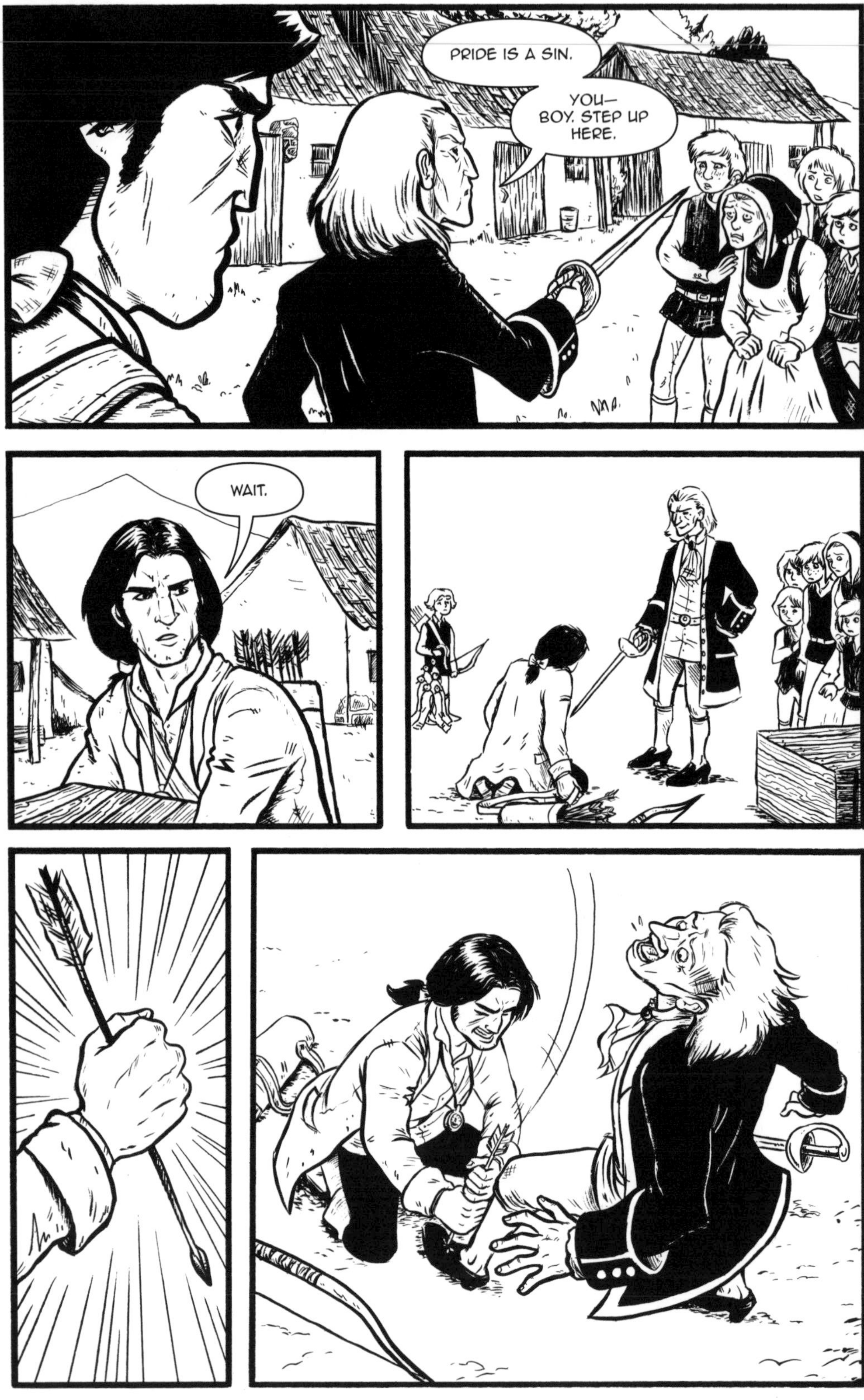
PRIDE IS A SIN.
YOU— BOY. STEP UP HERE.
WAIT.

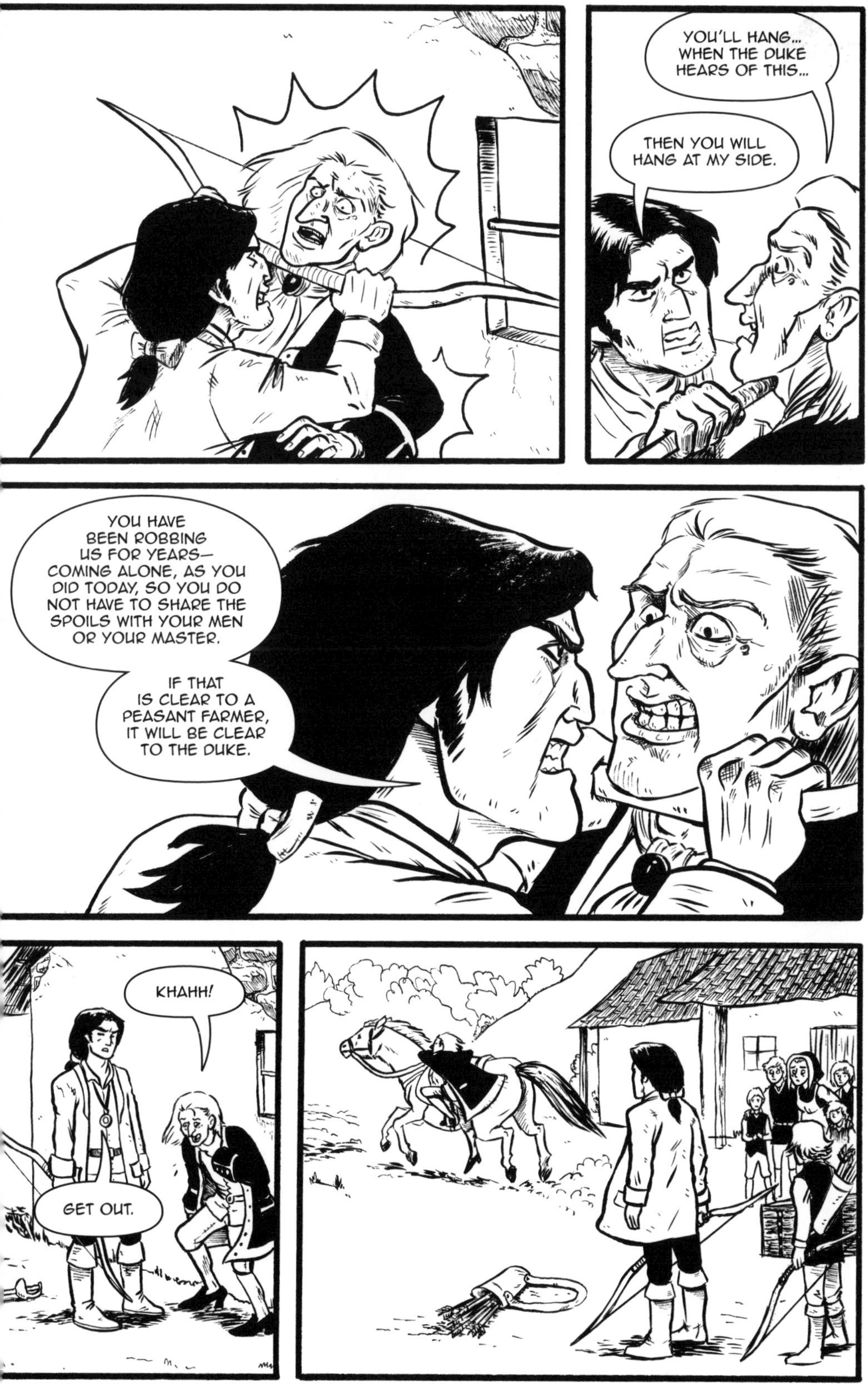
YOU'LL HANG... WHEN THE DUKE HEARS OF THIS...
THEN YOU WILL HANG AT MY SIDE.
YOU HAVE BEEN ROBBING US FOR YEARS— COMING ALONE, AS YOU DID TODAY, SO YOU DO NOT HAVE TO SHARE THE SPOILS WITH YOUR MEN OR YOUR MASTER.
IF THAT IS CLEAR TO A PEASANT FARMER, IT WILL BE CLEAR TO THE DUKE.
KHAHH!
GET OUT.

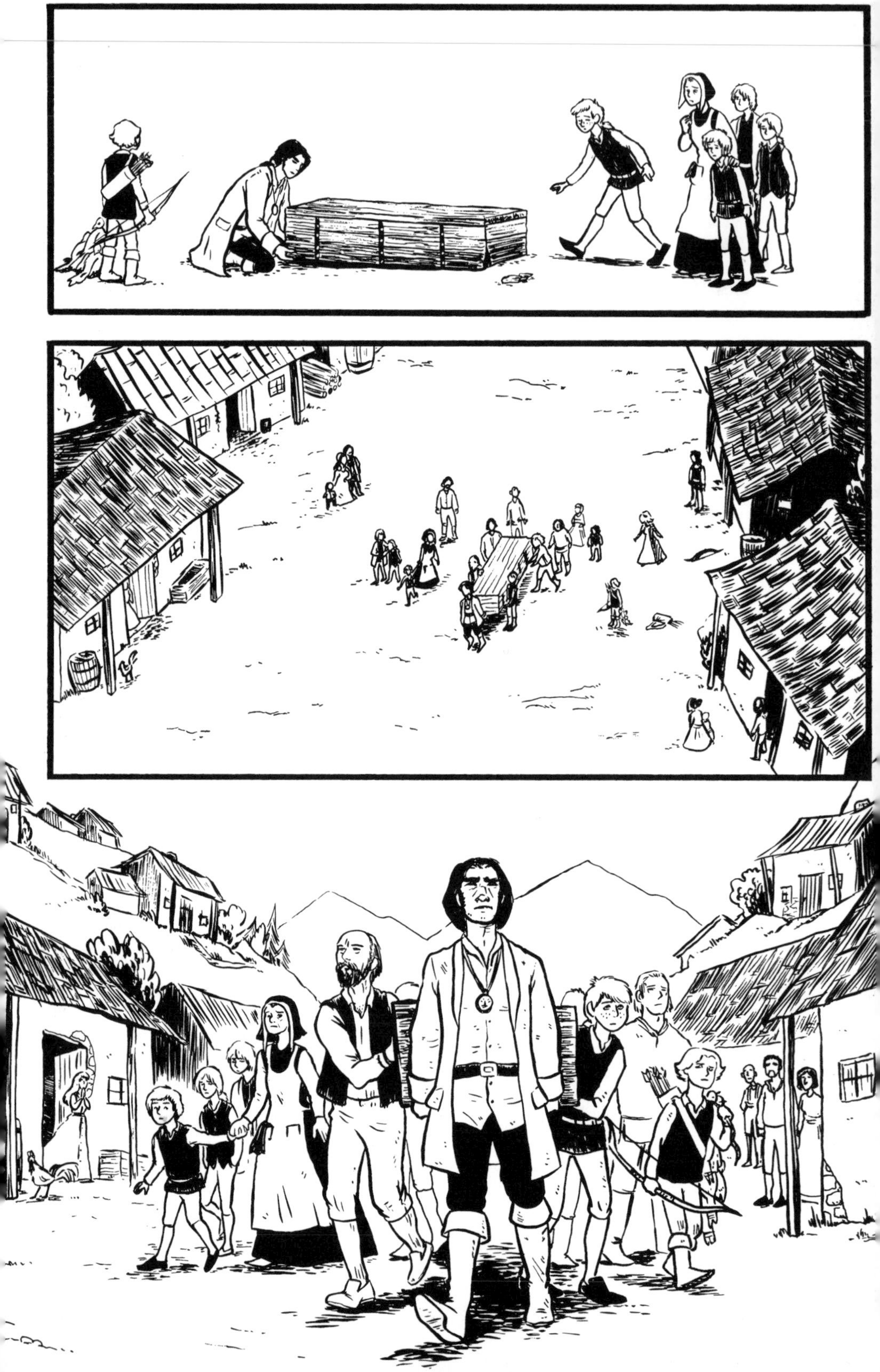

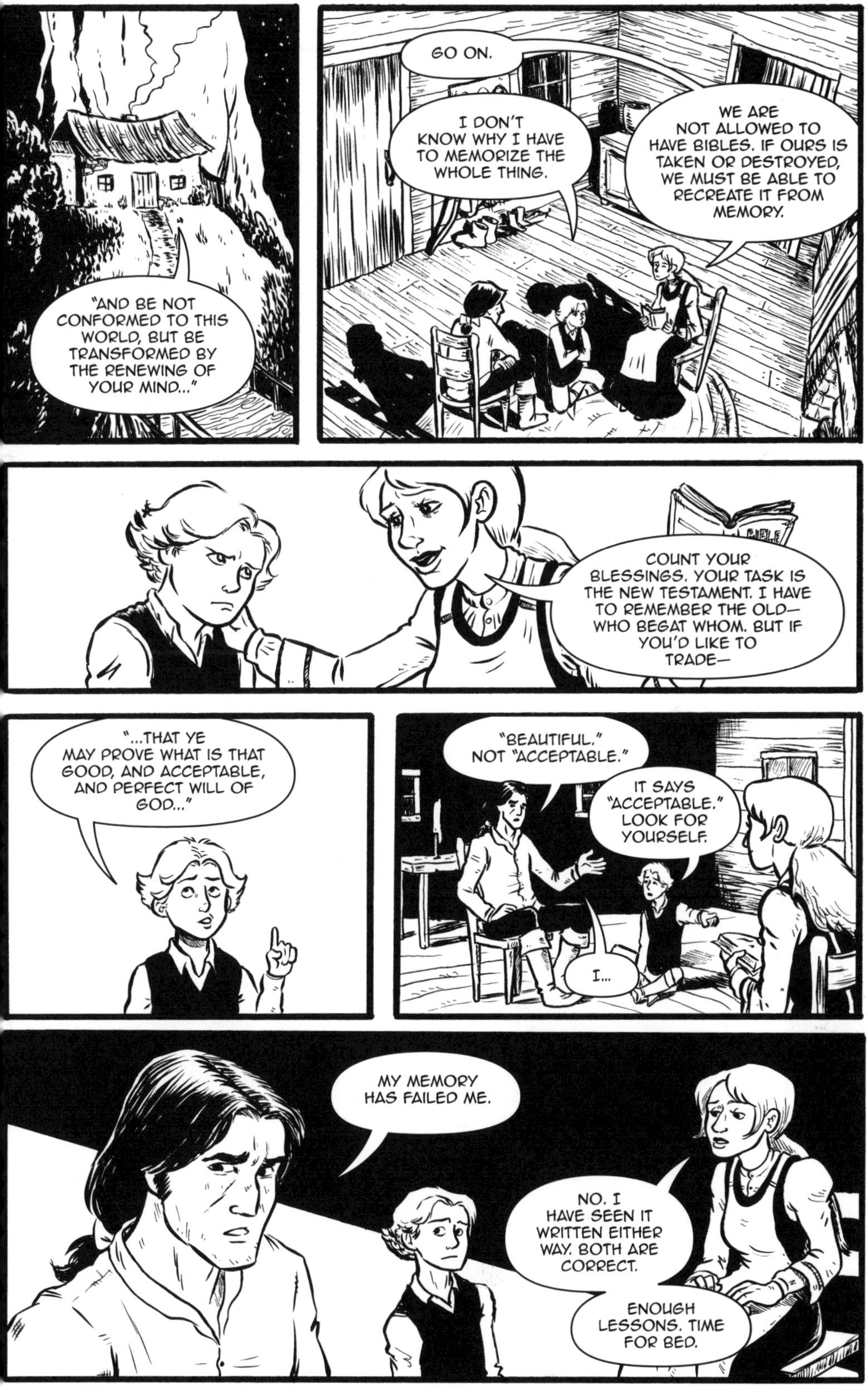
"AND BE NOT CONFORMED TO THIS WORLD, BUT BE TRANSFORMED BY THE RENEWING OF YOUR MIND..."
GO ON.
I DON'T KNOW WHY I HAVE TO MEMORIZE THE WHOLE THING.
WE ARE NOT ALLOWED TO HAVE BIBLES. IF OURS IS TAKEN OR DESTROYED, WE MUST BE ABLE TO RECREATE IT FROM MEMORY.
COUNT YOUR BLESSINGS. YOUR TASK IS THE NEW TESTAMENT. I HAVE TO REMEMBER THE OLD— WHO BEGAT WHOM. BUT IF YOU'D LIKE TO TRADE—
"...THAT YE MAY PROVE WHAT IS THAT GOOD, AND ACCEPTABLE, AND PERFECT WILL OF GOD..."
"BEAUTIFUL." NOT "ACCEPTABLE."
IT SAYS "ACCEPTABLE." LOOK FOR YOURSELF.
I...
MY MEMORY HAS FAILED ME.
NO. I HAVE SEEN IT WRITTEN EITHER WAY. BOTH ARE CORRECT.
ENOUGH LESSONS. TIME FOR BED.

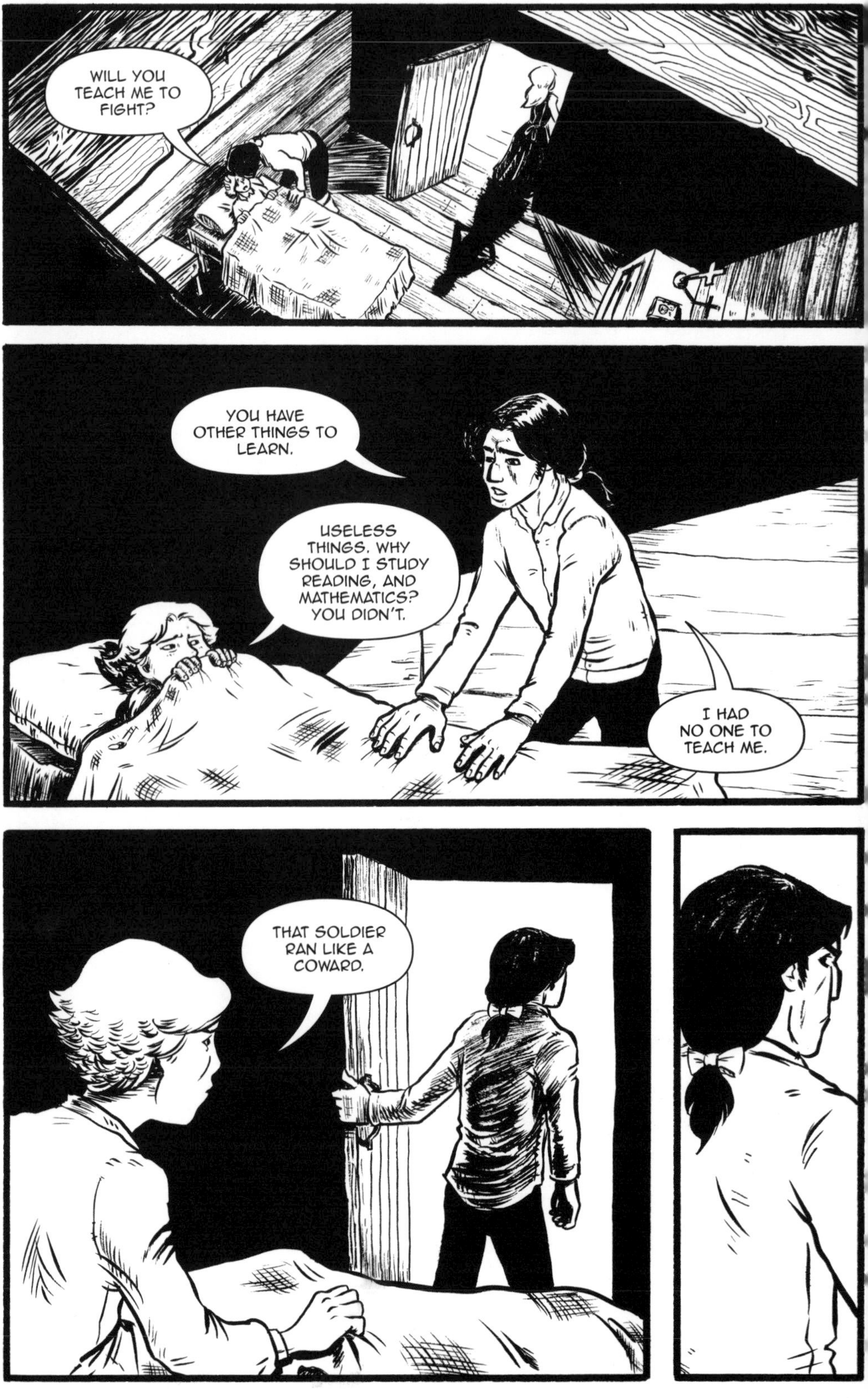
WILL YOU TEACH ME TO FIGHT?
YOU HAVE OTHER THINGS TO LEARN.
USELESS THINGS. WHY SHOULD I STUDY READING, AND MATHEMATICS? YOU DIDN'T.
I HAD NO ONE TO TEACH ME.
THAT SOLDIER RAN LIKE A COWARD.

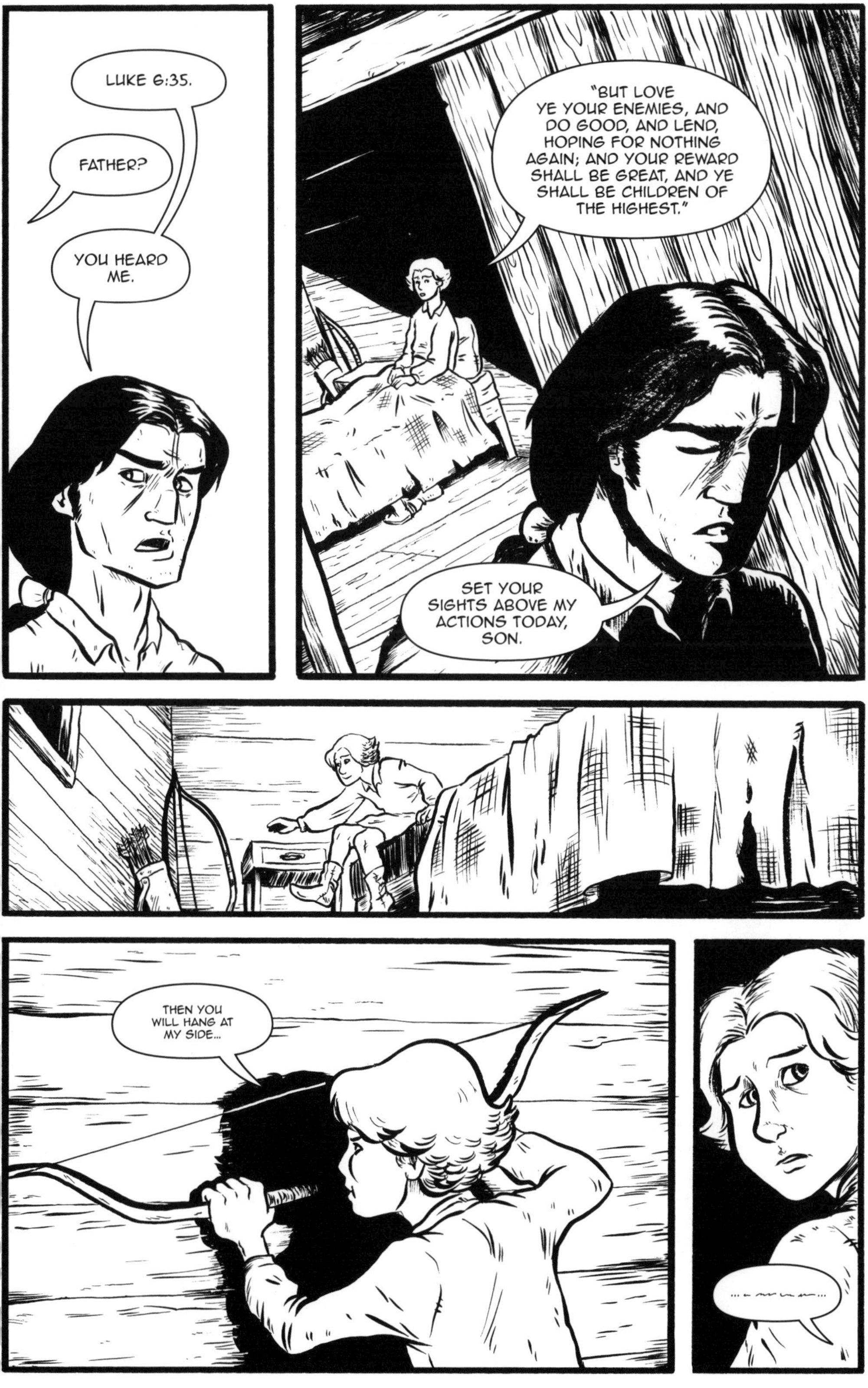
LUKE 6:35.
FATHER?
YOU HEARD ME.
"BUT LOVE YE YOUR ENEMIES, AND DO GOOD, AND LEND, HOPING FOR NOTHING AGAIN; AND YOUR REWARD SHALL BE GREAT, AND YE SHALL BE CHILDREN OF THE HIGHEST."
SET YOUR SIGHTS ABOVE MY ACTIONS TODAY, SON.
THEN YOU WILL HANG AT MY SIDE...

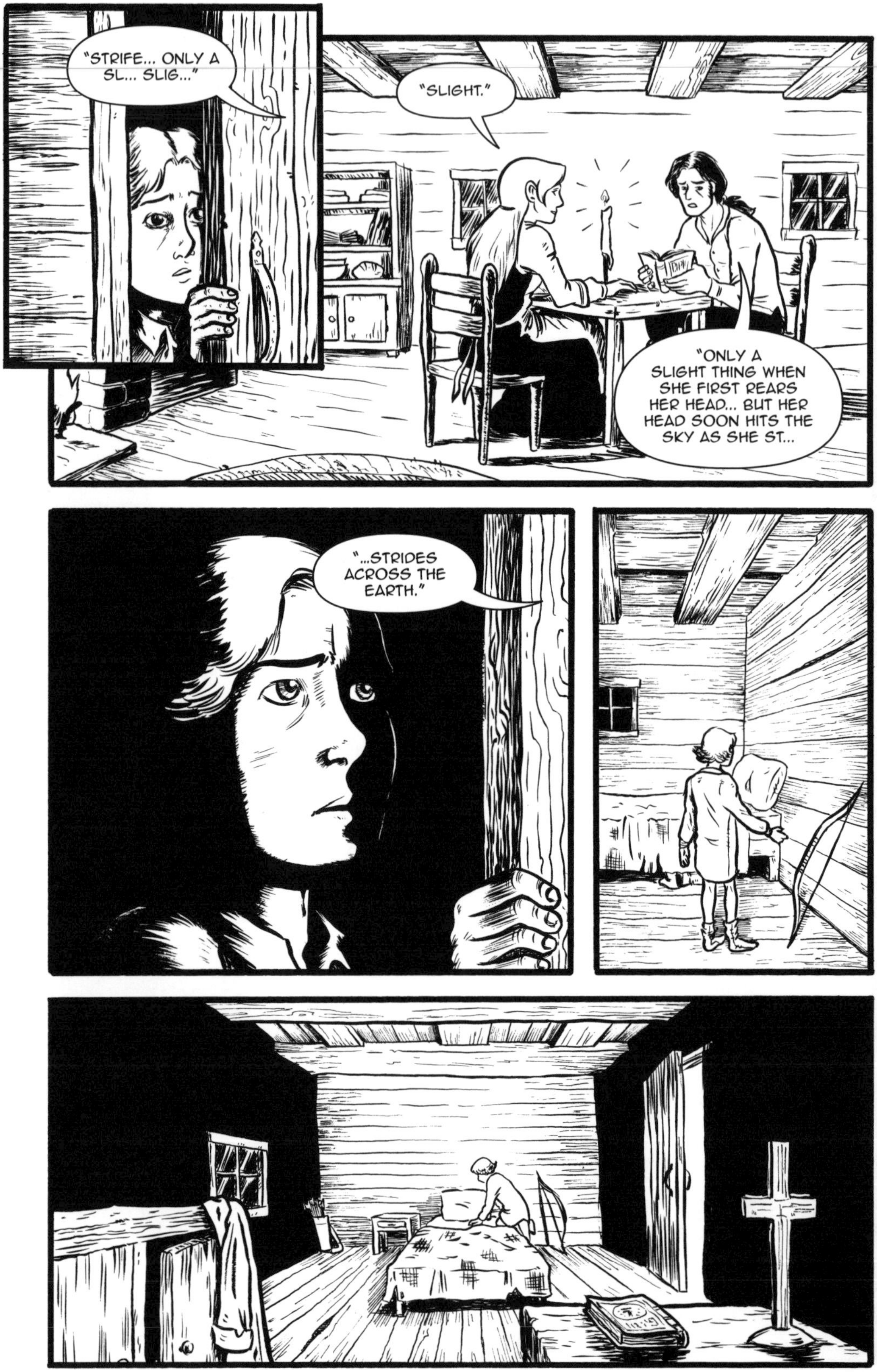
"STRIFE... ONLY A SL... SLIG..."
"SLIGHT."
"ONLY A SLIGHT THING WHEN SHE FIRST REARS HER HEAD... BUT HER HEAD SOON HITS THE SKY AS SHE ST...
"...STRIDES ACROSS THE EARTH."

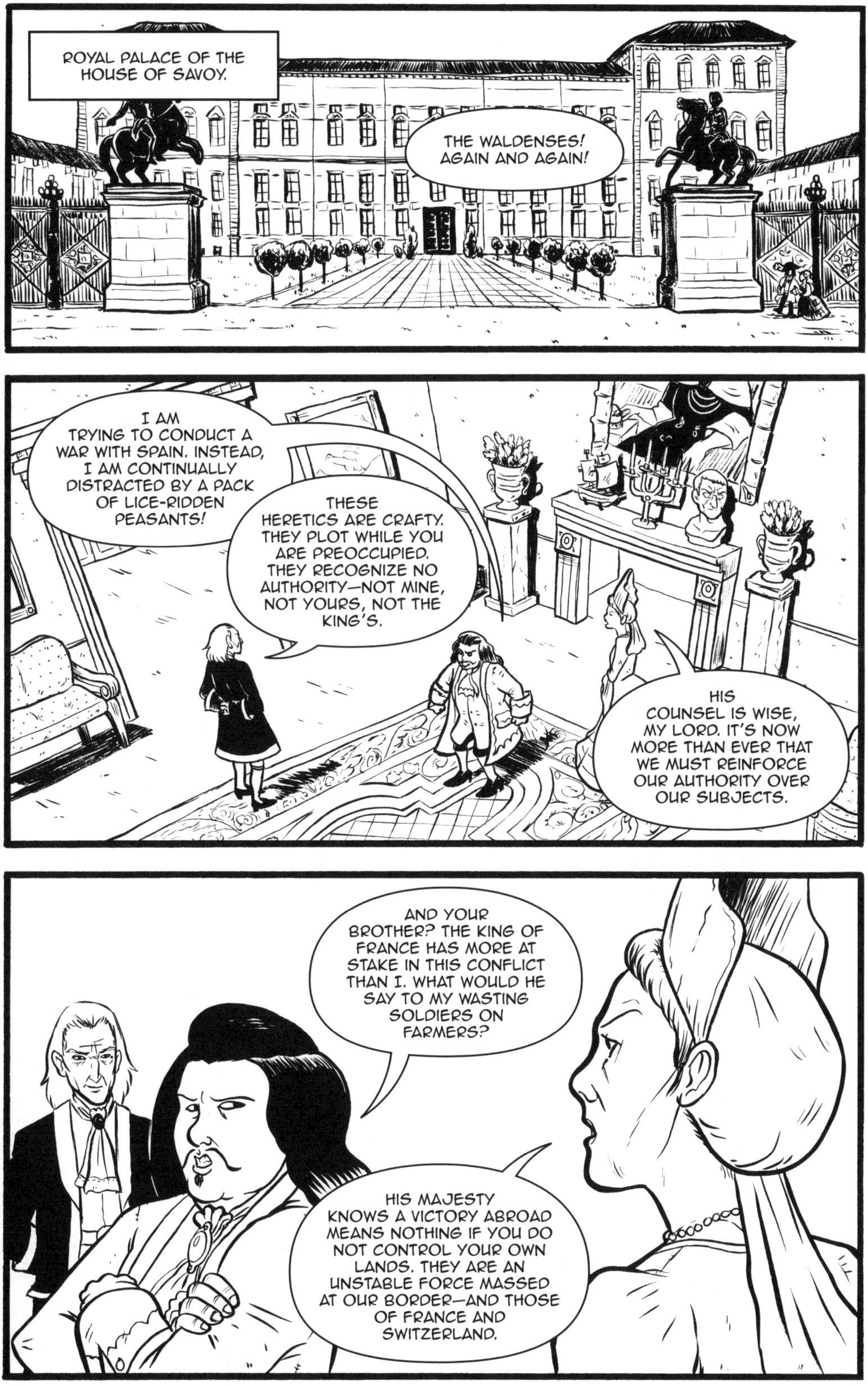
ROYAL PALACE OF THE HOUSE OF SAVOY.
THE WALDENSES! AGAIN AND AGAIN!
I AM TRYING TO CONDUCT A WAR WITH SPAIN. INSTEAD, I AM CONTINUALLY DISTRACTED BY A PACK OF LICE-RIDDEN PEASANTS!
THESE HERETICS ARE CRAFTY. THEY PLOT WHILE YOU ARE PREOCCUPIED. THEY RECOGNIZE NO AUTHORITY—NOT MINE, NOT YOURS, NOT THE KING'S.
HIS COUNSEL IS WISE, MY LORD. IT'S NOW MORE THAN EVER THAT WE MUST REINFORCE OUR AUTHORITY OVER OUR SUBJECTS.
AND YOUR BROTHER? THE KING OF FRANCE HAS MORE AT STAKE IN THIS CONFLICT THAN I. WHAT WOULD HE SAY TO MY WASTING SOLDIERS ON FARMERS?
HIS MAJESTY KNOWS A VICTORY ABROAD MEANS NOTHING IF YOU DO NOT CONTROL YOUR OWN LANDS. THEY ARE AN UNSTABLE FORCE MASSED AT OUR BORDER—AND THOSE OF FRANCE AND SWITZERLAND.

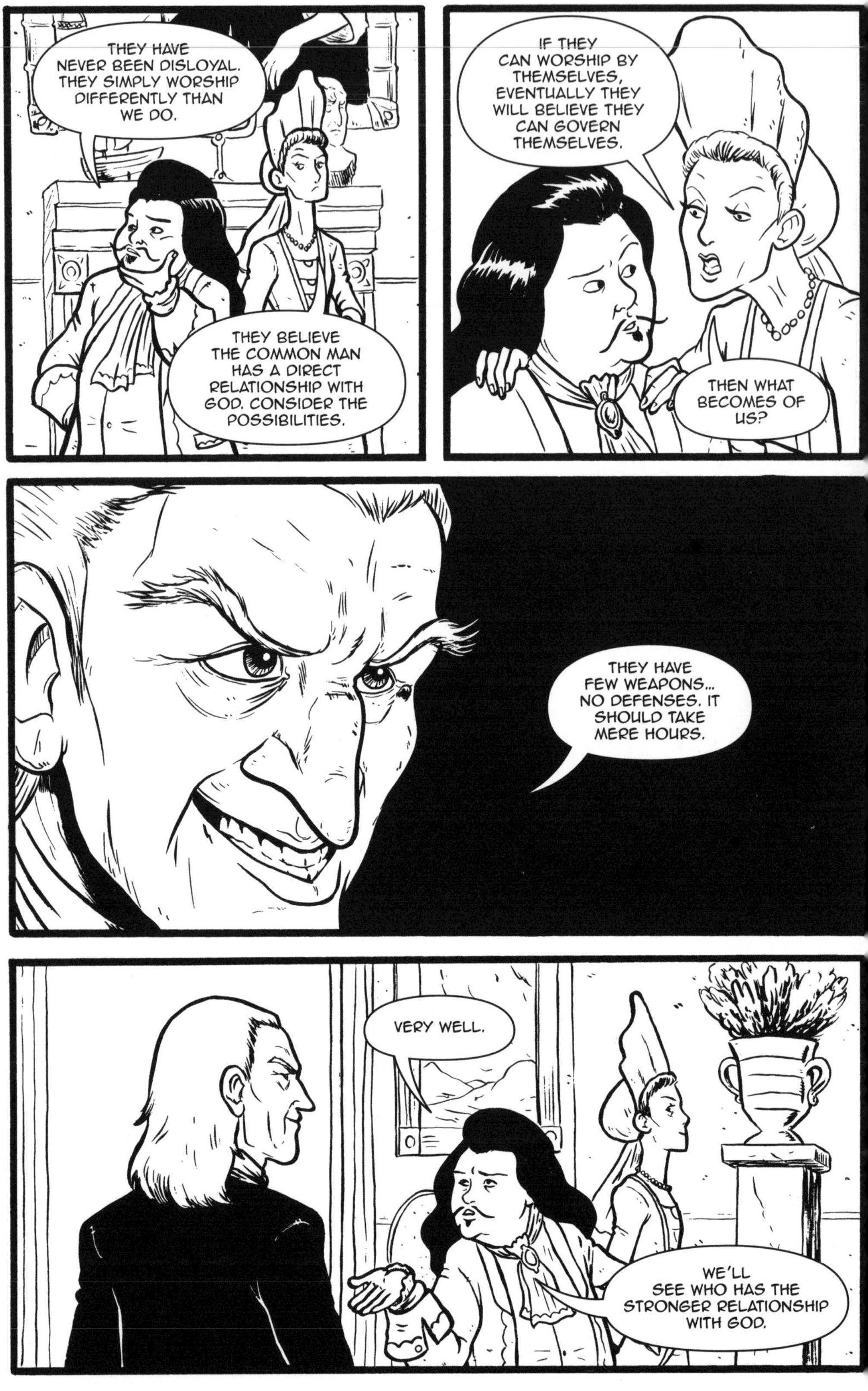
THEY HAVE NEVER BEEN DISLOYAL. THEY SIMPLY WORSHIP DIFFERENTLY THAN WE DO.
THEY BELIEVE THE COMMON MAN HAS A DIRECT RELATIONSHIP WITH GOD. CONSIDER THE POSSIBILITIES.
IF THEY CAN WORSHIP BY THEMSELVES, EVENTUALLY THEY WILL BELIEVE THEY CAN GOVERN THEMSELVES.
THEN WHAT BECOMES OF US?
THEY HAVE FEW WEAPONS... NO DEFENSES. IT SHOULD TAKE MERE HOURS.
VERY WELL.
WE'LL SEE WHO HAS THE STRONGER RELATIONSHIP WITH GOD.

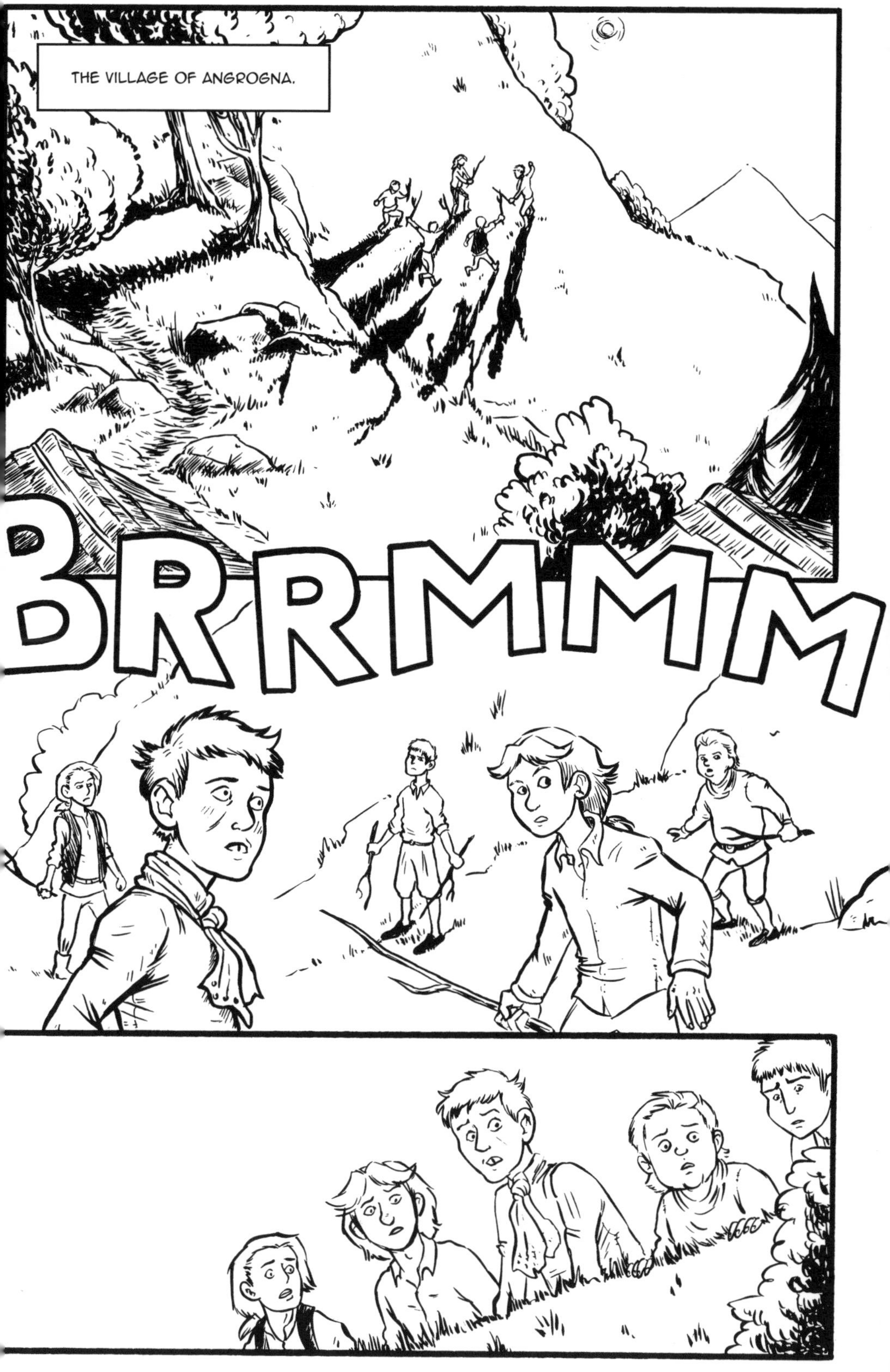
THE VILLAGE OF ANGROGNA.
BRRMMM

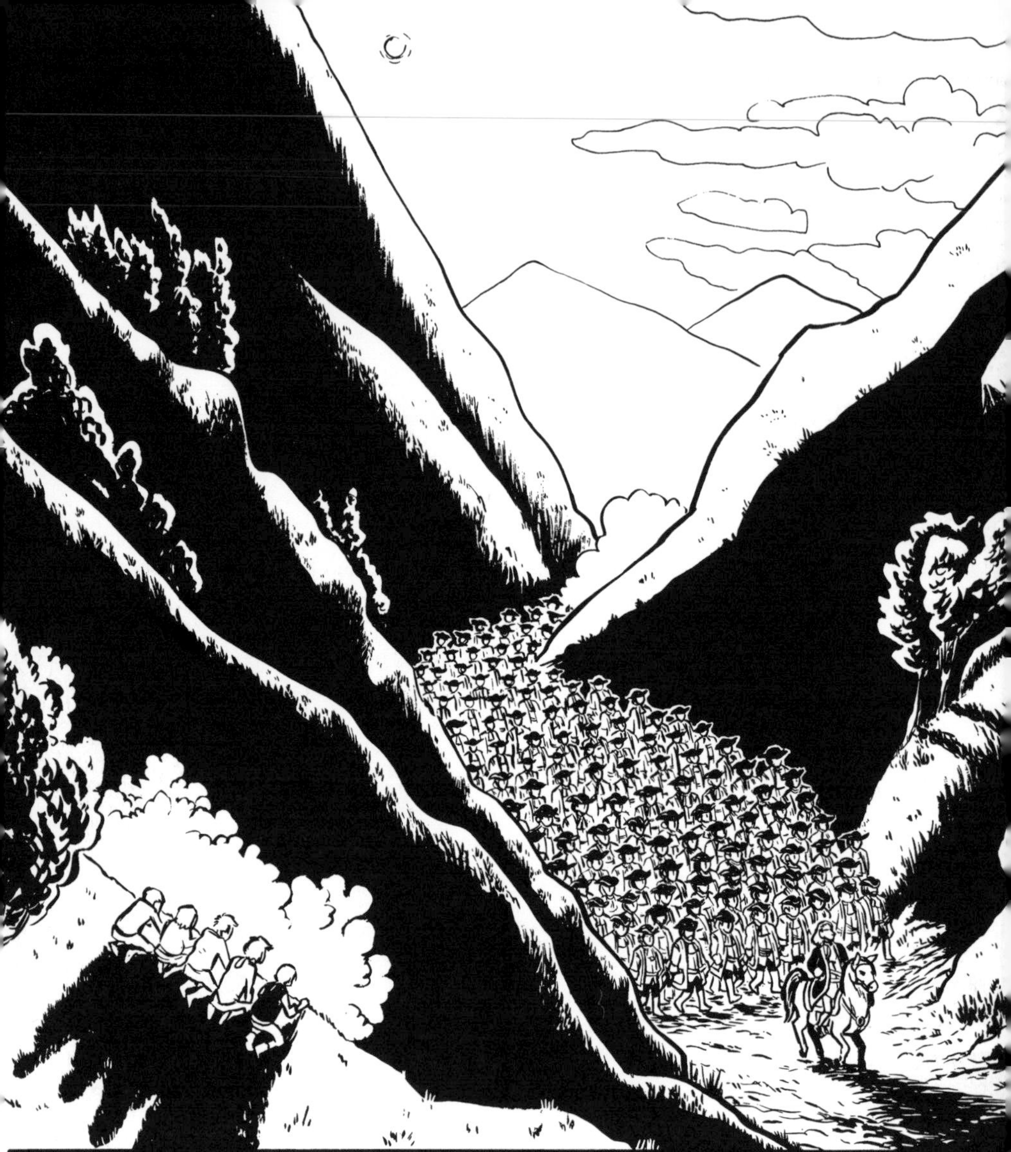

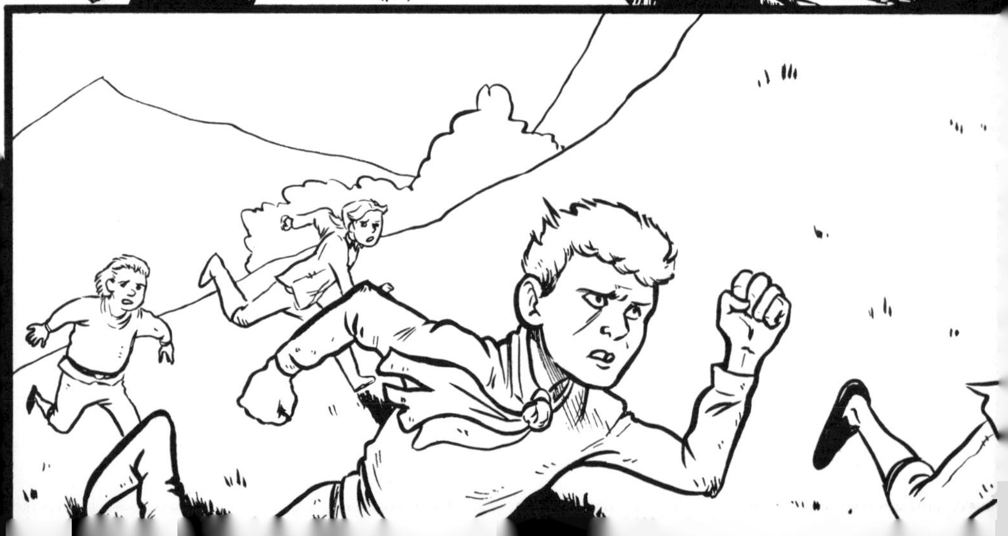

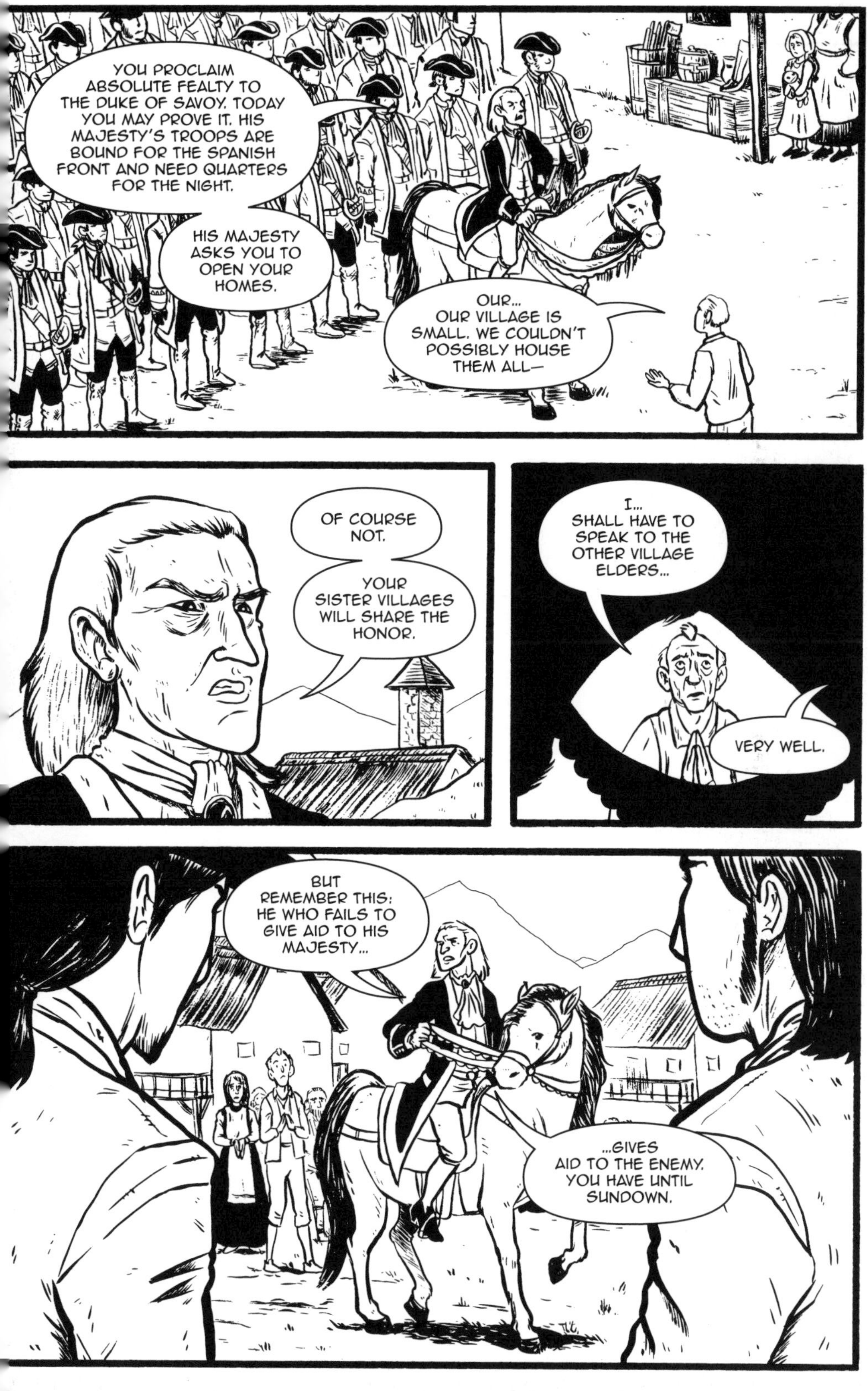
YOU PROCLAIM ABSOLUTE FEALTY TO THE DUKE OF SAVOY. TODAY YOU MAY PROVE IT. HIS MAJESTY'S TROOPS ARE BOUND FOR THE SPANISH FRONT AND NEED QUARTERS FOR THE NIGHT.
HIS MAJESTY ASKS YOU TO OPEN YOUR HOMES.
OUR... OUR VILLAGE IS SMALL. WE COULDN'T POSSIBLY HOUSE THEM ALL—
OF COURSE NOT.
YOUR SISTER VILLAGES WILL SHARE THE HONOR.
I... SHALL HAVE TO SPEAK TO THE OTHER VILLAGE ELDERS...
VERY WELL.
BUT REMEMBER THIS: HE WHO FAILS TO GIVE AID TO HIS MAJESTY...
...GIVES AID TO THE ENEMY. YOU HAVE UNTIL SUNDOWN.

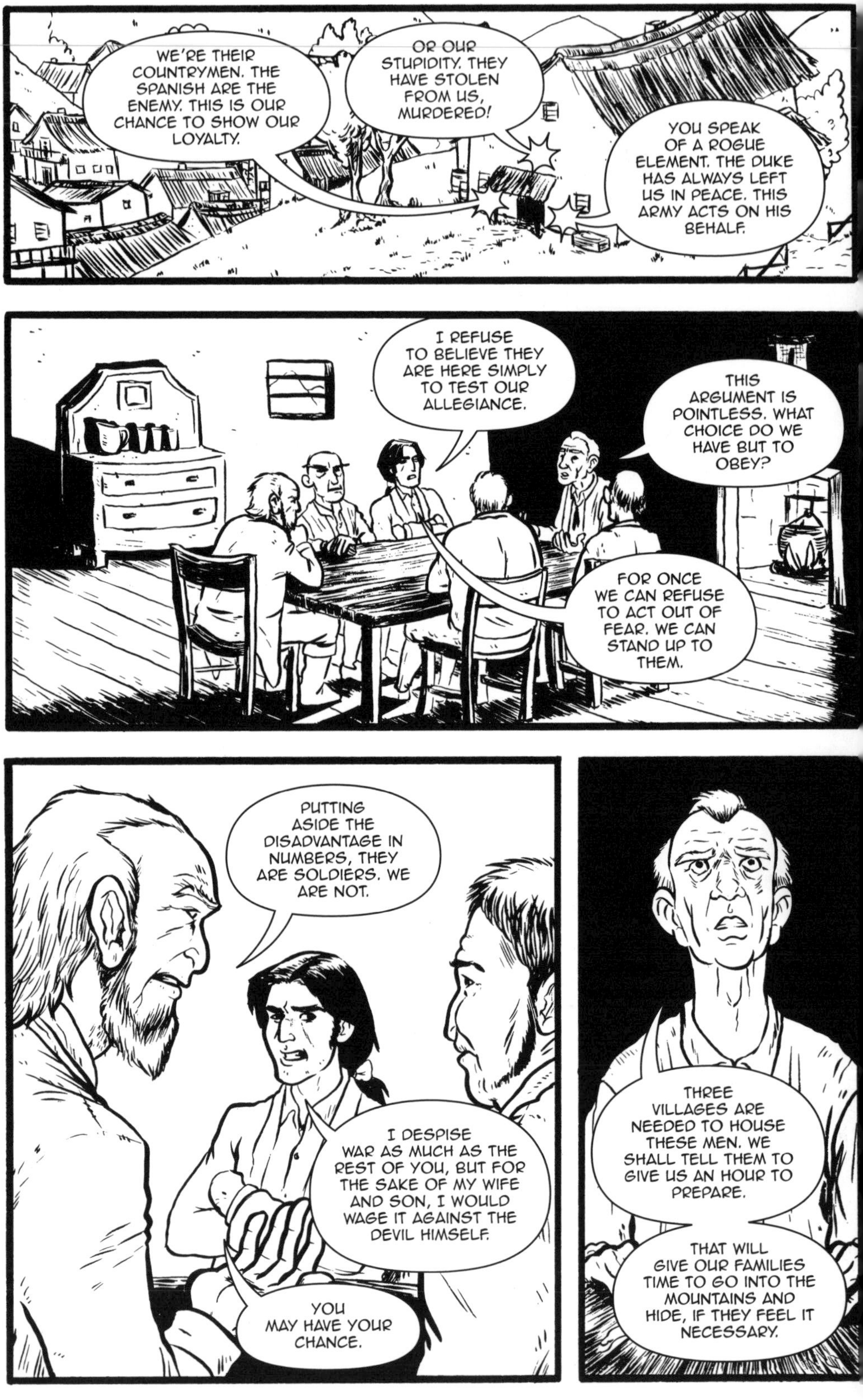
WE'RE THEIR COUNTRYMEN. THE SPANISH ARE THE ENEMY. THIS IS OUR CHANCE TO SHOW OUR LOYALTY.
OR OUR STUPIDITY. THEY HAVE STOLEN FROM US, MURDERED!
YOU SPEAK OF A ROGUE ELEMENT. THE DUKE HAS ALWAYS LEFT US IN PEACE. THIS ARMY ACTS ON HIS BEHALF.
I REFUSE TO BELIEVE THEY ARE HERE SIMPLY TO TEST OUR ALLEGIANCE.
THIS ARGUMENT IS POINTLESS. WHAT CHOICE DO WE HAVE BUT TO OBEY?
FOR ONCE WE CAN REFUSE TO ACT OUT OF FEAR. WE CAN STAND UP TO THEM.
PUTTING ASIDE THE DISADVANTAGE IN NUMBERS, THEY ARE SOLDIERS. WE ARE NOT.
I DESPISE WAR AS MUCH AS THE REST OF YOU, BUT FOR THE SAKE OF MY WIFE AND SON, I WOULD WAGE IT AGAINST THE DEVIL HIMSELF.
YOU MAY HAVE YOUR CHANCE.
THREE VILLAGES ARE NEEDED TO HOUSE THESE MEN. WE SHALL TELL THEM TO GIVE US AN HOUR TO PREPARE.
THAT WILL GIVE OUR FAMILIES TIME TO GO INTO THE MOUNTAINS AND HIDE, IF THEY FEEL IT NECESSARY.

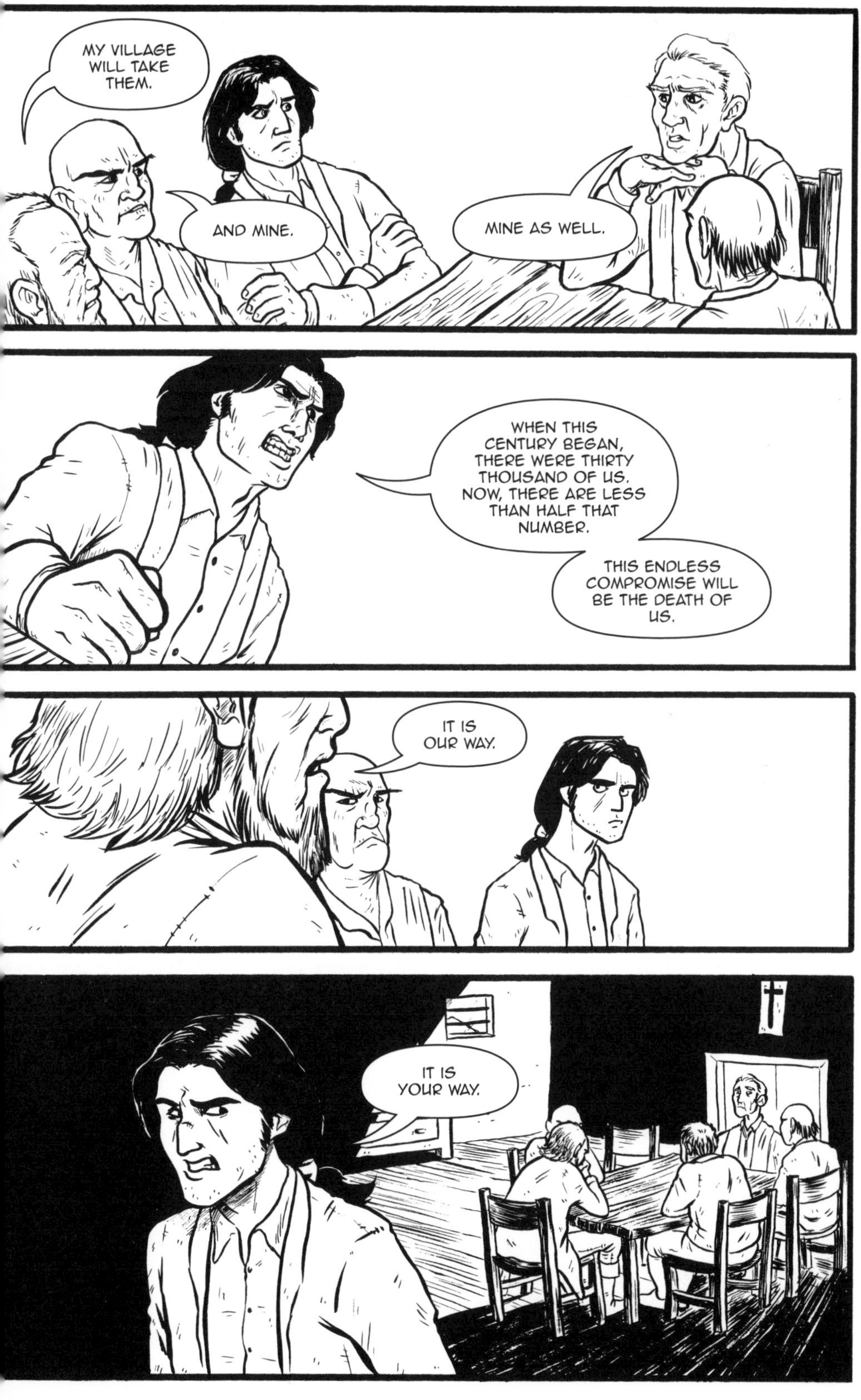
MY VILLAGE WILL TAKE THEM.
AND MINE.
MINE AS WELL.
WHEN THIS CENTURY BEGAN, THERE WERE THIRTY THOUSAND OF US. NOW, THERE ARE LESS THAN HALF THAT NUMBER.
THIS ENDLESS COMPROMISE WILL BE THE DEATH OF US.
IT IS OUR WAY.
IT IS YOUR WAY.

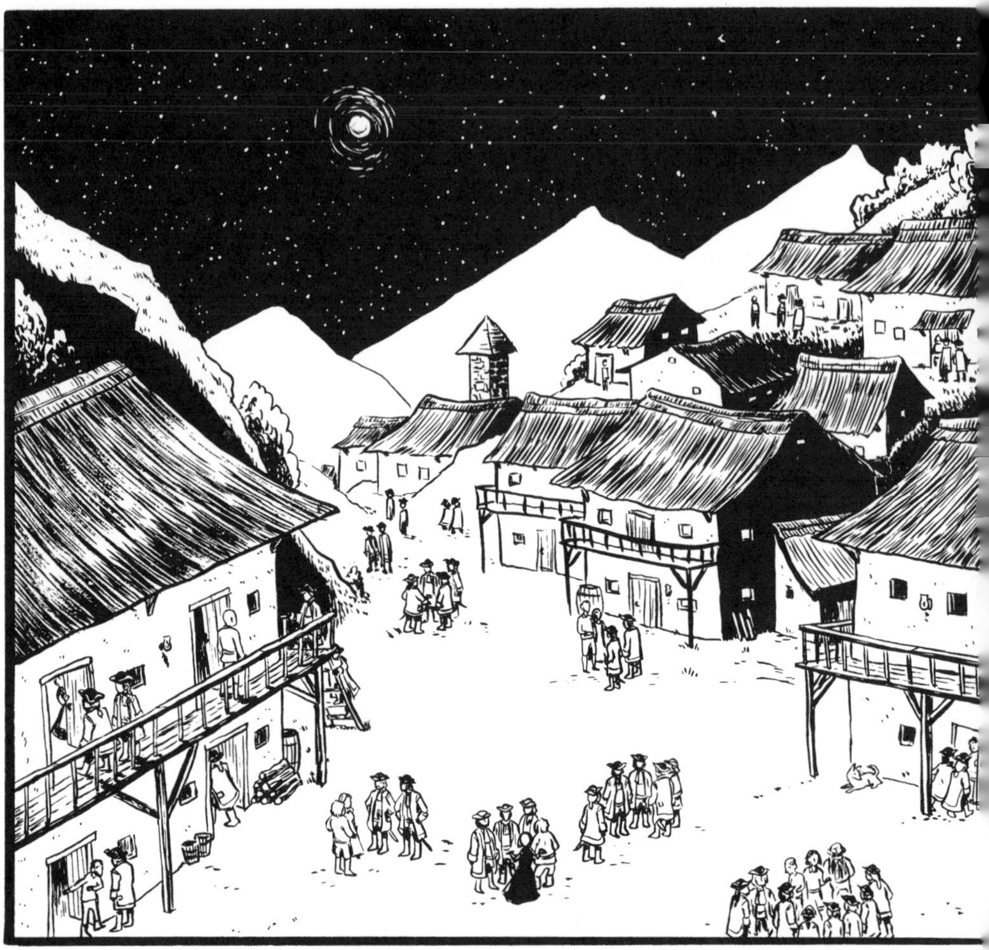

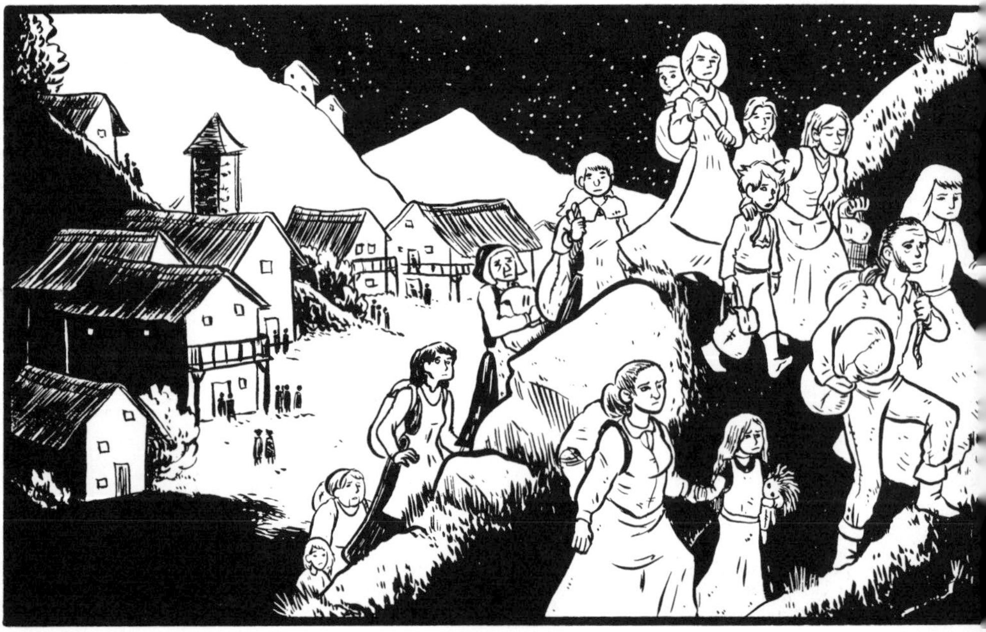

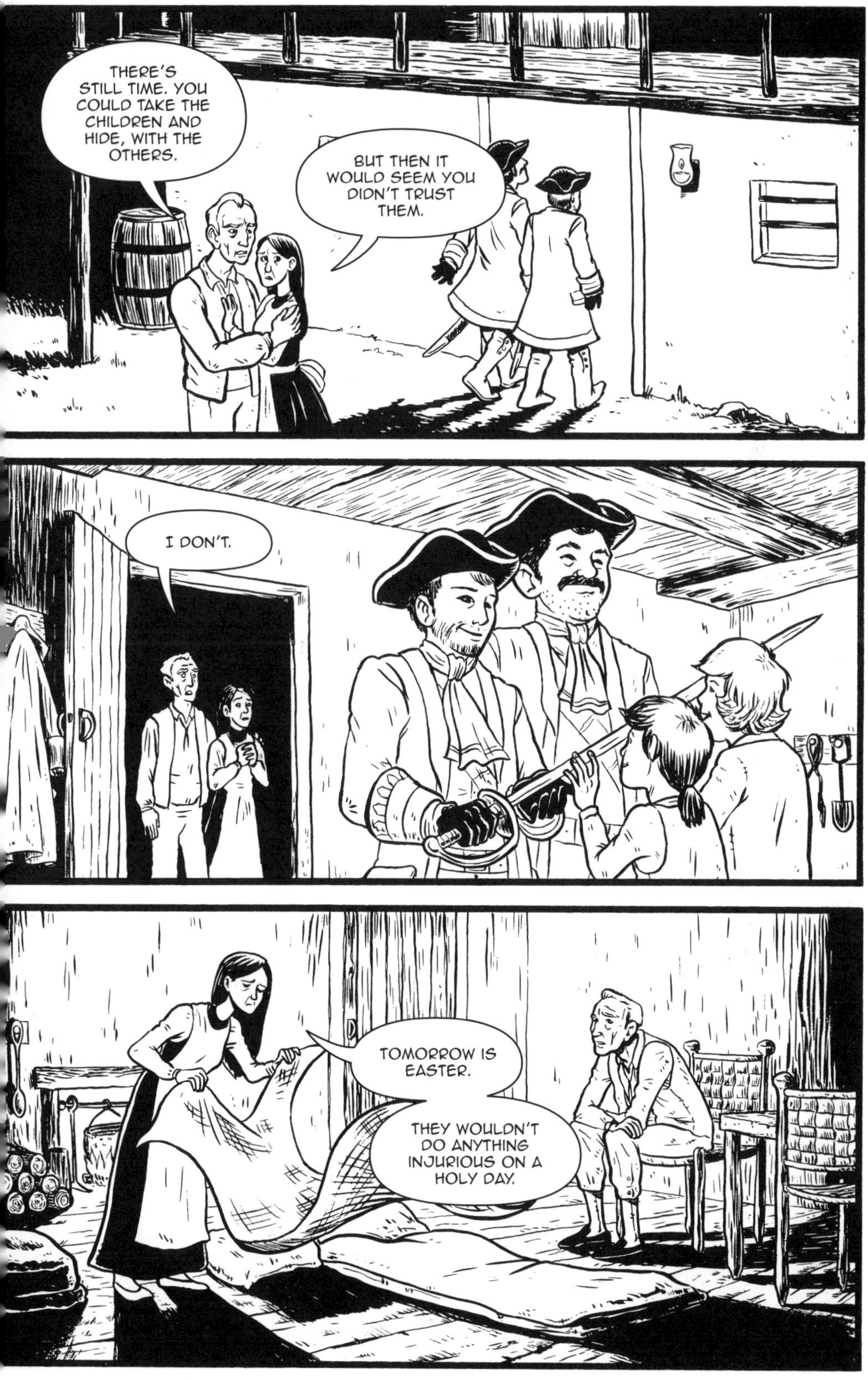
THERE'S STILL TIME. YOU COULD TAKE THE CHILDREN AND HIDE, WITH THE OTHERS.
BUT THEN IT WOULD SEEM YOU DIDN'T TRUST THEM.
I DON'T.
TOMORROW IS EASTER.
THEY WOULDN'T DO ANYTHING INJURIOUS ON A HOLY DAY.

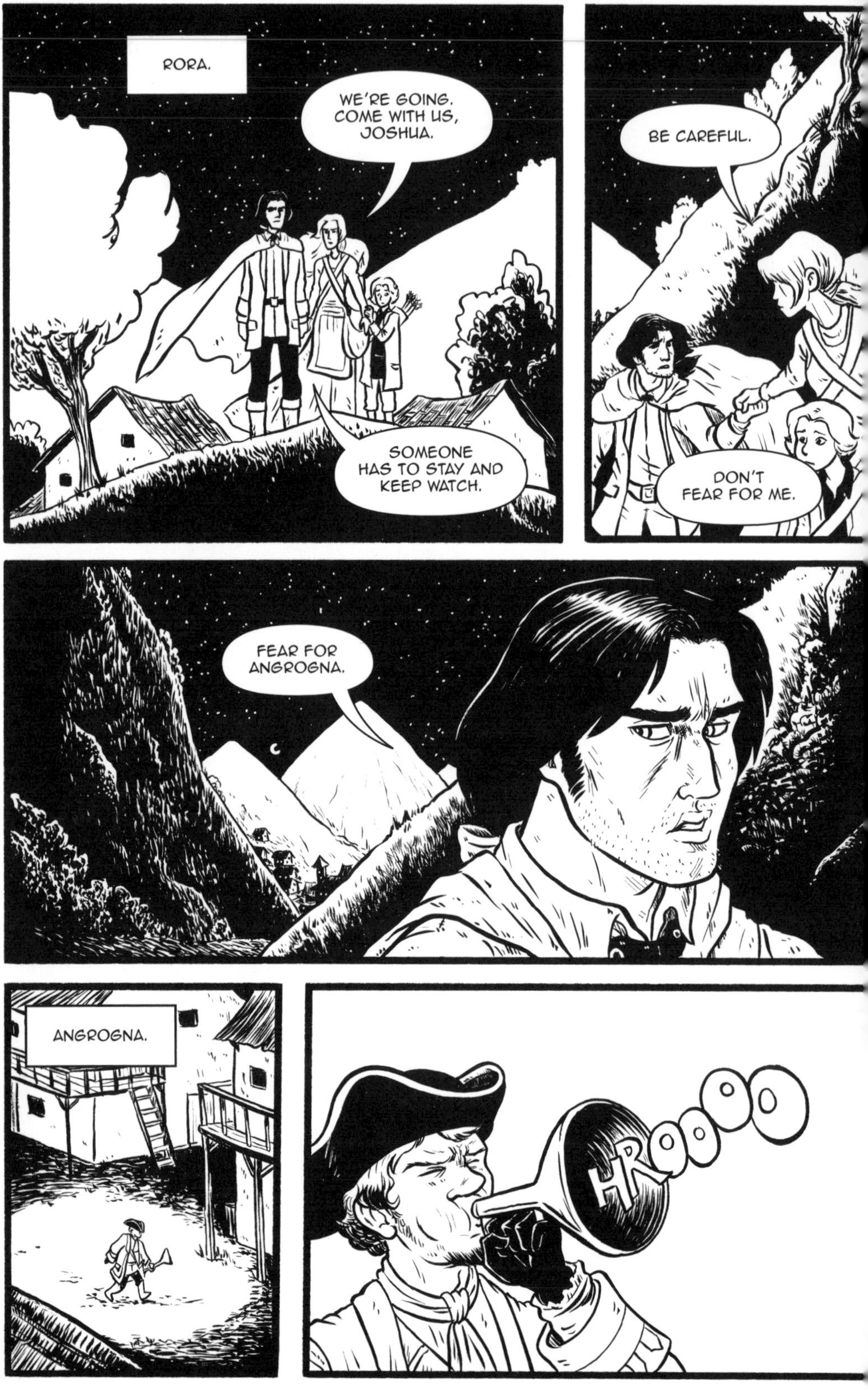
RORA.
WE'RE GOING. COME WITH US, JOSHUA.
SOMEONE HAS TO STAY AND KEEP WATCH.
BE CAREFUL.
DON'T FEAR FOR ME.
FEAR FOR ANGROGNA.
ANGROGNA.
HROOOO

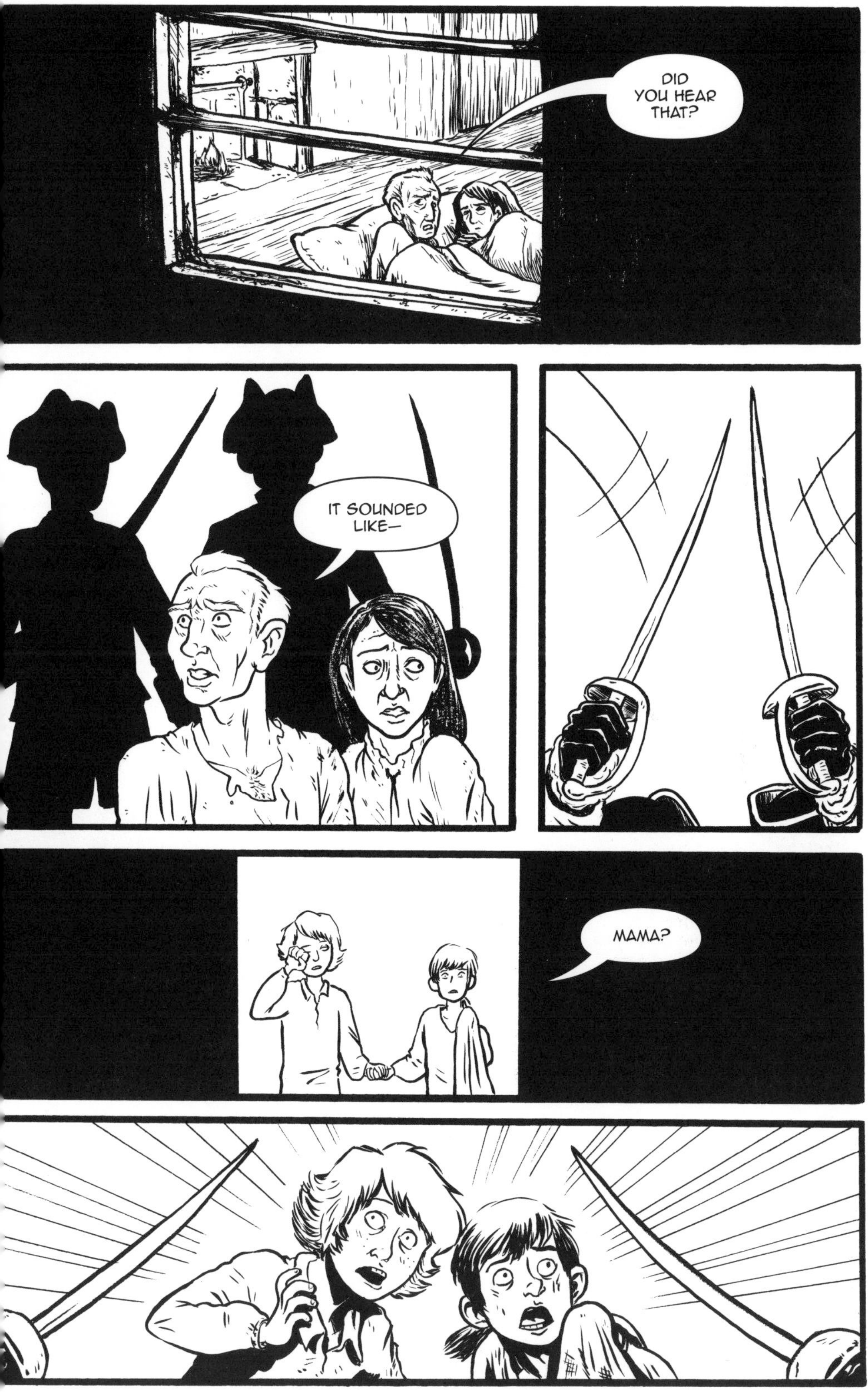
DID YOU HEAR THAT?
IT SOUNDED LIKE—
MAMA?

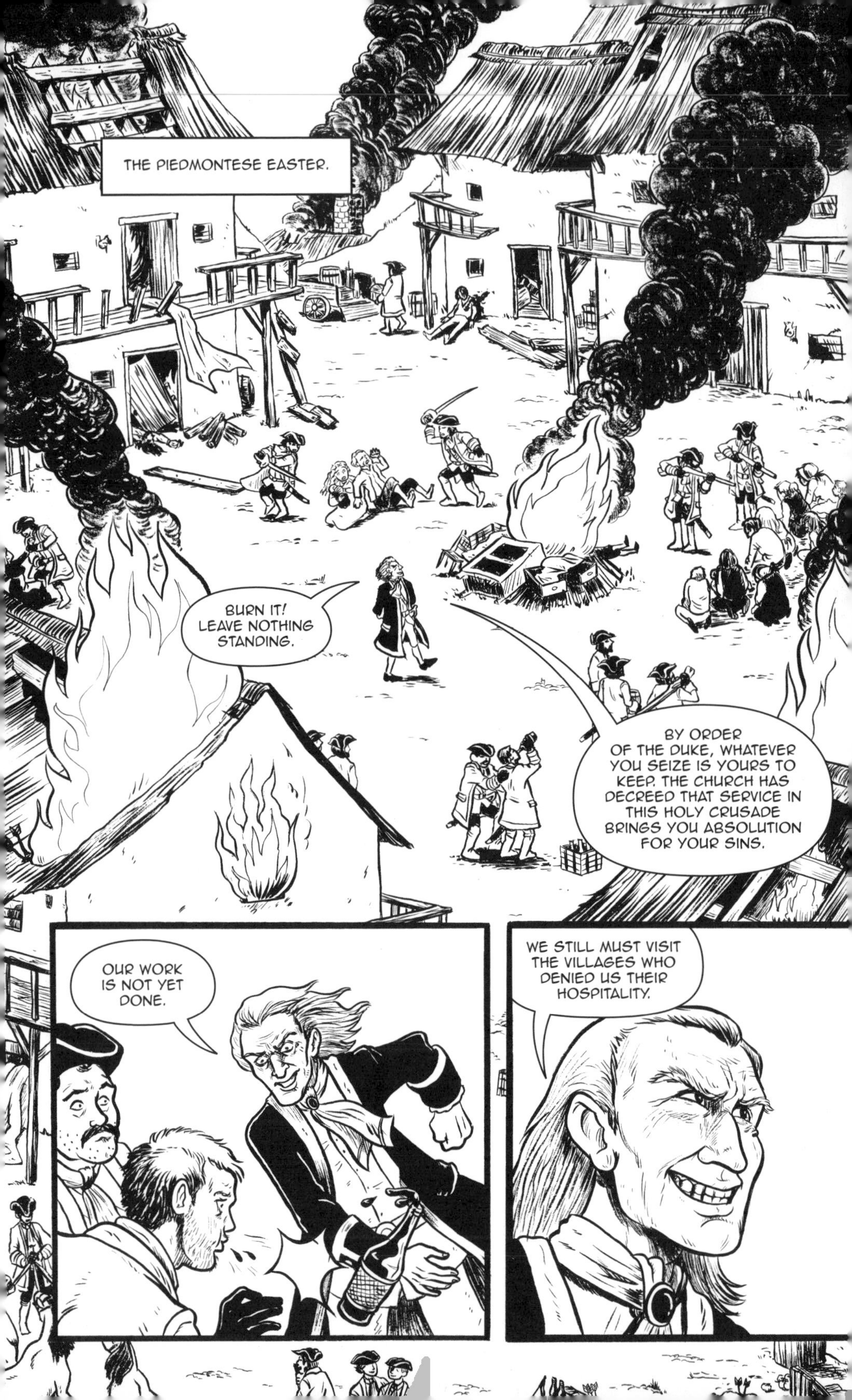
THE PIEDMONTESE EASTER.
BURN IT! LEAVE NOTHING STANDING.
BY ORDER OF THE DUKE, WHATEVER YOU SEIZE IS YOURS TO KEEP. THE CHURCH HAS DECREED THAT SERVICE IN THIS HOLY CRUSADE BRINGS YOU ABSOLUTION FOR YOUR SINS.
OUR WORK IS NOT YET DONE.
WE STILL MUST VISIT THE VILLAGES WHO DENIED US THEIR HOSPITALITY.

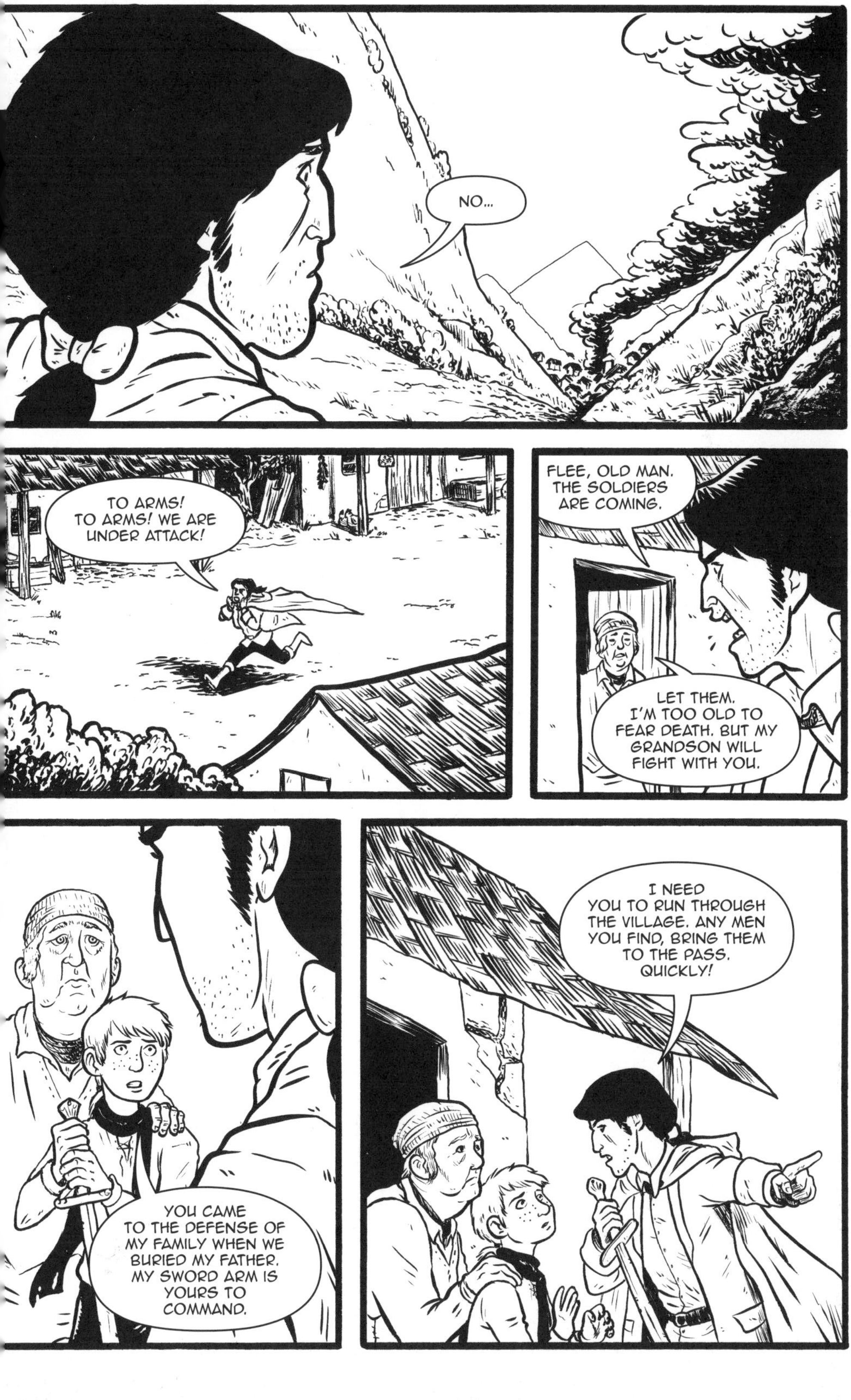
NO...
TO ARMS! TO ARMS! WE ARE UNDER ATTACK!
FLEE, OLD MAN. THE SOLDIERS ARE COMING.
LET THEM. I'M TOO OLD TO FEAR DEATH. BUT MY GRANDSON WILL FIGHT WITH YOU.
YOU CAME TO THE DEFENSE OF MY FAMILY WHEN WE BURIED MY FATHER. MY SWORD ARM IS YOURS TO COMMAND.
I NEED YOU TO RUN THROUGH THE VILLAGE. ANY MEN YOU FIND, BRING THEM TO THE PASS. QUICKLY!

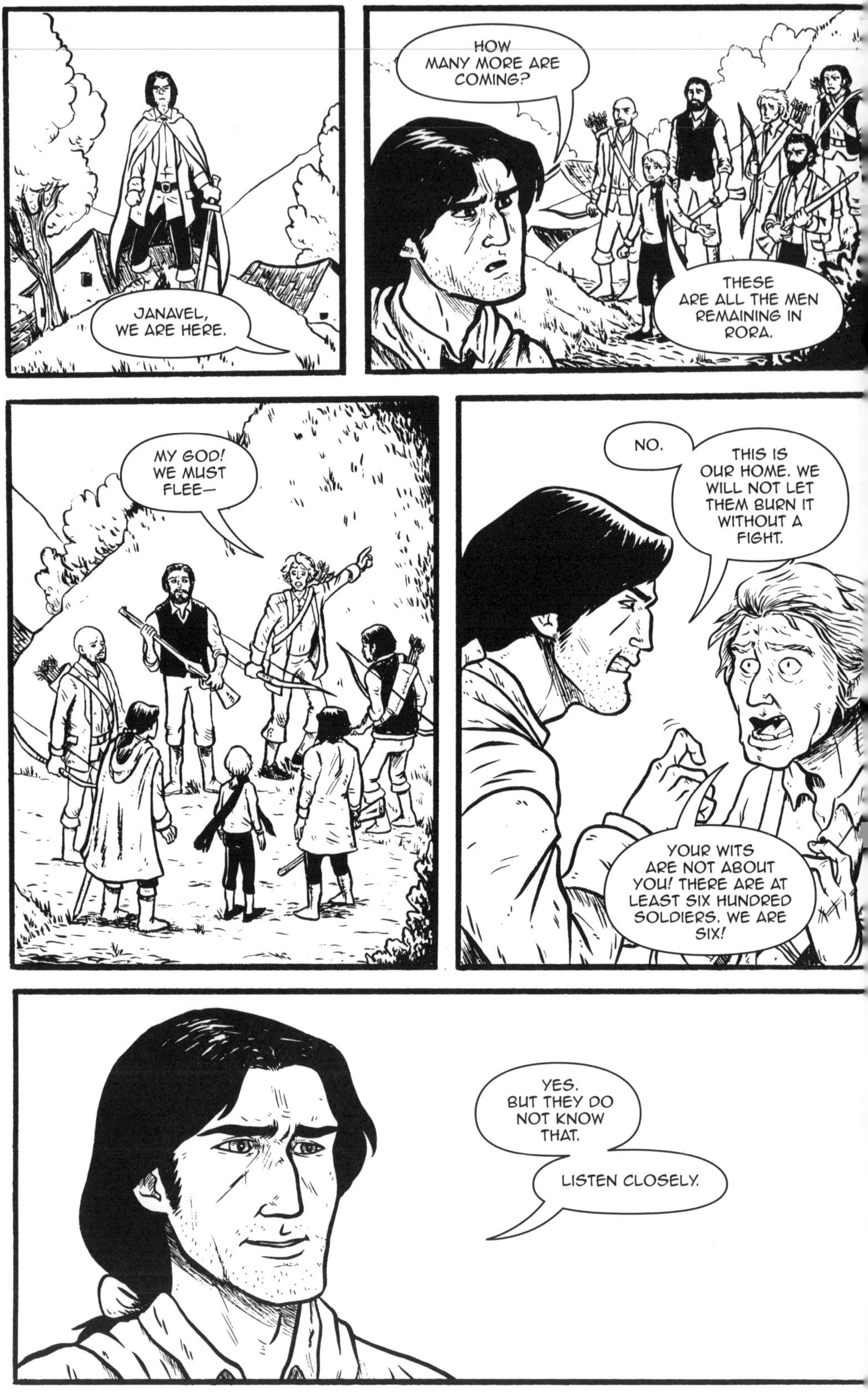
JANAVEL, WE ARE HERE.
HOW MANY MORE ARE COMING?
THESE ARE ALL THE MEN REMAINING IN RORA.
MY GOD! WE MUST FLEE—
NO.
THIS IS OUR HOME. WE WILL NOT LET THEM BURN IT WITHOUT A FIGHT.
YOUR WITS ARE NOT ABOUT YOU! THERE ARE AT LEAST SIX HUNDRED SOLDIERS. WE ARE SIX!
YES. BUT THEY DO NOT KNOW THAT.
LISTEN CLOSELY.

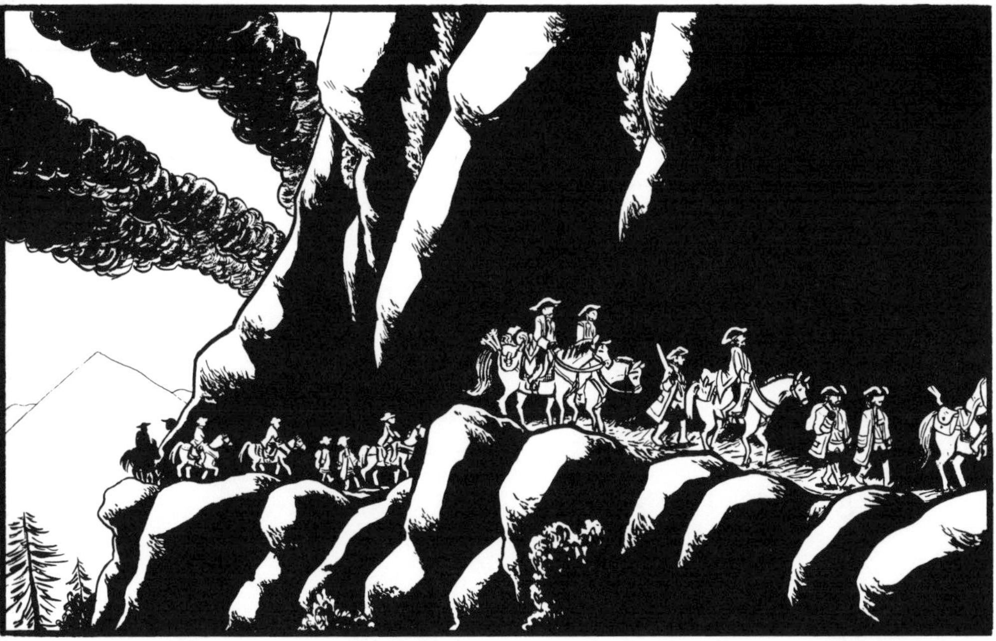

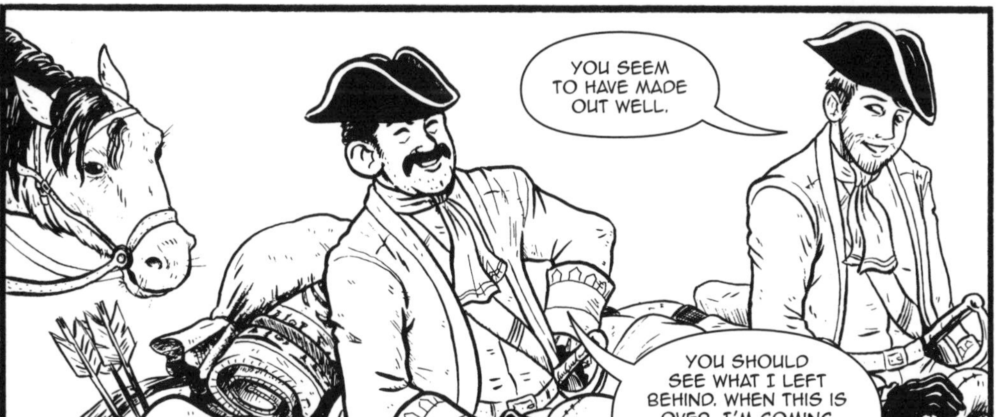
YOU SEEM TO HAVE MADE OUT WELL.
YOU SHOULD SEE WHAT I LEFT BEHIND. WHEN THIS IS OVER, I'M COMING BACK WITH AN OXCART! HA HA—

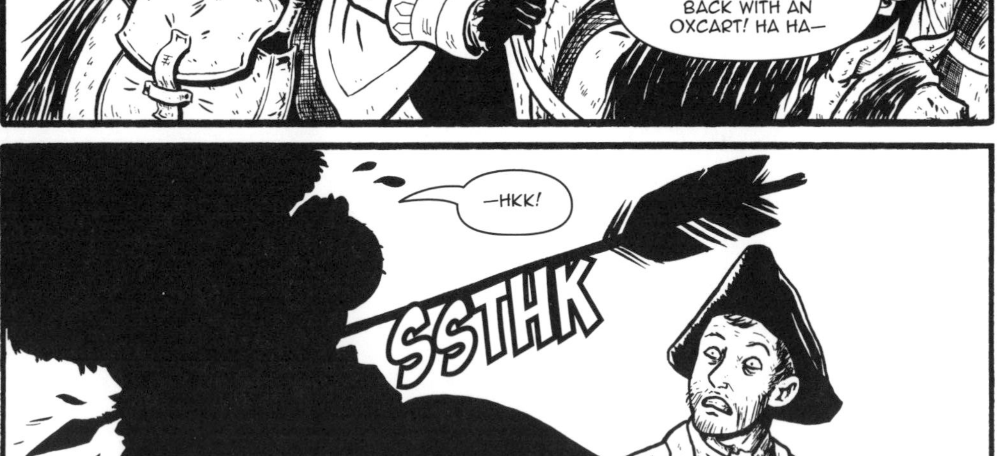
—HKK!
SSTHK

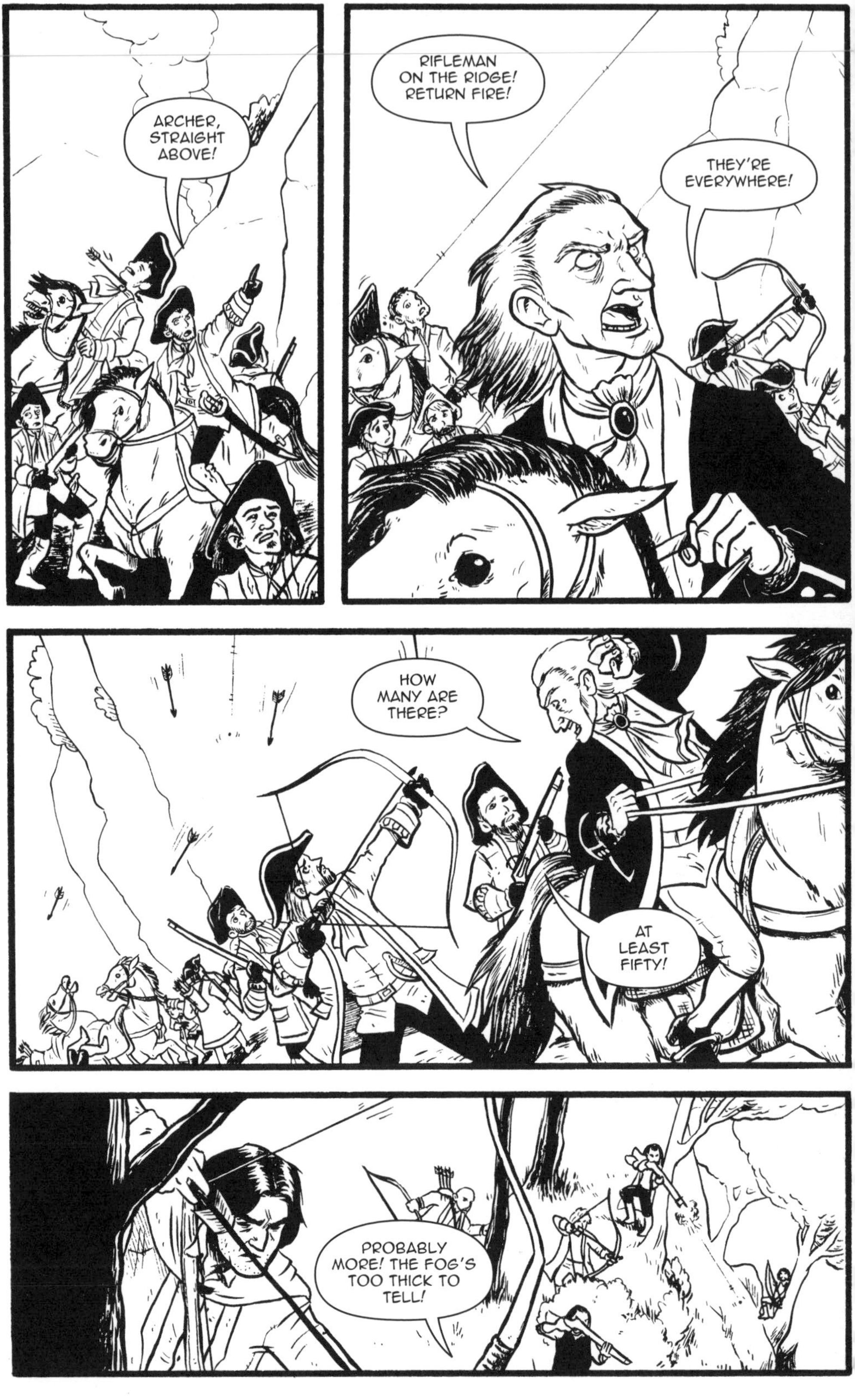
ARCHER, STRAIGHT ABOVE!
RIFLEMAN ON THE RIDGE! RETURN FIRE!
THEY'RE EVERYWHERE!
HOW MANY ARE THERE?
AT LEAST FIFTY!
PROBABLY MORE! THE FOG'S TOO THICK TO TELL!

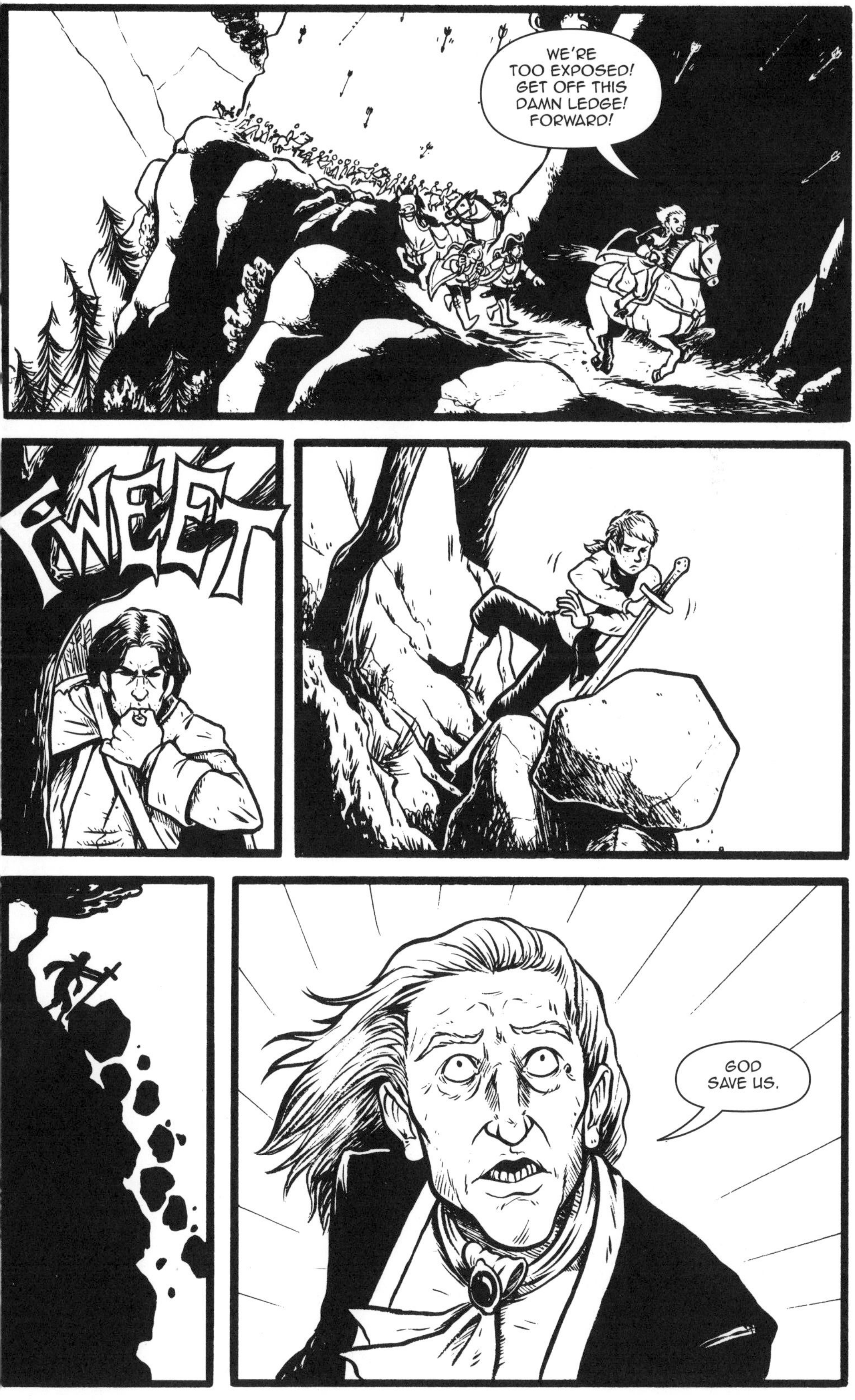
WE'RE TOO EXPOSED! GET OFF THIS DAMN LEDGE! FORWARD!
FWEET
GOD SAVE US.

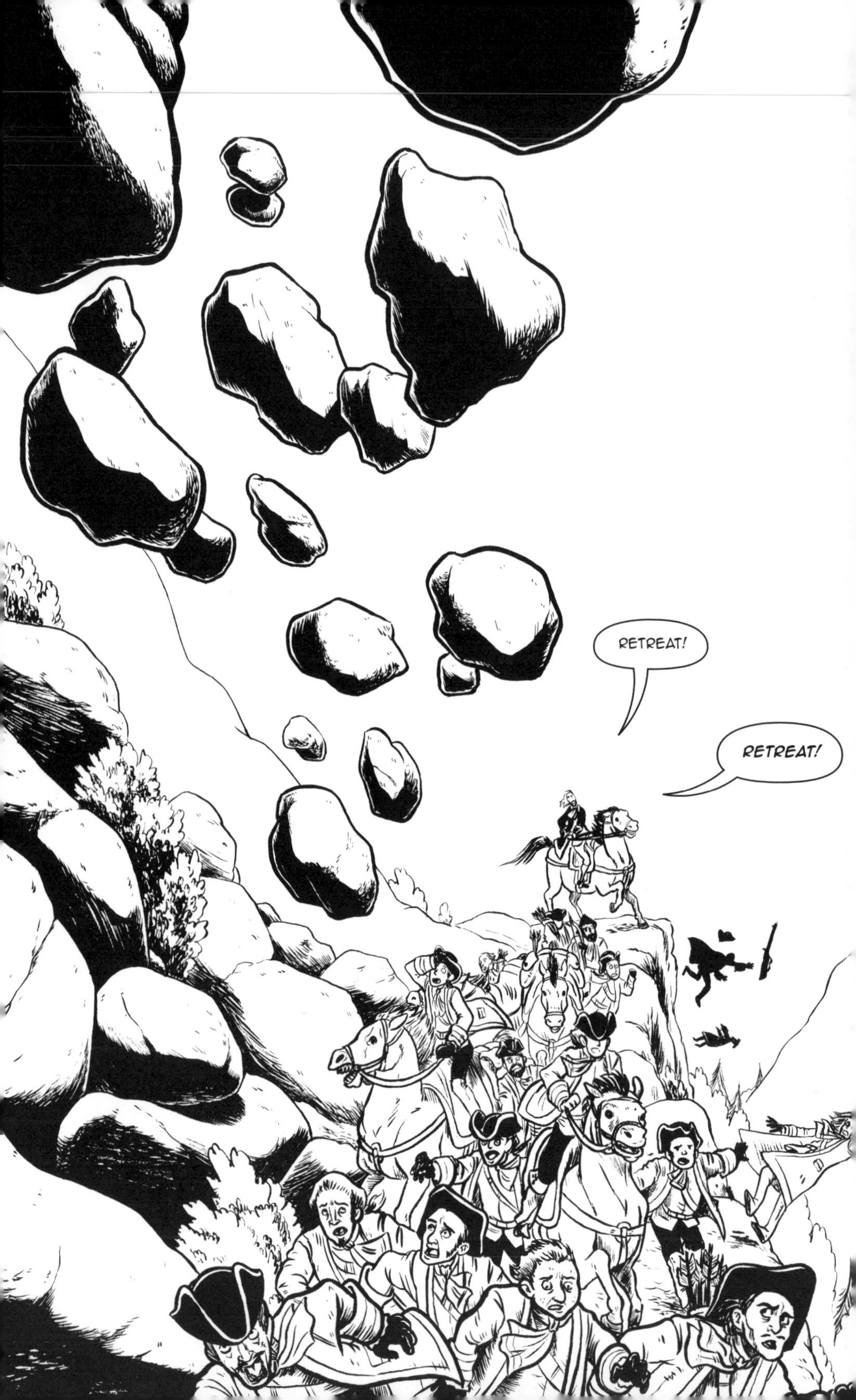
RETREAT!
RETREAT!

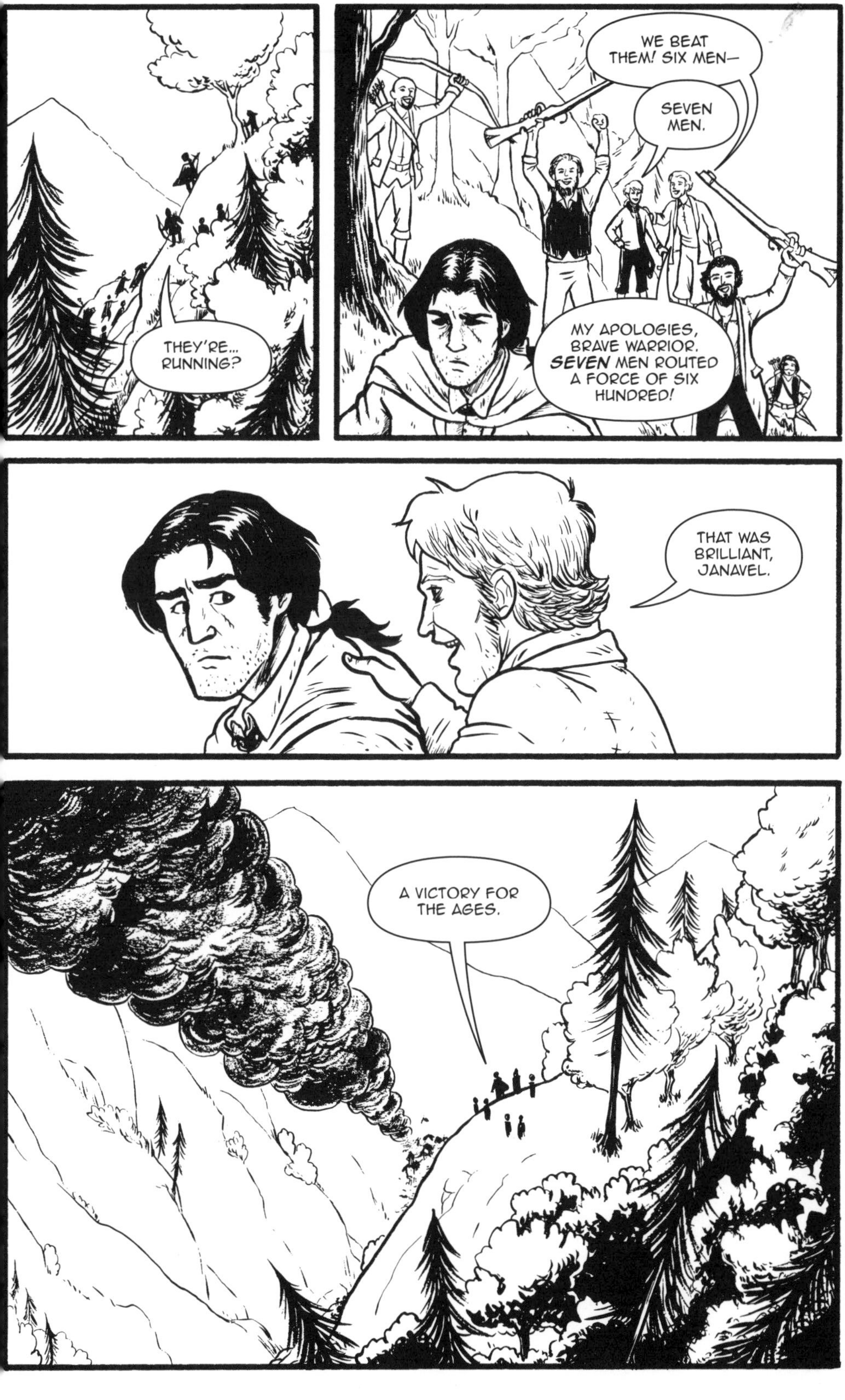
THEY'RE... RUNNING?
WE BEAT THEM! SIX MEN—
SEVEN MEN.
MY APOLOGIES, BRAVE WARRIOR. SEVEN MEN ROUTED A FORCE OF SIX HUNDRED!
THAT WAS BRILLIANT, JANAVEL.
A VICTORY FOR THE AGES.

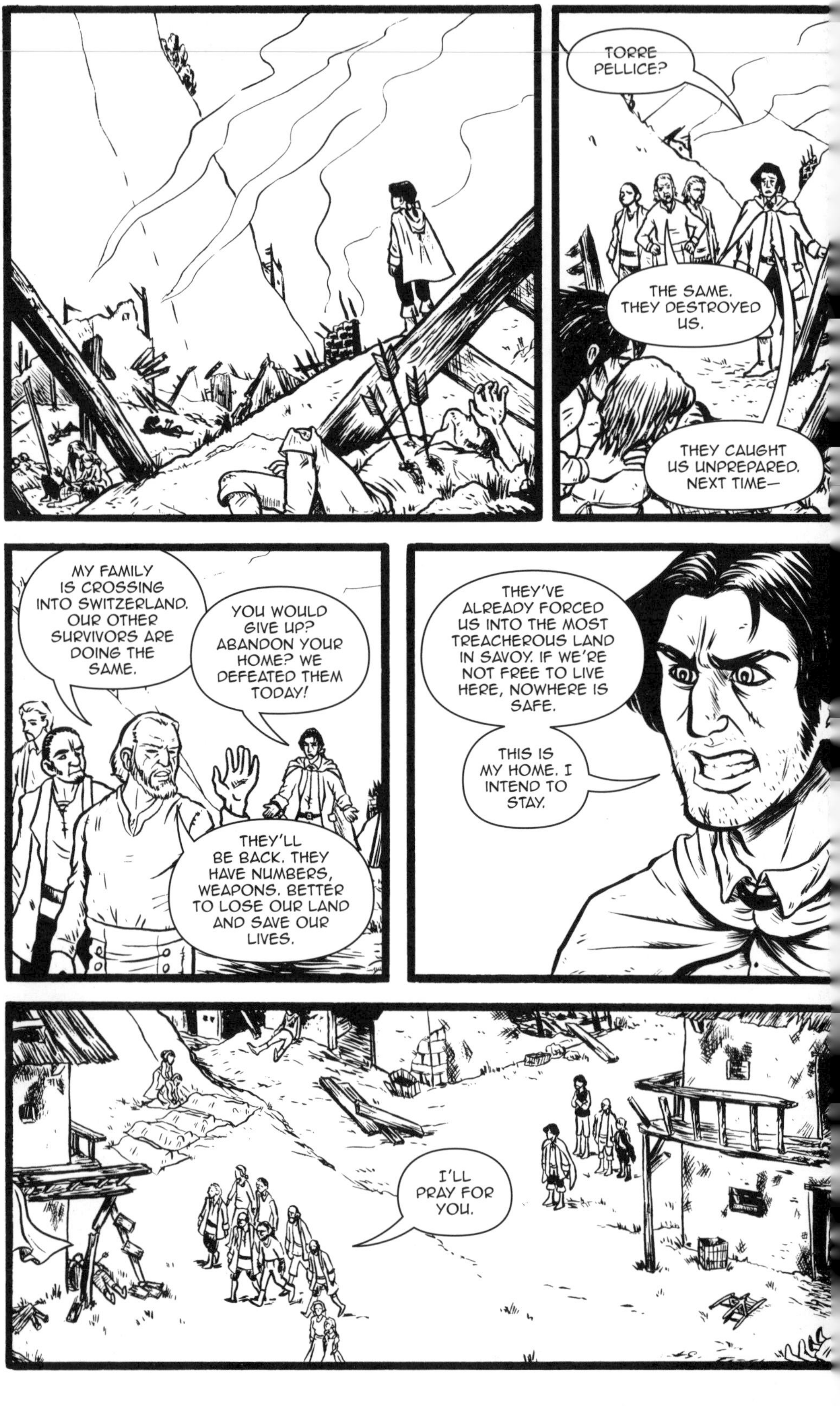
TORRE PELLICE?
THE SAME. THEY DESTROYED US.
THEY CAUGHT US UNPREPARED. NEXT TIME—
MY FAMILY IS CROSSING INTO SWITZERLAND. OUR OTHER SURVIVORS ARE DOING THE SAME.
YOU WOULD GIVE UP? ABANDON YOUR HOME? WE DEFEATED THEM TODAY!
THEY'LL BE BACK. THEY HAVE NUMBERS, WEAPONS. BETTER TO LOSE OUR LAND AND SAVE OUR LIVES.
THEY'VE ALREADY FORCED US INTO THE MOST TREACHEROUS LAND IN SAVOY. IF WE'RE NOT FREE TO LIVE HERE, NOWHERE IS SAFE.
THIS IS MY HOME. I INTEND TO STAY.
I'LL PRAY FOR YOU.

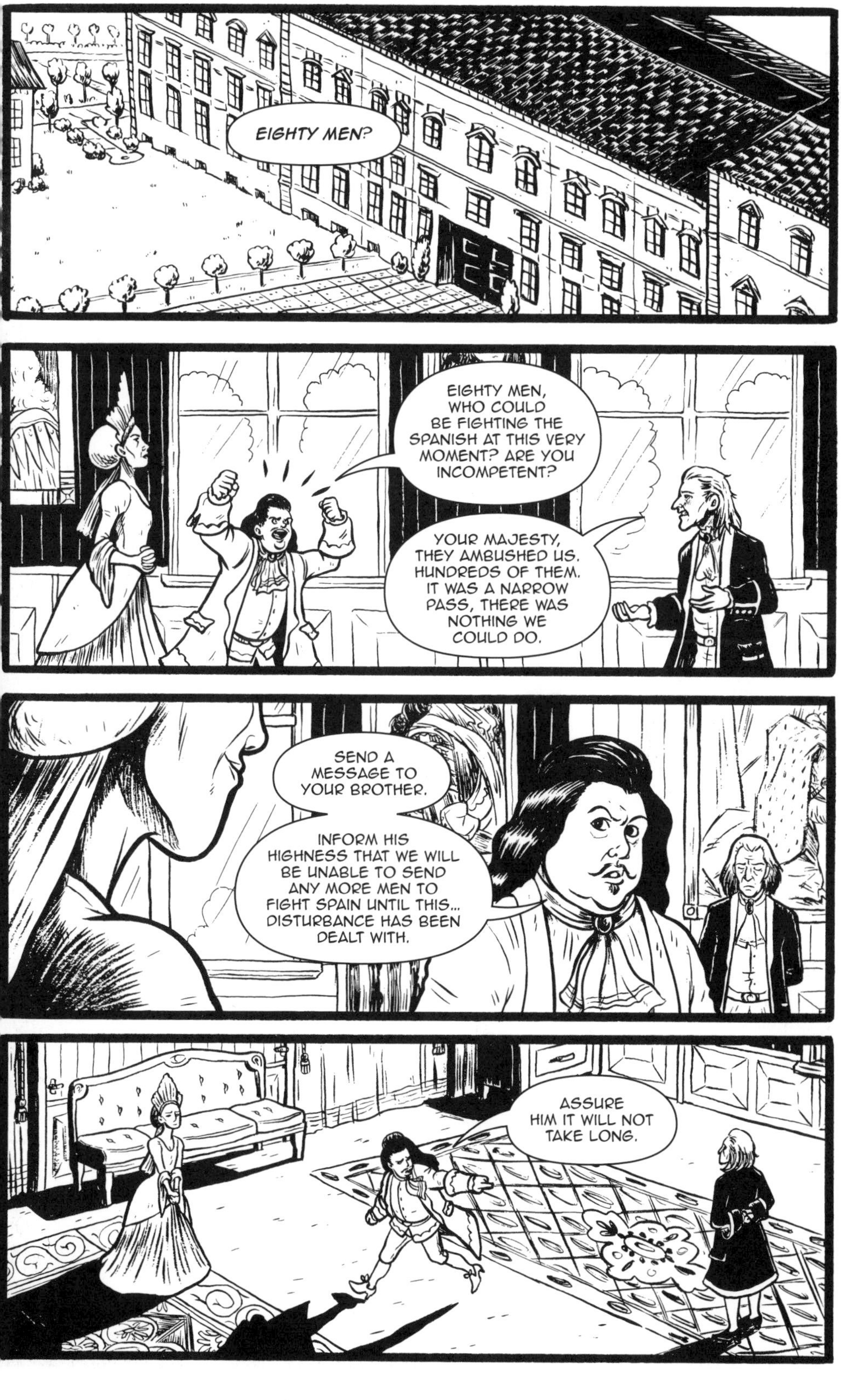
EIGHTY MEN?
EIGHTY MEN, WHO COULD BE FIGHTING THE SPANISH AT THIS VERY MOMENT? ARE YOU INCOMPETENT?
YOUR MAJESTY, THEY AMBUSHED US. HUNDREDS OF THEM. IT WAS A NARROW PASS, THERE WAS NOTHING WE COULD DO.
SEND A MESSAGE TO YOUR BROTHER.
INFORM HIS HIGHNESS THAT WE WILL BE UNABLE TO SEND ANY MORE MEN TO FIGHT SPAIN UNTIL THIS... DISTURBANCE HAS BEEN DEALT WITH.
ASSURE HIM IT WILL NOT TAKE LONG.

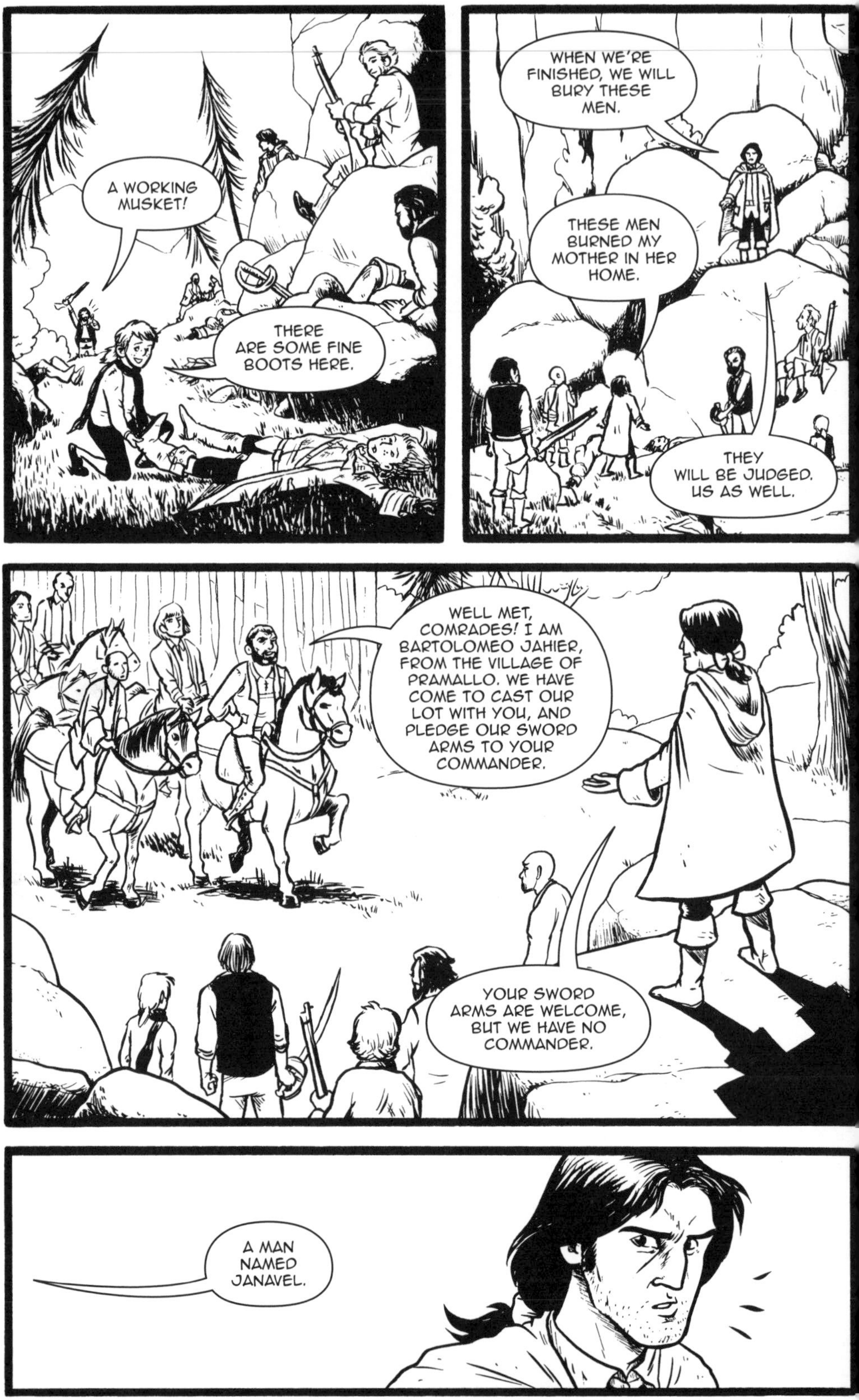
A WORKING MUSKET!
THERE ARE SOME FINE BOOTS HERE.
WHEN WE'RE FINISHED, WE WILL BURY THESE MEN.
THESE MEN BURNED MY MOTHER IN HER HOME.
THEY WILL BE JUDGED. US AS WELL.
WELL MET, COMRADES! I AM BARTOLOMEO JAHIER, FROM THE VILLAGE OF PRAMALLO. WE HAVE COME TO CAST OUR LOT WITH YOU, AND PLEDGE OUR SWORD ARMS TO YOUR COMMANDER.
YOUR SWORD ARMS ARE WELCOME, BUT WE HAVE NO COMMANDER.
A MAN NAMED JANAVEL.

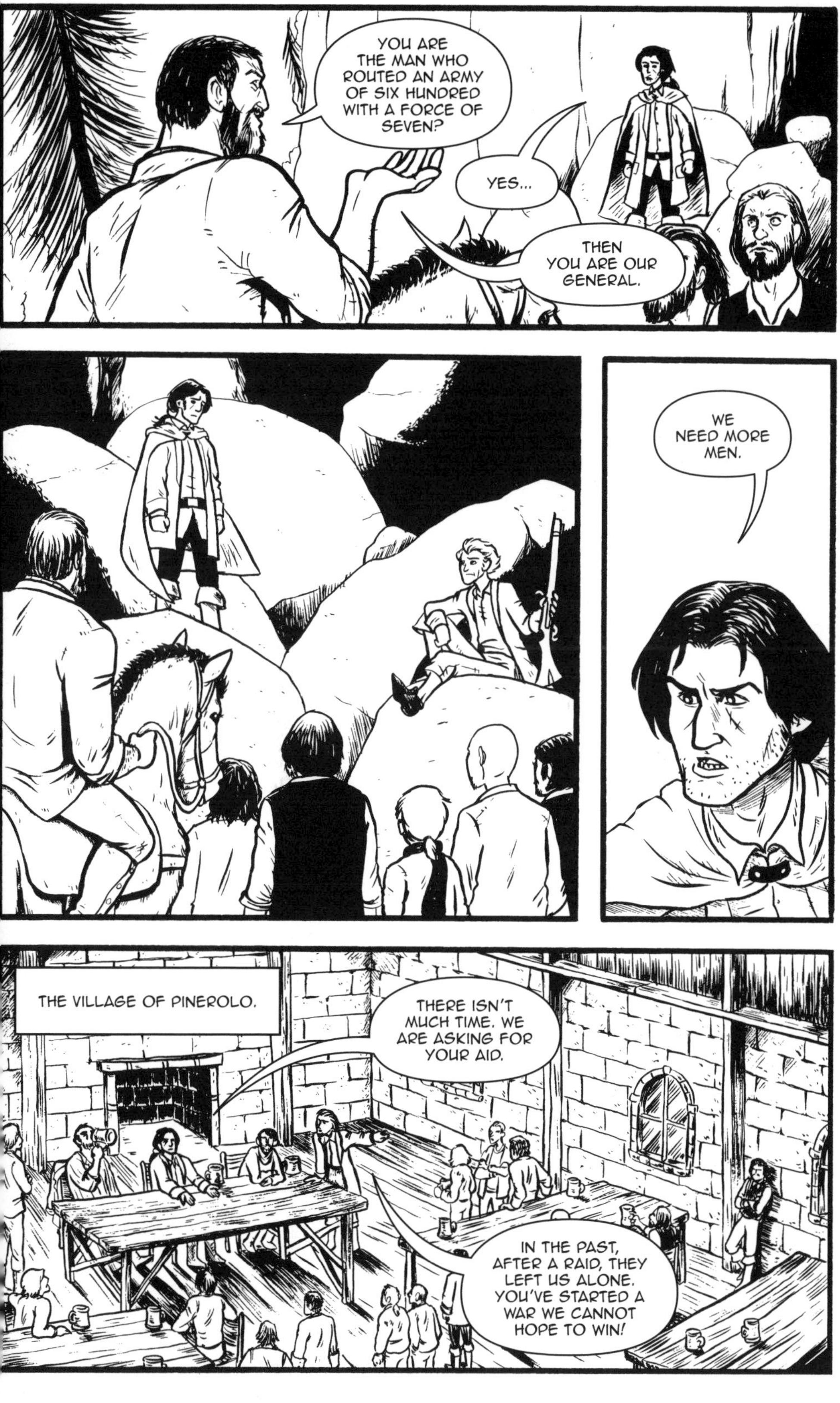
YOU ARE THE MAN WHO ROUTED AN ARMY OF SIX HUNDRED WITH A FORCE OF SEVEN?
YES...
THEN YOU ARE OUR GENERAL.
WE NEED MORE MEN.
THE VILLAGE OF PINEROLO.
THERE ISN'T MUCH TIME. WE ARE ASKING FOR YOUR AID.
IN THE PAST, AFTER A RAID, THEY LEFT US ALONE. YOU'VE STARTED A WAR WE CANNOT HOPE TO WIN!

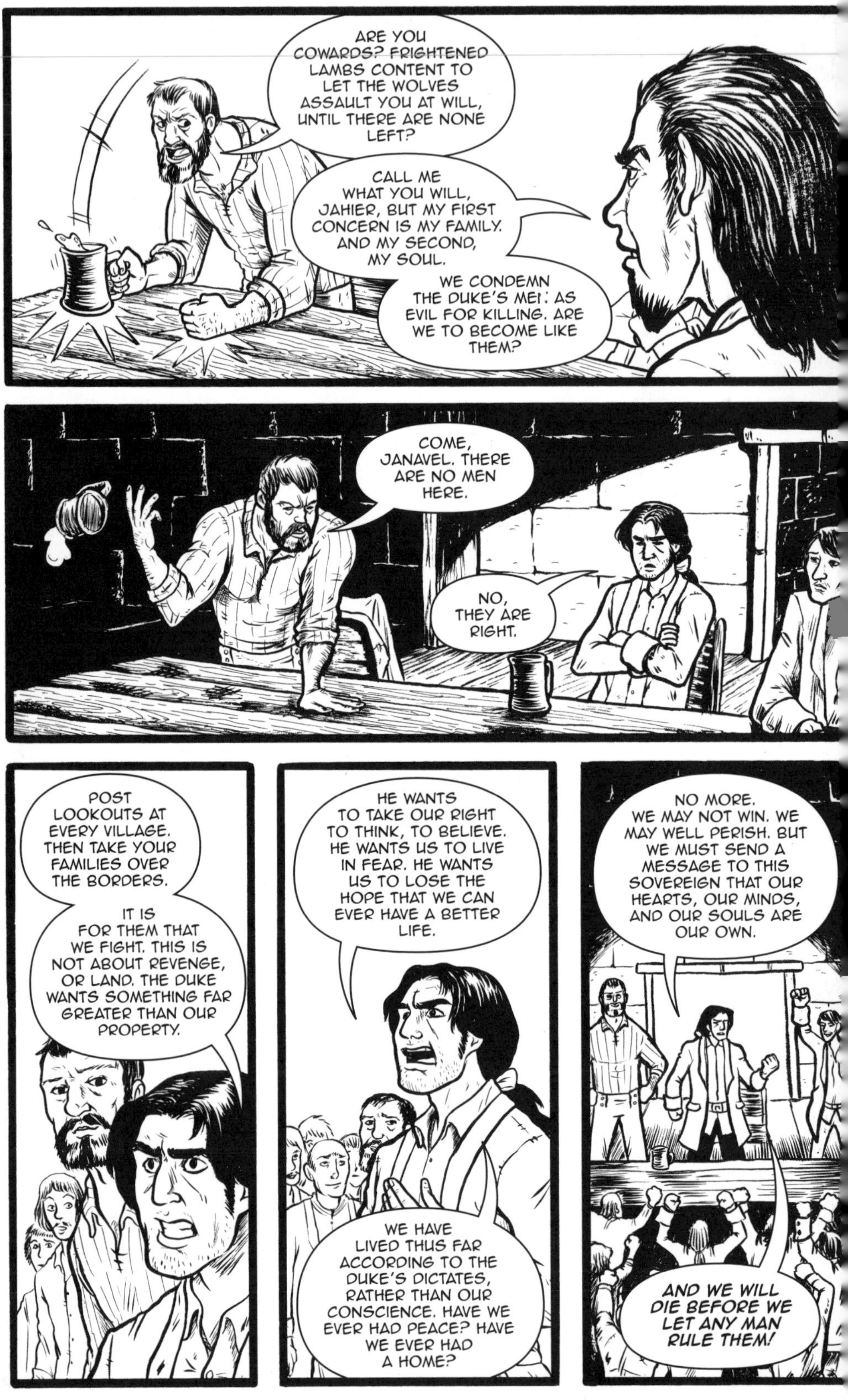
ARE YOU COWARDS? FRIGHTENED LAMBS CONTENT TO LET THE WOLVES ASSAULT YOU AT WILL, UNTIL THERE ARE NONE LEFT?
CALL ME WHAT YOU WILL, JAHIER, BUT MY FIRST CONCERN IS MY FAMILY. AND MY SECOND, MY SOUL.
WE CONDEMN THE DUKE'S MEN AS EVIL FOR KILLING. ARE WE TO BECOME LIKE THEM?
COME, JANAVEL. THERE ARE NO MEN HERE.
NO, THEY ARE RIGHT.
POST LOOKOUTS AT EVERY VILLAGE. THEN TAKE YOUR FAMILIES OVER THE BORDERS.
IT IS FOR THEM THAT WE FIGHT. THIS IS NOT ABOUT REVENGE, OR LAND. THE DUKE WANTS SOMETHING FAR GREATER THAN OUR PROPERTY.
HE WANTS TO TAKE OUR RIGHT TO THINK, TO BELIEVE. HE WANTS US TO LIVE IN FEAR. HE WANTS US TO LOSE THE HOPE THAT WE CAN EVER HAVE A BETTER LIFE.
WE HAVE LIVED THUS FAR ACCORDING TO THE DUKE'S DICTATES, RATHER THAN OUR CONSCIENCE. HAVE WE EVER HAD PEACE? HAVE WE EVER HAD A HOME?
NO MORE. WE MAY NOT WIN. WE MAY WELL PERISH. BUT WE MUST SEND A MESSAGE TO THIS SOVEREIGN THAT OUR HEARTS, OUR MINDS, AND OUR SOULS ARE OUR OWN.
AND WE WILL DIE BEFORE WE LET ANY MAN RULE THEM!

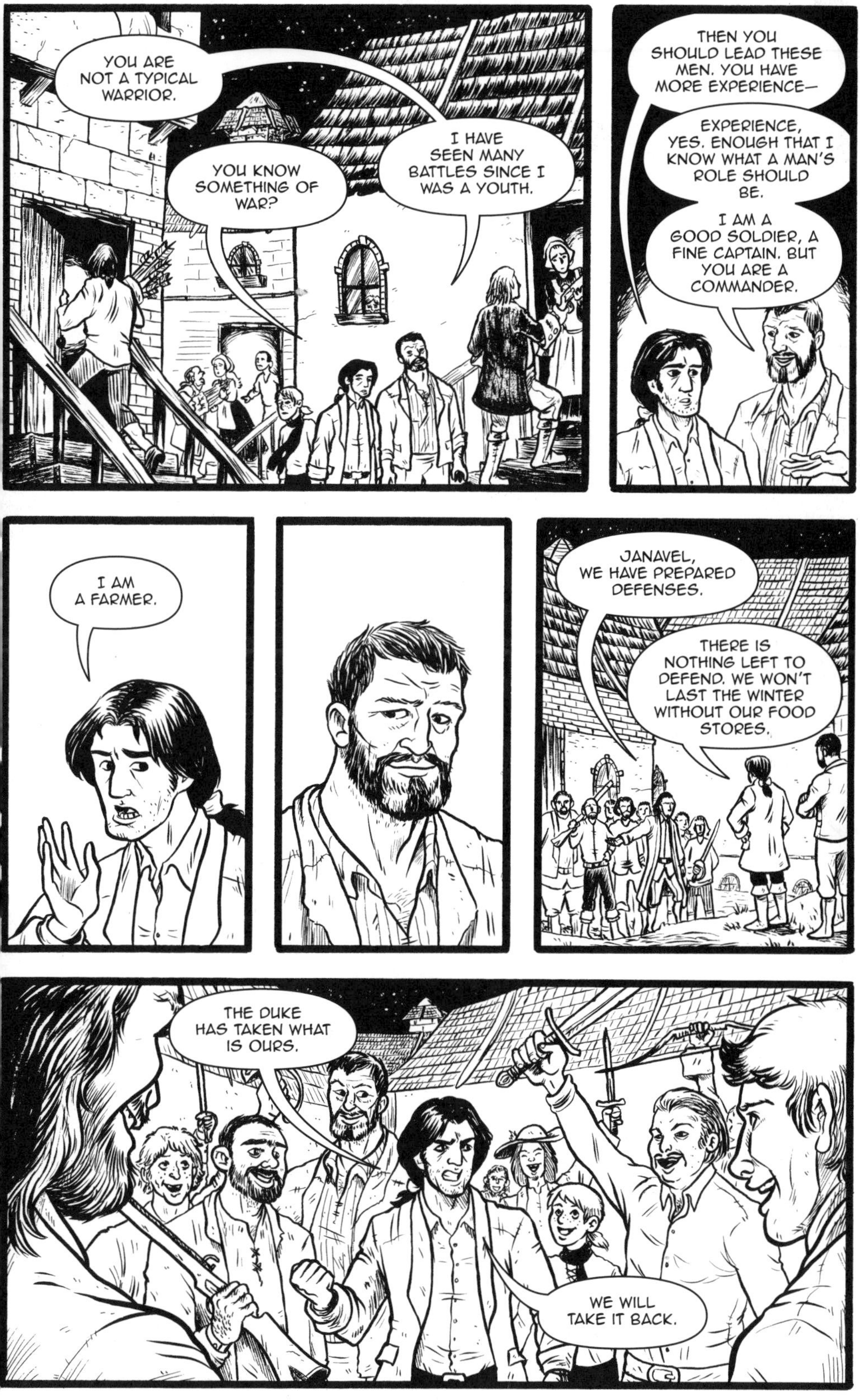
YOU ARE NOT A TYPICAL WARRIOR.
YOU KNOW SOMETHING OF WAR?
I HAVE SEEN MANY BATTLES SINCE I WAS A YOUTH.
THEN YOU SHOULD LEAD THESE MEN. YOU HAVE MORE EXPERIENCE—
EXPERIENCE, YES. ENOUGH THAT I KNOW WHAT A MAN'S ROLE SHOULD BE.
I AM A GOOD SOLDIER, A FINE CAPTAIN. BUT YOU ARE A COMMANDER.
I AM A FARMER.
JANAVEL, WE HAVE PREPARED DEFENSES.
THERE IS NOTHING LEFT TO DEFEND. WE WON'T LAST THE WINTER WITHOUT OUR FOOD STORES.
THE DUKE HAS TAKEN WHAT IS OURS.
WE WILL TAKE IT BACK.

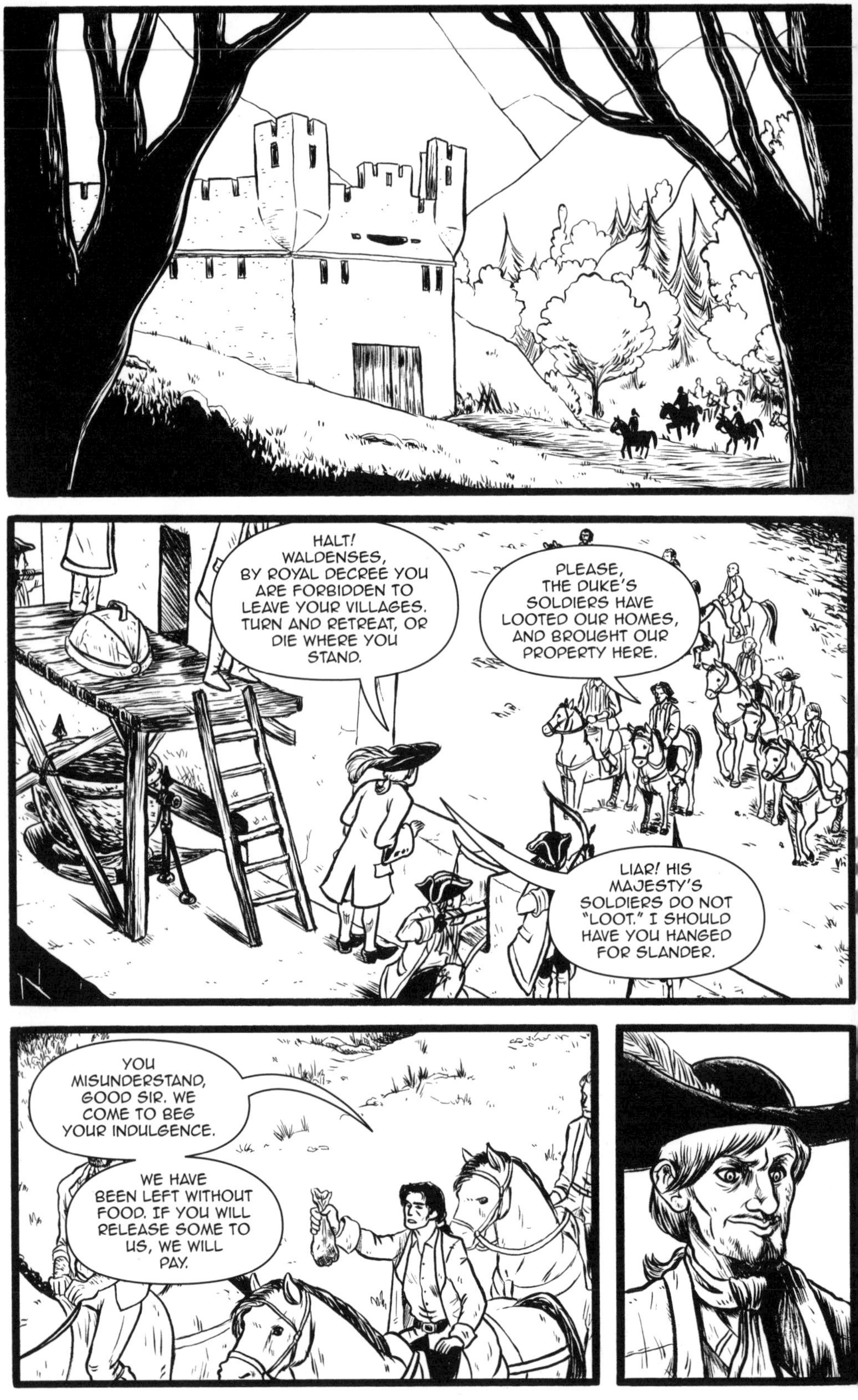
HALT! WALDENSES, BY ROYAL DECREE YOU ARE FORBIDDEN TO LEAVE YOUR VILLAGES. TURN AND RETREAT, OR DIE WHERE YOU STAND.
PLEASE, THE DUKE'S SOLDIERS HAVE LOOTED OUR HOMES, AND BROUGHT OUR PROPERTY HERE.
LIAR! HIS MAJESTY'S SOLDIERS DO NOT "LOOT." I SHOULD HAVE YOU HANGED FOR SLANDER.
YOU MISUNDERSTAND, GOOD SIR. WE COME TO BEG YOUR INDULGENCE.
WE HAVE BEEN LEFT WITHOUT FOOD. IF YOU WILL RELEASE SOME TO US, WE WILL PAY.

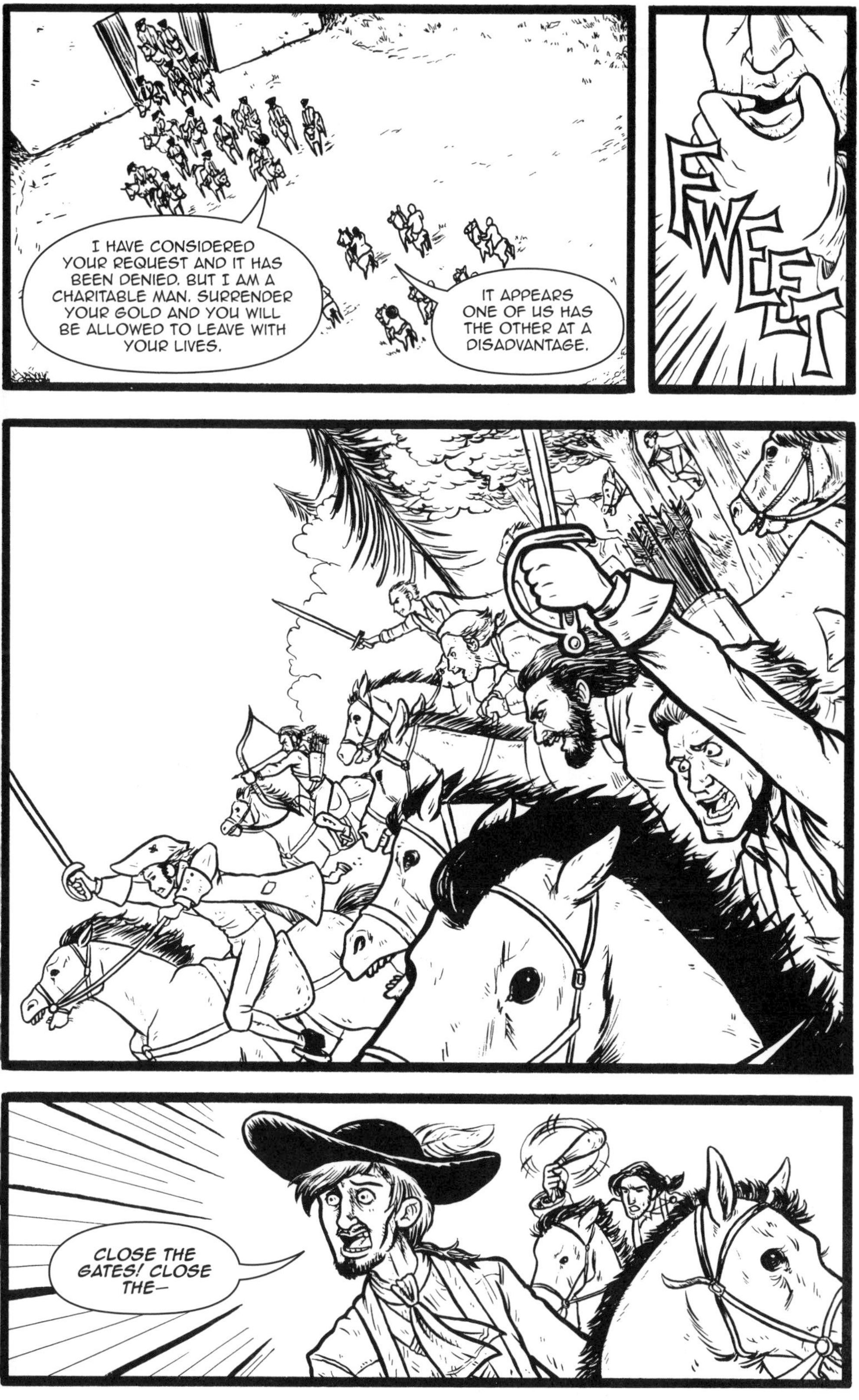
I HAVE CONSIDERED YOUR REQUEST AND IT HAS BEEN DENIED. BUT I AM A CHARITABLE MAN. SURRENDER YOUR GOLD AND YOU WILL BE ALLOWED TO LEAVE WITH YOUR LIVES.
IT APPEARS ONE OF US HAS THE OTHER AT A DISADVANTAGE.
FWEET
CLOSE THE GATES! CLOSE THE—

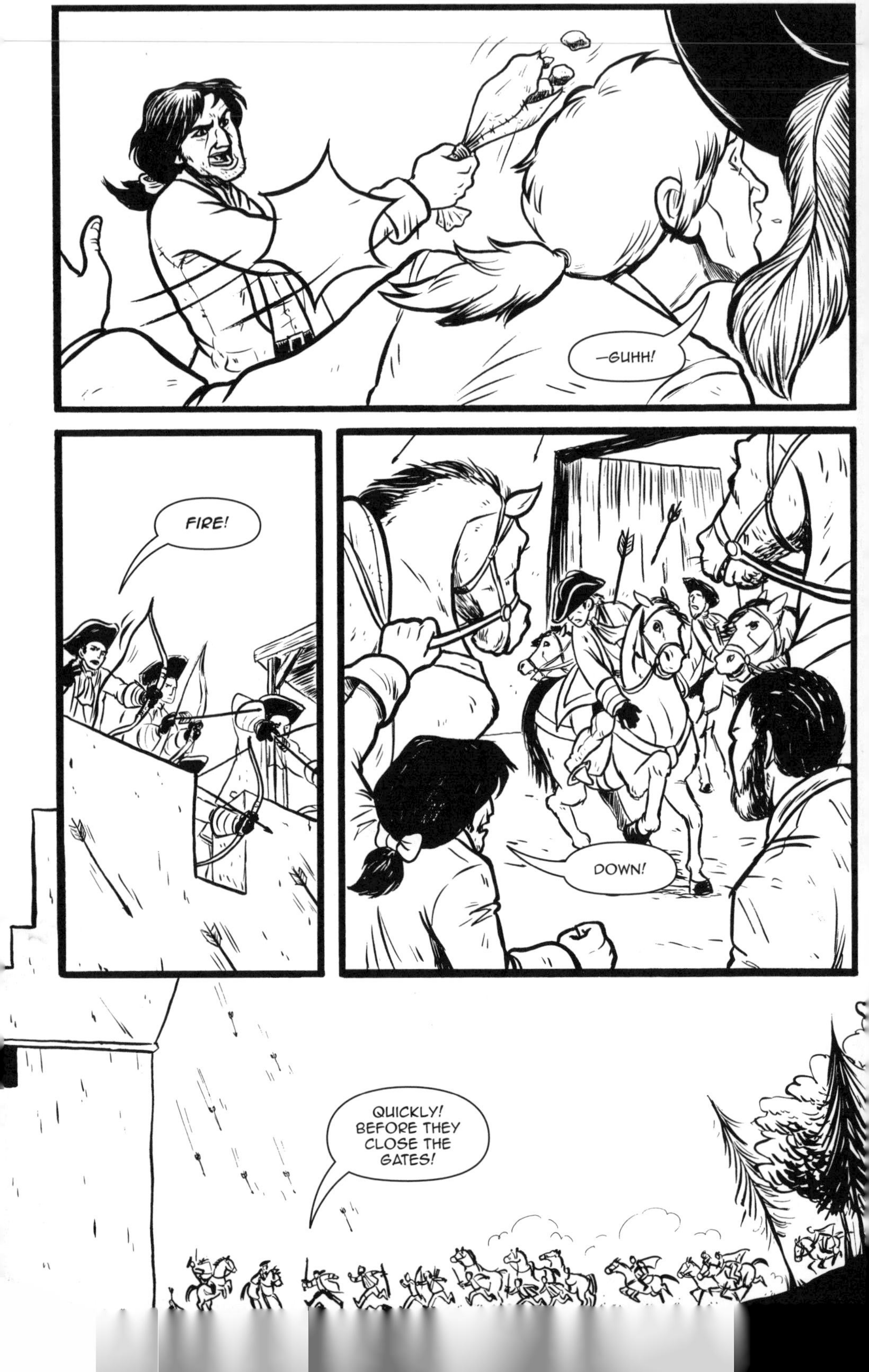
—GUHH!
FIRE!
DOWN!
QUICKLY! BEFORE THEY CLOSE THE GATES!

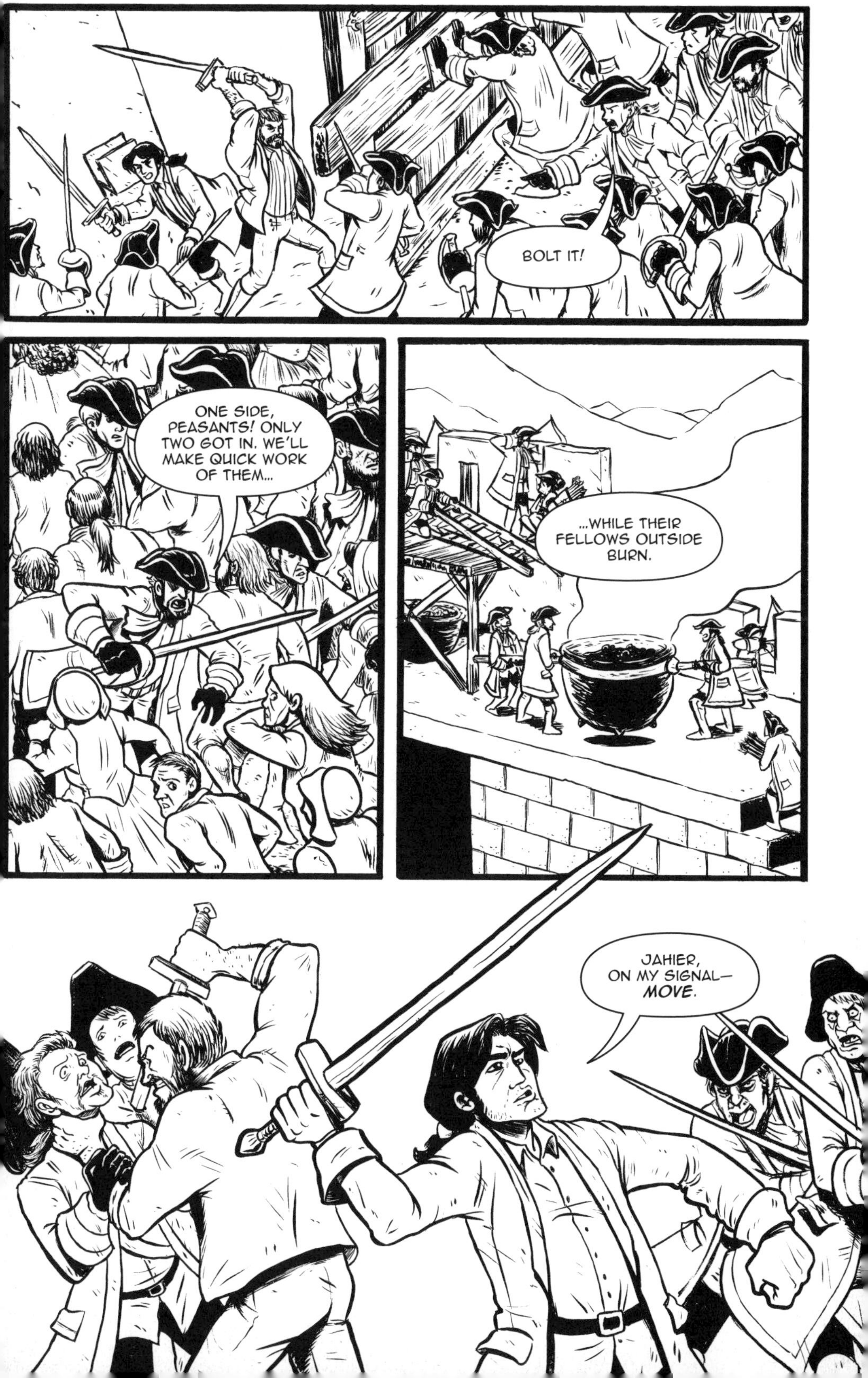
BOLT IT!
ONE SIDE, PEASANTS! ONLY TWO GOT IN. WE'LL MAKE QUICK WORK OF THEM...
...WHILE THEIR FELLOWS OUTSIDE BURN.
JAHIER, ON MY SIGNAL—
MOVE.

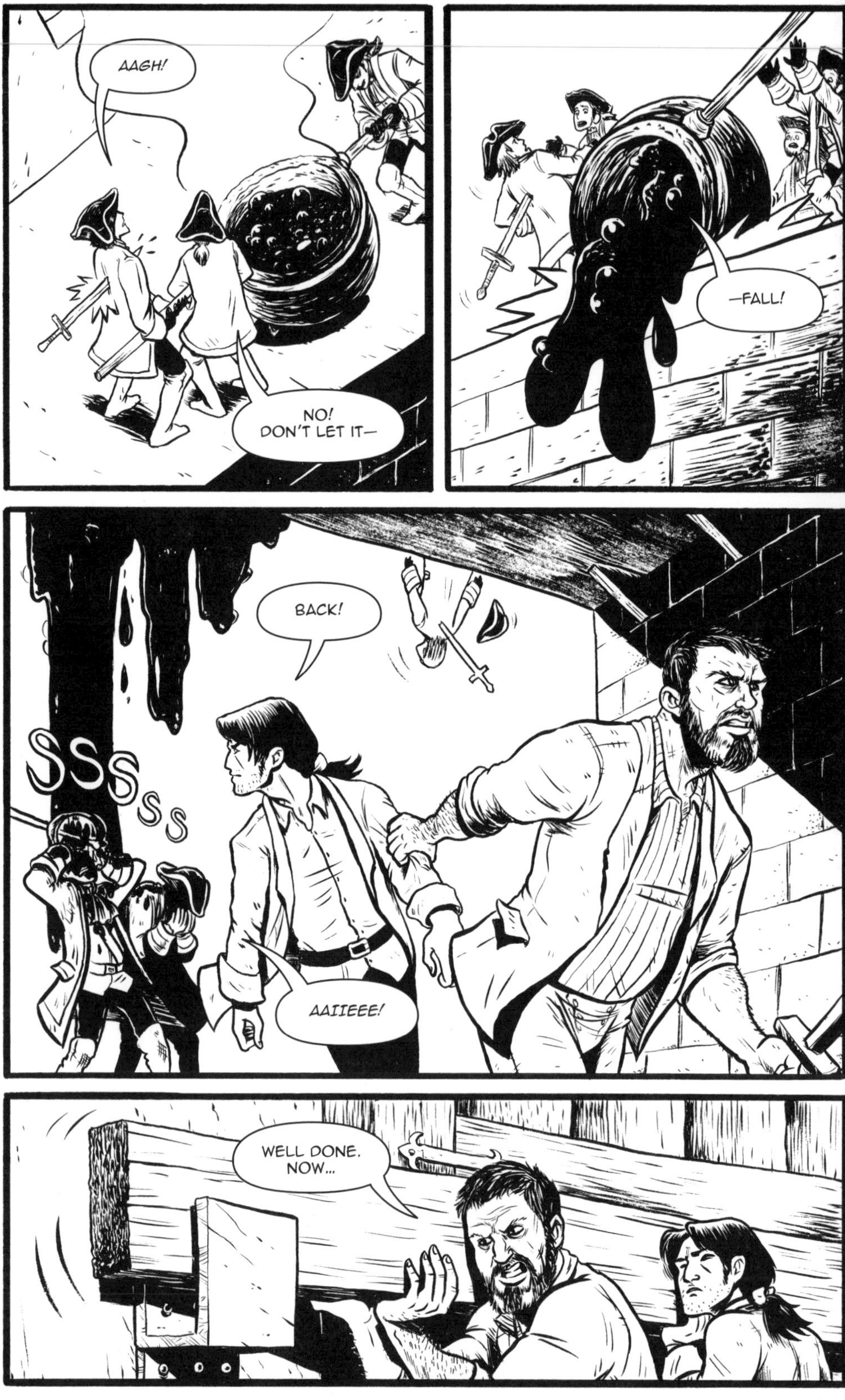
AAGH!
NO! DON'T LET IT—
—FALL!
BACK!
SSSSS
AAIIEEE!
WELL DONE. NOW...

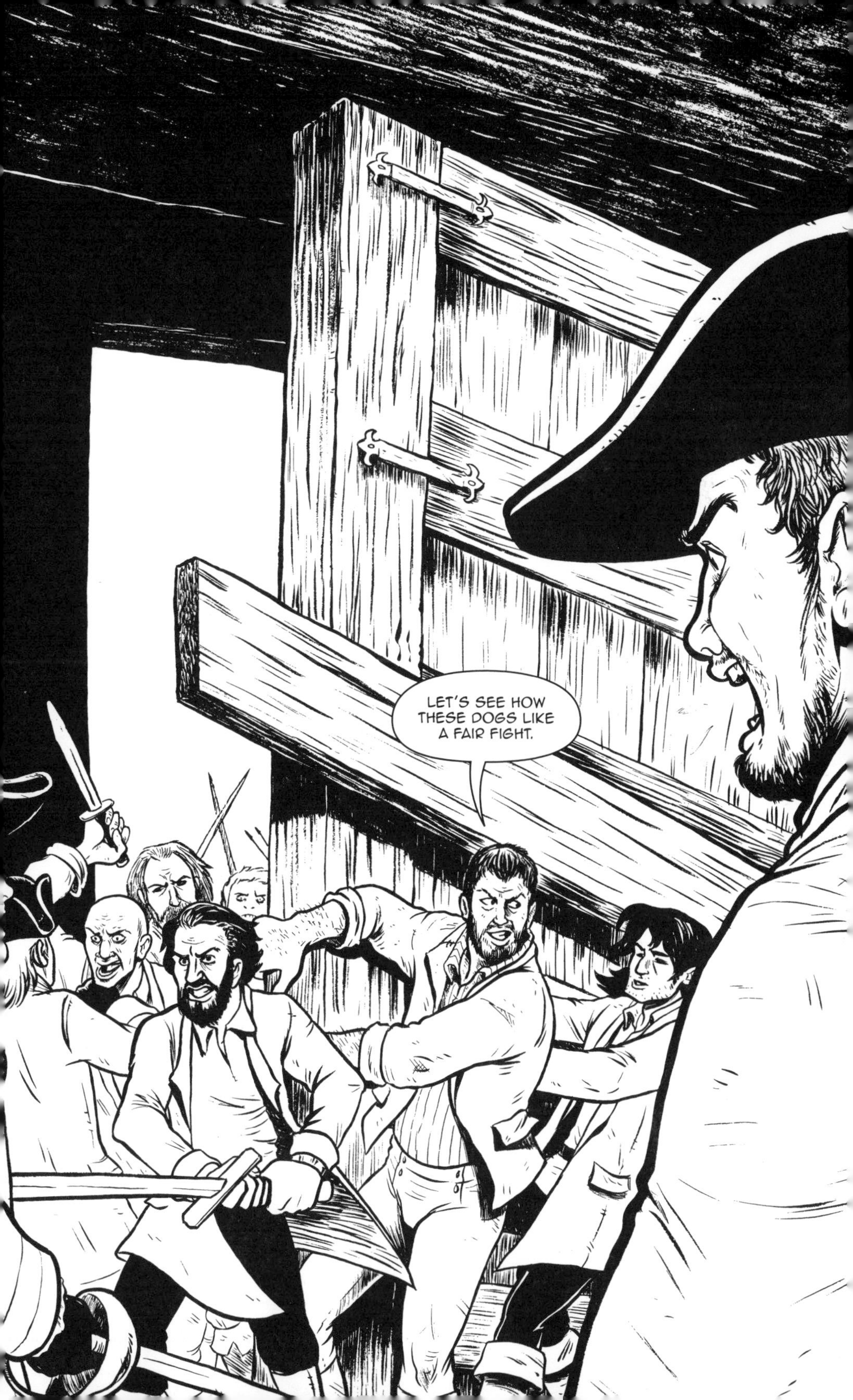
LET'S SEE HOW THESE DOGS LIKE A FAIR FIGHT.

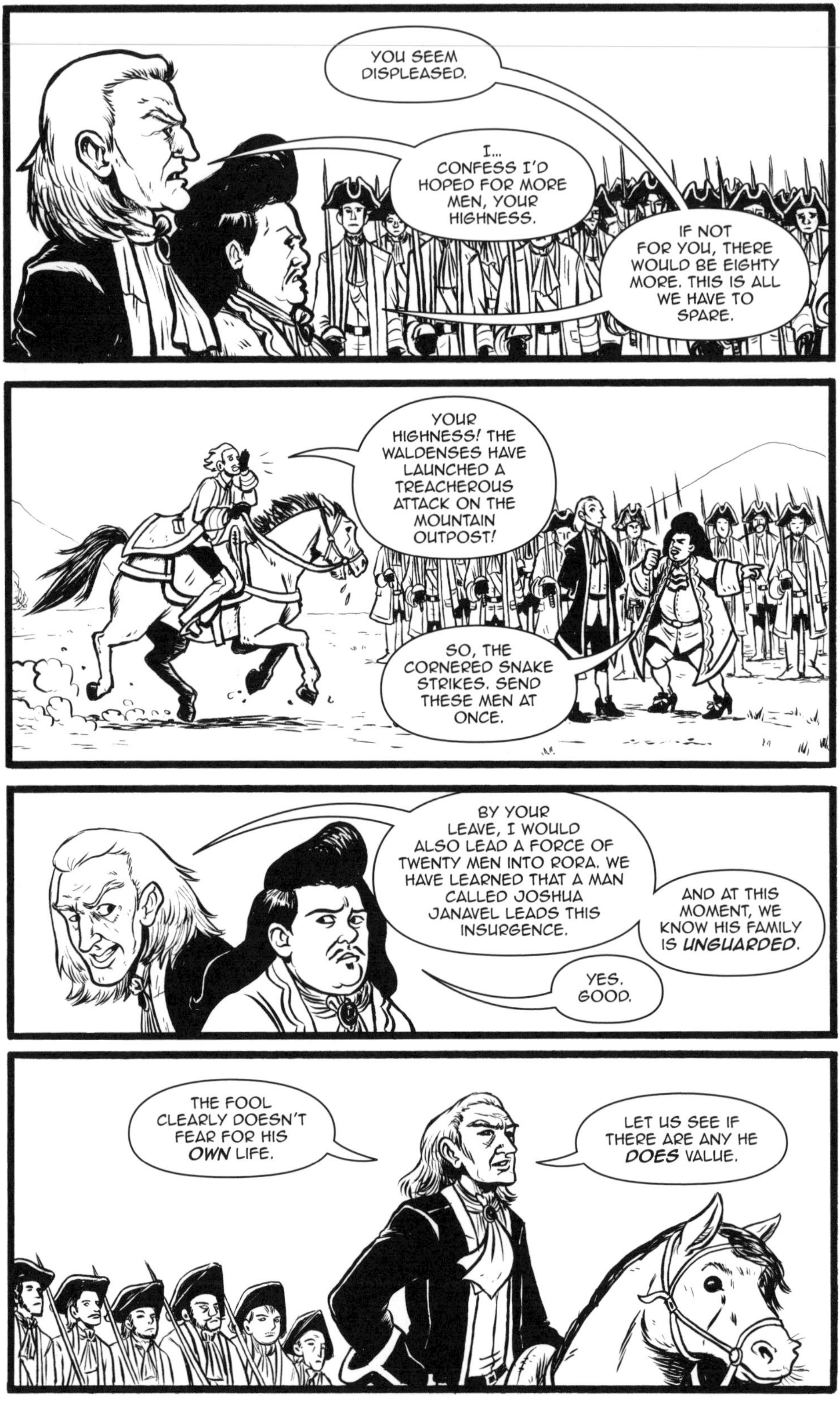
YOU SEEM DISPLEASED.
I... CONFESS I'D HOPED FOR MORE MEN, YOUR HIGHNESS.
IF NOT FOR YOU, THERE WOULD BE EIGHTY MORE. THIS IS ALL WE HAVE TO SPARE.
YOUR HIGHNESS! THE WALDENSES HAVE LAUNCHED A TREACHEROUS ATTACK ON THE MOUNTAIN OUTPOST!
SO, THE CORNERED SNAKE STRIKES. SEND THESE MEN AT ONCE.
BY YOUR LEAVE, I WOULD ALSO LEAD A FORCE OF TWENTY MEN INTO RORA. WE HAVE LEARNED THAT A MAN CALLED JOSHUA JANAVEL LEADS THIS INSURGENCE.
AND AT THIS MOMENT, WE KNOW HIS FAMILY IS UNGUARDED.
YES. GOOD.
THE FOOL CLEARLY DOESN'T FEAR FOR HIS OWN LIFE.
LET US SEE IF THERE ARE ANY HE DOES VALUE.

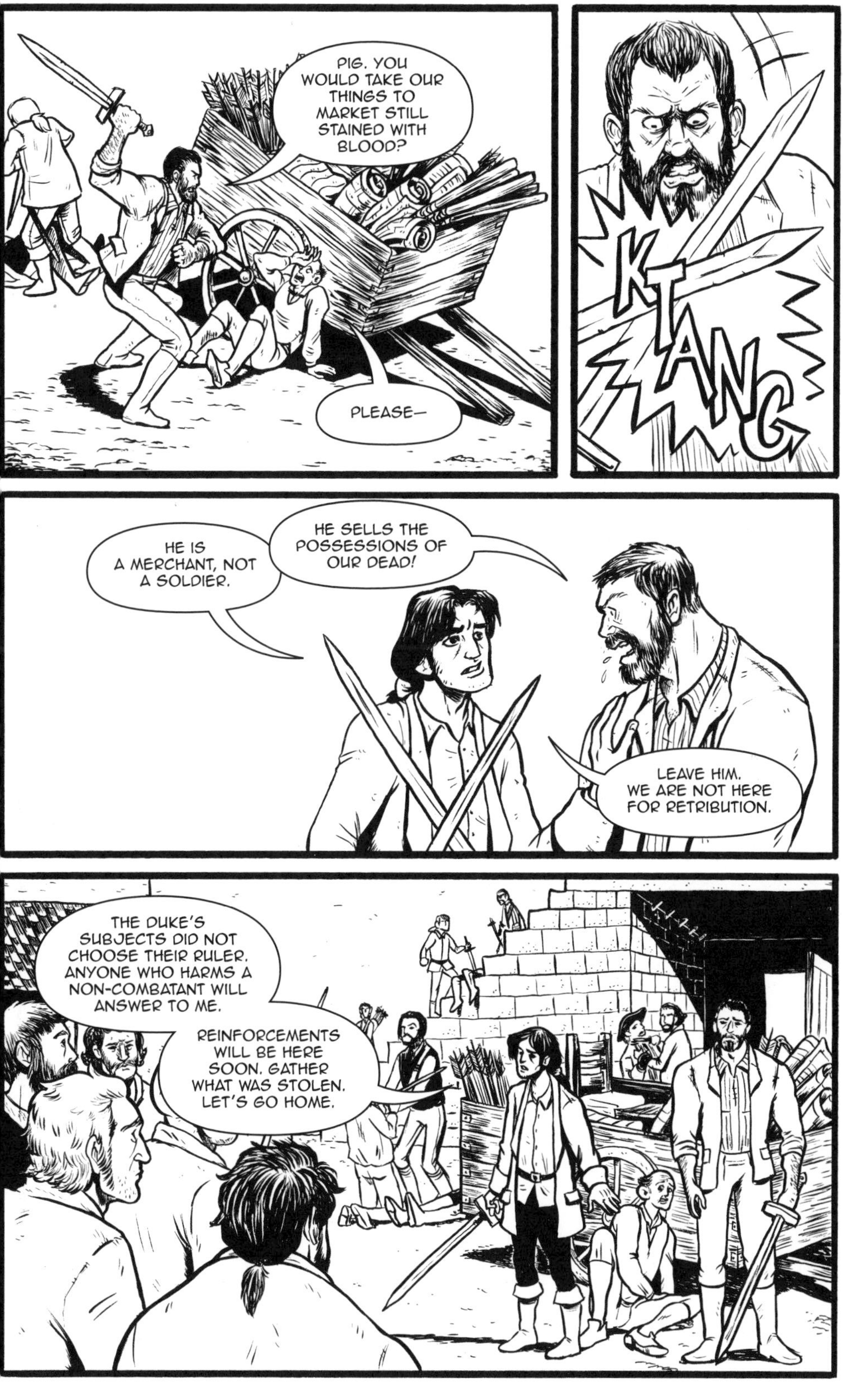
PIG. YOU WOULD TAKE OUR THINGS TO MARKET STILL STAINED WITH BLOOD?
PLEASE—
KTANG
HE IS A MERCHANT, NOT A SOLDIER.
HE SELLS THE POSSESSIONS OF OUR DEAD!
LEAVE HIM. WE ARE NOT HERE FOR RETRIBUTION.
THE DUKE'S SUBJECTS DID NOT CHOOSE THEIR RULER. ANYONE WHO HARMS A NON-COMBATANT WILL ANSWER TO ME.
REINFORCEMENTS WILL BE HERE SOON. GATHER WHAT WAS STOLEN. LET'S GO HOME.

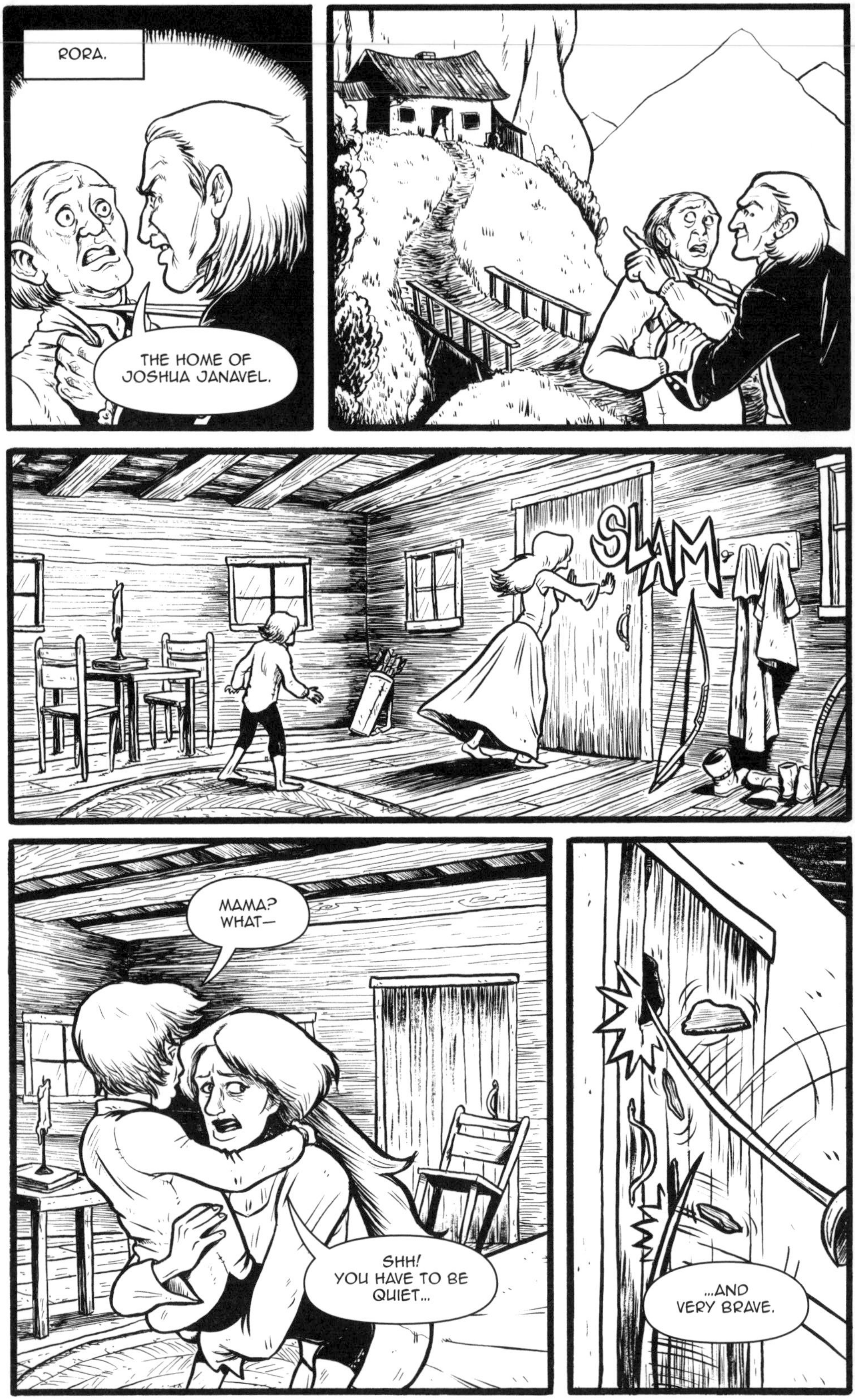
RORA.
THE HOME OF JOSHUA JANAVEL.
SLAM
MAMA? WHAT—
SHH! YOU HAVE TO BE QUIET...
...AND VERY BRAVE.

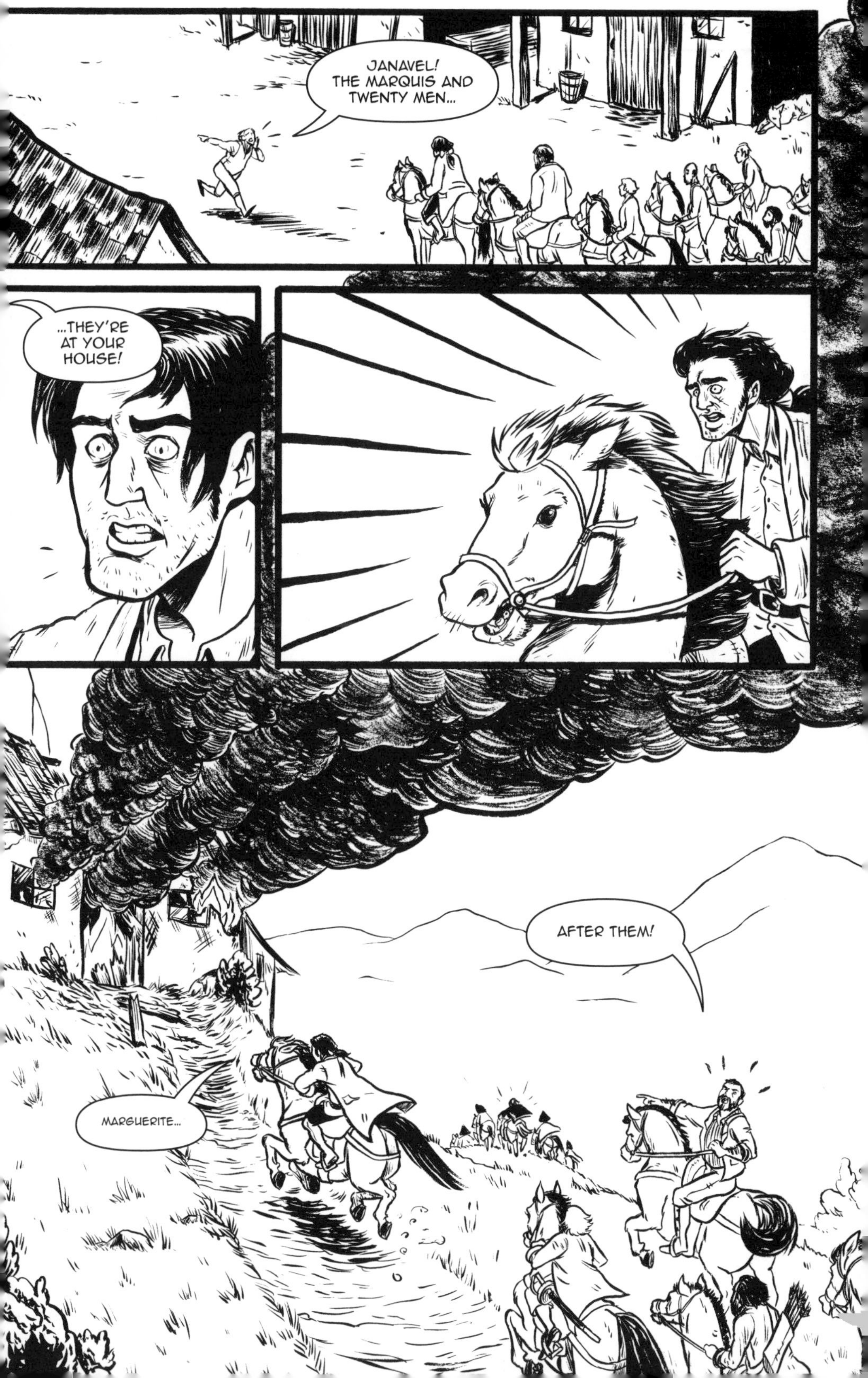
JANAVEL! THE MARQUIS AND TWENTY MEN...
...THEY'RE AT YOUR HOUSE!
AFTER THEM!
MARGUERITE...

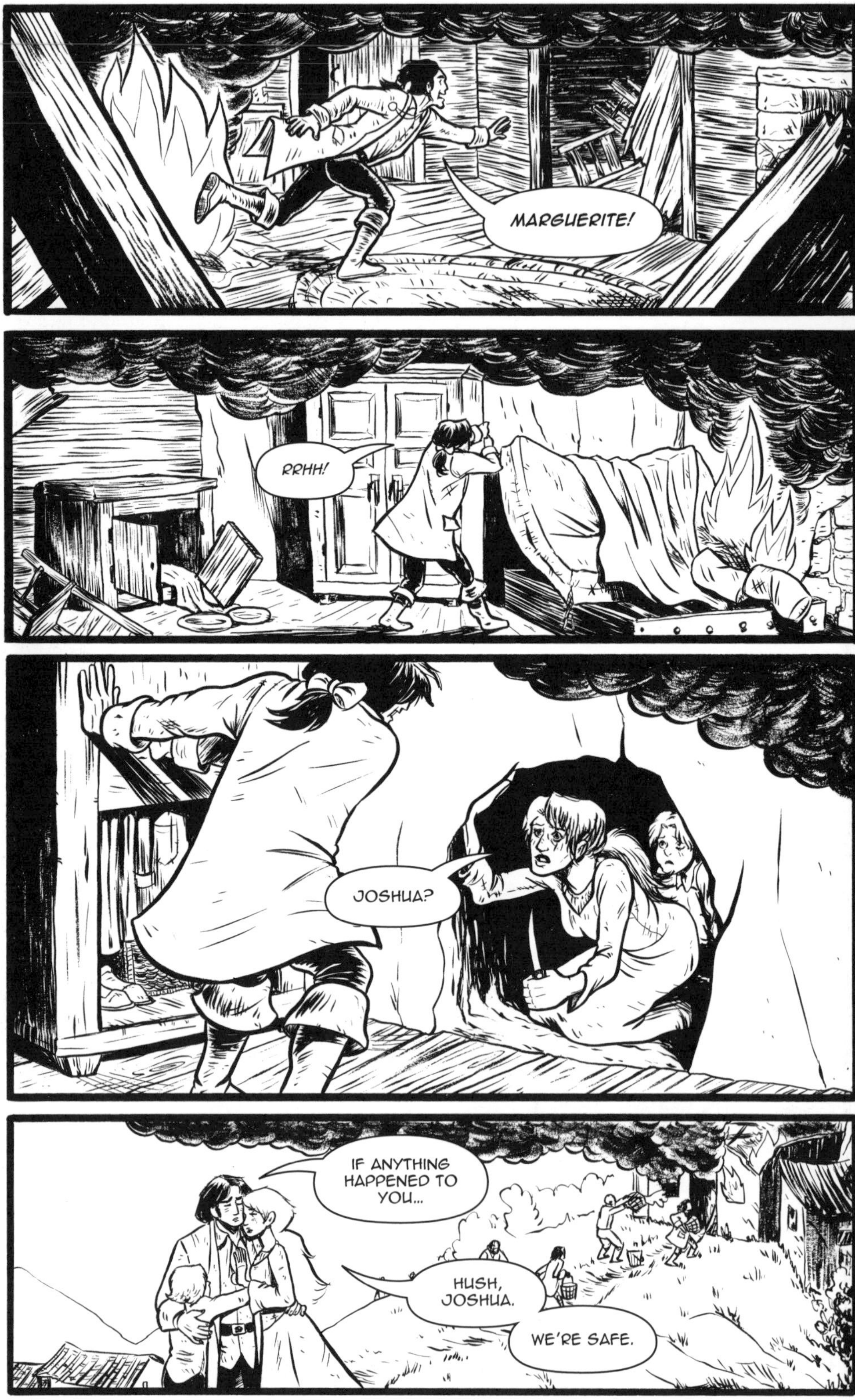
MARGUERITE!
RRHH!
JOSHUA?
IF ANYTHING HAPPENED TO YOU...
HUSH, JOSHUA.
WE'RE SAFE.

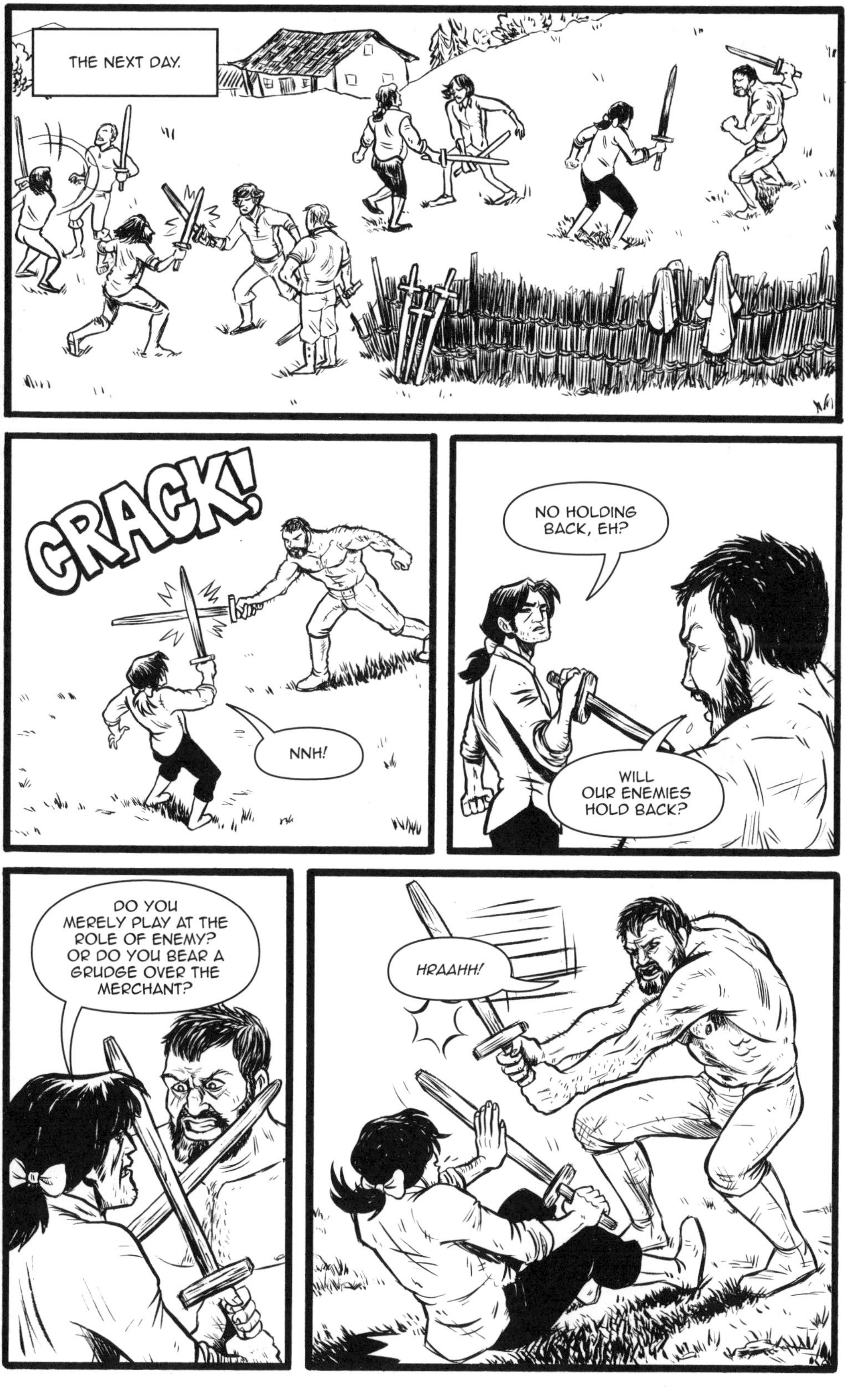
THE NEXT DAY.
CRACK!
NNH!
NO HOLDING BACK, EH?
WILL OUR ENEMIES HOLD BACK?
DO YOU MERELY PLAY AT THE ROLE OF ENEMY? OR DO YOU BEAR A GRUDGE OVER THE MERCHANT?
HRAAHH!

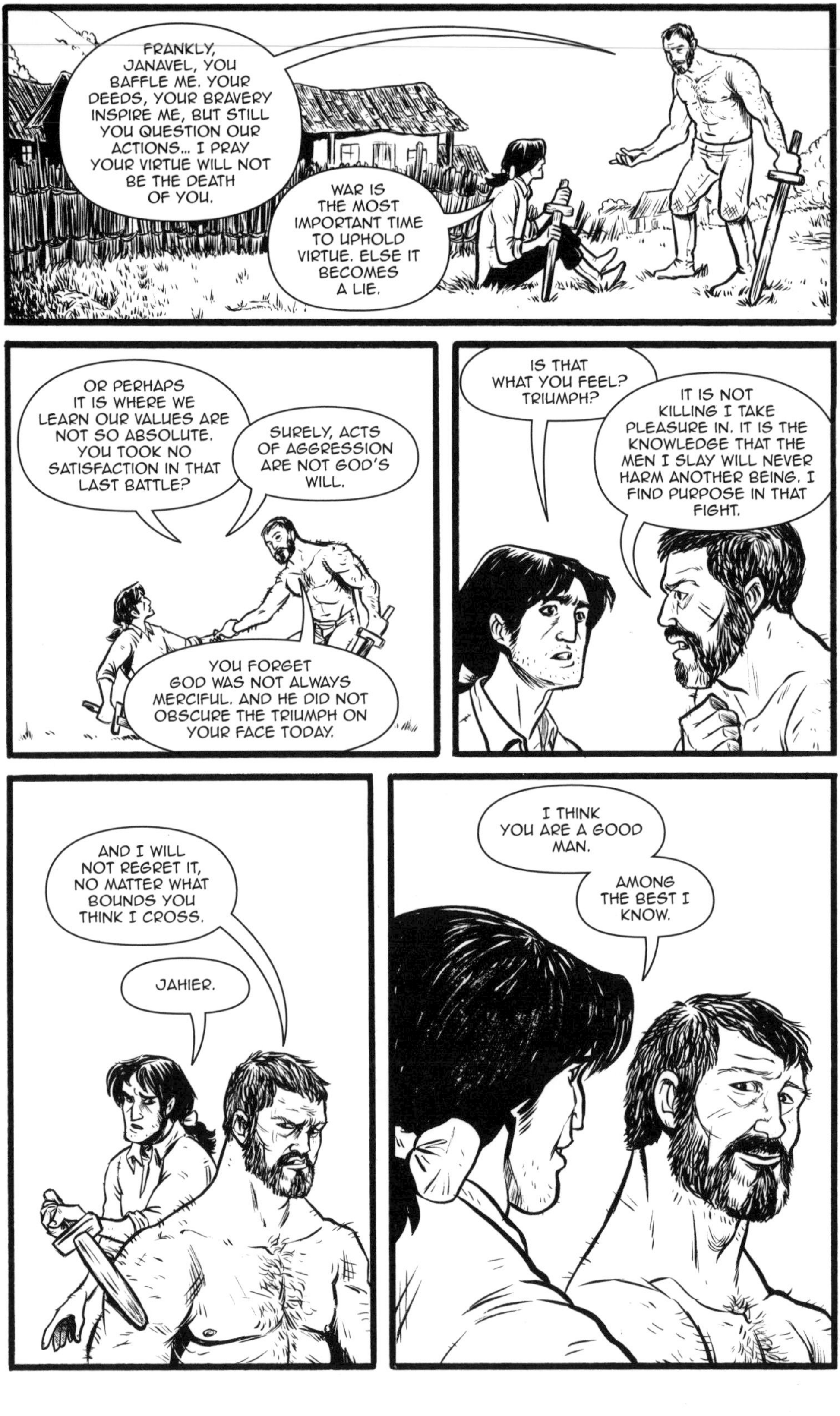
FRANKLY, JANAVEL, YOU BAFFLE ME. YOUR DEEDS, YOUR BRAVERY INSPIRE ME, BUT STILL YOU QUESTION OUR ACTIONS... I PRAY YOUR VIRTUE WILL NOT BE THE DEATH OF YOU.
WAR IS THE MOST IMPORTANT TIME TO UPHOLD VIRTUE. ELSE IT BECOMES A LIE.
OR PERHAPS IT IS WHERE WE LEARN OUR VALUES ARE NOT SO ABSOLUTE. YOU TOOK NO SATISFACTION IN THAT LAST BATTLE?
SURELY, ACTS OF AGGRESSION ARE NOT GOD'S WILL.
YOU FORGET GOD WAS NOT ALWAYS MERCIFUL. AND HE DID NOT OBSCURE THE TRIUMPH ON YOUR FACE TODAY.
IS THAT WHAT YOU FEEL? TRIUMPH?
IT IS NOT KILLING I TAKE PLEASURE IN. IT IS THE KNOWLEDGE THAT THE MEN I SLAY WILL NEVER HARM ANOTHER BEING. I FIND PURPOSE IN THAT FIGHT.
AND I WILL NOT REGRET IT, NO MATTER WHAT BOUNDS YOU THINK I CROSS.
JAHIER.
I THINK YOU ARE A GOOD MAN.
AMONG THE BEST I KNOW.

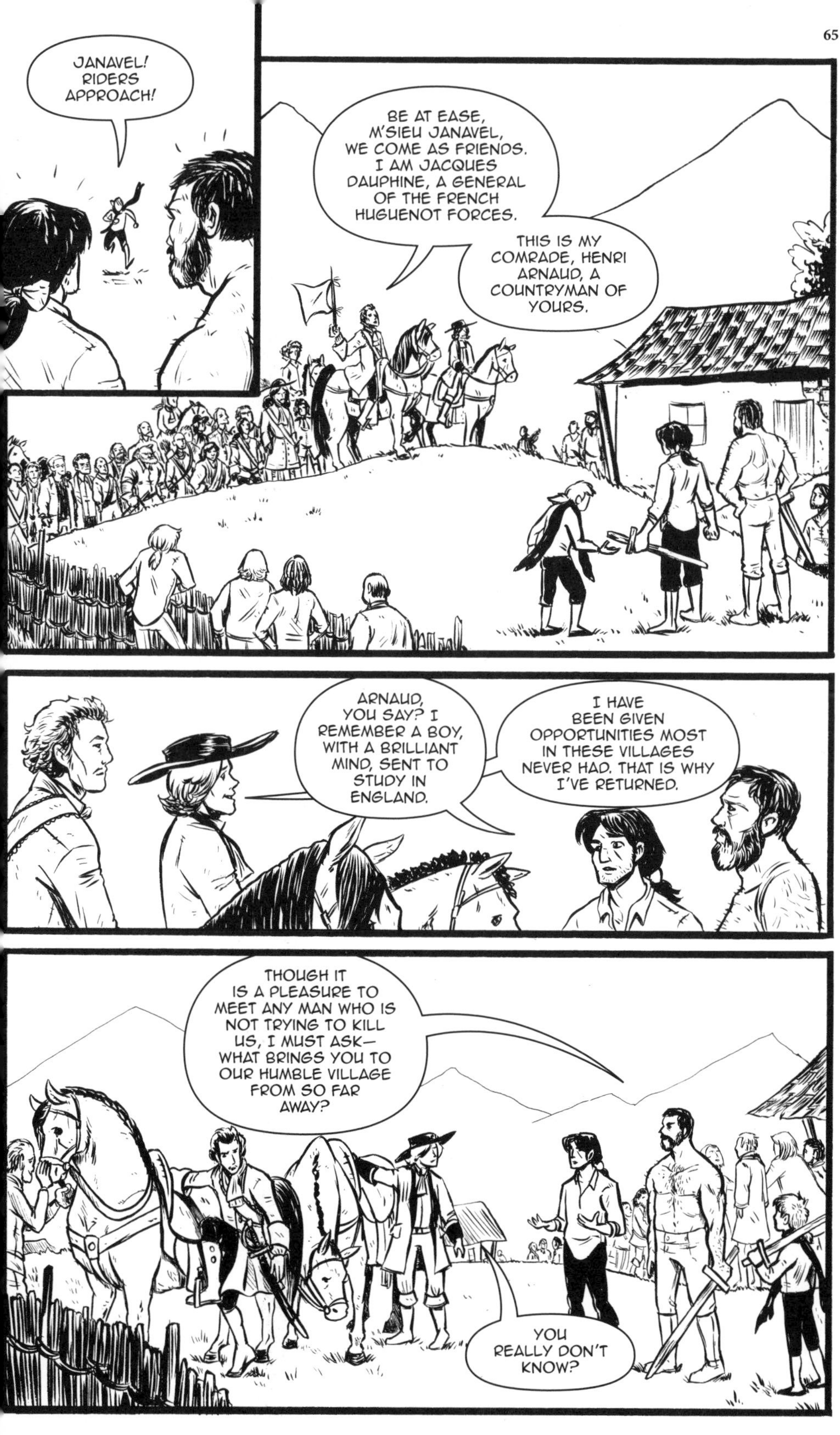
JANAVEL! RIDERS APPROACH!
BE AT EASE, M'SIEU JANAVEL, WE COME AS FRIENDS. I AM JACQUES DAUPHINE, A GENERAL OF THE FRENCH HUGUENOT FORCES.
THIS IS MY COMRADE, HENRI ARNAUD, A COUNTRYMAN OF YOURS.
ARNAUD, YOU SAY? I REMEMBER A BOY, WITH A BRILLIANT MIND, SENT TO STUDY IN ENGLAND.
I HAVE BEEN GIVEN OPPORTUNITIES MOST IN THESE VILLAGES NEVER HAD. THAT IS WHY I'VE RETURNED.
THOUGH IT IS A PLEASURE TO MEET ANY MAN WHO IS NOT TRYING TO KILL US, I MUST ASK— WHAT BRINGS YOU TO OUR HUMBLE VILLAGE FROM SO FAR AWAY?
YOU REALLY DON'T KNOW?

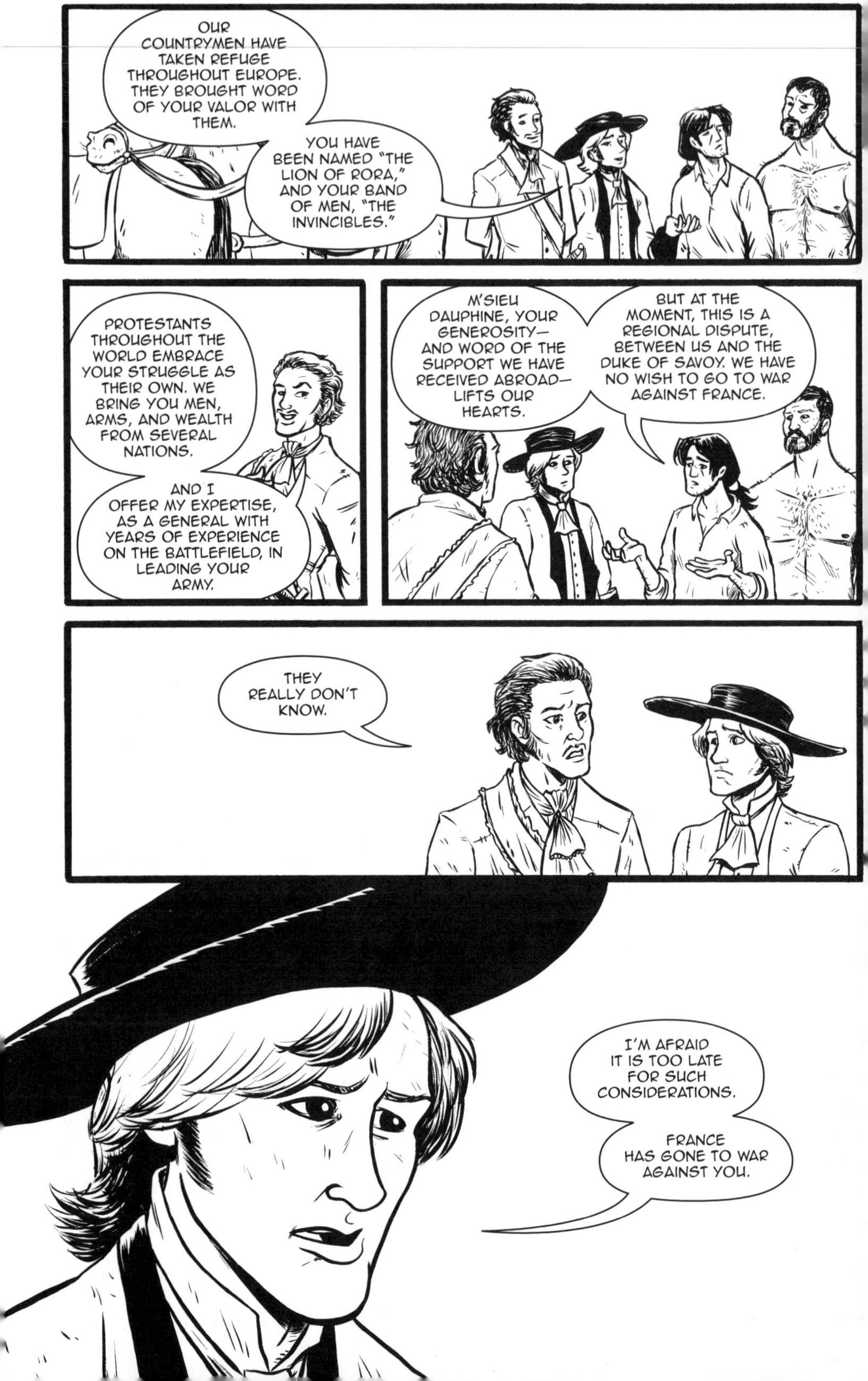
OUR COUNTRYMEN HAVE TAKEN REFUGE THROUGHOUT EUROPE. THEY BROUGHT WORD OF YOUR VALOR WITH THEM.
YOU HAVE BEEN NAMED "THE LION OF RORA," AND YOUR BAND OF MEN, "THE INVINCIBLES."
PROTESTANTS THROUGHOUT THE WORLD EMBRACE YOUR STRUGGLE AS THEIR OWN. WE BRING YOU MEN, ARMS, AND WEALTH FROM SEVERAL NATIONS.
AND I OFFER MY EXPERTISE, AS A GENERAL WITH YEARS OF EXPERIENCE ON THE BATTLEFIELD, IN LEADING YOUR ARMY.
M'SIEU DAUPHINE, YOUR GENEROSITY— AND WORD OF THE SUPPORT WE HAVE RECEIVED ABROAD— LIFTS OUR HEARTS.
BUT AT THE MOMENT, THIS IS A REGIONAL DISPUTE, BETWEEN US AND THE DUKE OF SAVOY. WE HAVE NO WISH TO GO TO WAR AGAINST FRANCE.
THEY REALLY DON'T KNOW.
I'M AFRAID IT IS TOO LATE FOR SUCH CONSIDERATIONS.
FRANCE HAS GONE TO WAR AGAINST YOU.

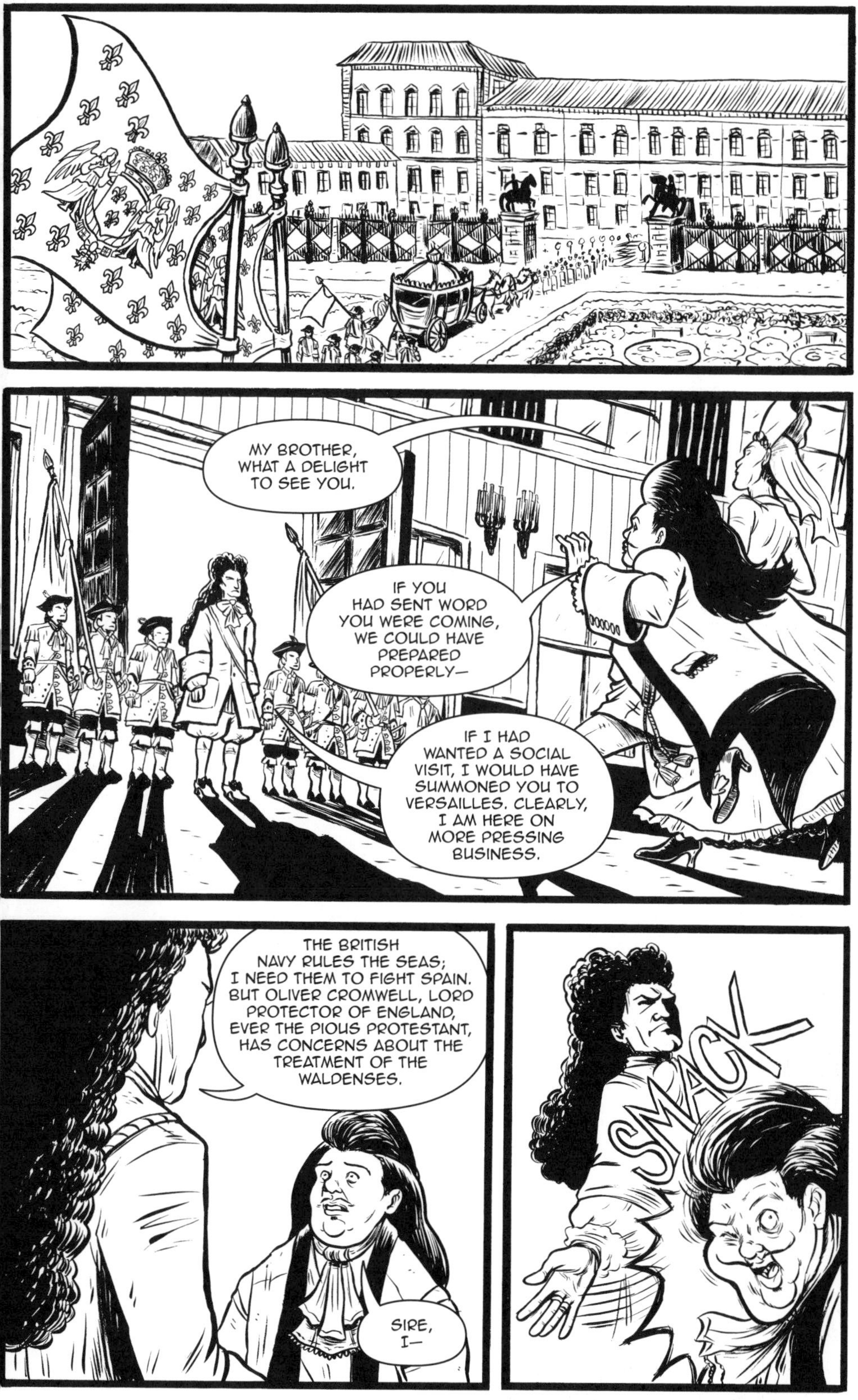
MY BROTHER, WHAT A DELIGHT TO SEE YOU.
IF YOU HAD SENT WORD YOU WERE COMING, WE COULD HAVE PREPARED PROPERLY—
IF I HAD WANTED A SOCIAL VISIT, I WOULD HAVE SUMMONED YOU TO VERSAILLES. CLEARLY, I AM HERE ON MORE PRESSING BUSINESS.
THE BRITISH NAVY RULES THE SEAS; I NEED THEM TO FIGHT SPAIN. BUT OLIVER CROMWELL, LORD PROTECTOR OF ENGLAND, EVER THE PIOUS PROTESTANT, HAS CONCERNS ABOUT THE TREATMENT OF THE WALDENSES.
SIRE, I—
SMACK

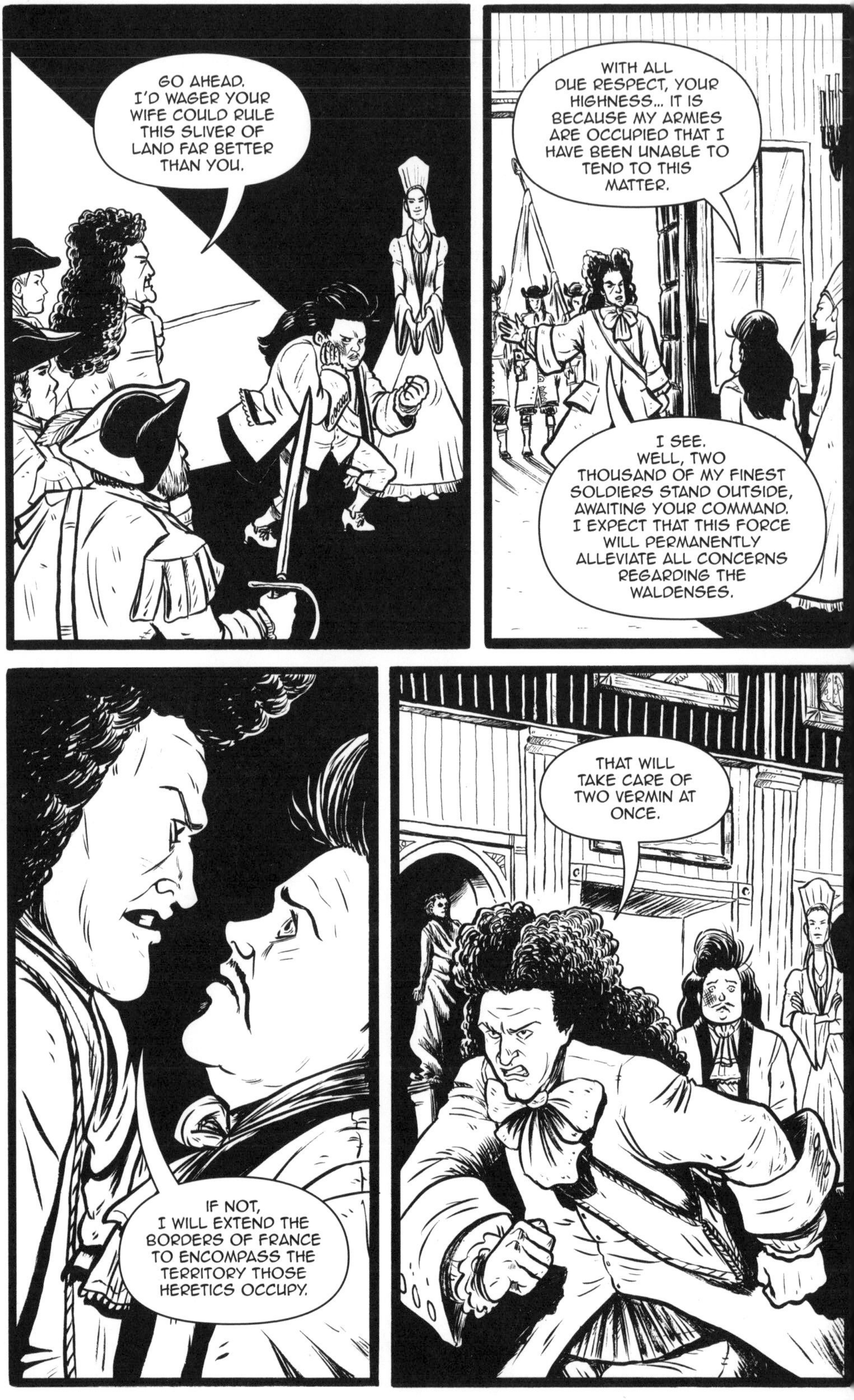
GO AHEAD. I'D WAGER YOUR WIFE COULD RULE THIS SLIVER OF LAND FAR BETTER THAN YOU.
WITH ALL DUE RESPECT, YOUR HIGHNESS... IT IS BECAUSE MY ARMIES ARE OCCUPIED THAT I HAVE BEEN UNABLE TO TEND TO THIS MATTER.
I SEE. WELL, TWO THOUSAND OF MY FINEST SOLDIERS STAND OUTSIDE, AWAITING YOUR COMMAND. I EXPECT THAT THIS FORCE WILL PERMANENTLY ALLEVIATE ALL CONCERNS REGARDING THE WALDENSES.
IF NOT, I WILL EXTEND THE BORDERS OF FRANCE TO ENCOMPASS THE TERRITORY THOSE HERETICS OCCUPY.
THAT WILL TAKE CARE OF TWO VERMIN AT ONCE.

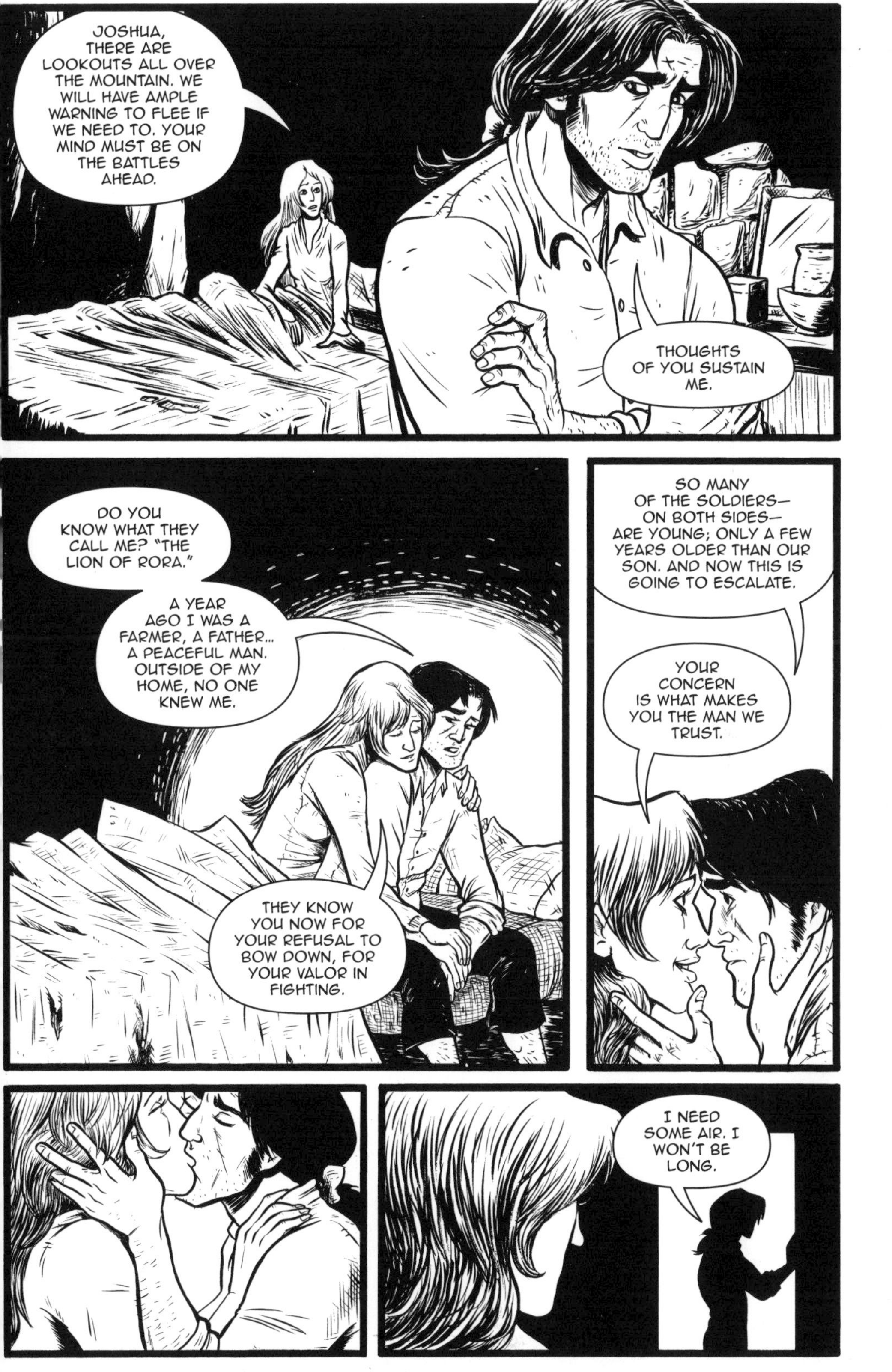
JOSHUA, THERE ARE LOOKOUTS ALL OVER THE MOUNTAIN. WE WILL HAVE AMPLE WARNING TO FLEE IF WE NEED TO. YOUR MIND MUST BE ON THE BATTLES AHEAD.
THOUGHTS OF YOU SUSTAIN ME.
DO YOU KNOW WHAT THEY CALL ME? "THE LION OF RORA."
A YEAR AGO I WAS A FARMER, A FATHER... A PEACEFUL MAN. OUTSIDE OF MY HOME, NO ONE KNEW ME.
THEY KNOW YOU NOW FOR YOUR REFUSAL TO BOW DOWN, FOR YOUR VALOR IN FIGHTING.
SO MANY OF THE SOLDIERS— ON BOTH SIDES— ARE YOUNG; ONLY A FEW YEARS OLDER THAN OUR SON. AND NOW THIS IS GOING TO ESCALATE.
YOUR CONCERN IS WHAT MAKES YOU THE MAN WE TRUST.
I NEED SOME AIR. I WON'T BE LONG.

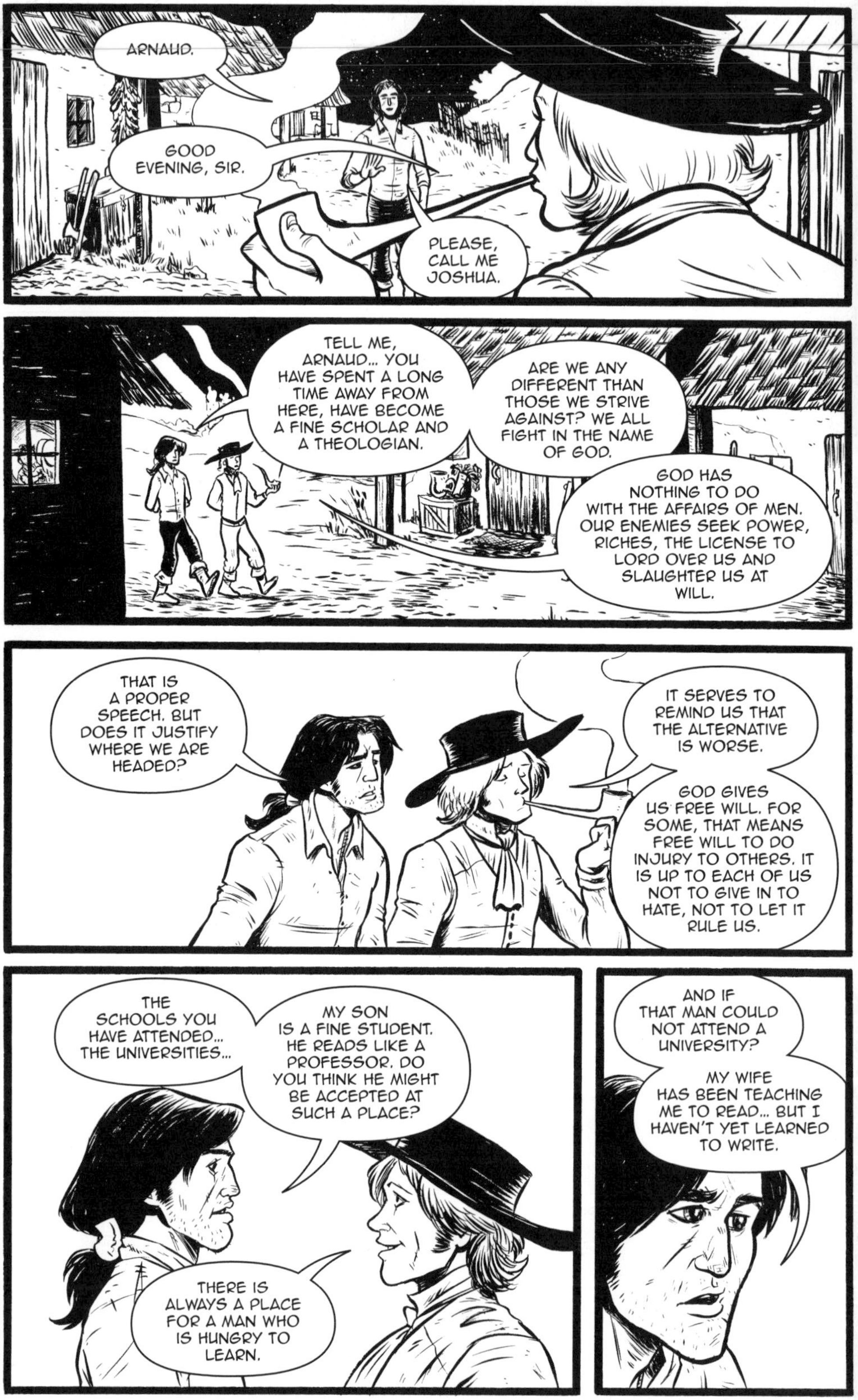
ARNAUD.
GOOD EVENING, SIR.
PLEASE, CALL ME JOSHUA.
TELL ME, ARNAUD... YOU HAVE SPENT A LONG TIME AWAY FROM HERE, HAVE BECOME A FINE SCHOLAR AND A THEOLOGIAN.
ARE WE ANY DIFFERENT THAN THOSE WE STRIVE AGAINST? WE ALL FIGHT IN THE NAME OF GOD.
GOD HAS NOTHING TO DO WITH THE AFFAIRS OF MEN. OUR ENEMIES SEEK POWER, RICHES, THE LICENSE TO LORD OVER US AND SLAUGHTER US AT WILL.
THAT IS A PROPER SPEECH. BUT DOES IT JUSTIFY WHERE WE ARE HEADED?
IT SERVES TO REMIND US THAT THE ALTERNATIVE IS WORSE.
GOD GIVES US FREE WILL. FOR SOME, THAT MEANS FREE WILL TO DO INJURY TO OTHERS. IT IS UP TO EACH OF US NOT TO GIVE IN TO HATE, NOT TO LET IT RULE US.
THE SCHOOLS YOU HAVE ATTENDED... THE UNIVERSITIES...
MY SON IS A FINE STUDENT. HE READS LIKE A PROFESSOR. DO YOU THINK HE MIGHT BE ACCEPTED AT SUCH A PLACE?
THERE IS ALWAYS A PLACE FOR A MAN WHO IS HUNGRY TO LEARN.
AND IF THAT MAN COULD NOT ATTEND A UNIVERSITY?
MY WIFE HAS BEEN TEACHING ME TO READ... BUT I HAVEN'T YET LEARNED TO WRITE.

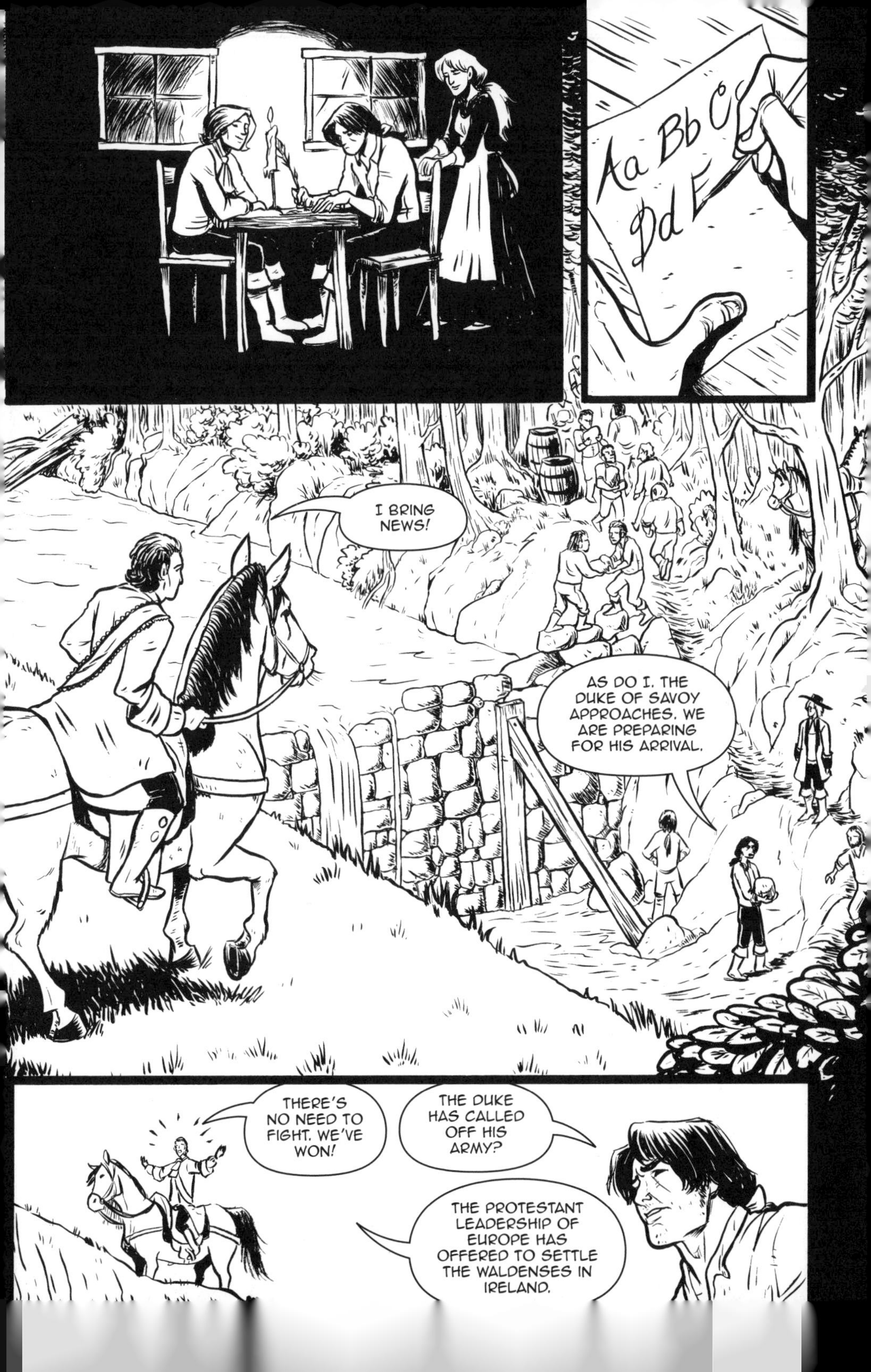
Aa Bb Cc
Dd E
I BRING NEWS!
AS DO I. THE DUKE OF SAVOY APPROACHES. WE ARE PREPARING FOR HIS ARRIVAL.
THERE'S NO NEED TO FIGHT. WE'VE WON!
THE DUKE HAS CALLED OFF HIS ARMY?
THE PROTESTANT LEADERSHIP OF EUROPE HAS OFFERED TO SETTLE THE WALDENSES IN IRELAND.

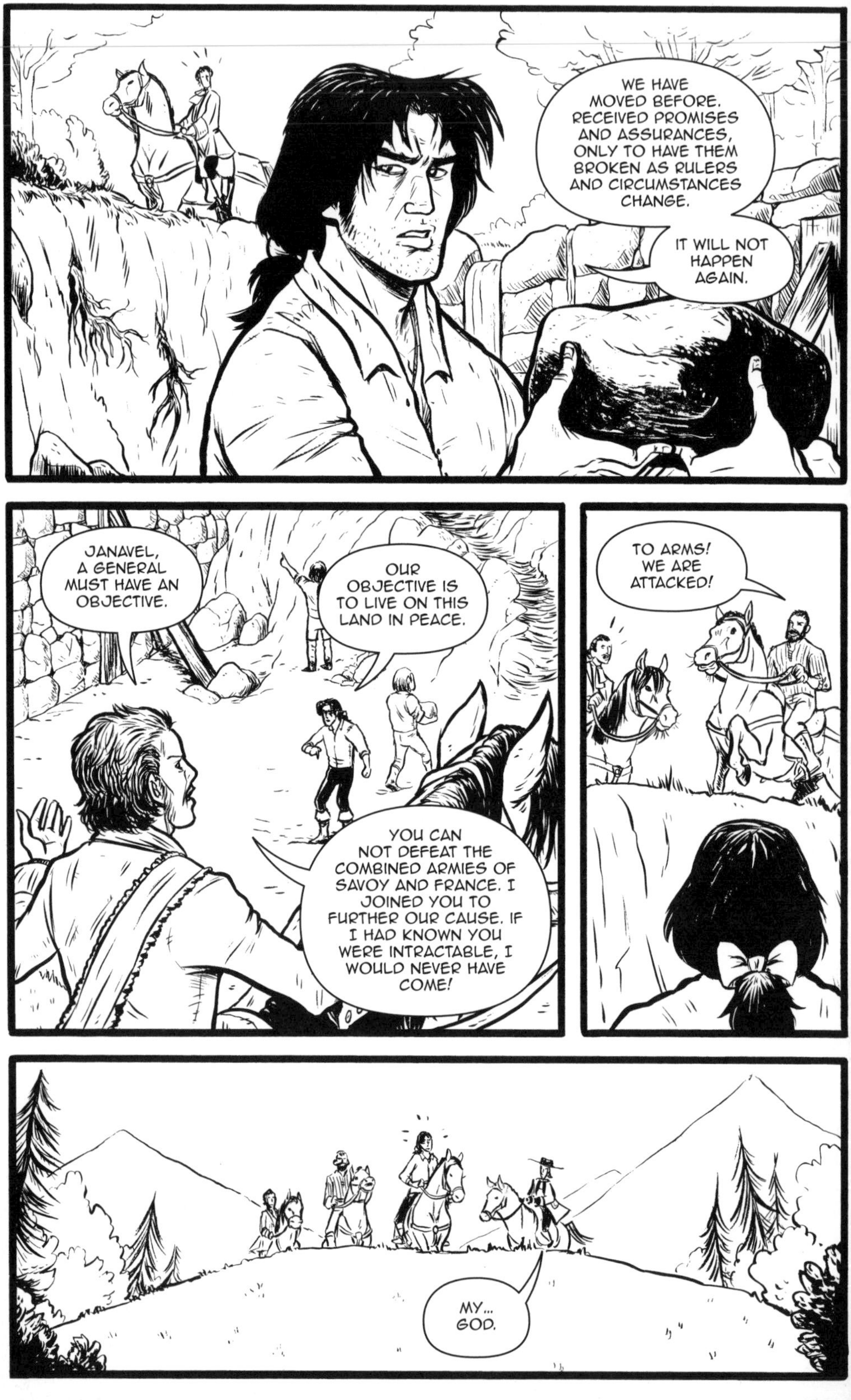
WE HAVE MOVED BEFORE. RECEIVED PROMISES AND ASSURANCES, ONLY TO HAVE THEM BROKEN AS RULERS AND CIRCUMSTANCES CHANGE.
IT WILL NOT HAPPEN AGAIN.
JANAVEL, A GENERAL MUST HAVE AN OBJECTIVE.
OUR OBJECTIVE IS TO LIVE ON THIS LAND IN PEACE.
YOU CAN NOT DEFEAT THE COMBINED ARMIES OF SAVOY AND FRANCE. I JOINED YOU TO FURTHER OUR CAUSE. IF I HAD KNOWN YOU WERE INTRACTABLE, I WOULD NEVER HAVE COME!
TO ARMS! WE ARE ATTACKED!
MY... GOD.

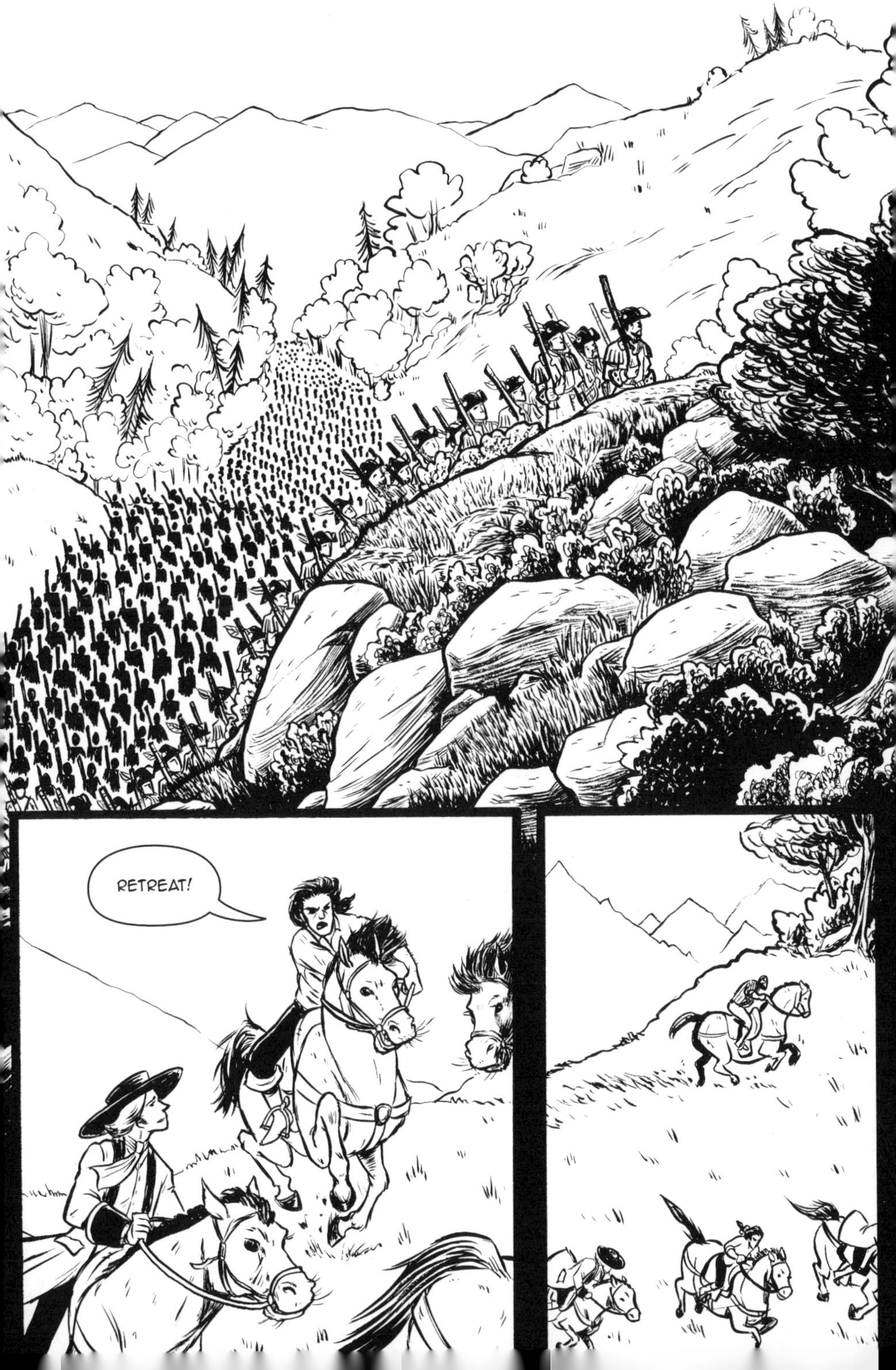
RETREAT!

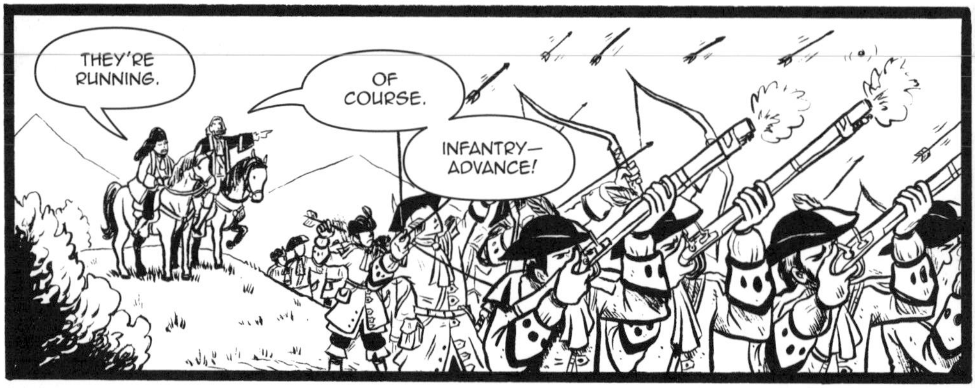
THEY'RE RUNNING.
OF COURSE.
INFANTRY— ADVANCE!

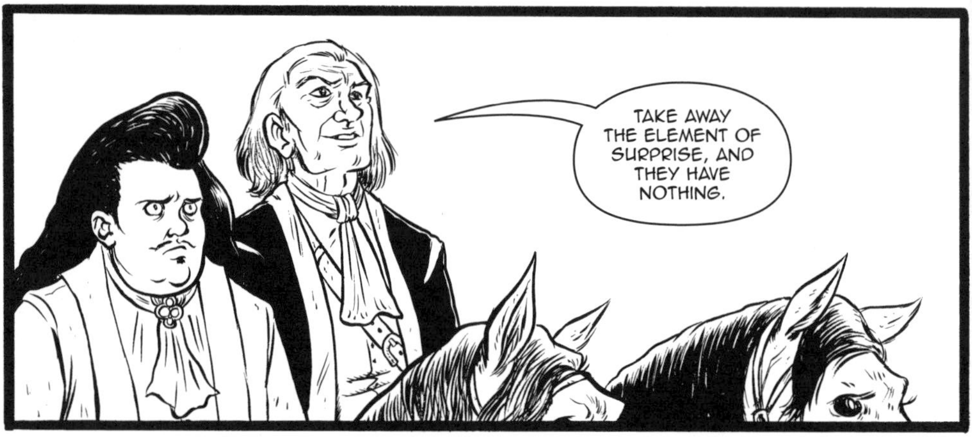
TAKE AWAY THE ELEMENT OF SURPRISE, AND THEY HAVE NOTHING.

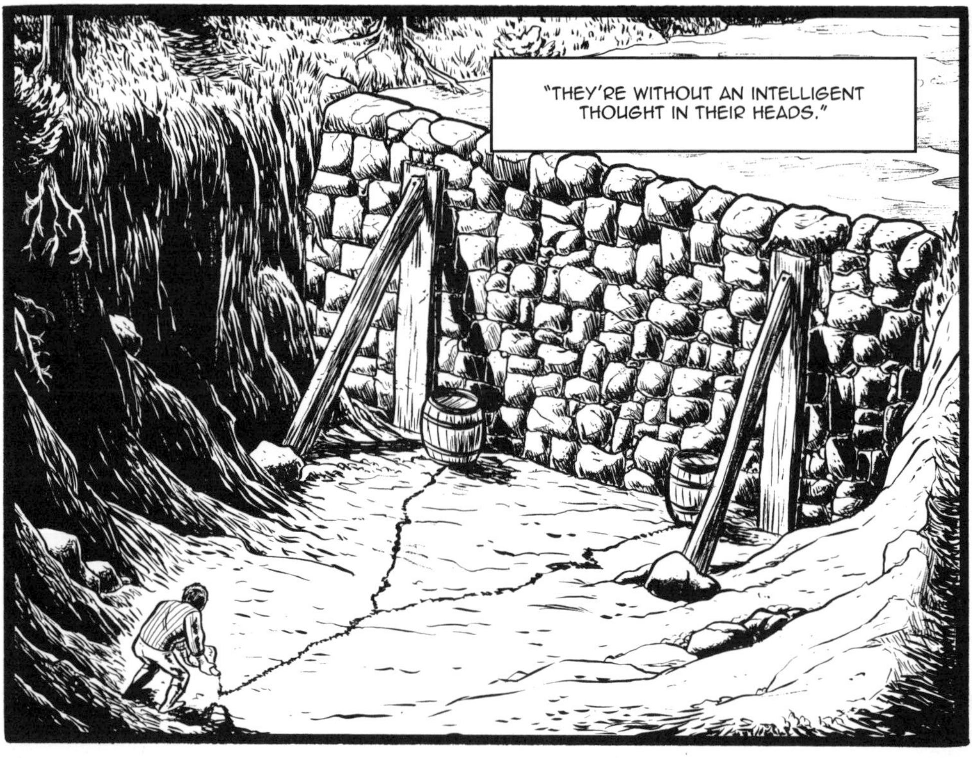
"THEY'RE WITHOUT AN INTELLIGENT THOUGHT IN THEIR HEADS."

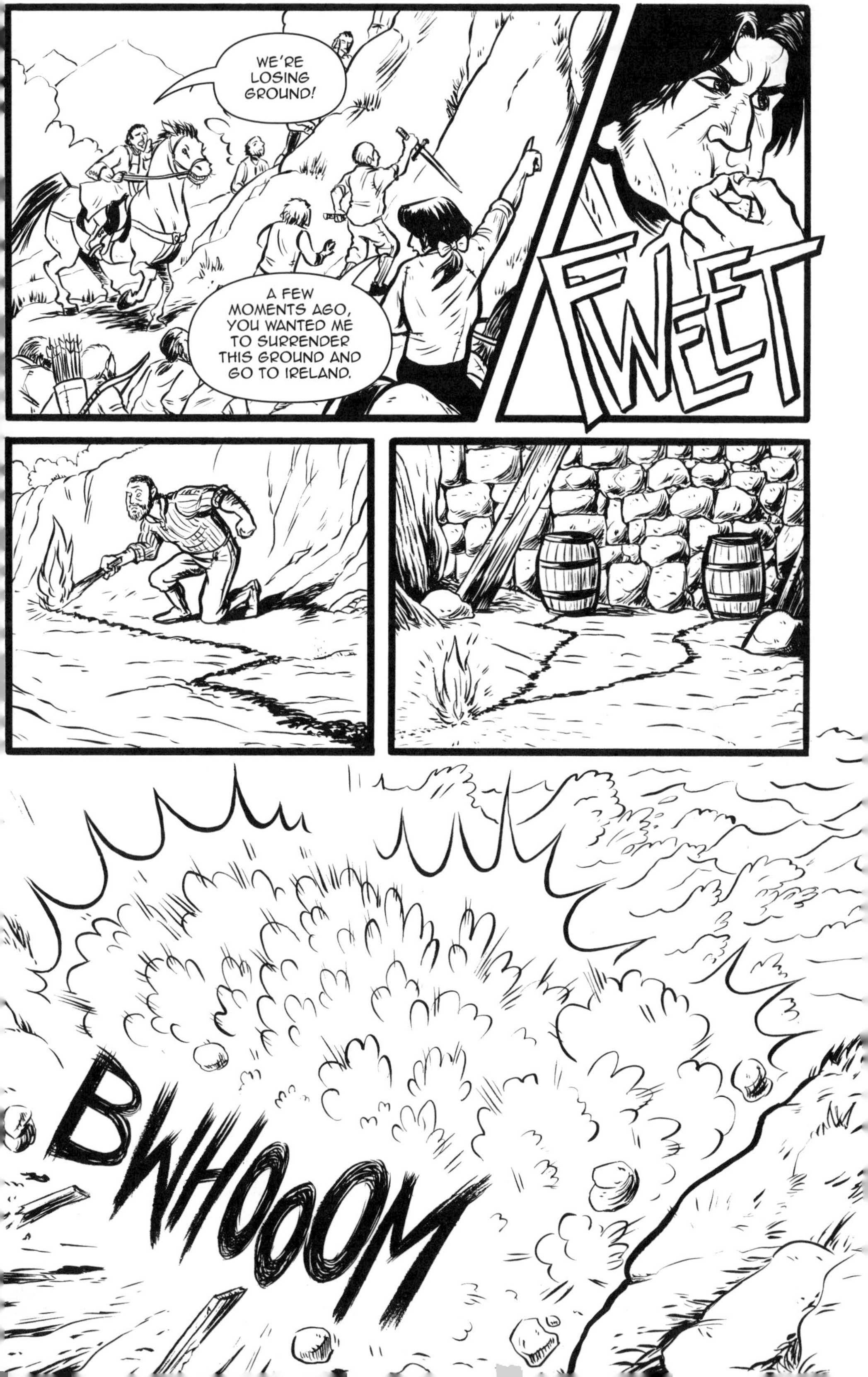
WE'RE LOSING GROUND!
A FEW MOMENTS AGO, YOU WANTED ME TO SURRENDER THIS GROUND AND GO TO IRELAND.
FWEET
BWHOOOM

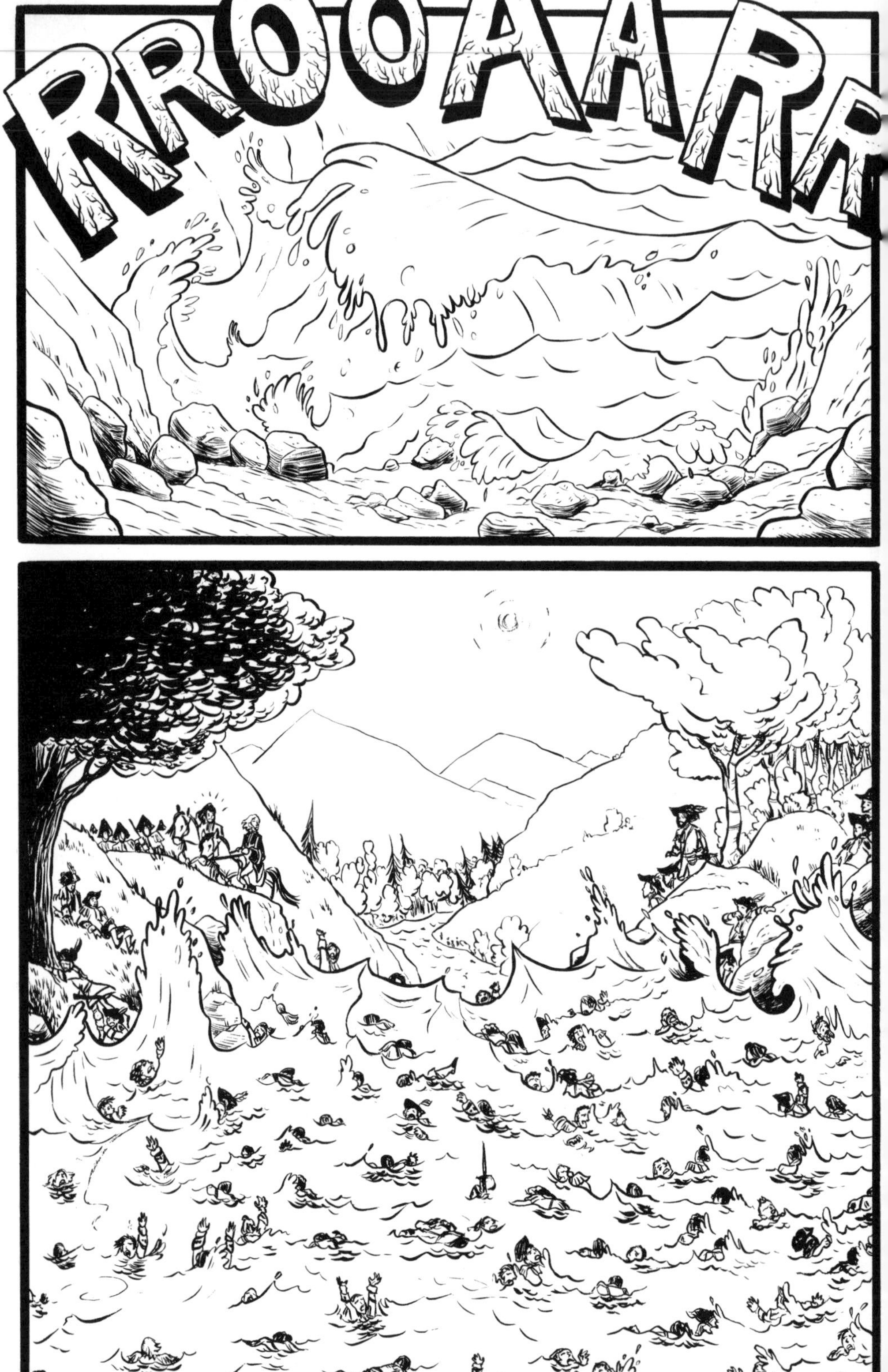
RROOAARR

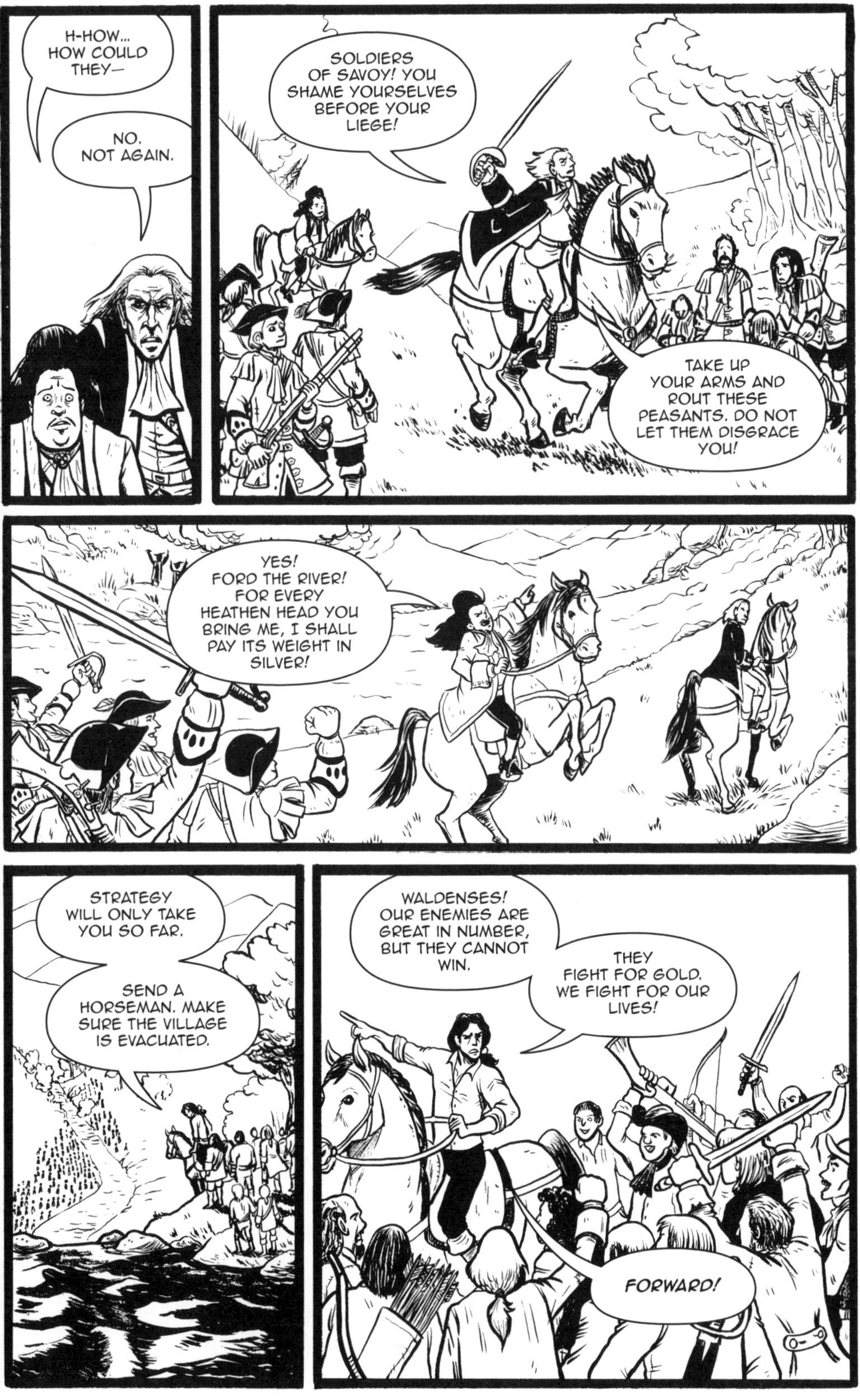
H-HOW... HOW COULD THEY—
NO. NOT AGAIN.
SOLDIERS OF SAVOY! YOU SHAME YOURSELVES BEFORE YOUR LIEGE!
TAKE UP YOUR ARMS AND ROUT THESE PEASANTS. DO NOT LET THEM DISGRACE YOU!
YES! FORD THE RIVER! FOR EVERY HEATHEN HEAD YOU BRING ME, I SHALL PAY ITS WEIGHT IN SILVER!
STRATEGY WILL ONLY TAKE YOU SO FAR.
SEND A HORSEMAN. MAKE SURE THE VILLAGE IS EVACUATED.
WALDENSES! OUR ENEMIES ARE GREAT IN NUMBER, BUT THEY CANNOT WIN.
THEY FIGHT FOR GOLD. WE FIGHT FOR OUR LIVES!
FORWARD!

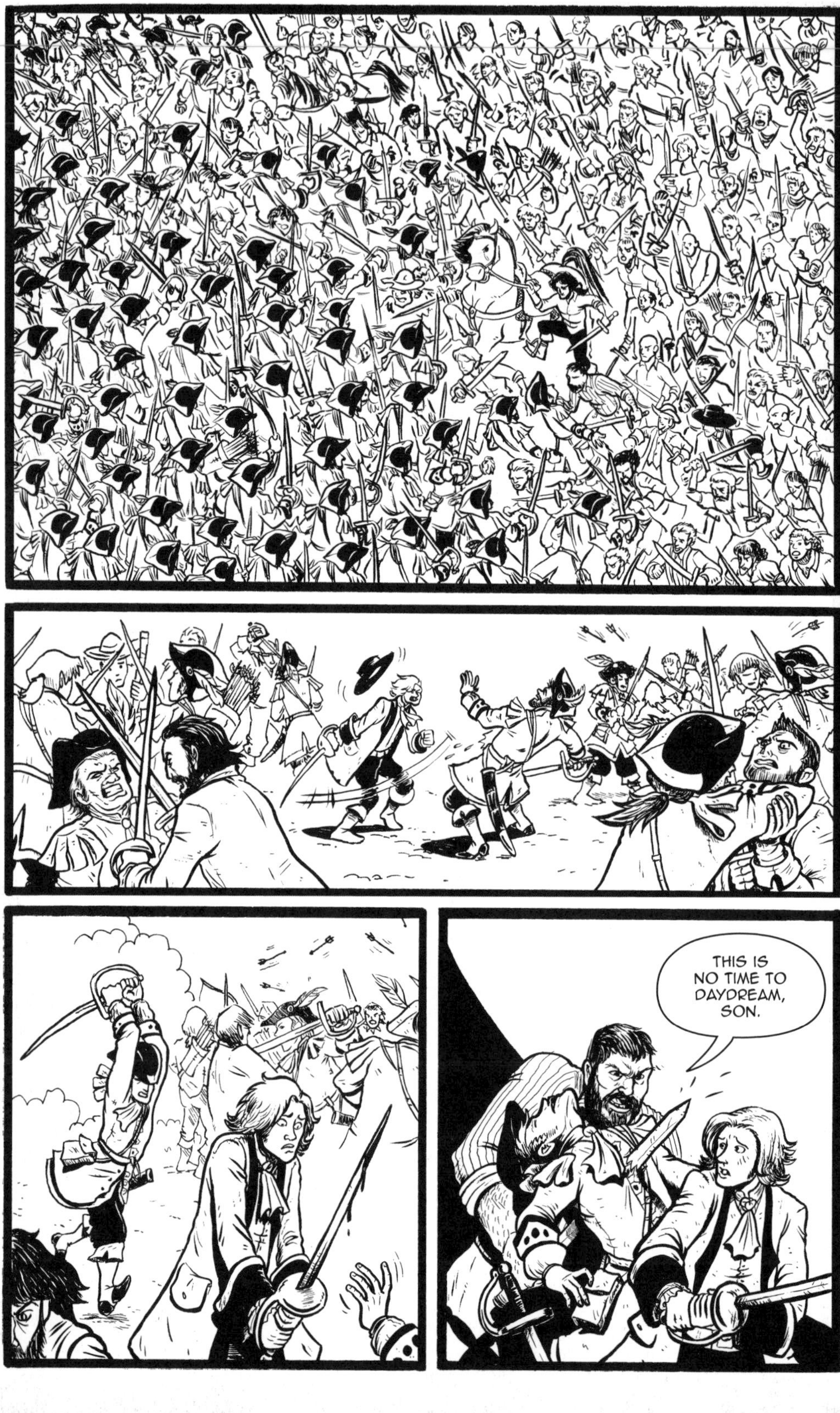
THIS IS
NO TIME TO
DAYDREAM,
SON.

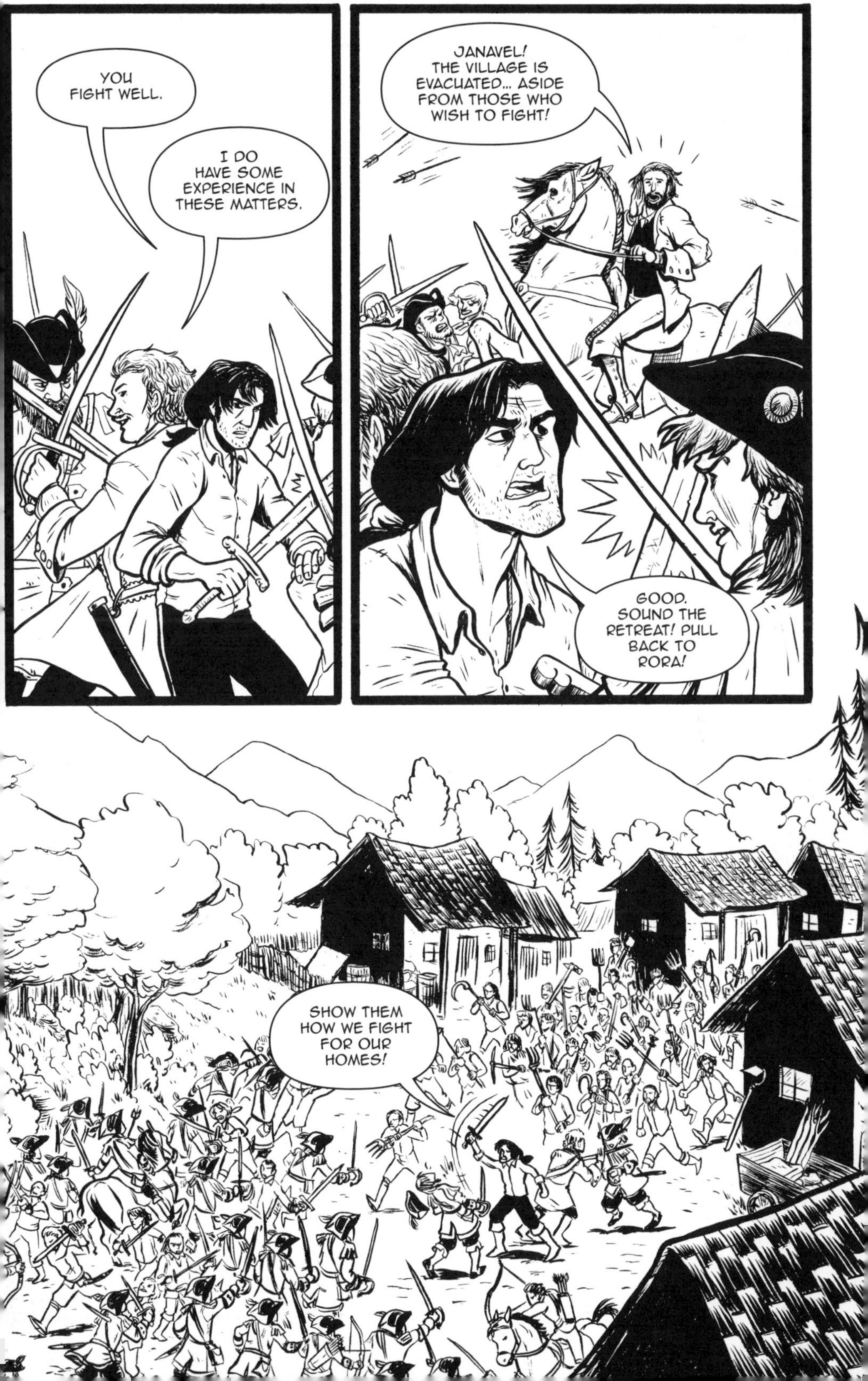
YOU FIGHT WELL.
I DO HAVE SOME EXPERIENCE IN THESE MATTERS.
JANAVEL! THE VILLAGE IS EVACUATED... ASIDE FROM THOSE WHO WISH TO FIGHT!
GOOD. SOUND THE RETREAT! PULL BACK TO RORA!
SHOW THEM HOW WE FIGHT FOR OUR HOMES!

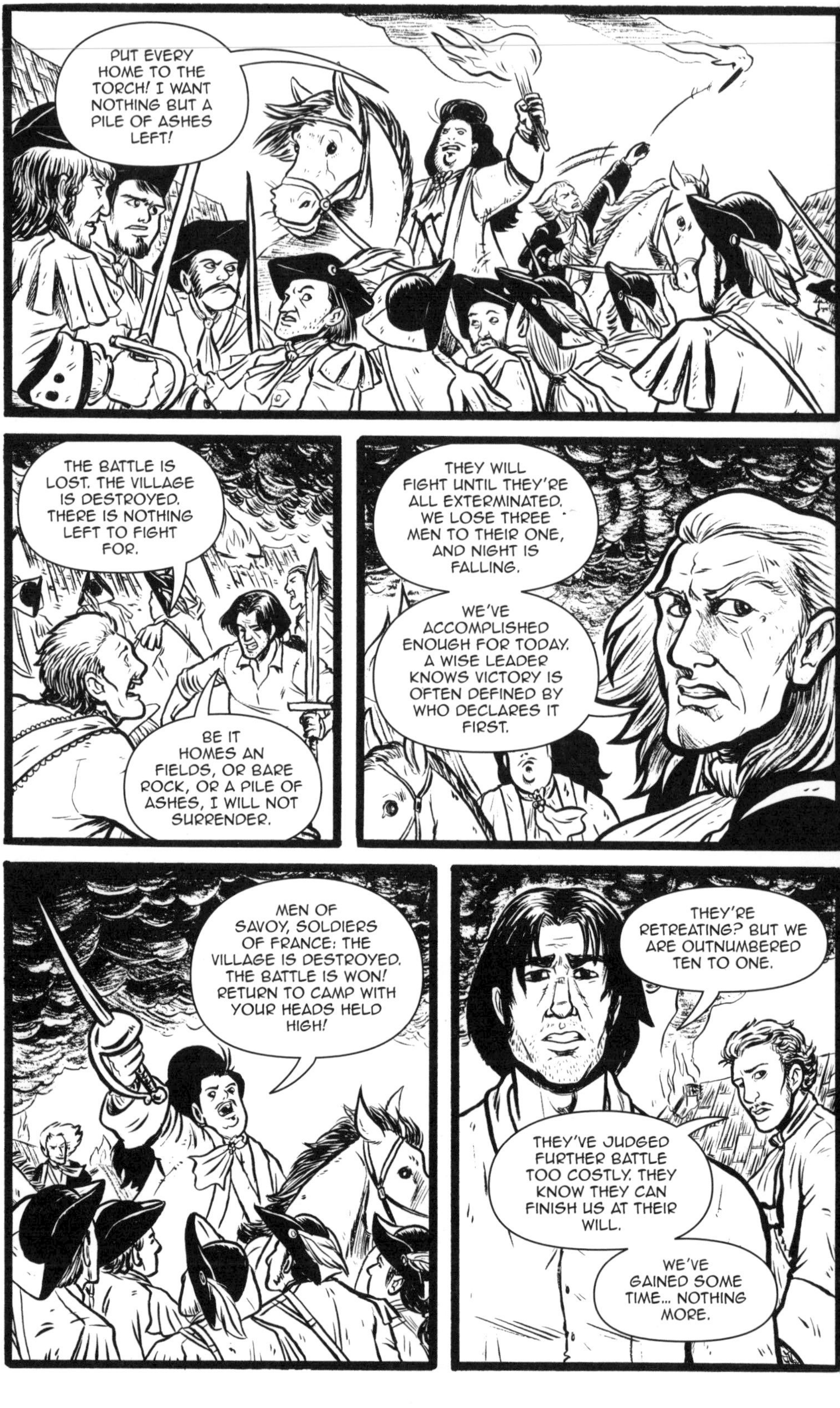
PUT EVERY HOME TO THE TORCH! I WANT NOTHING BUT A PILE OF ASHES LEFT!
THE BATTLE IS LOST. THE VILLAGE IS DESTROYED. THERE IS NOTHING LEFT TO FIGHT FOR.
BE IT HOMES AN FIELDS, OR BARE ROCK, OR A PILE OF ASHES, I WILL NOT SURRENDER.
THEY WILL FIGHT UNTIL THEY'RE ALL EXTERMINATED. WE LOSE THREE MEN TO THEIR ONE, AND NIGHT IS FALLING.
WE'VE ACCOMPLISHED ENOUGH FOR TODAY. A WISE LEADER KNOWS VICTORY IS OFTEN DEFINED BY WHO DECLARES IT FIRST.
MEN OF SAVOY, SOLDIERS OF FRANCE: THE VILLAGE IS DESTROYED. THE BATTLE IS WON! RETURN TO CAMP WITH YOUR HEADS HELD HIGH!
THEY'RE RETREATING? BUT WE ARE OUTNUMBERED TEN TO ONE.
THEY'VE JUDGED FURTHER BATTLE TOO COSTLY. THEY KNOW THEY CAN FINISH US AT THEIR WILL.
WE'VE GAINED SOME TIME... NOTHING MORE.

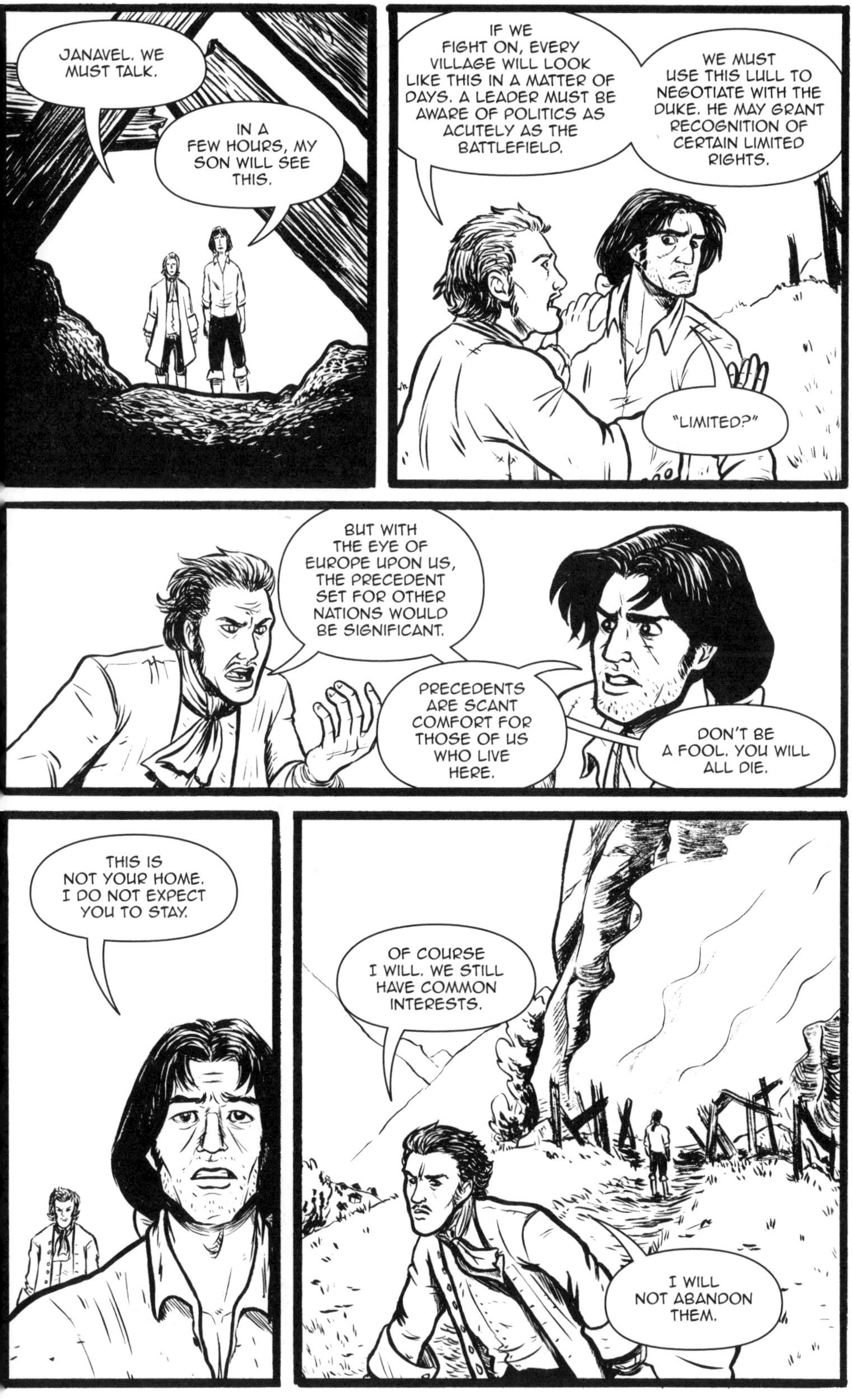
JANAVEL. WE MUST TALK.
IN A FEW HOURS, MY SON WILL SEE THIS.
IF WE FIGHT ON, EVERY VILLAGE WILL LOOK LIKE THIS IN A MATTER OF DAYS. A LEADER MUST BE AWARE OF POLITICS AS ACUTELY AS THE BATTLEFIELD.
WE MUST USE THIS LULL TO NEGOTIATE WITH THE DUKE. HE MAY GRANT RECOGNITION OF CERTAIN LIMITED RIGHTS.
"LIMITED?"
BUT WITH THE EYE OF EUROPE UPON US, THE PRECEDENT SET FOR OTHER NATIONS WOULD BE SIGNIFICANT.
PRECEDENTS ARE SCANT COMFORT FOR THOSE OF US WHO LIVE HERE.
DON'T BE A FOOL. YOU WILL ALL DIE.
THIS IS NOT YOUR HOME. I DO NOT EXPECT YOU TO STAY.
OF COURSE I WILL. WE STILL HAVE COMMON INTERESTS.
I WILL NOT ABANDON THEM.

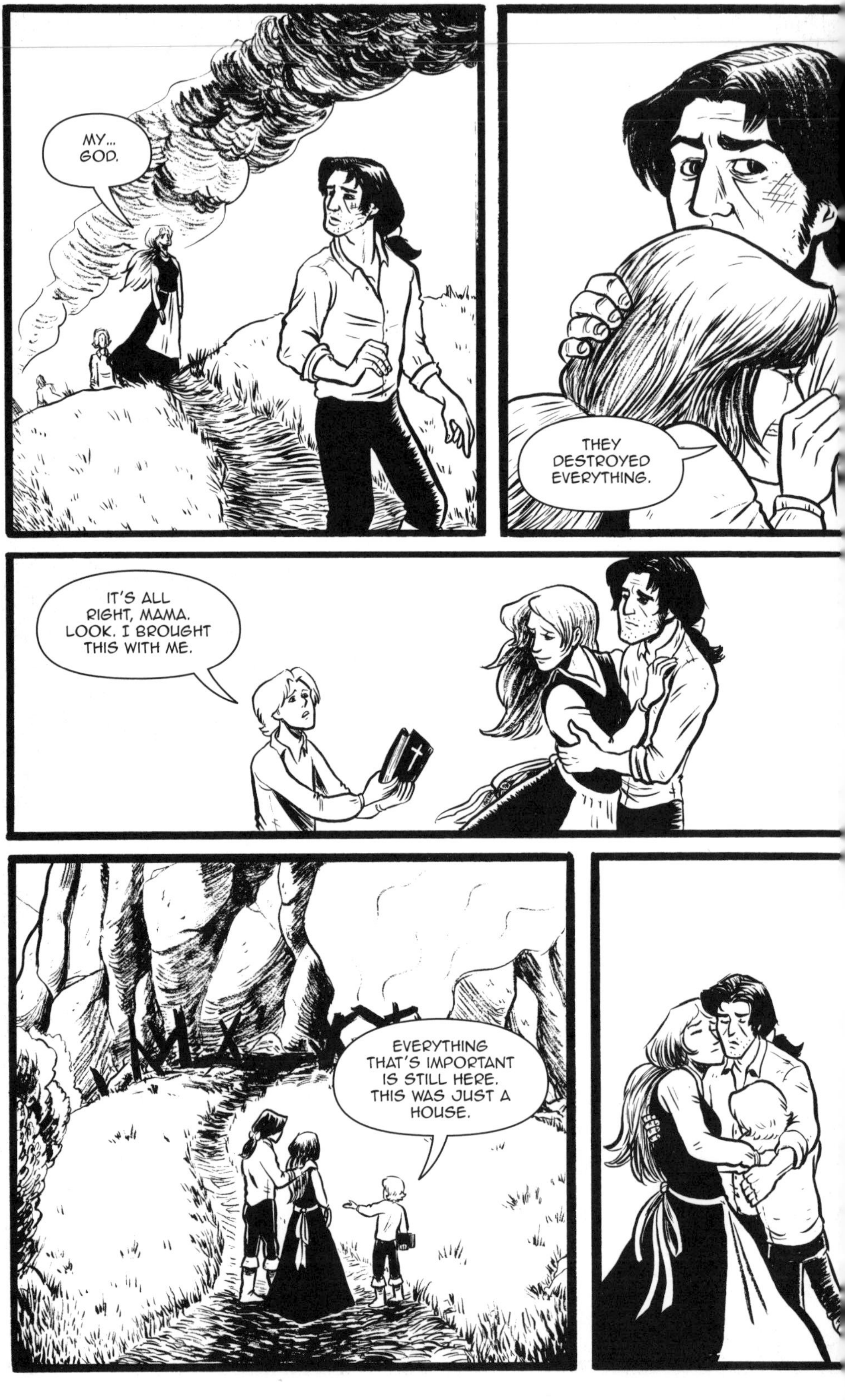
MY... GOD.
THEY DESTROYED EVERYTHING.
IT'S ALL RIGHT, MAMA. LOOK. I BROUGHT THIS WITH ME.
EVERYTHING THAT'S IMPORTANT IS STILL HERE. THIS WAS JUST A HOUSE.

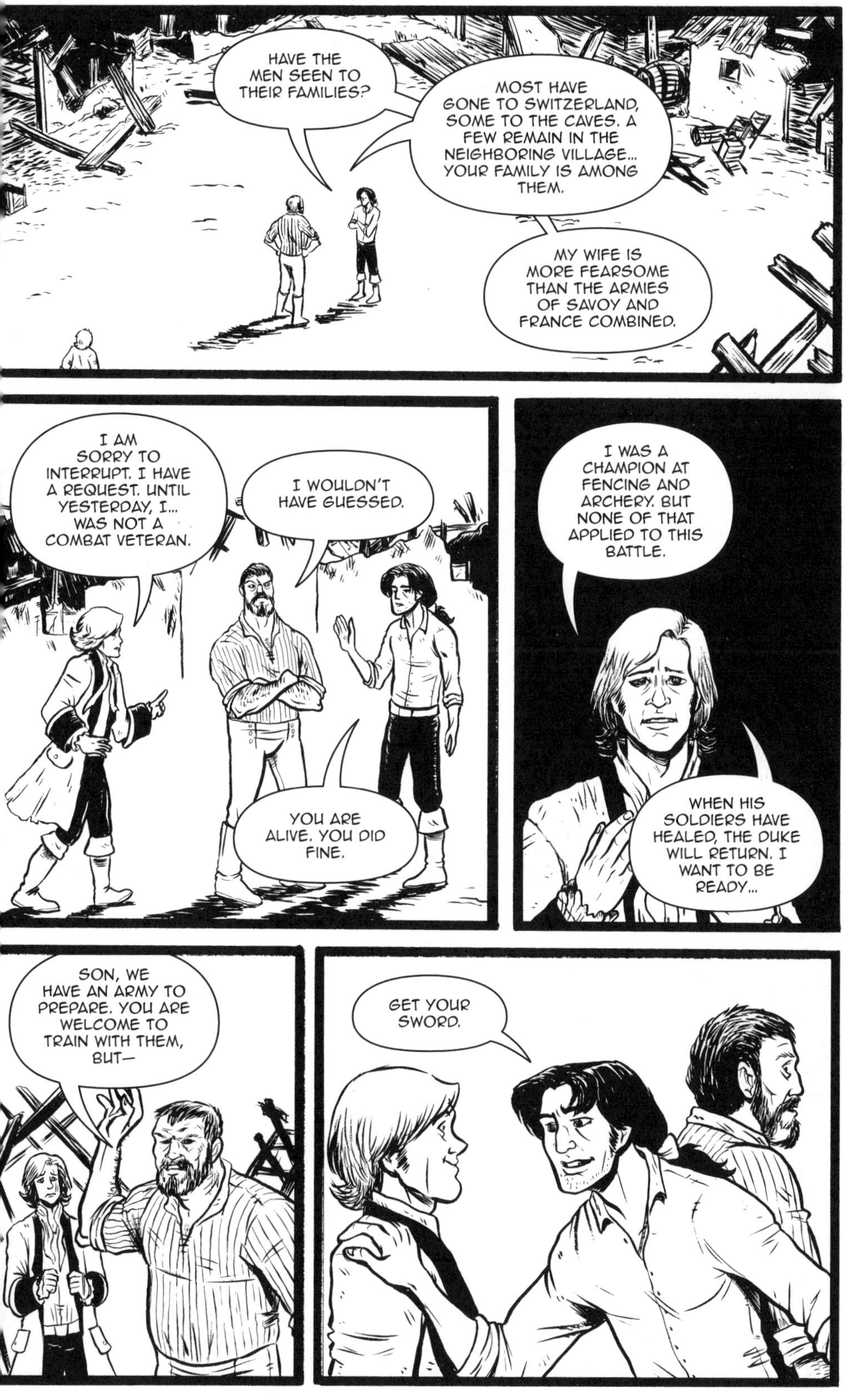
HAVE THE MEN SEEN TO THEIR FAMILIES?
MOST HAVE GONE TO SWITZERLAND, SOME TO THE CAVES. A FEW REMAIN IN THE NEIGHBORING VILLAGE... YOUR FAMILY IS AMONG THEM.
MY WIFE IS MORE FEARSOME THAN THE ARMIES OF SAVOY AND FRANCE COMBINED.
I AM SORRY TO INTERRUPT. I HAVE A REQUEST. UNTIL YESTERDAY, I... WAS NOT A COMBAT VETERAN.
I WOULDN'T HAVE GUESSED.
YOU ARE ALIVE. YOU DID FINE.
I WAS A CHAMPION AT FENCING AND ARCHERY. BUT NONE OF THAT APPLIED TO THIS BATTLE.
WHEN HIS SOLDIERS HAVE HEALED, THE DUKE WILL RETURN. I WANT TO BE READY...
SON, WE HAVE AN ARMY TO PREPARE. YOU ARE WELCOME TO TRAIN WITH THEM, BUT—
GET YOUR SWORD.

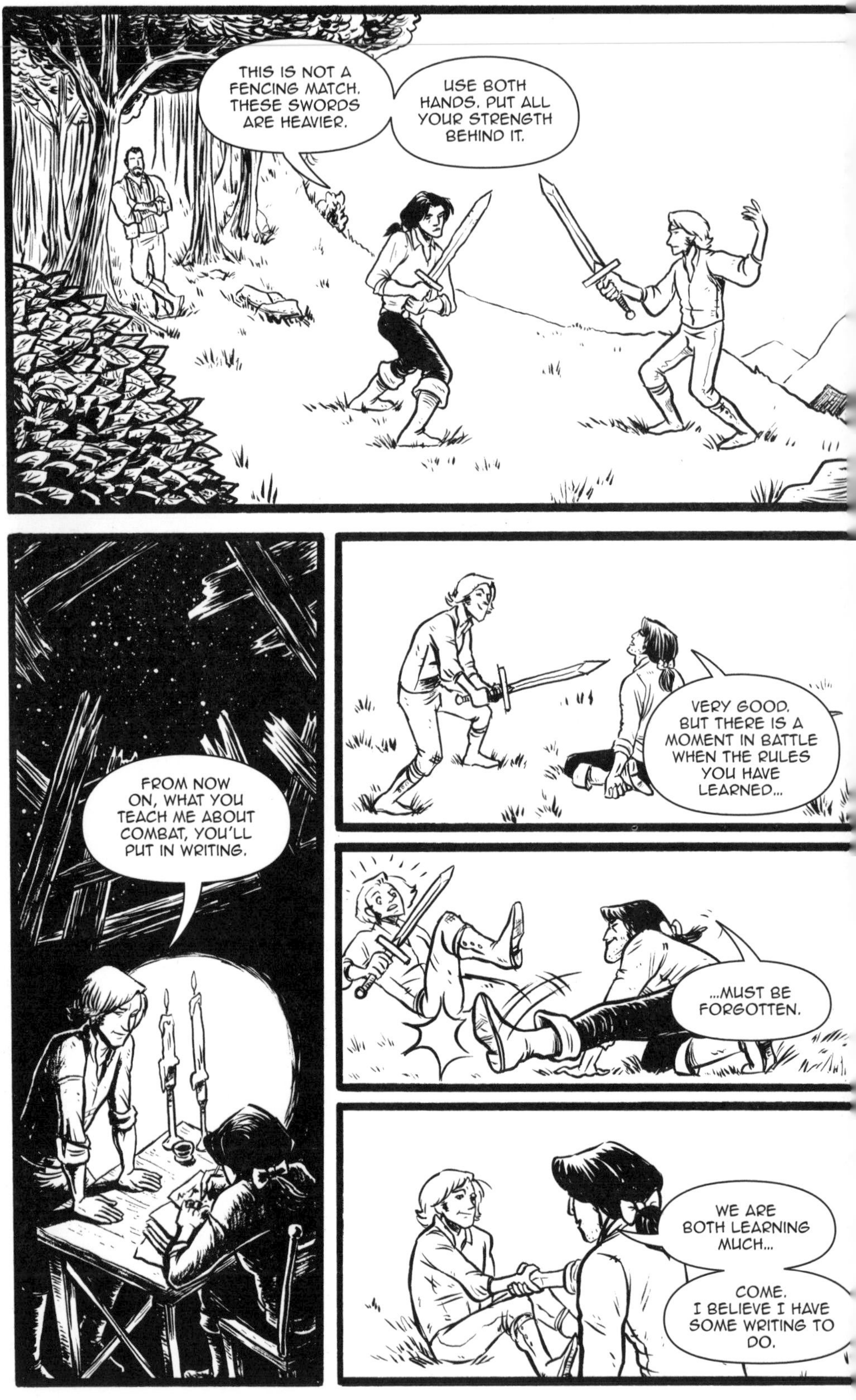
THIS IS NOT A FENCING MATCH. THESE SWORDS ARE HEAVIER.
USE BOTH HANDS. PUT ALL YOUR STRENGTH BEHIND IT.
FROM NOW ON, WHAT YOU TEACH ME ABOUT COMBAT, YOU'LL PUT IN WRITING.
VERY GOOD. BUT THERE IS A MOMENT IN BATTLE WHEN THE RULES YOU HAVE LEARNED...
...MUST BE FORGOTTEN.
WE ARE BOTH LEARNING MUCH...
COME. I BELIEVE I HAVE SOME WRITING TO DO.

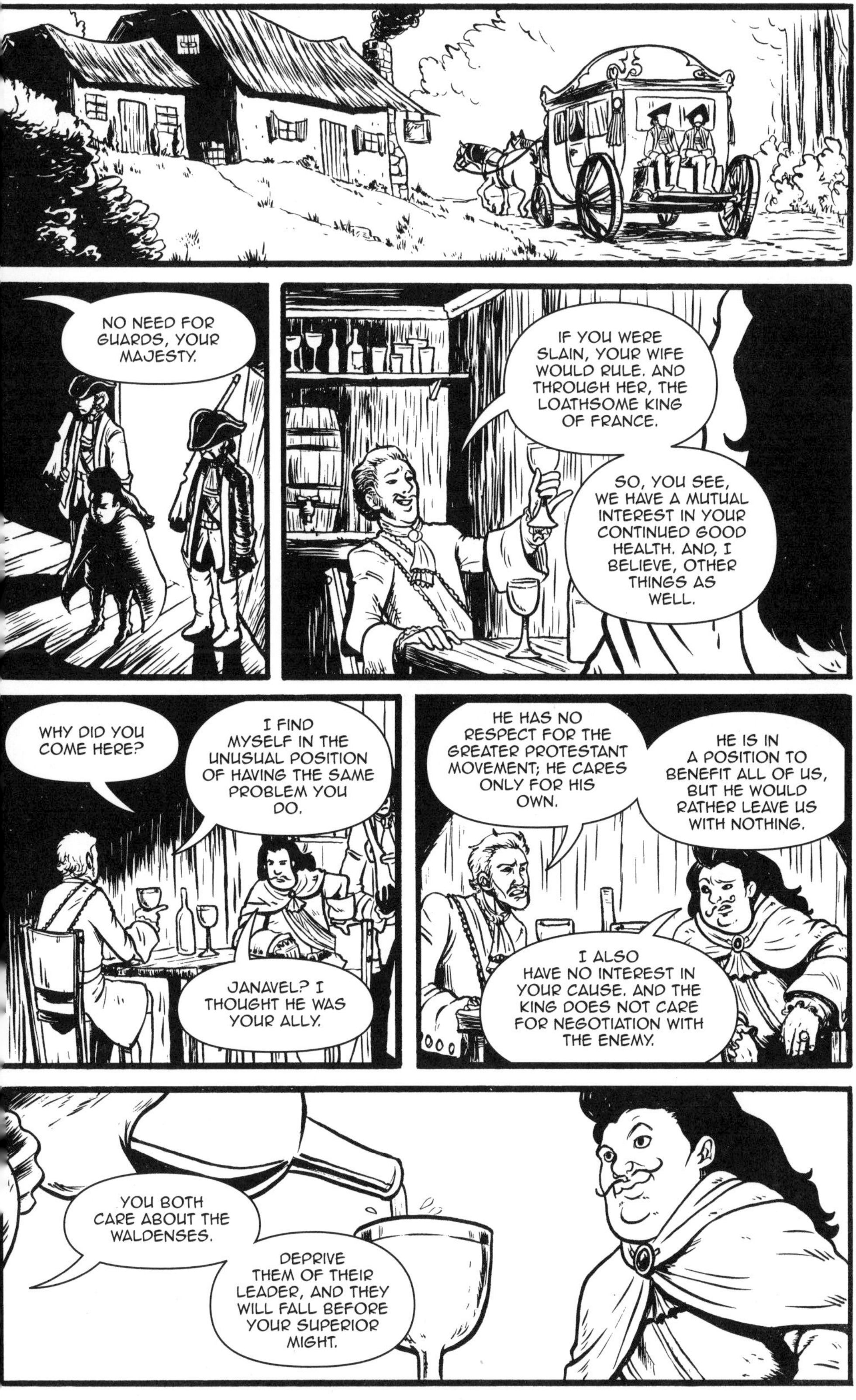
NO NEED FOR GUARDS, YOUR MAJESTY.
IF YOU WERE SLAIN, YOUR WIFE WOULD RULE. AND THROUGH HER, THE LOATHSOME KING OF FRANCE.
SO, YOU SEE, WE HAVE A MUTUAL INTEREST IN YOUR CONTINUED GOOD HEALTH. AND, I BELIEVE, OTHER THINGS AS WELL.
WHY DID YOU COME HERE?
I FIND MYSELF IN THE UNUSUAL POSITION OF HAVING THE SAME PROBLEM YOU DO.
JANAVEL? I THOUGHT HE WAS YOUR ALLY.
HE HAS NO RESPECT FOR THE GREATER PROTESTANT MOVEMENT; HE CARES ONLY FOR HIS OWN.
HE IS IN A POSITION TO BENEFIT ALL OF US, BUT HE WOULD RATHER LEAVE US WITH NOTHING.
I ALSO HAVE NO INTEREST IN YOUR CAUSE. AND THE KING DOES NOT CARE FOR NEGOTIATION WITH THE ENEMY.
YOU BOTH CARE ABOUT THE WALDENSES.
DEPRIVE THEM OF THEIR LEADER, AND THEY WILL FALL BEFORE YOUR SUPERIOR MIGHT.

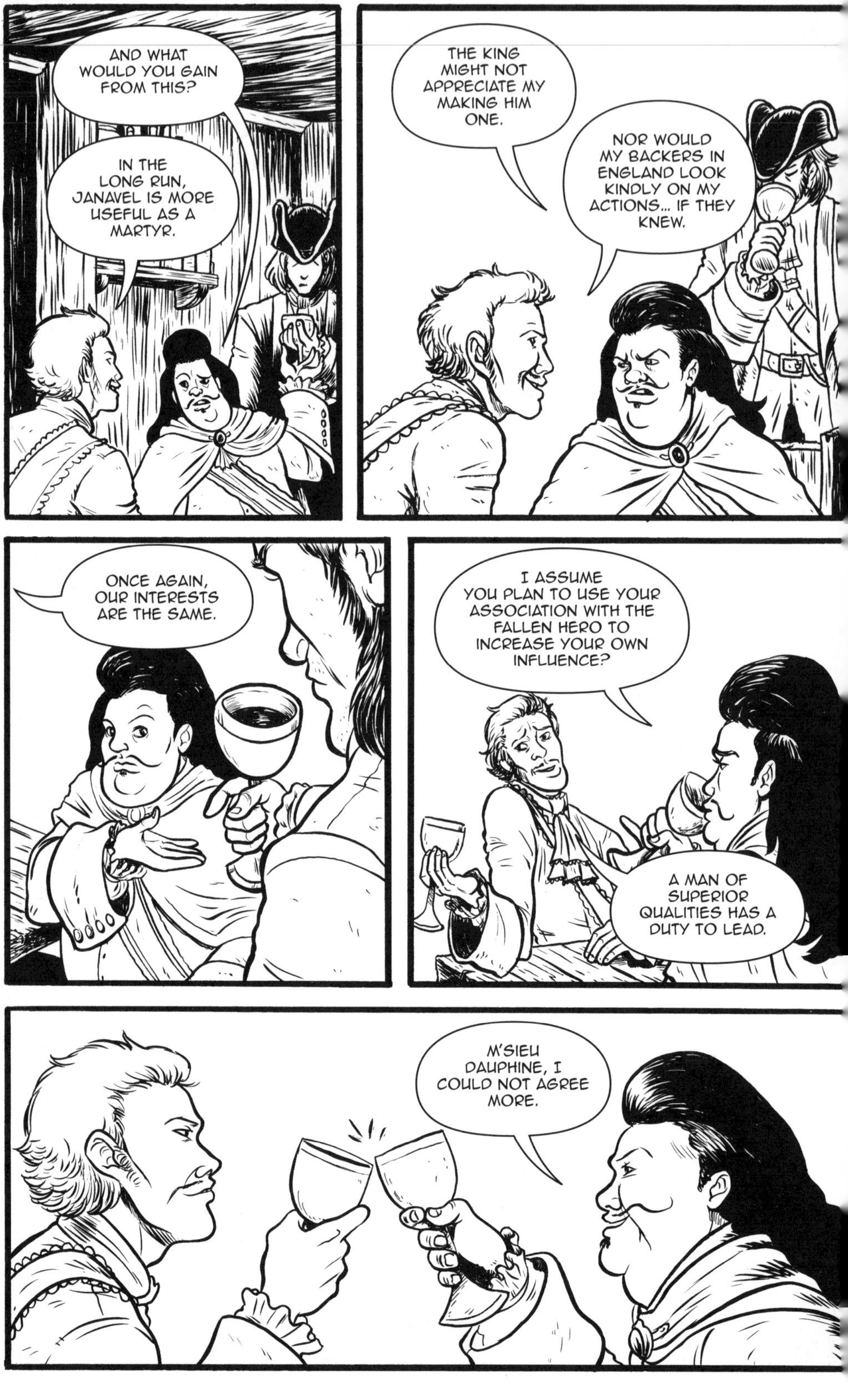
AND WHAT WOULD YOU GAIN FROM THIS?
IN THE LONG RUN, JANAVEL IS MORE USEFUL AS A MARTYR.
THE KING MIGHT NOT APPRECIATE MY MAKING HIM ONE.
NOR WOULD MY BACKERS IN ENGLAND LOOK KINDLY ON MY ACTIONS... IF THEY KNEW.
ONCE AGAIN, OUR INTERESTS ARE THE SAME.
I ASSUME YOU PLAN TO USE YOUR ASSOCIATION WITH THE FALLEN HERO TO INCREASE YOUR OWN INFLUENCE?
A MAN OF SUPERIOR QUALITIES HAS A DUTY TO LEAD.
M'SIEU DAUPHINE, I COULD NOT AGREE MORE.

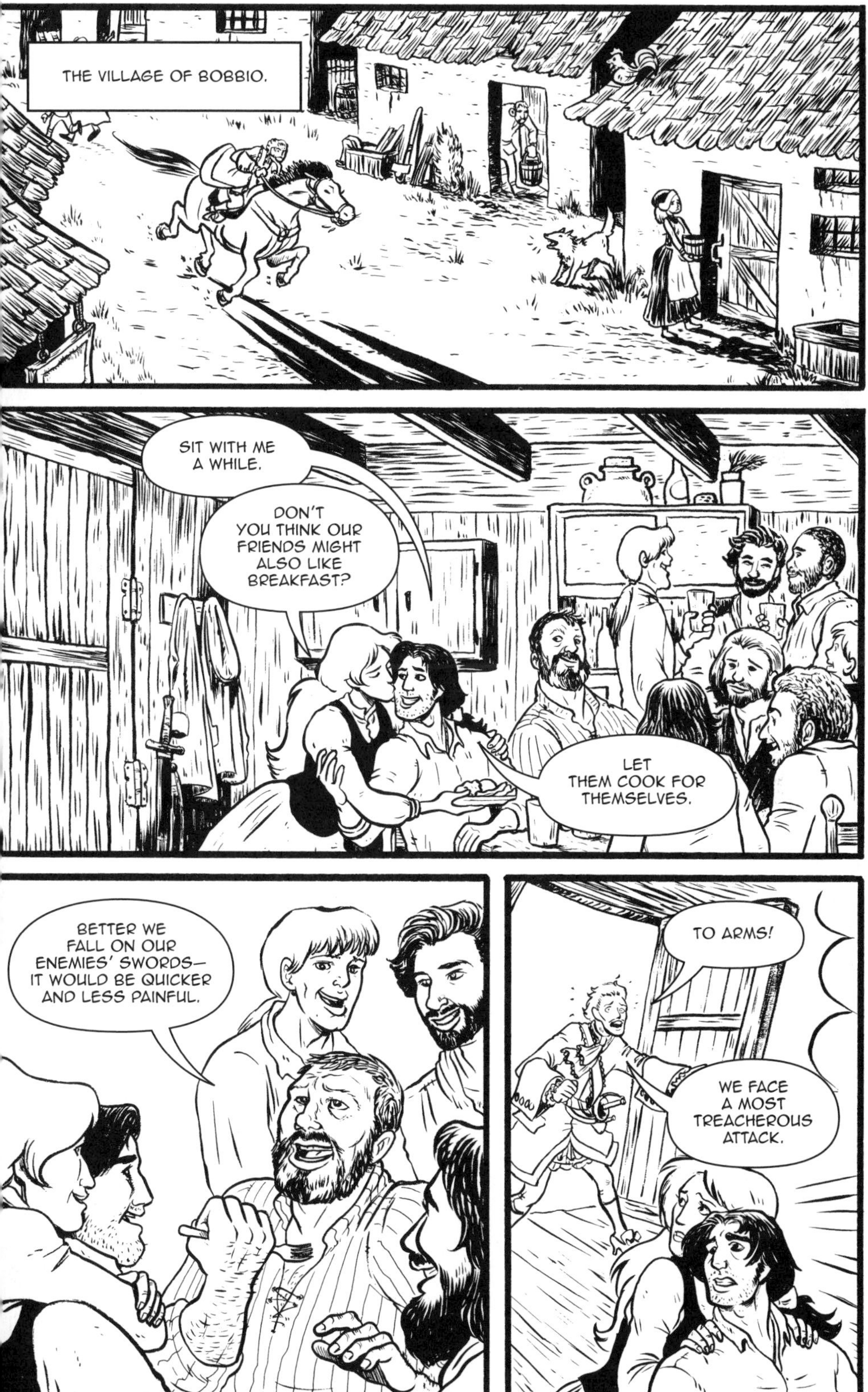
THE VILLAGE OF BOBBIO.
SIT WITH ME A WHILE.
DON'T YOU THINK OUR FRIENDS MIGHT ALSO LIKE BREAKFAST?
LET THEM COOK FOR THEMSELVES.
BETTER WE FALL ON OUR ENEMIES' SWORDS— IT WOULD BE QUICKER AND LESS PAINFUL.
TO ARMS!
WE FACE A MOST TREACHEROUS ATTACK.

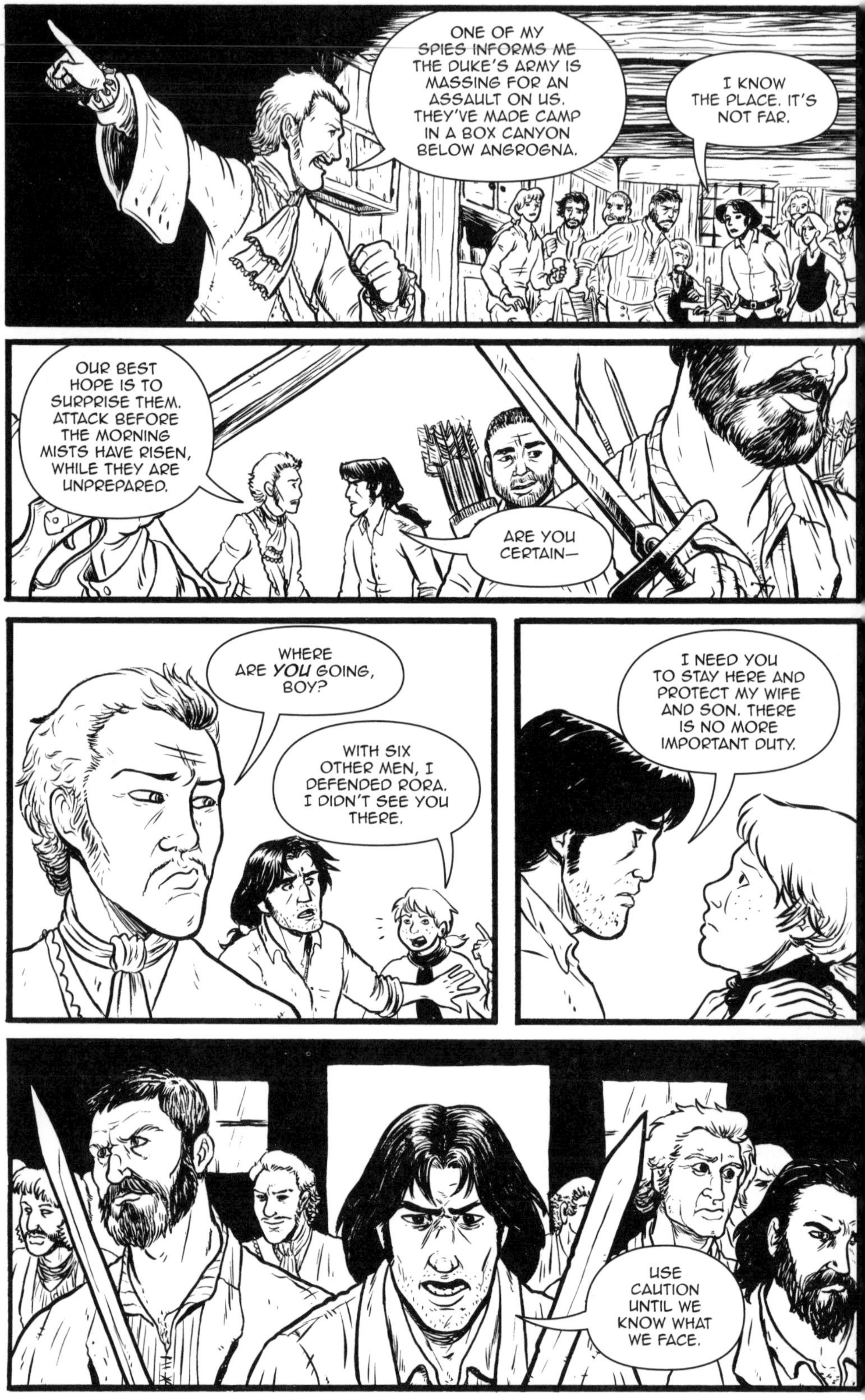
ONE OF MY SPIES INFORMS ME THE DUKE'S ARMY IS MASSING FOR AN ASSAULT ON US. THEY'VE MADE CAMP IN A BOX CANYON BELOW ANGROGNA.
I KNOW THE PLACE. IT'S NOT FAR.
OUR BEST HOPE IS TO SURPRISE THEM. ATTACK BEFORE THE MORNING MISTS HAVE RISEN, WHILE THEY ARE UNPREPARED.
ARE YOU CERTAIN—
WHERE ARE *YOU* GOING, BOY?
WITH SIX OTHER MEN, I DEFENDED RORA. I DIDN'T SEE YOU THERE.
I NEED YOU TO STAY HERE AND PROTECT MY WIFE AND SON. THERE IS NO MORE IMPORTANT DUTY.
USE CAUTION UNTIL WE KNOW WHAT WE FACE.

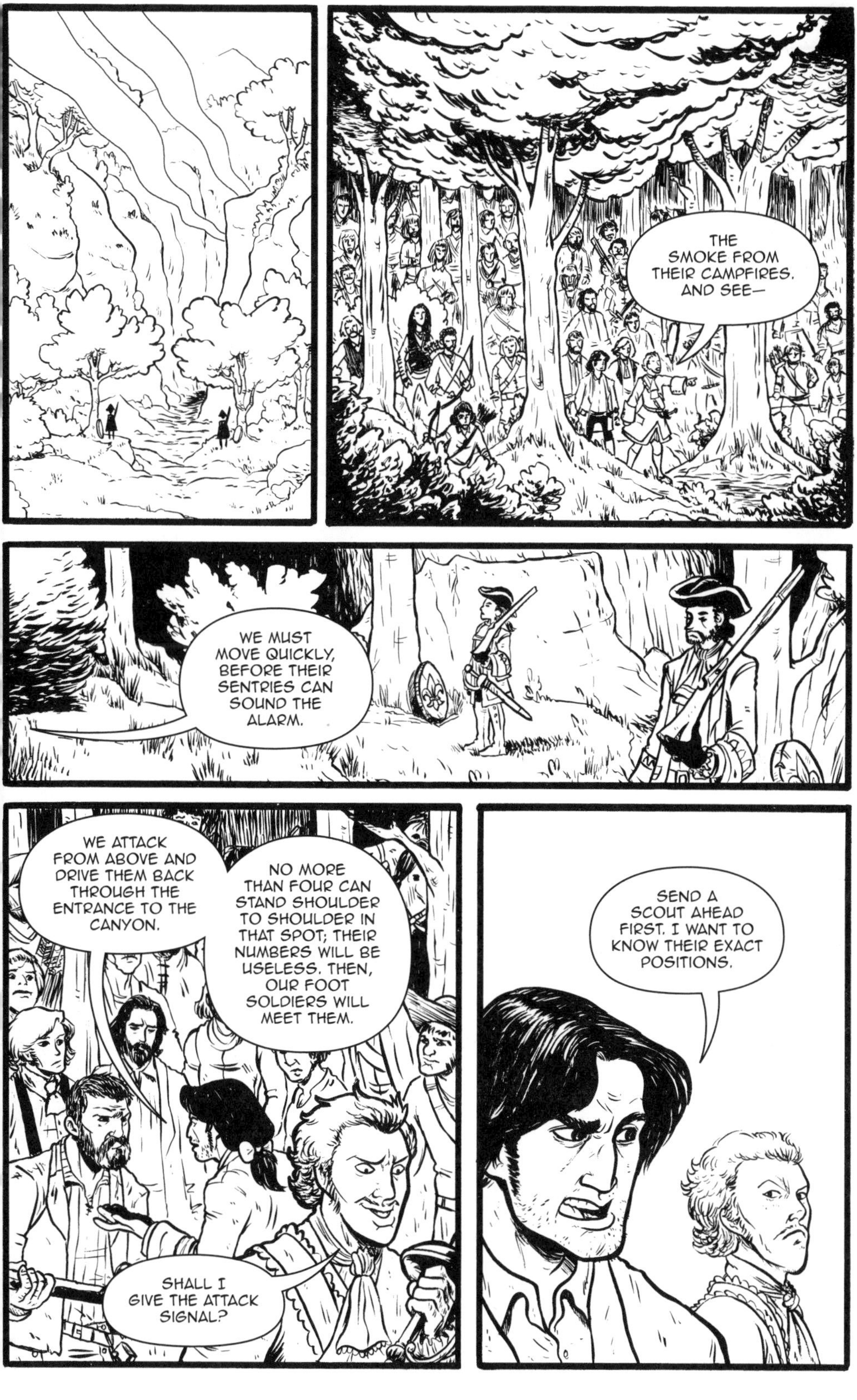
THE SMOKE FROM THEIR CAMPFIRES. AND SEE—
WE MUST MOVE QUICKLY, BEFORE THEIR SENTRIES CAN SOUND THE ALARM.
WE ATTACK FROM ABOVE AND DRIVE THEM BACK THROUGH THE ENTRANCE TO THE CANYON.
NO MORE THAN FOUR CAN STAND SHOULDER TO SHOULDER IN THAT SPOT; THEIR NUMBERS WILL BE USELESS. THEN, OUR FOOT SOLDIERS WILL MEET THEM.
SHALL I GIVE THE ATTACK SIGNAL?
SEND A SCOUT AHEAD FIRST. I WANT TO KNOW THEIR EXACT POSITIONS.

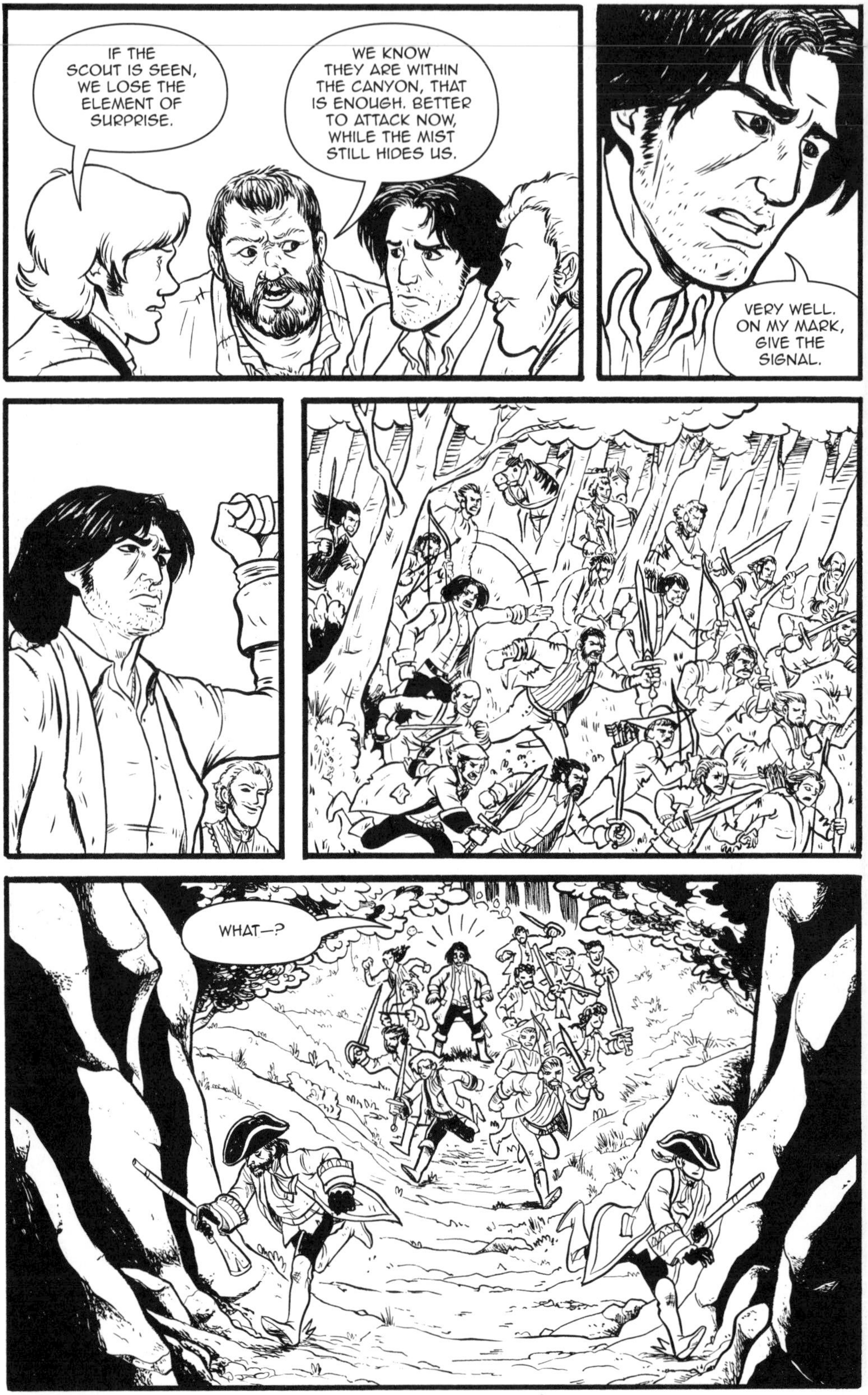
IF THE SCOUT IS SEEN, WE LOSE THE ELEMENT OF SURPRISE.
WE KNOW THEY ARE WITHIN THE CANYON, THAT IS ENOUGH. BETTER TO ATTACK NOW, WHILE THE MIST STILL HIDES US.
VERY WELL. ON MY MARK, GIVE THE SIGNAL.
WHAT—?

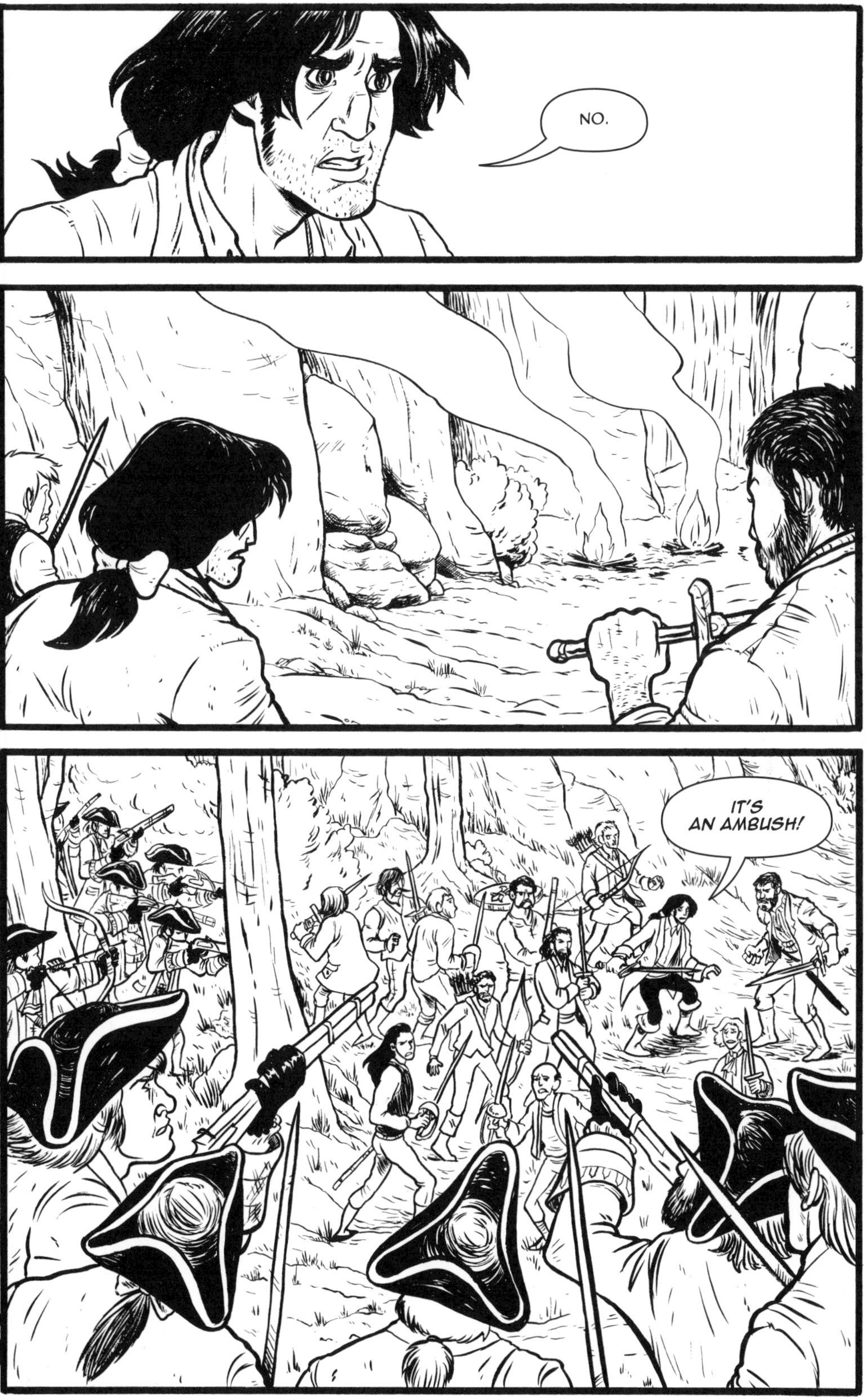
NO.
IT'S AN AMBUSH!

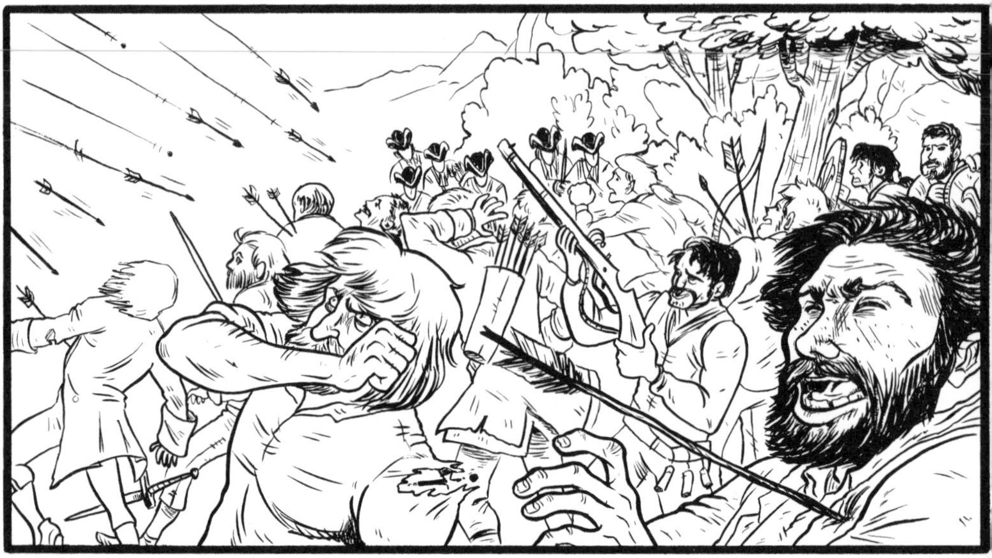

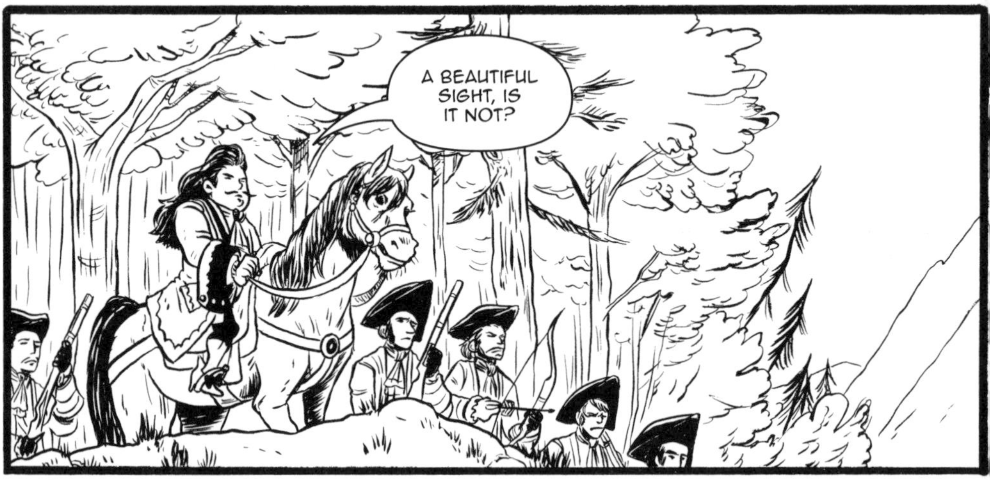
A BEAUTIFUL SIGHT, IS IT NOT?

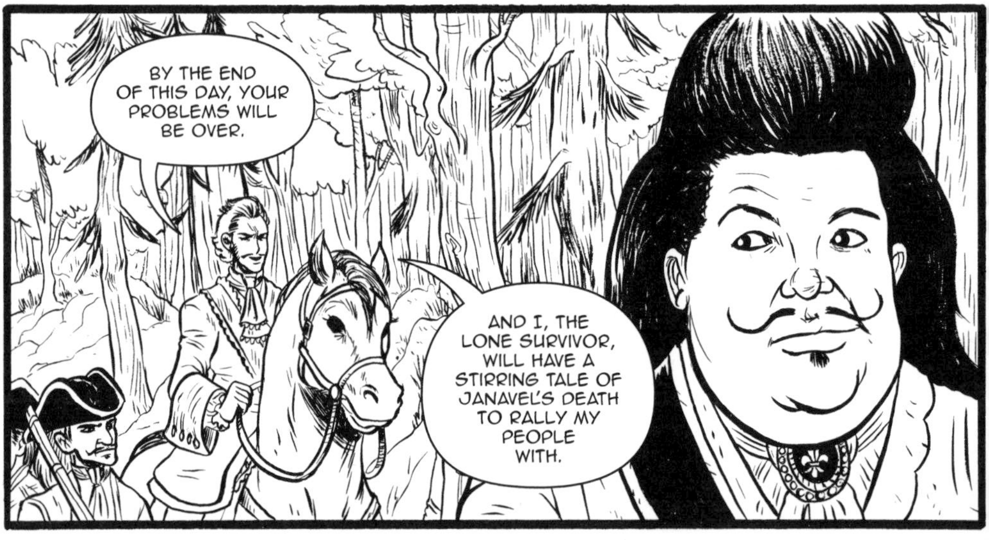
BY THE END OF THIS DAY, YOUR PROBLEMS WILL BE OVER.
AND I, THE LONE SURVIVOR, WILL HAVE A STIRRING TALE OF JANAVEL'S DEATH TO RALLY MY PEOPLE WITH.

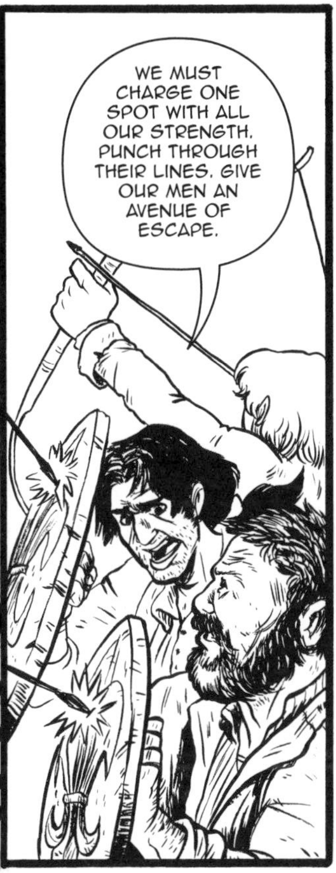
WE MUST CHARGE ONE SPOT WITH ALL OUR STRENGTH. PUNCH THROUGH THEIR LINES. GIVE OUR MEN AN AVENUE OF ESCAPE.

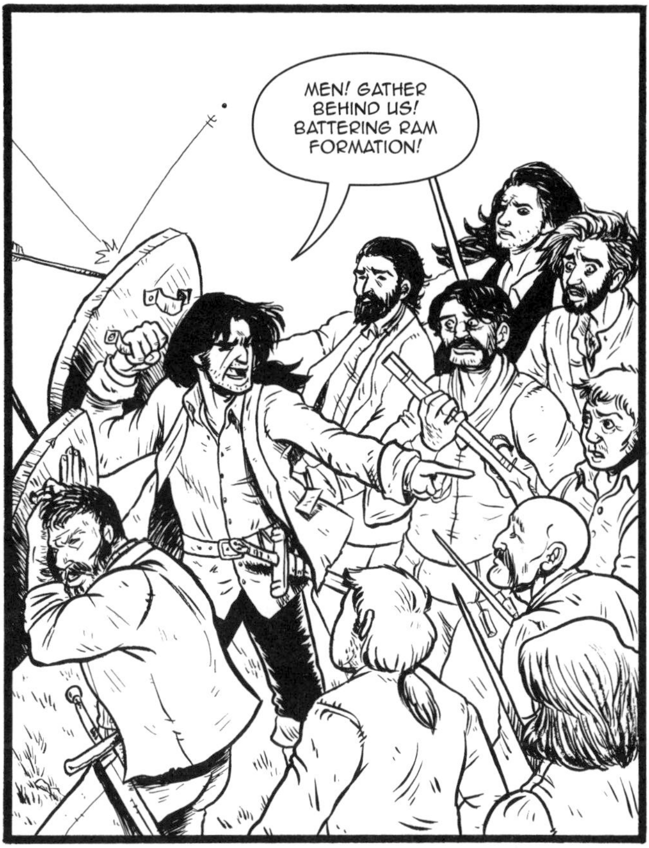
MEN! GATHER BEHIND US! BATTERING RAM FORMATION!

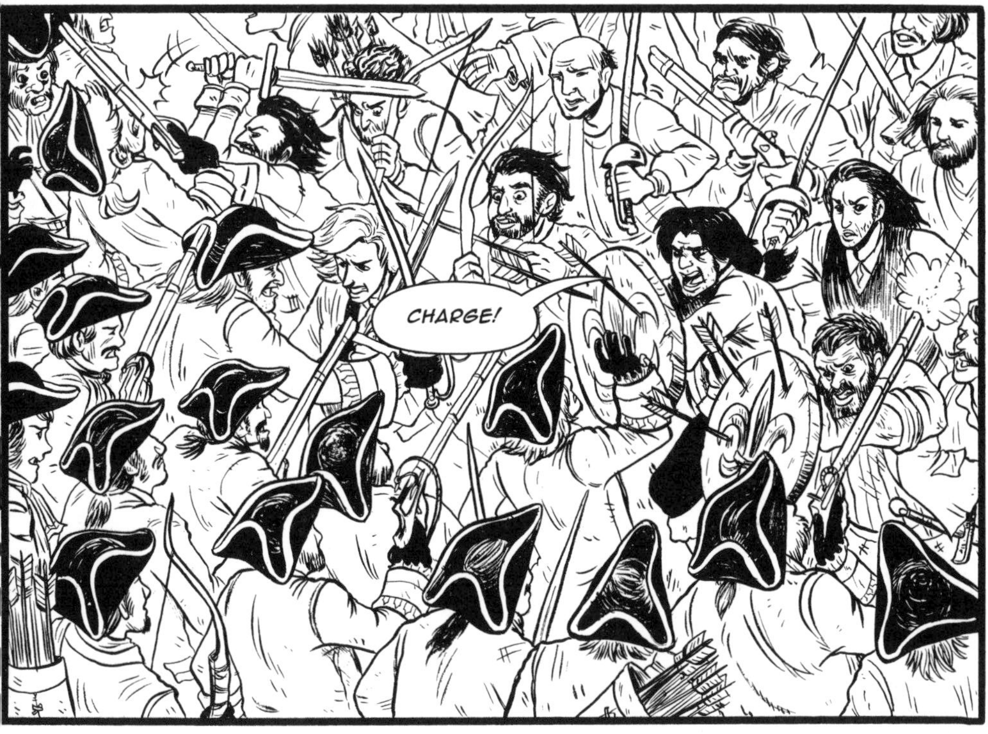
CHARGE!

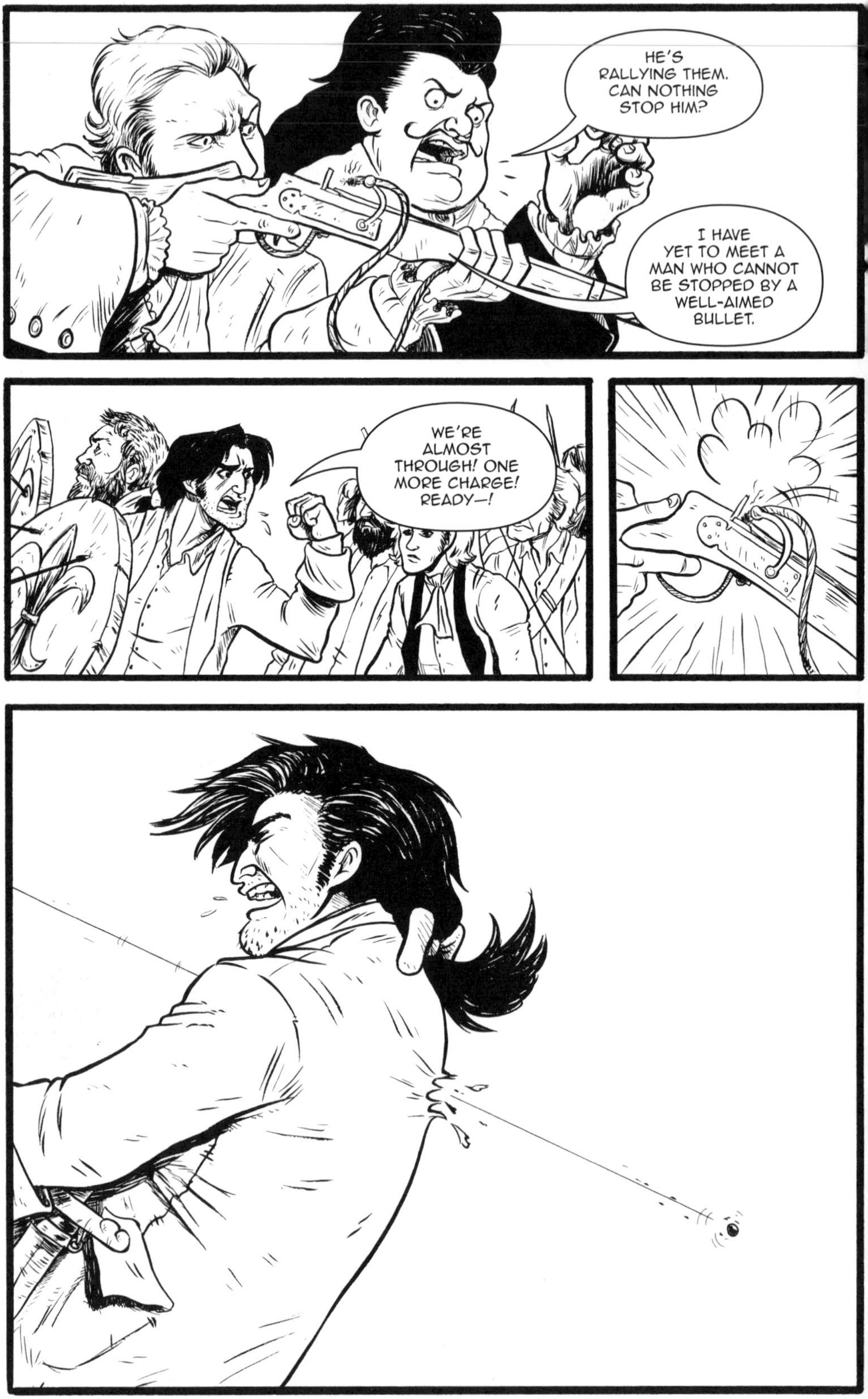
HE'S RALLYING THEM. CAN NOTHING STOP HIM?
I HAVE YET TO MEET A MAN WHO CANNOT BE STOPPED BY A WELL-AIMED BULLET.
WE'RE ALMOST THROUGH! ONE MORE CHARGE! READY—!

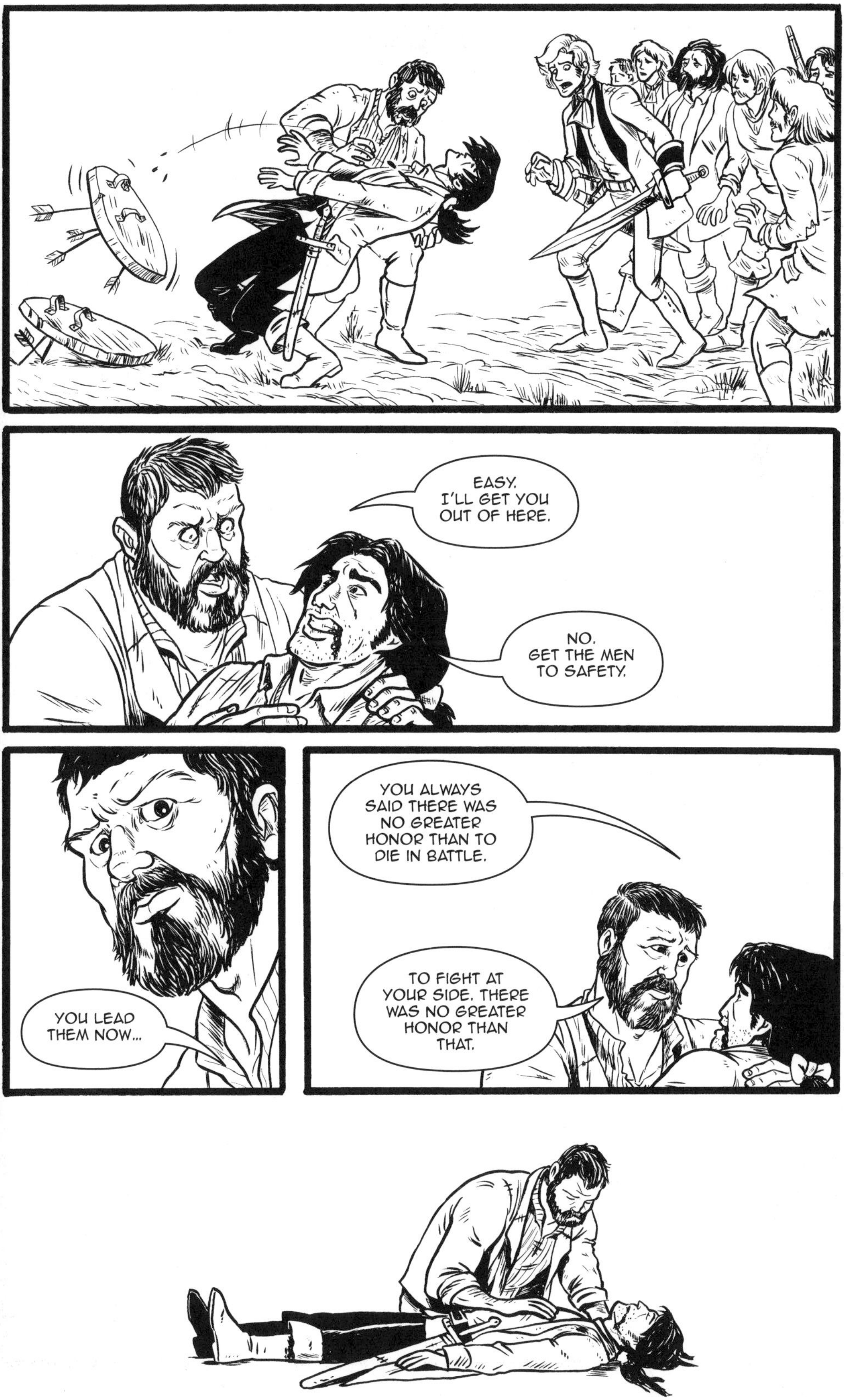
EASY. I'LL GET YOU OUT OF HERE.
NO. GET THE MEN TO SAFETY.
YOU LEAD THEM NOW...
YOU ALWAYS SAID THERE WAS NO GREATER HONOR THAN TO DIE IN BATTLE.
TO FIGHT AT YOUR SIDE. THERE WAS NO GREATER HONOR THAN THAT.

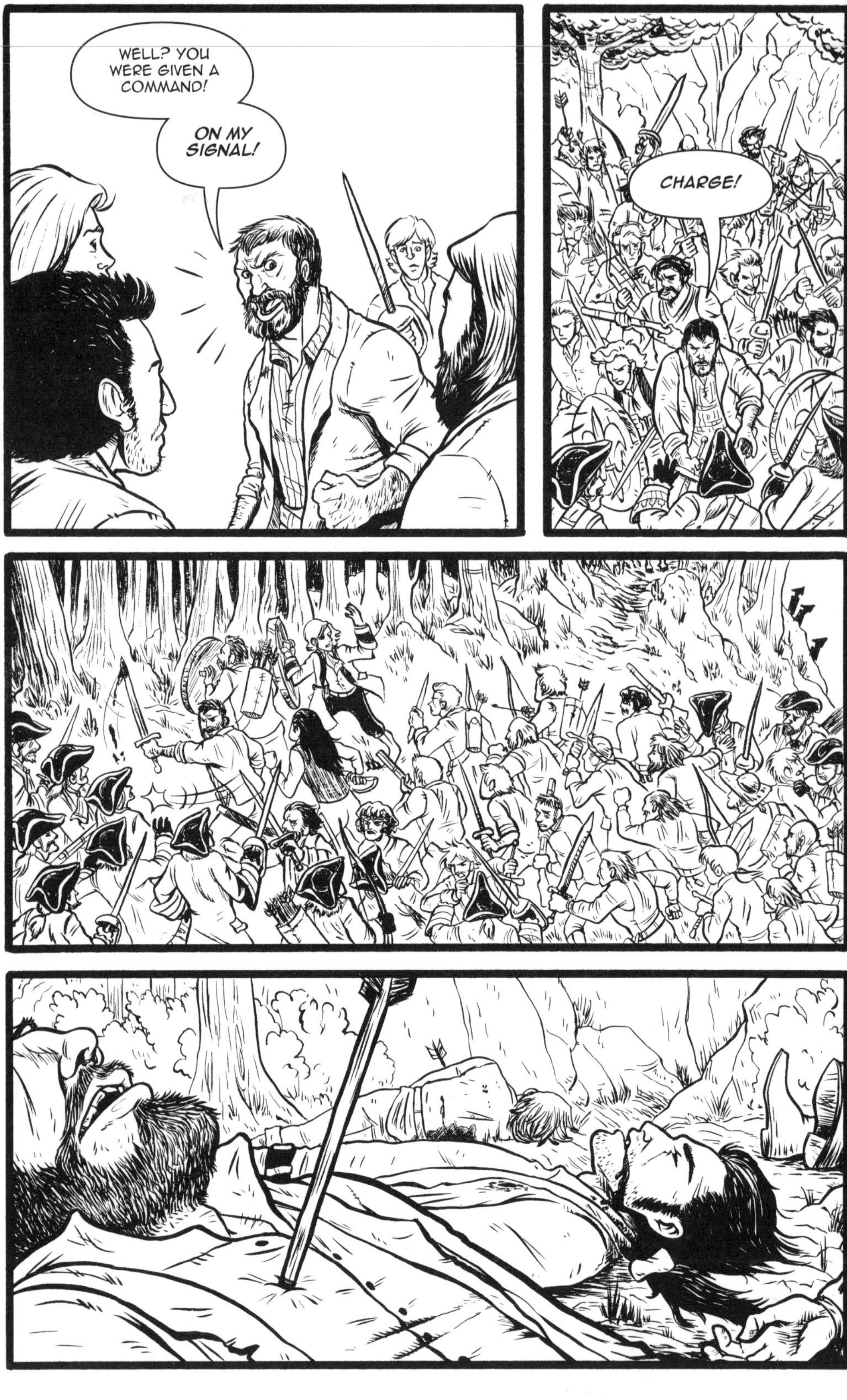
WELL? YOU WERE GIVEN A COMMAND!
ON MY SIGNAL!
CHARGE!

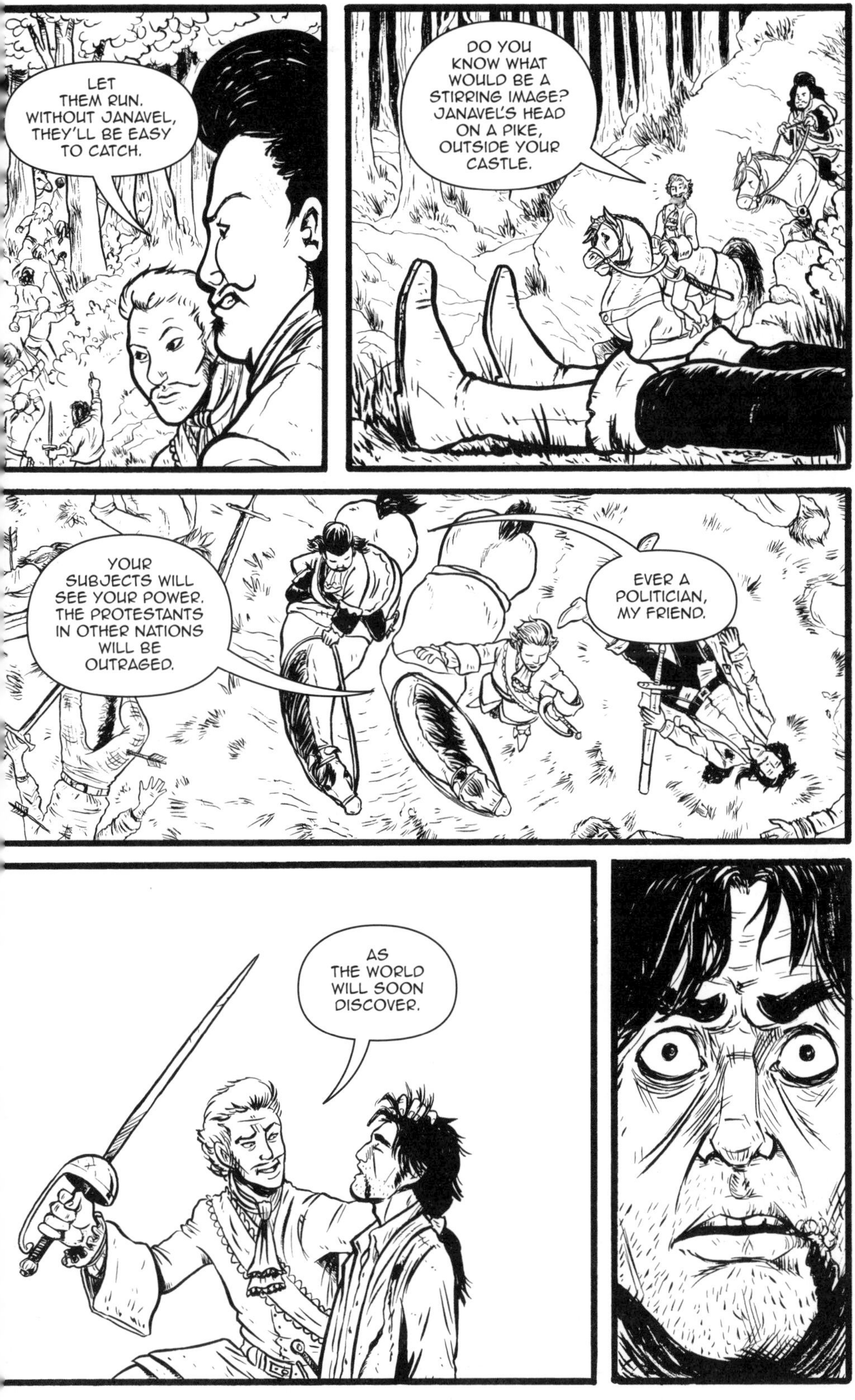
LET THEM RUN. WITHOUT JANAVEL, THEY'LL BE EASY TO CATCH.
DO YOU KNOW WHAT WOULD BE A STIRRING IMAGE? JANAVEL'S HEAD ON A PIKE, OUTSIDE YOUR CASTLE.
YOUR SUBJECTS WILL SEE YOUR POWER. THE PROTESTANTS IN OTHER NATIONS WILL BE OUTRAGED.
EVER A POLITICIAN, MY FRIEND.
AS THE WORLD WILL SOON DISCOVER.

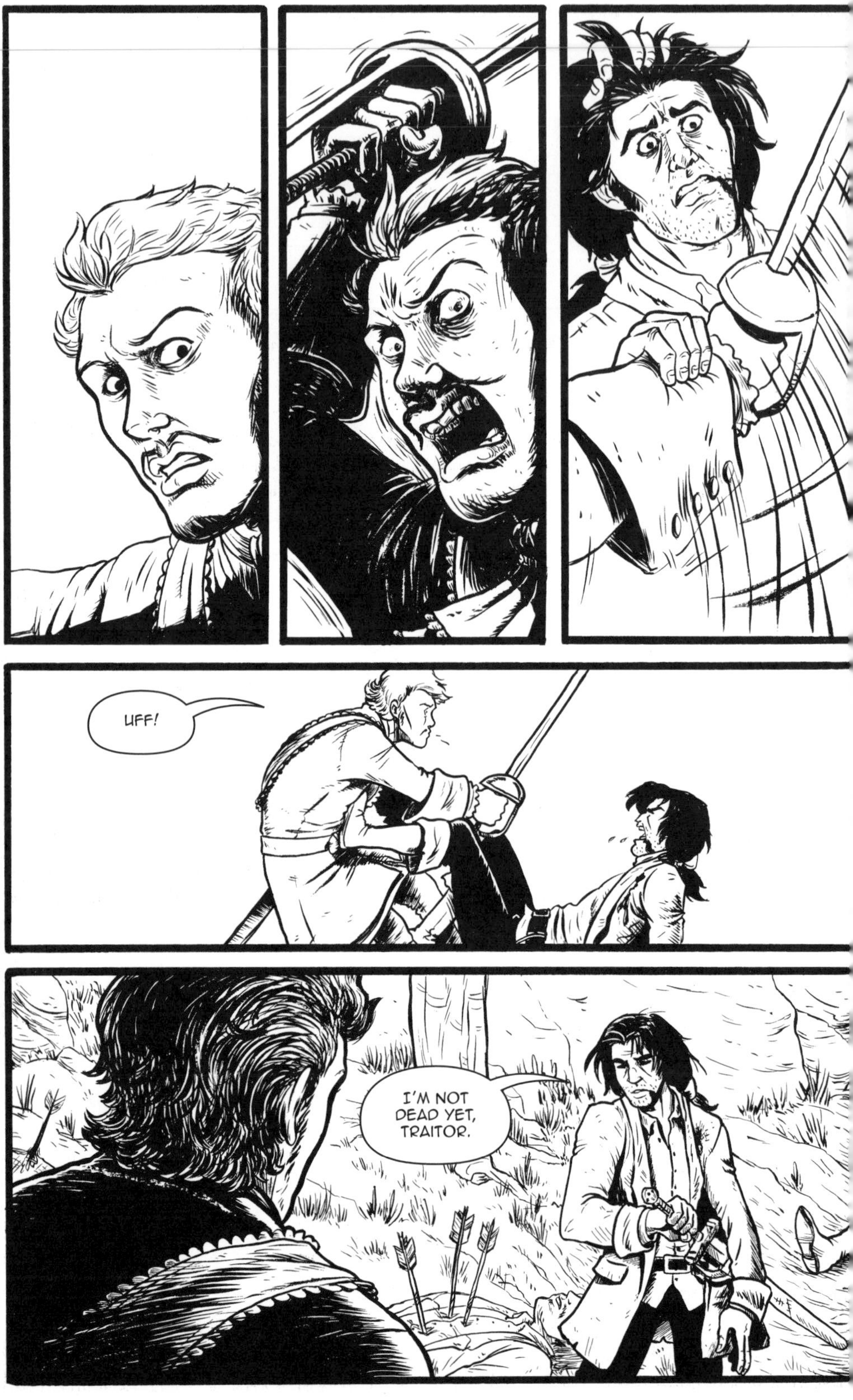
UFF!
I'M NOT DEAD YET, TRAITOR.

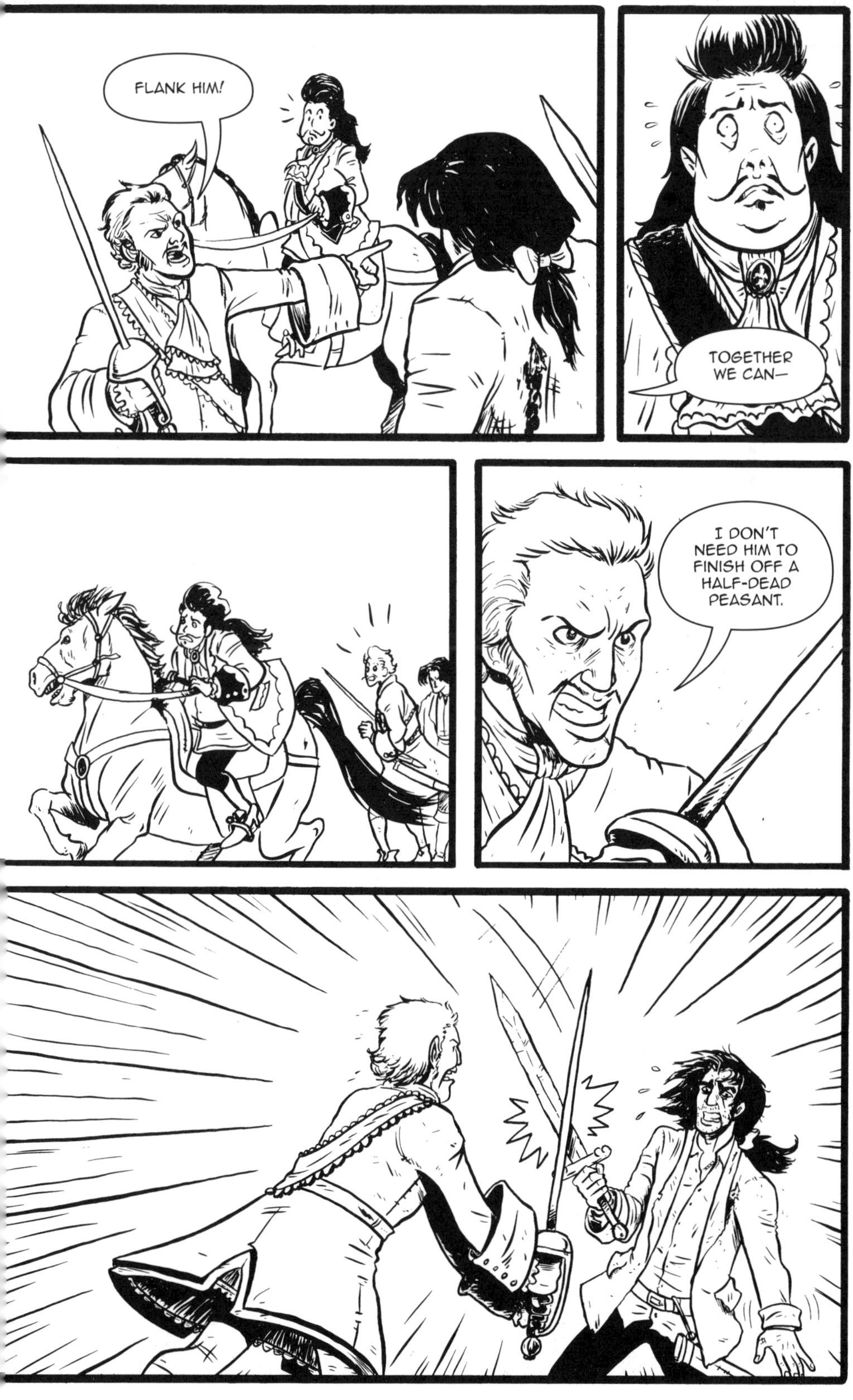
FLANK HIM!
TOGETHER WE CAN—
I DON'T NEED HIM TO FINISH OFF A HALF-DEAD PEASANT.

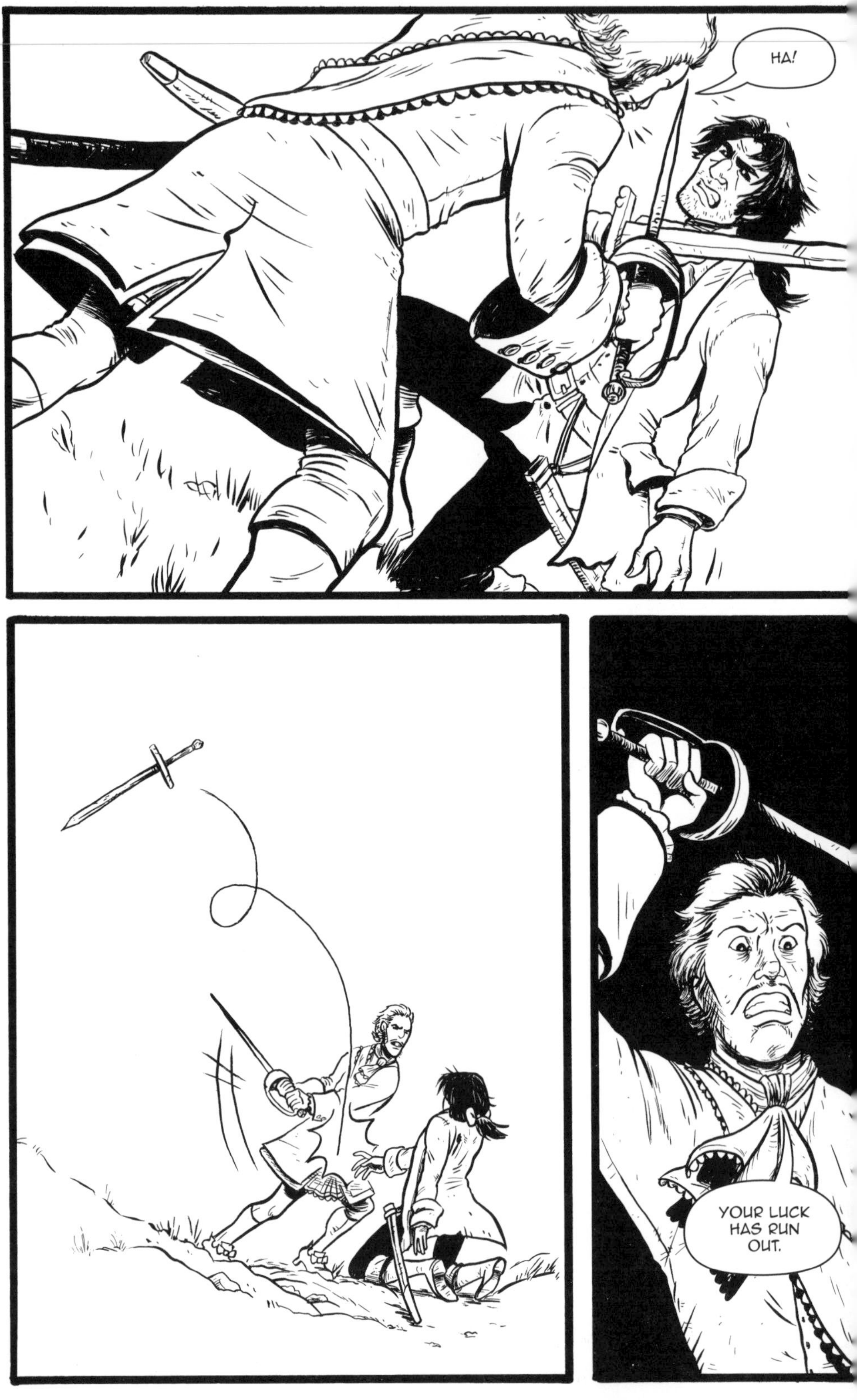
HA!
YOUR LUCK HAS RUN OUT.

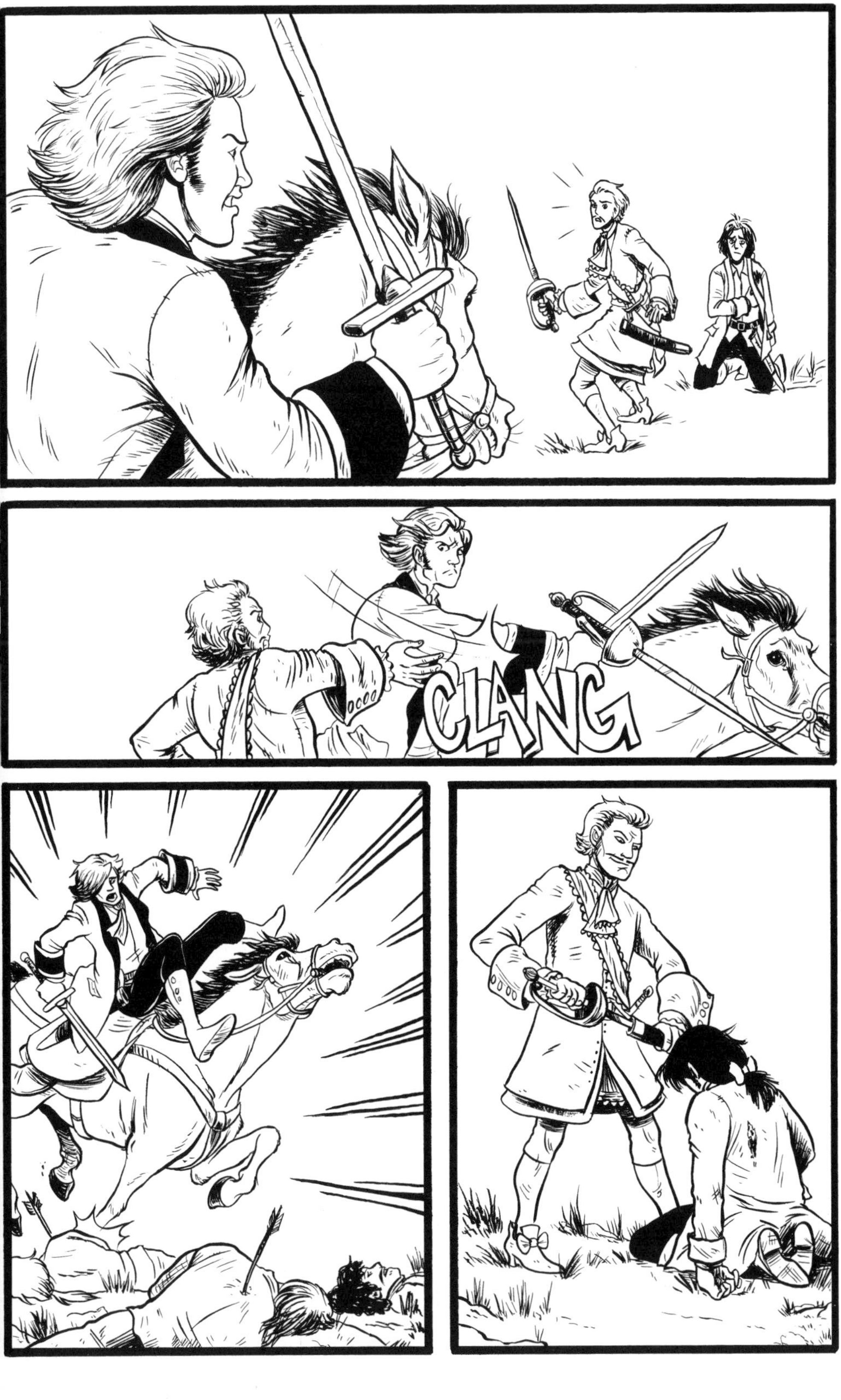
CLANG

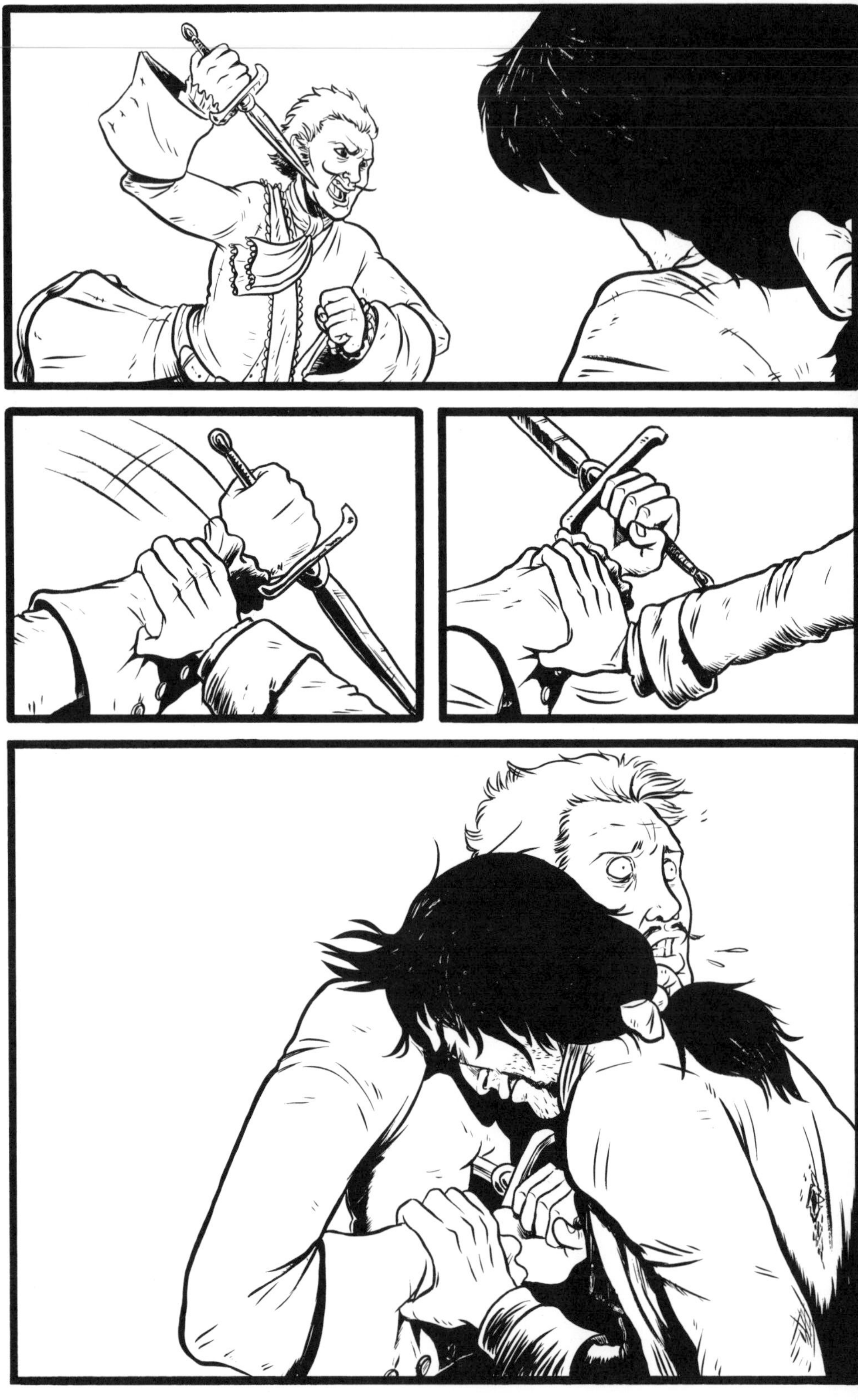

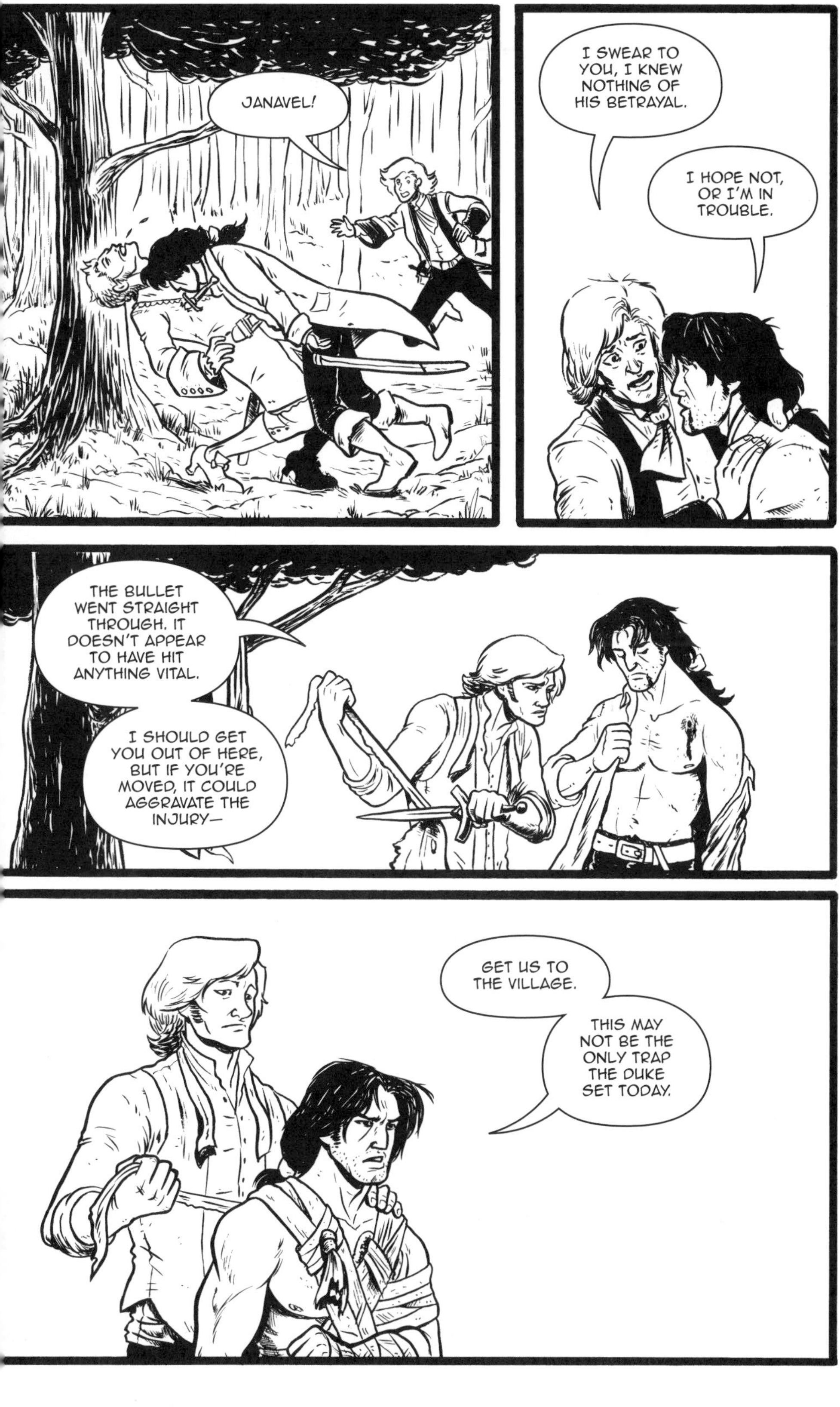
JANAVEL!
I SWEAR TO YOU, I KNEW NOTHING OF HIS BETRAYAL.
I HOPE NOT, OR I'M IN TROUBLE.
THE BULLET WENT STRAIGHT THROUGH. IT DOESN'T APPEAR TO HAVE HIT ANYTHING VITAL.
I SHOULD GET YOU OUT OF HERE, BUT IF YOU'RE MOVED, IT COULD AGGRAVATE THE INJURY—
GET US TO THE VILLAGE.
THIS MAY NOT BE THE ONLY TRAP THE DUKE SET TODAY.

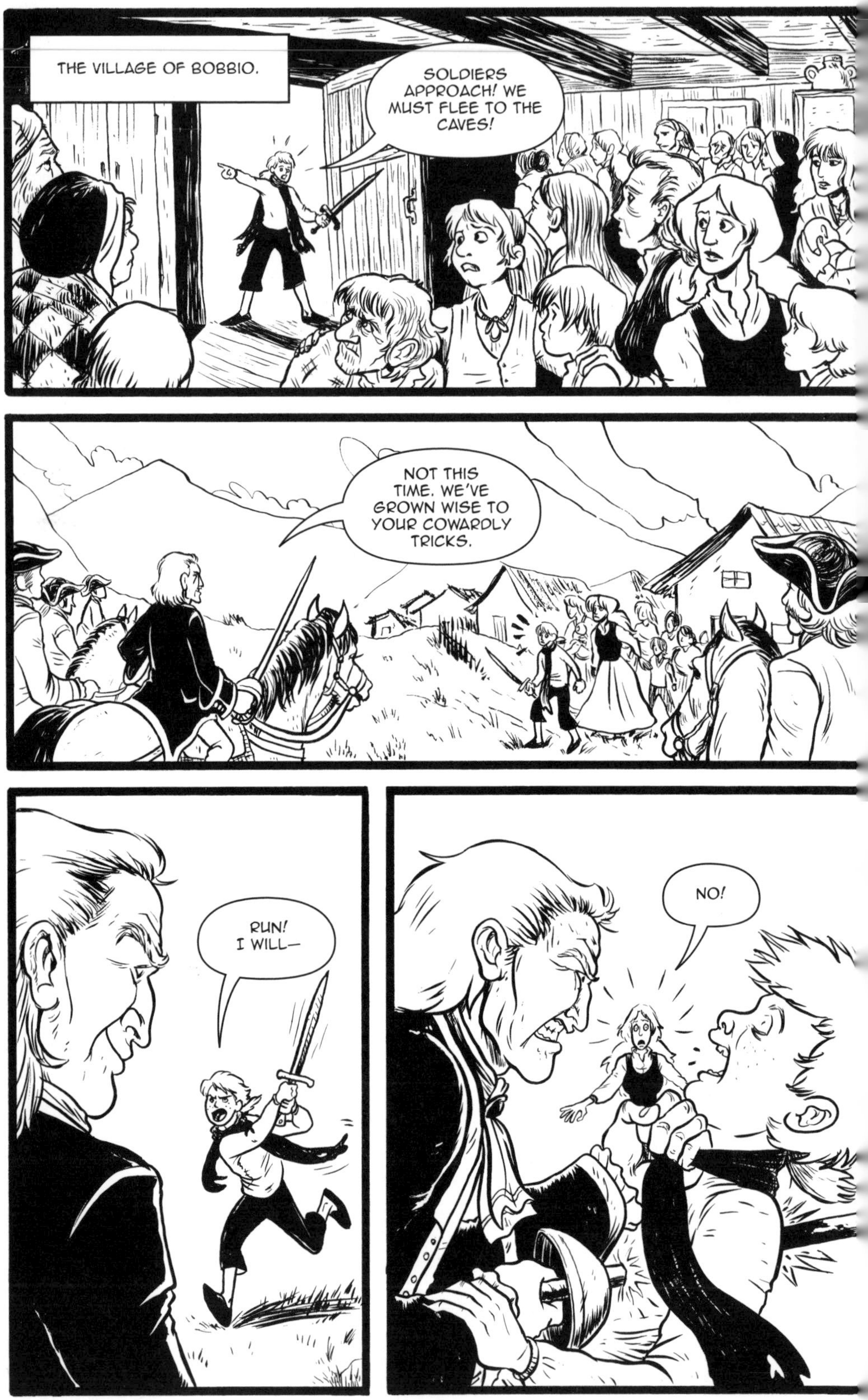
THE VILLAGE OF BOBBIO.
SOLDIERS APPROACH! WE MUST FLEE TO THE CAVES!
NOT THIS TIME. WE'VE GROWN WISE TO YOUR COWARDLY TRICKS.
RUN! I WILL—
NO!

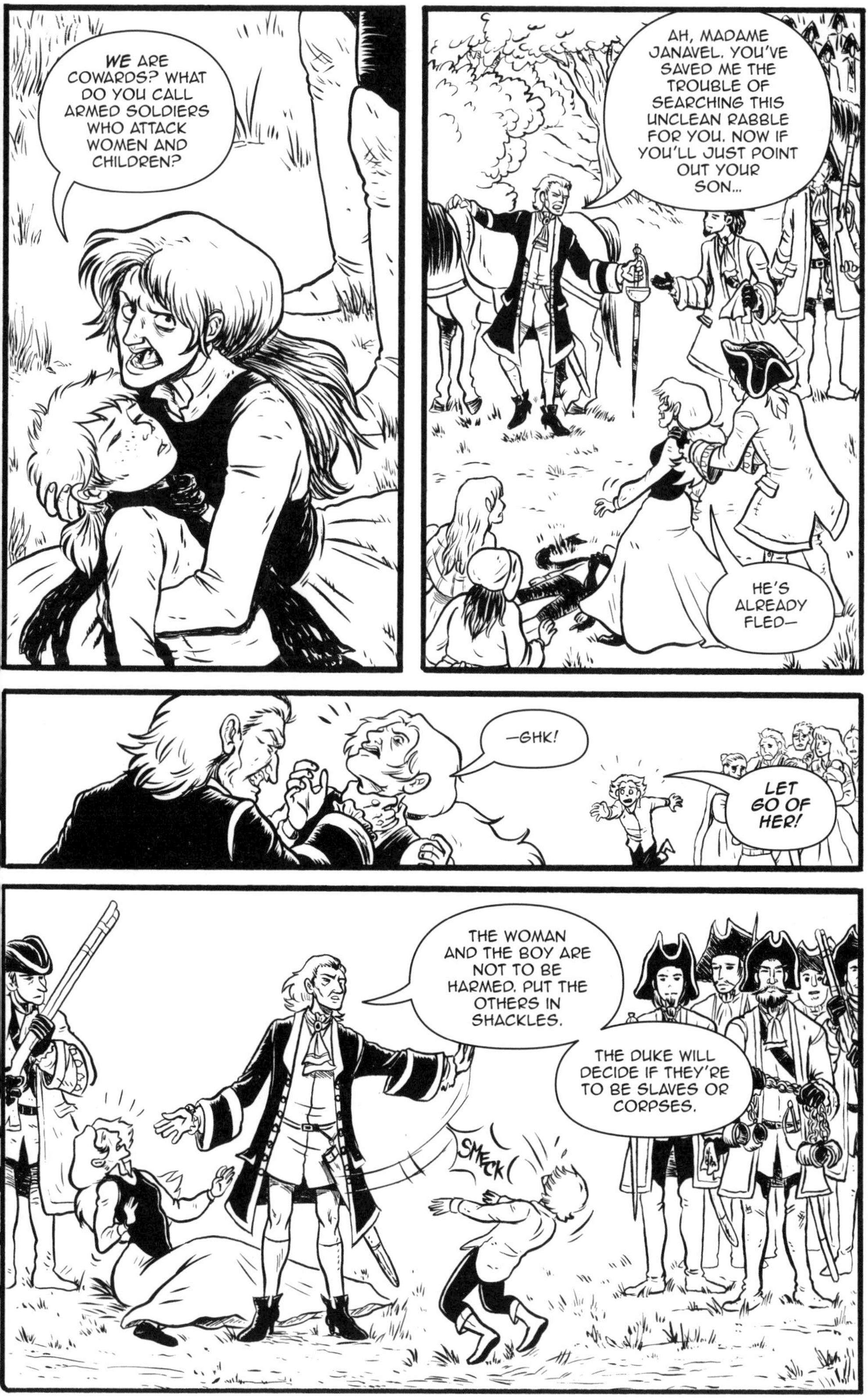
WE ARE COWARDS? WHAT DO YOU CALL ARMED SOLDIERS WHO ATTACK WOMEN AND CHILDREN?
AH, MADAME JANAVEL. YOU'VE SAVED ME THE TROUBLE OF SEARCHING THIS UNCLEAN RABBLE FOR YOU. NOW IF YOU'LL JUST POINT OUT YOUR SON...
HE'S ALREADY FLED—
—GHK!
LET GO OF HER!
THE WOMAN AND THE BOY ARE NOT TO BE HARMED. PUT THE OTHERS IN SHACKLES.
THE DUKE WILL DECIDE IF THEY'RE TO BE SLAVES OR CORPSES.
SMECK

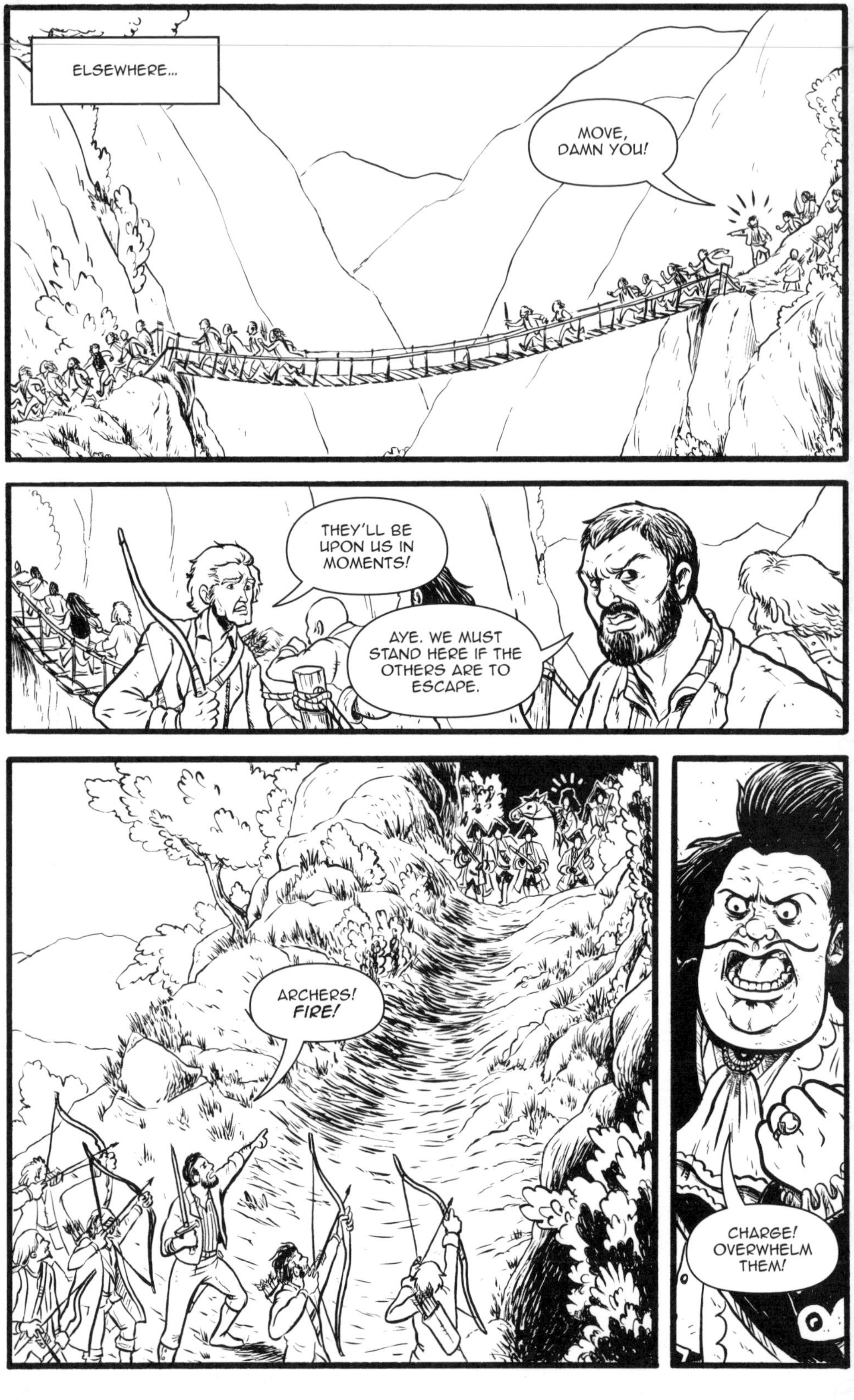
ELSEWHERE...
MOVE, DAMN YOU!
THEY'LL BE UPON US IN MOMENTS!
AYE. WE MUST STAND HERE IF THE OTHERS ARE TO ESCAPE.
ARCHERS! *FIRE!*
CHARGE! OVERWHELM THEM!

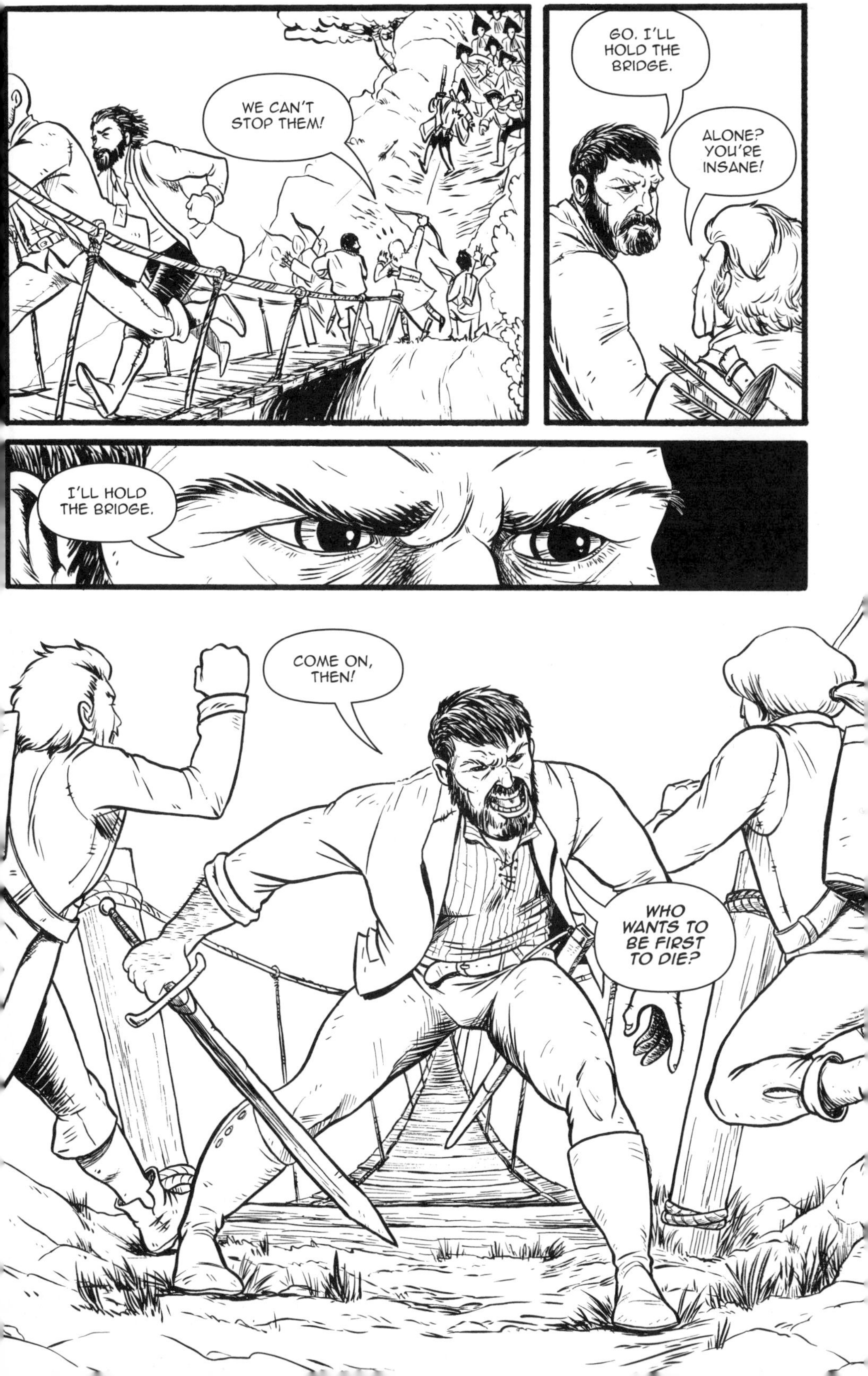
WE CAN'T STOP THEM!
GO. I'LL HOLD THE BRIDGE.
ALONE? YOU'RE INSANE!
I'LL HOLD THE BRIDGE.
COME ON, THEN!
WHO WANTS TO BE FIRST TO DIE?

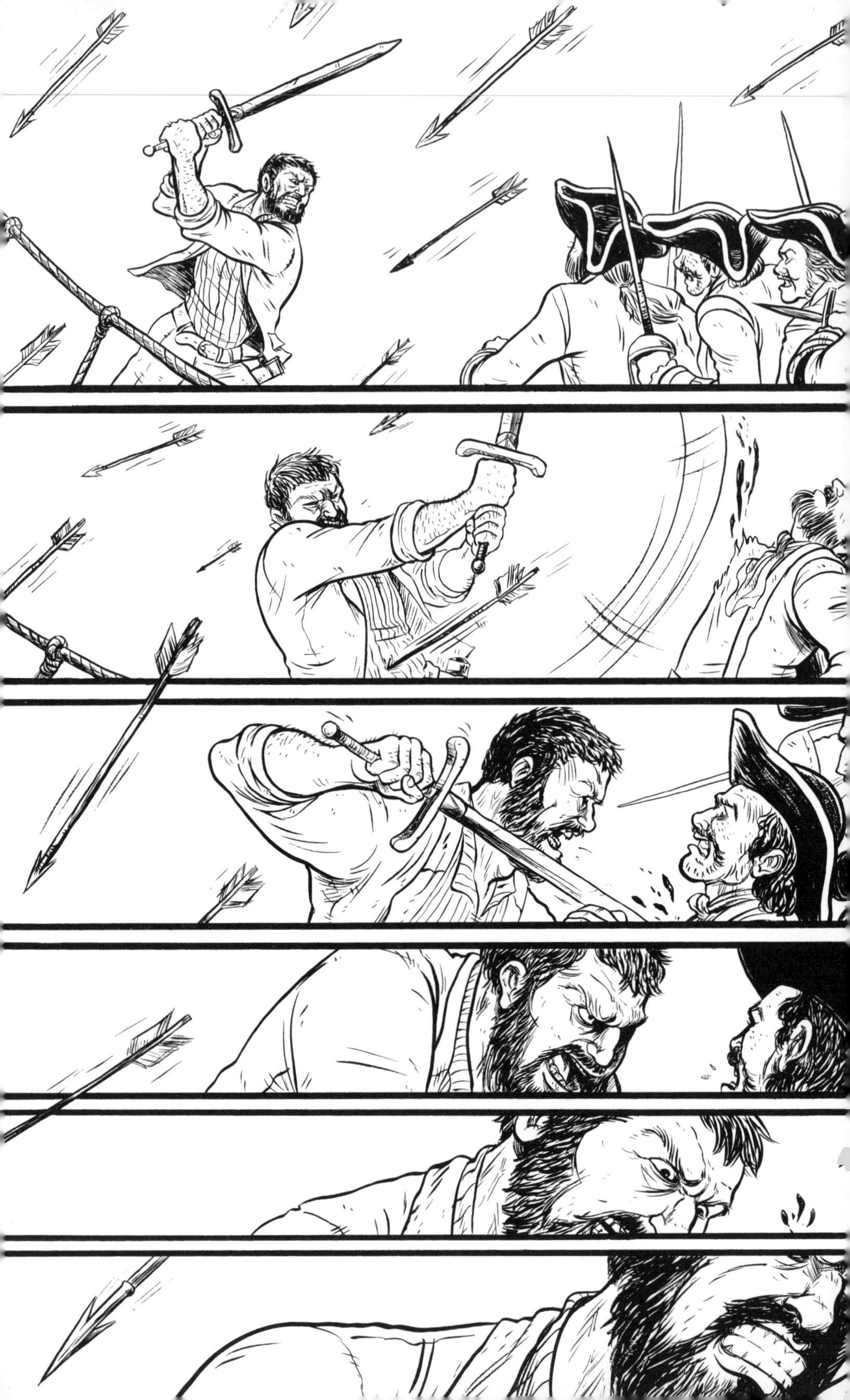

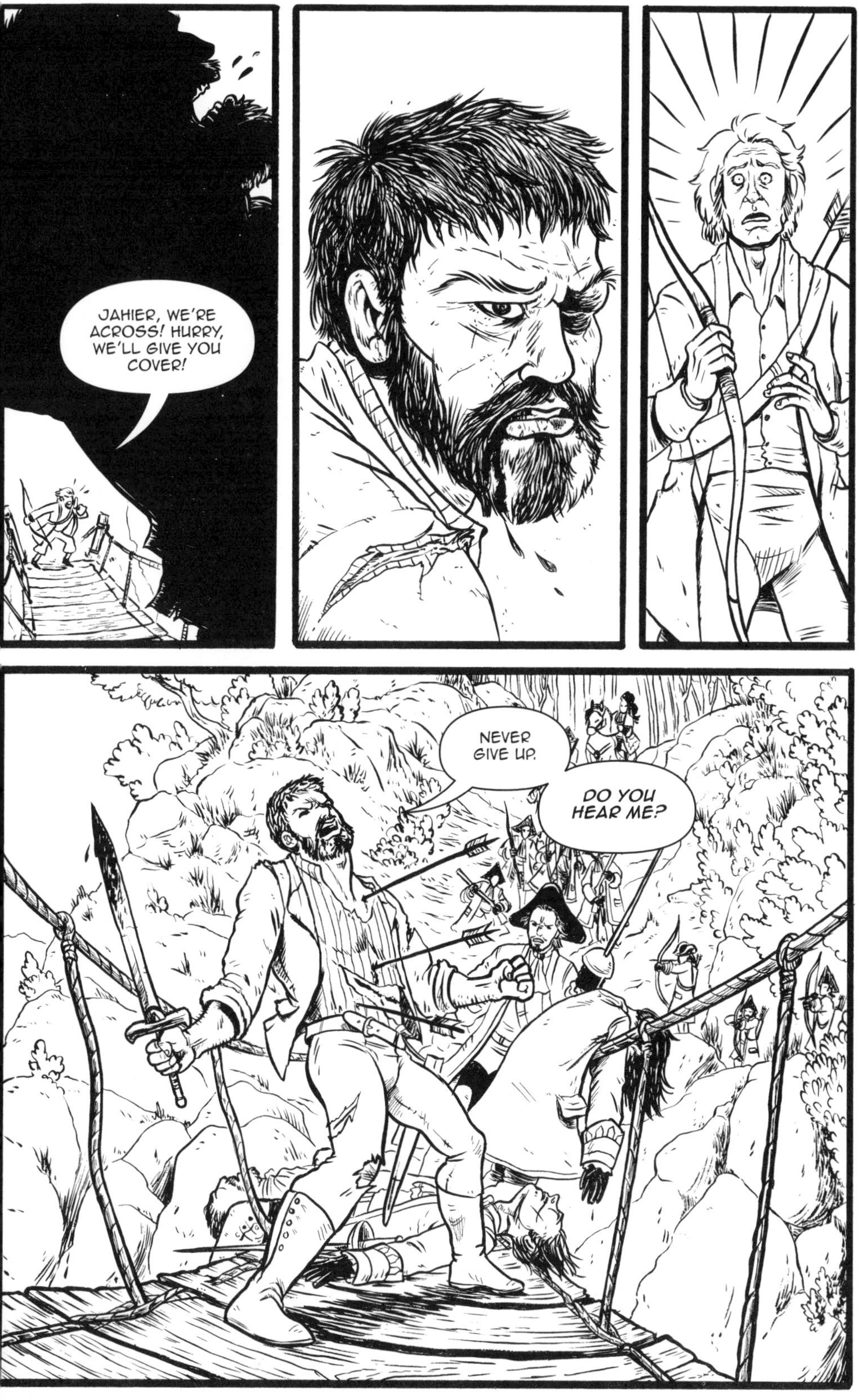
JAHIER, WE'RE ACROSS! HURRY, WE'LL GIVE YOU COVER!
NEVER GIVE UP.
DO YOU HEAR ME?

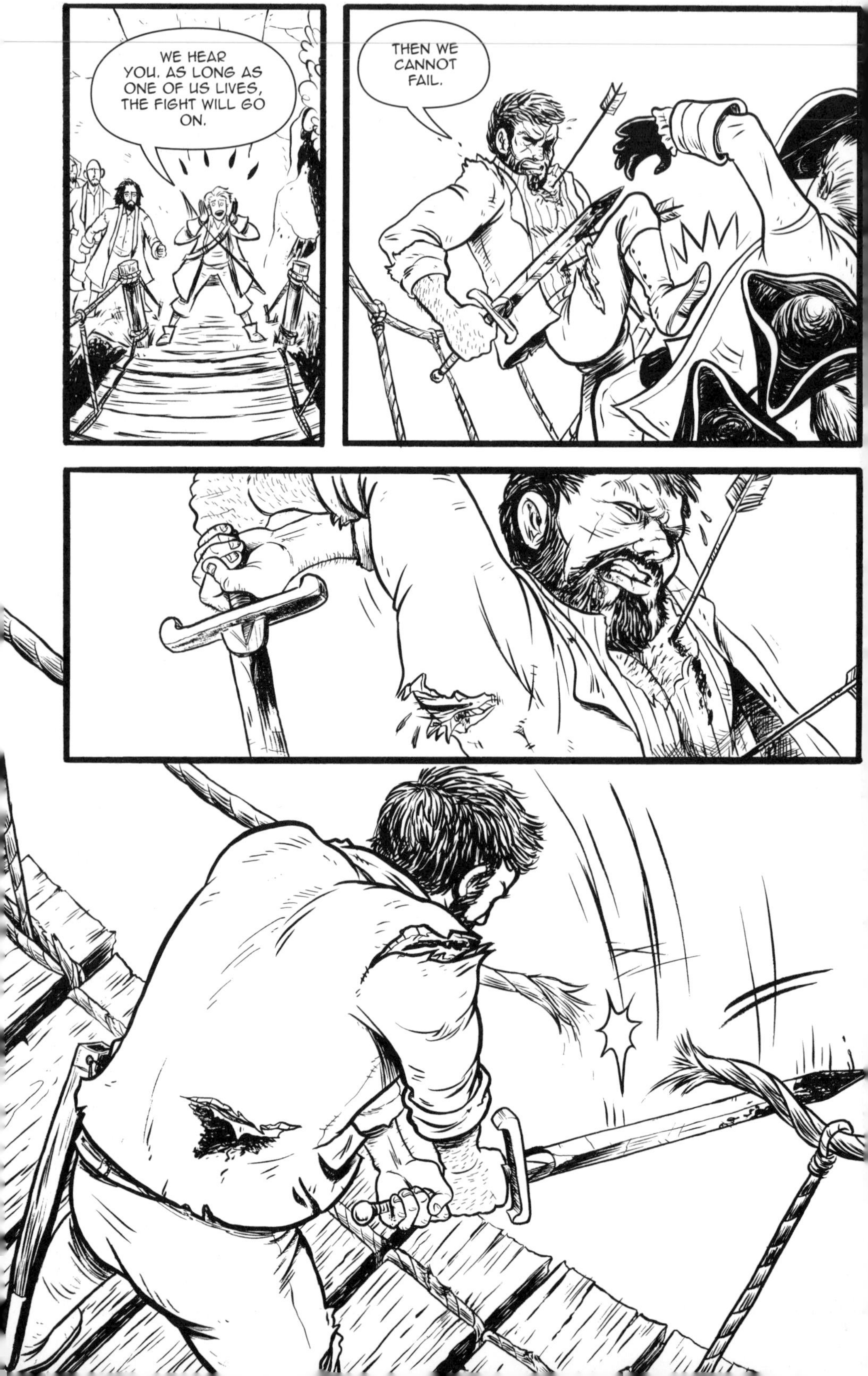
WE HEAR YOU. AS LONG AS ONE OF US LIVES, THE FIGHT WILL GO ON.
THEN WE CANNOT FAIL.

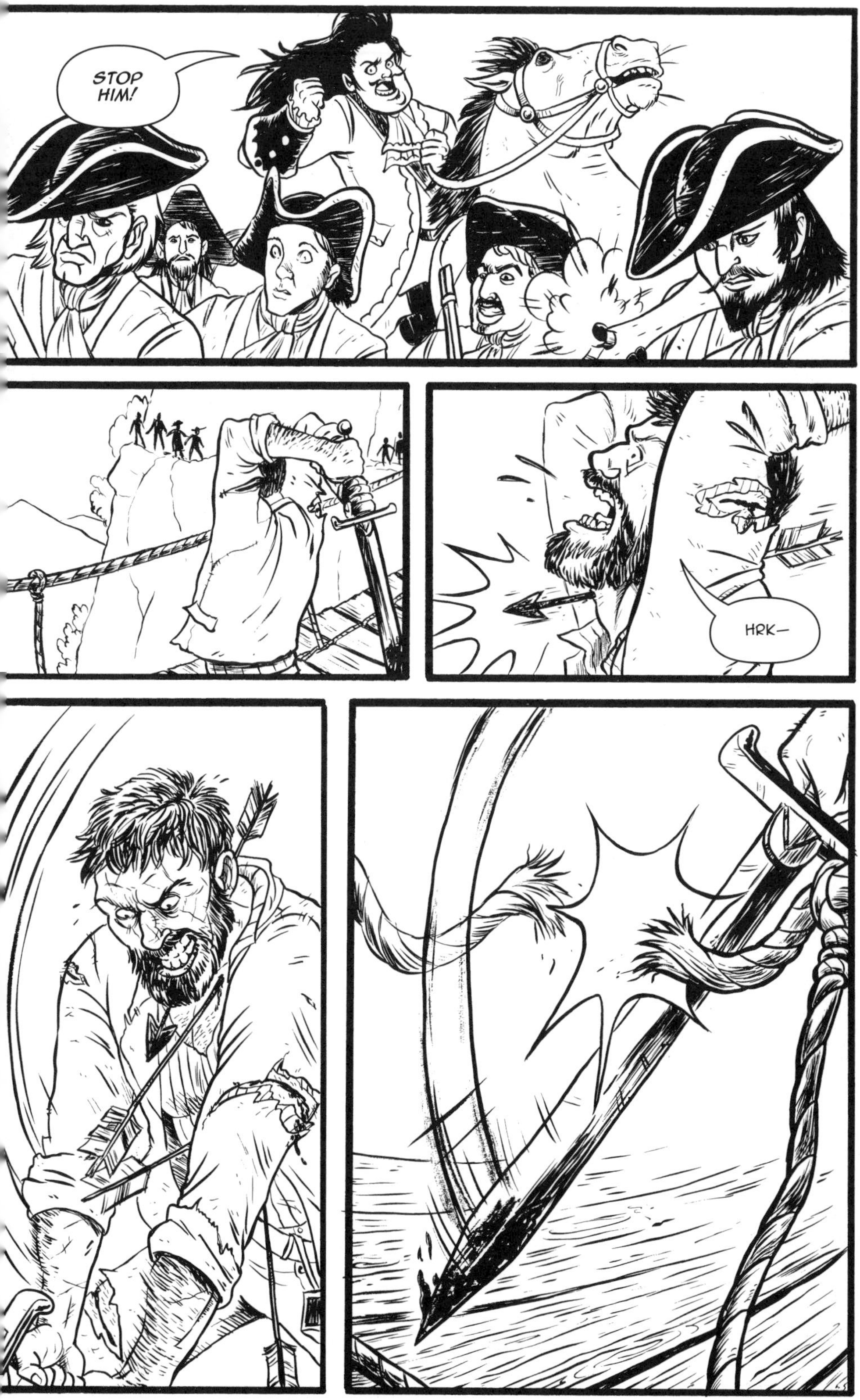
STOP HIM!
HRK—

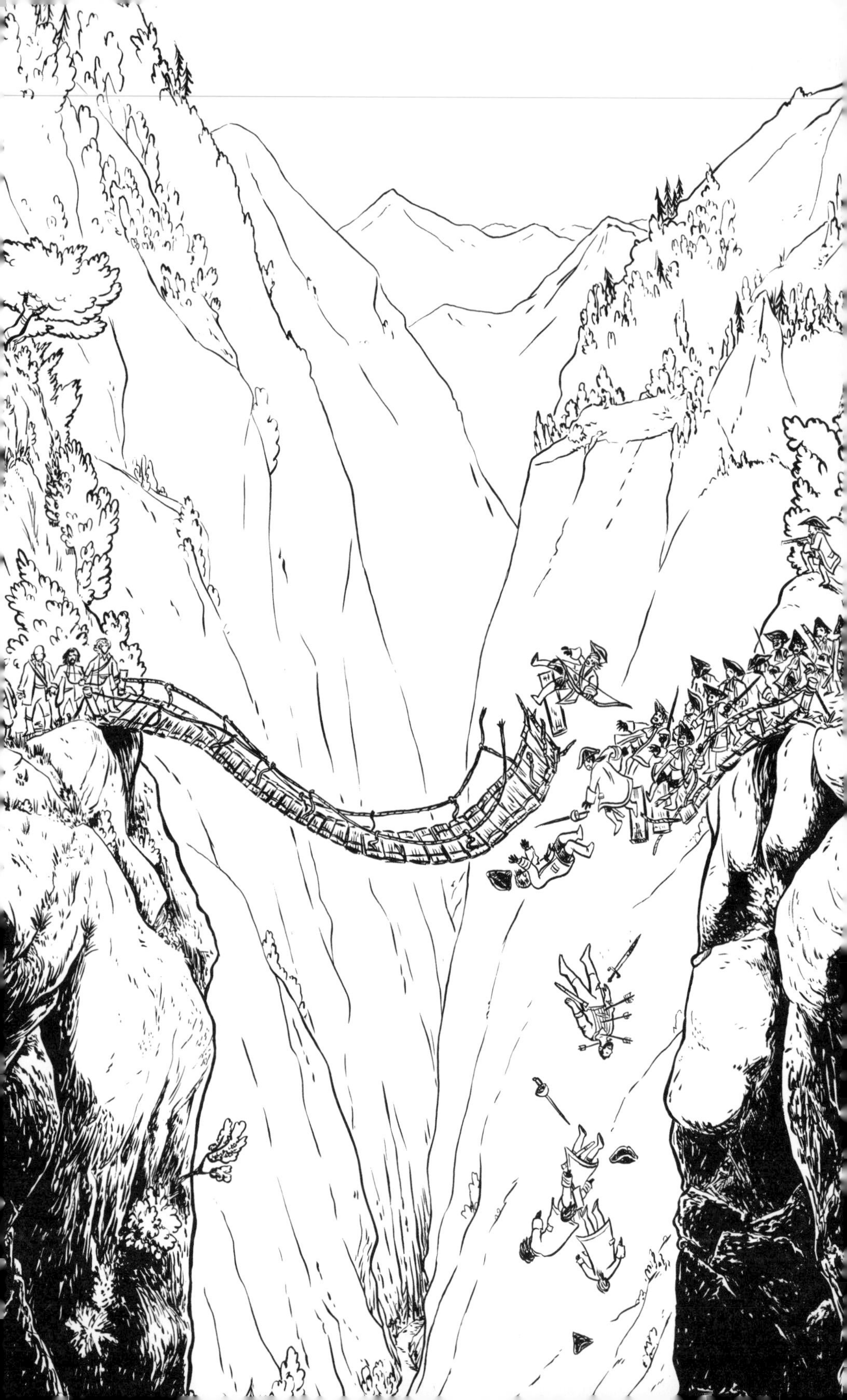

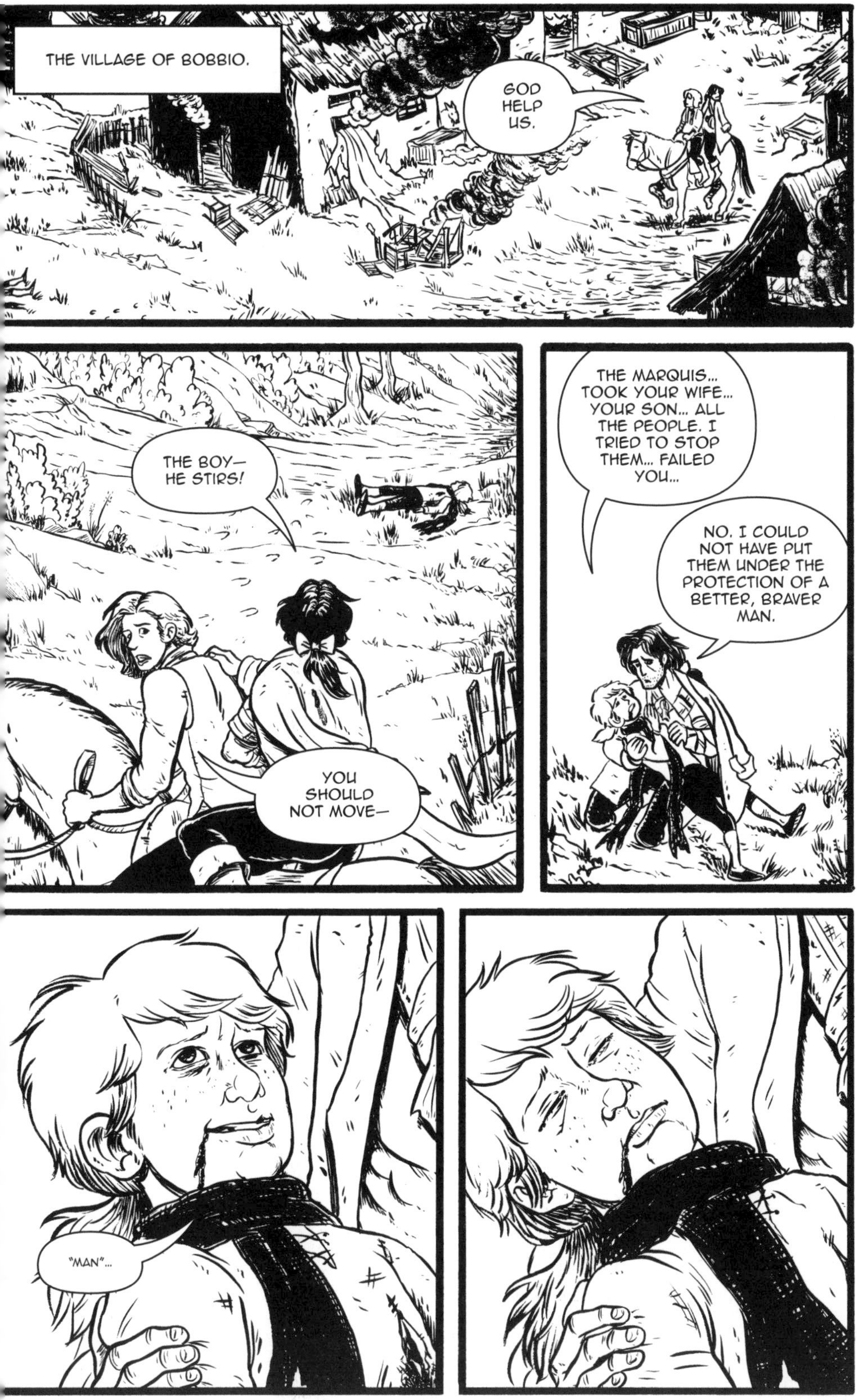
THE VILLAGE OF BOBBIO.
GOD HELP US.
THE BOY— HE STIRS!
YOU SHOULD NOT MOVE—
THE MARQUIS... TOOK YOUR WIFE... YOUR SON... ALL THE PEOPLE. I TRIED TO STOP THEM... FAILED YOU...
NO. I COULD NOT HAVE PUT THEM UNDER THE PROTECTION OF A BETTER, BRAVER MAN.
"MAN"...

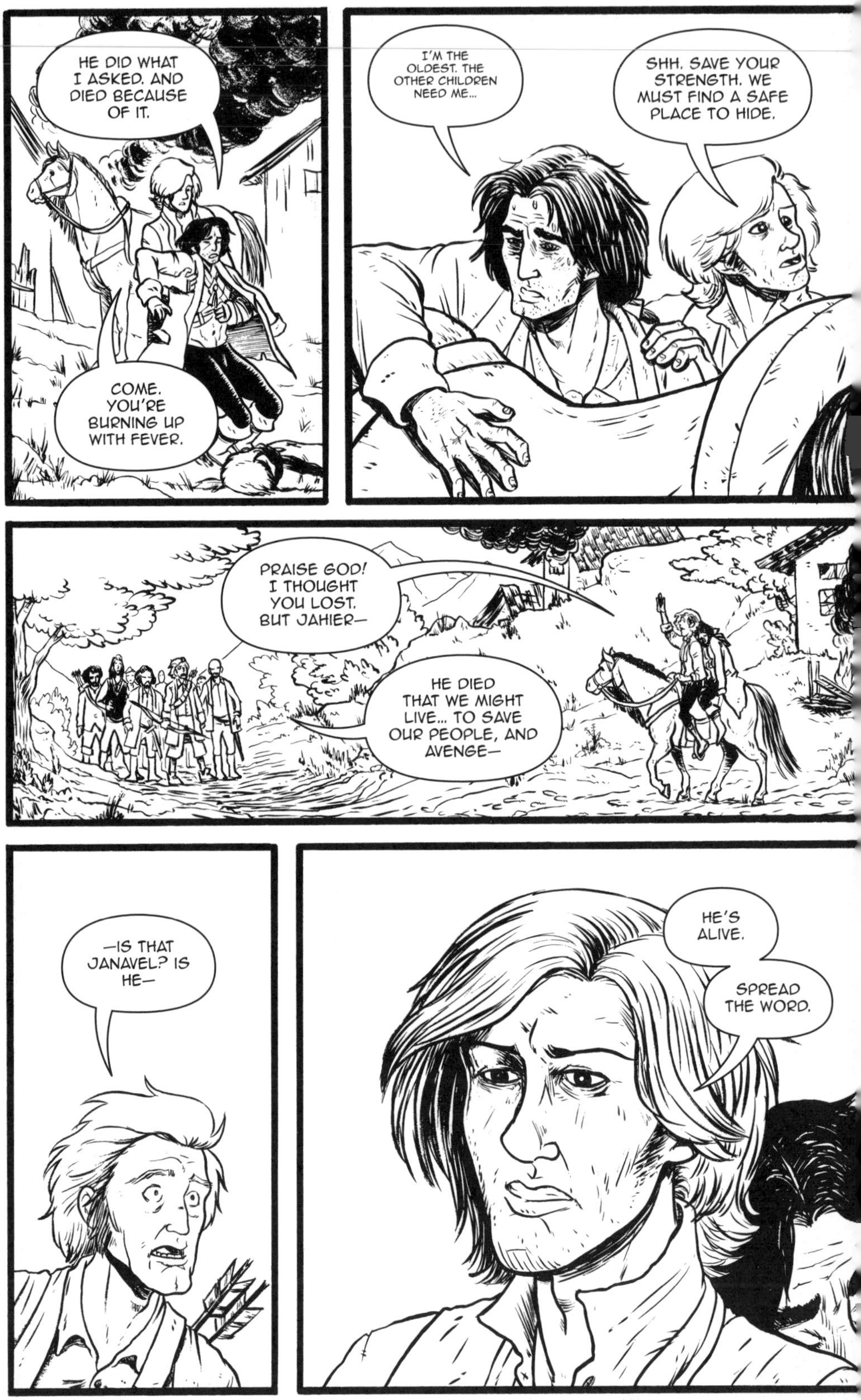
HE DID WHAT I ASKED. AND DIED BECAUSE OF IT.
COME. YOU'RE BURNING UP WITH FEVER.
I'M THE OLDEST. THE OTHER CHILDREN NEED ME...
SHH. SAVE YOUR STRENGTH. WE MUST FIND A SAFE PLACE TO HIDE.
PRAISE GOD! I THOUGHT YOU LOST. BUT JAHIER—
HE DIED THAT WE MIGHT LIVE... TO SAVE OUR PEOPLE, AND AVENGE—
—IS THAT JANAVEL? IS HE—
HE'S ALIVE.
SPREAD THE WORD.

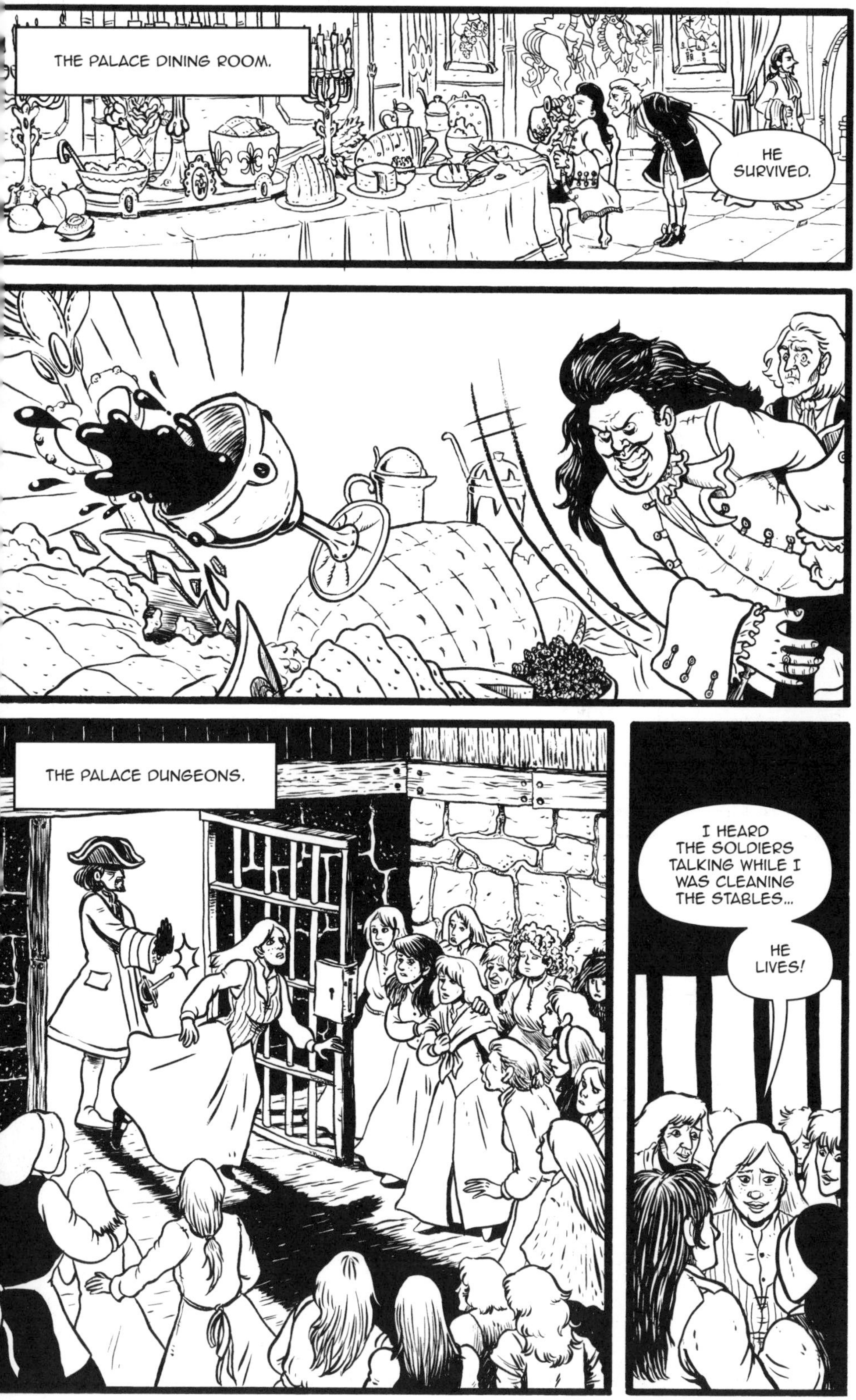
THE PALACE DINING ROOM.
HE SURVIVED.
THE PALACE DUNGEONS.
I HEARD THE SOLDIERS TALKING WHILE I WAS CLEANING THE STABLES...
HE LIVES!

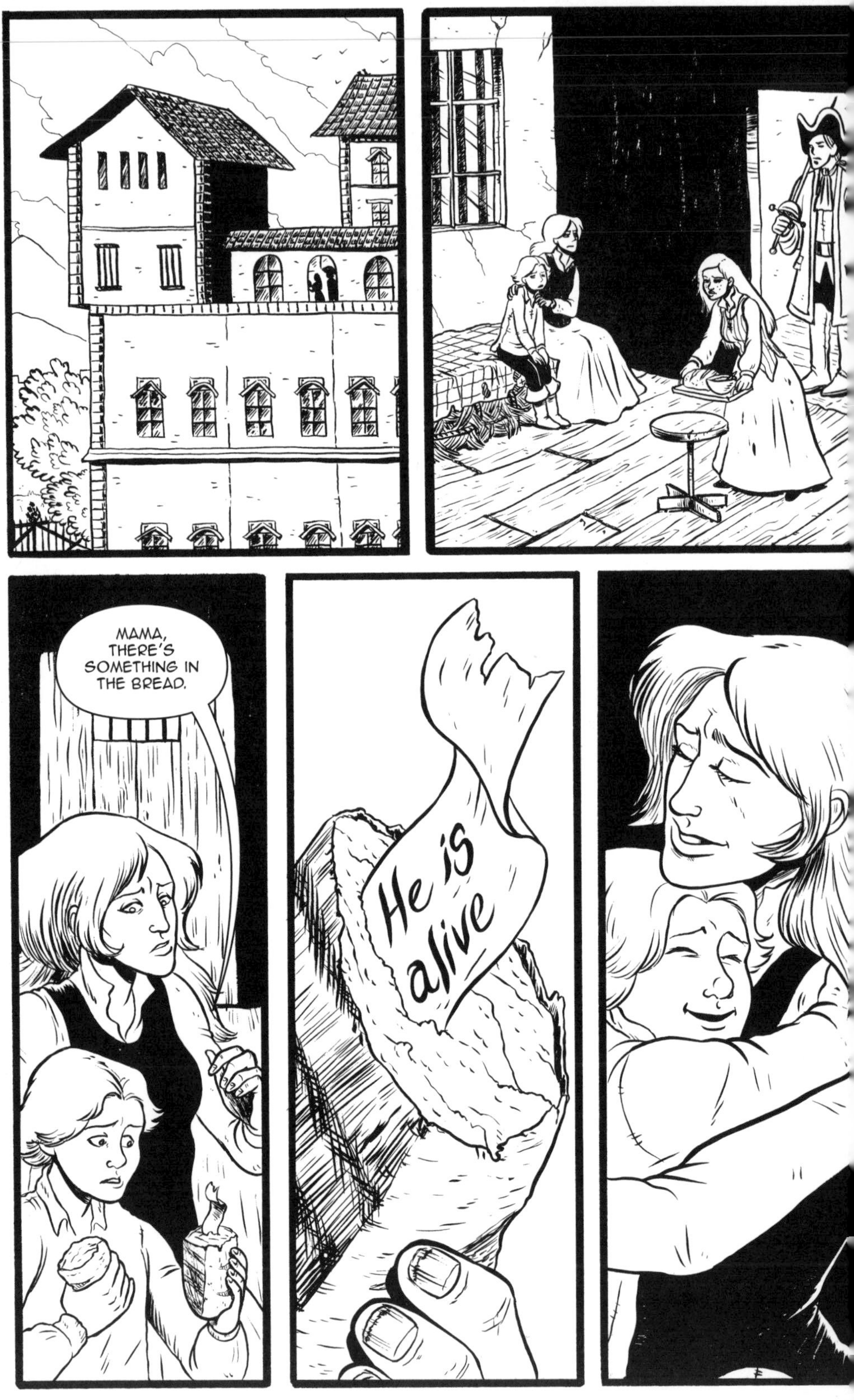
MAMA, THERE'S SOMETHING IN THE BREAD.
He is alive

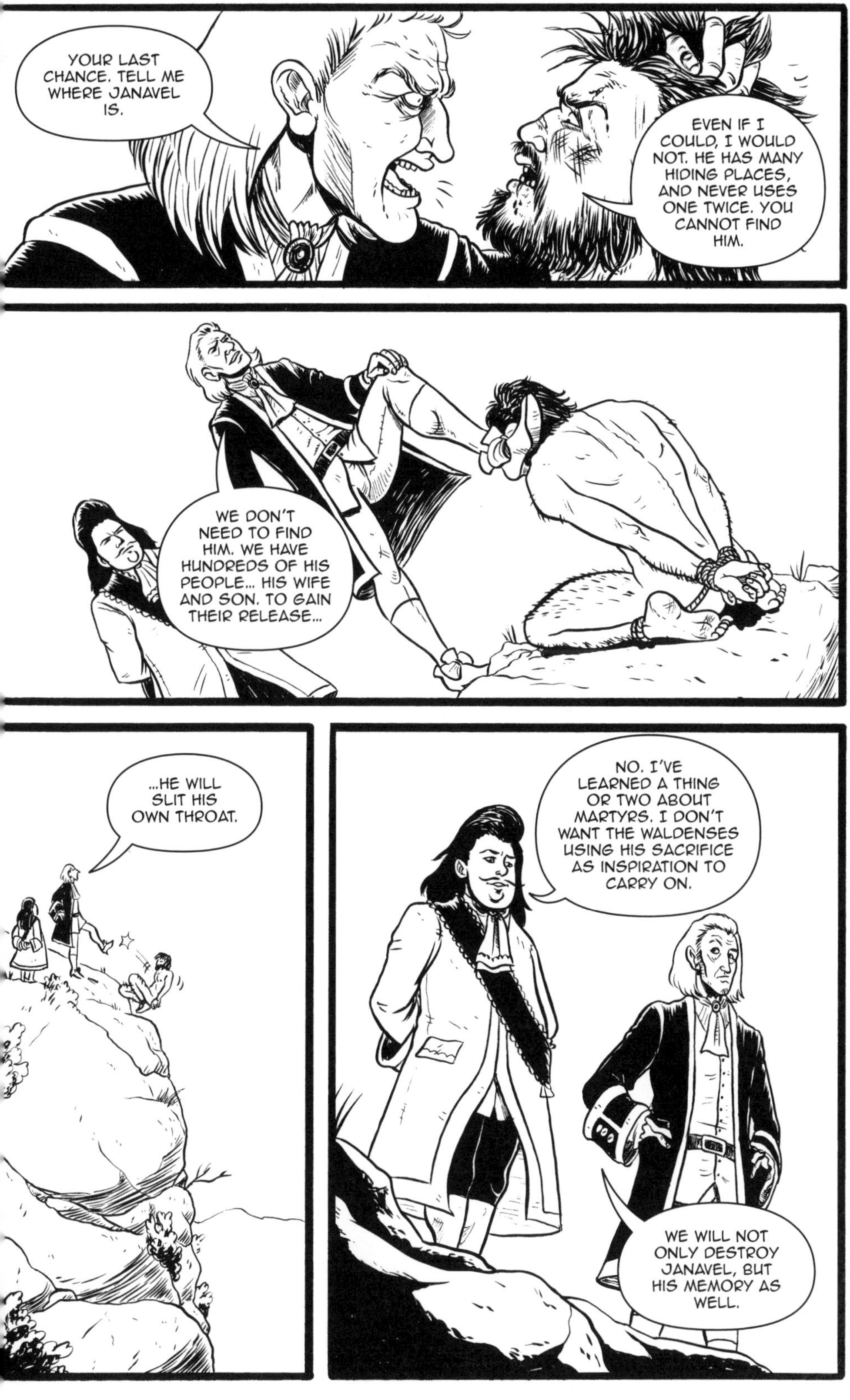
YOUR LAST CHANCE. TELL ME WHERE JANAVEL IS.
EVEN IF I COULD, I WOULD NOT. HE HAS MANY HIDING PLACES, AND NEVER USES ONE TWICE. YOU CANNOT FIND HIM.
WE DON'T NEED TO FIND HIM. WE HAVE HUNDREDS OF HIS PEOPLE... HIS WIFE AND SON. TO GAIN THEIR RELEASE...
...HE WILL SLIT HIS OWN THROAT.
NO. I'VE LEARNED A THING OR TWO ABOUT MARTYRS. I DON'T WANT THE WALDENSES USING HIS SACRIFICE AS INSPIRATION TO CARRY ON.
WE WILL NOT ONLY DESTROY JANAVEL, BUT HIS MEMORY AS WELL.

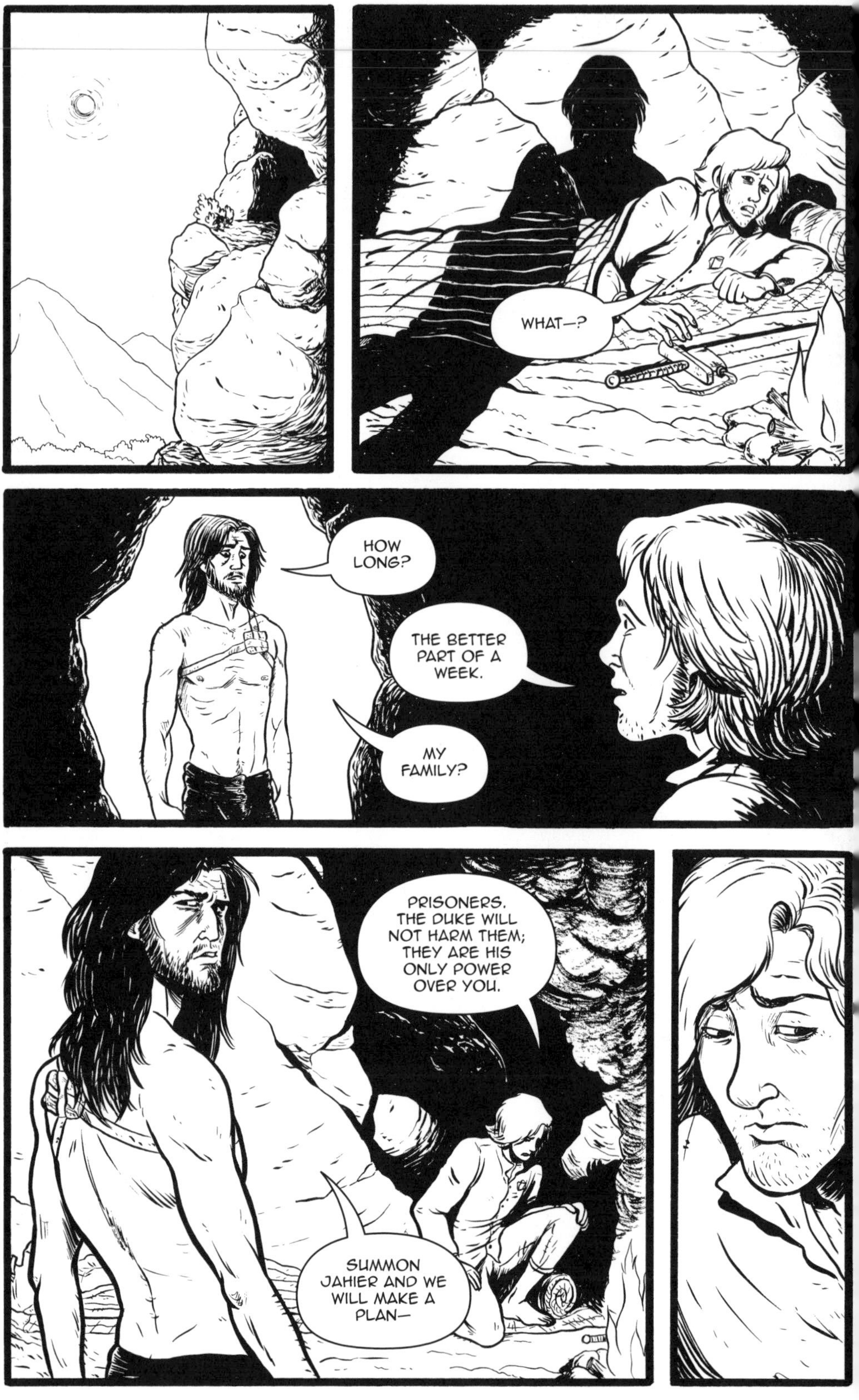
WHAT—?
HOW LONG?
THE BETTER PART OF A WEEK.
MY FAMILY?
PRISONERS. THE DUKE WILL NOT HARM THEM; THEY ARE HIS ONLY POWER OVER YOU.
SUMMON JAHIER AND WE WILL MAKE A PLAN—

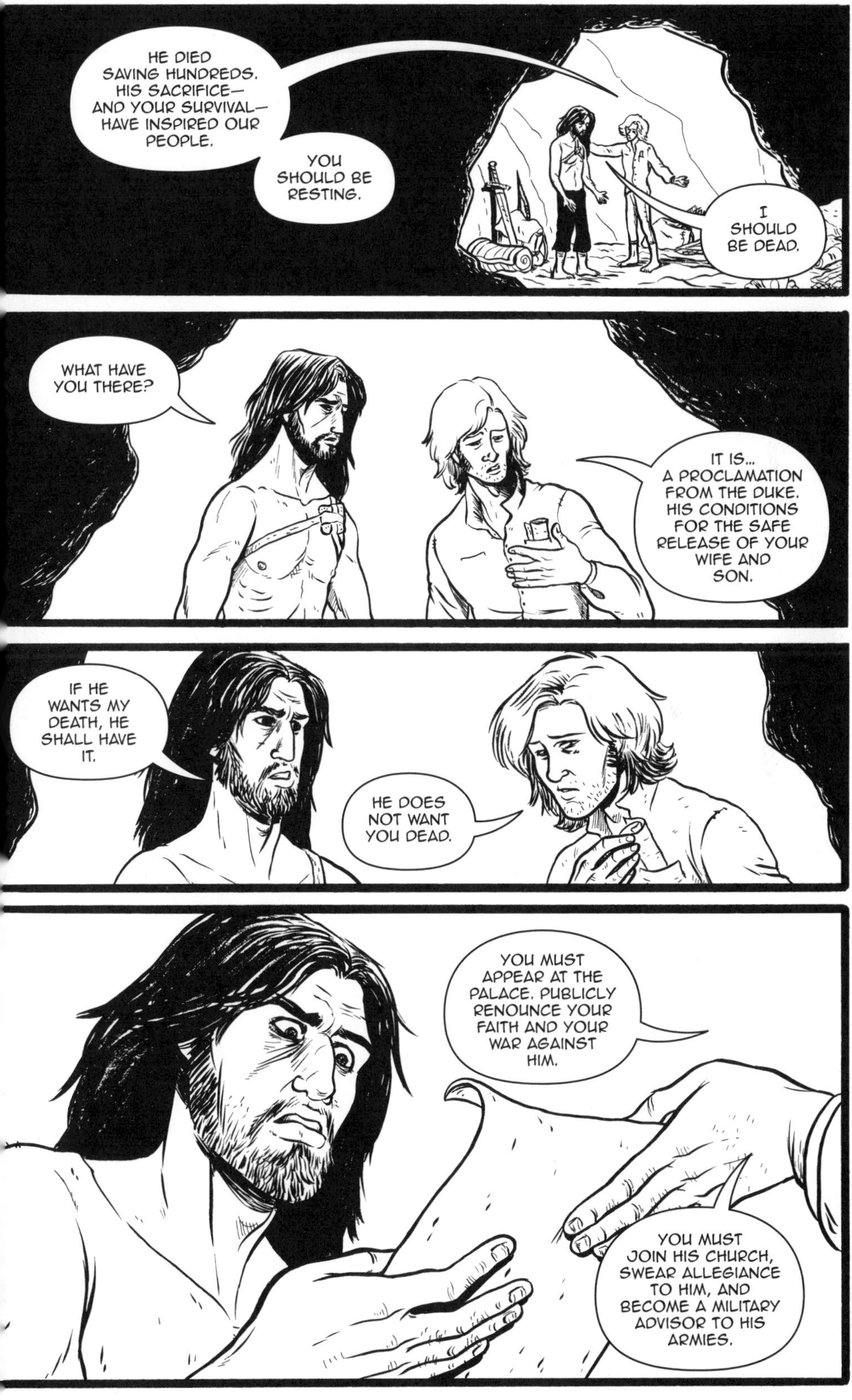
HE DIED SAVING HUNDREDS. HIS SACRIFICE— AND YOUR SURVIVAL— HAVE INSPIRED OUR PEOPLE.
YOU SHOULD BE RESTING.
I SHOULD BE DEAD.
WHAT HAVE YOU THERE?
IT IS... A PROCLAMATION FROM THE DUKE. HIS CONDITIONS FOR THE SAFE RELEASE OF YOUR WIFE AND SON.
IF HE WANTS MY DEATH, HE SHALL HAVE IT.
HE DOES NOT WANT YOU DEAD.
YOU MUST APPEAR AT THE PALACE. PUBLICLY RENOUNCE YOUR FAITH AND YOUR WAR AGAINST HIM.
YOU MUST JOIN HIS CHURCH, SWEAR ALLEGIANCE TO HIM, AND BECOME A MILITARY ADVISOR TO HIS ARMIES.

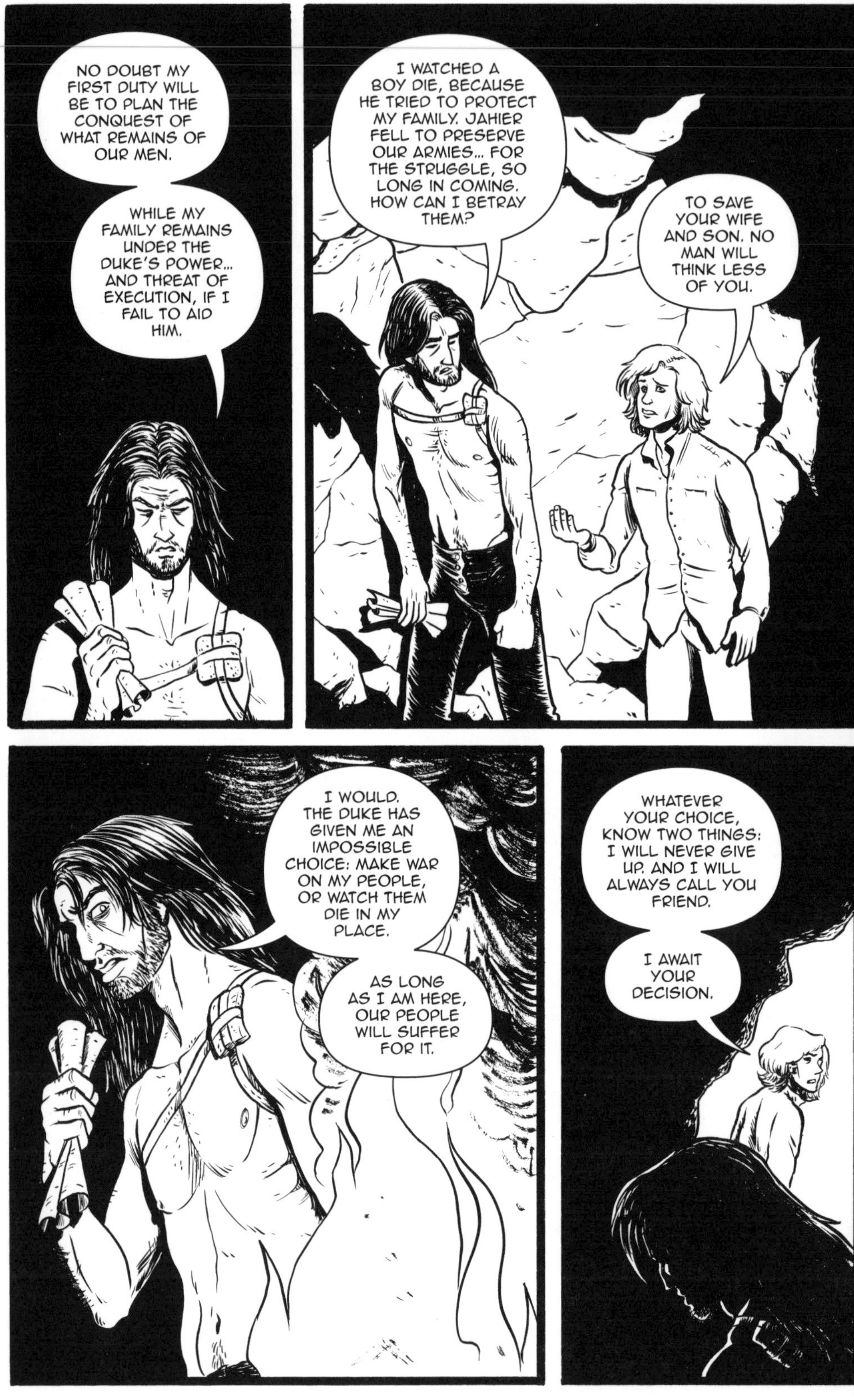
NO DOUBT MY FIRST DUTY WILL BE TO PLAN THE CONQUEST OF WHAT REMAINS OF OUR MEN.
WHILE MY FAMILY REMAINS UNDER THE DUKE'S POWER... AND THREAT OF EXECUTION, IF I FAIL TO AID HIM.
I WATCHED A BOY DIE, BECAUSE HE TRIED TO PROTECT MY FAMILY. JAHIER FELL TO PRESERVE OUR ARMIES... FOR THE STRUGGLE, SO LONG IN COMING. HOW CAN I BETRAY THEM?
TO SAVE YOUR WIFE AND SON. NO MAN WILL THINK LESS OF YOU.
I WOULD. THE DUKE HAS GIVEN ME AN IMPOSSIBLE CHOICE: MAKE WAR ON MY PEOPLE, OR WATCH THEM DIE IN MY PLACE.
AS LONG AS I AM HERE, OUR PEOPLE WILL SUFFER FOR IT.
WHATEVER YOUR CHOICE, KNOW TWO THINGS: I WILL NEVER GIVE UP. AND I WILL ALWAYS CALL YOU FRIEND.
I AWAIT YOUR DECISION.

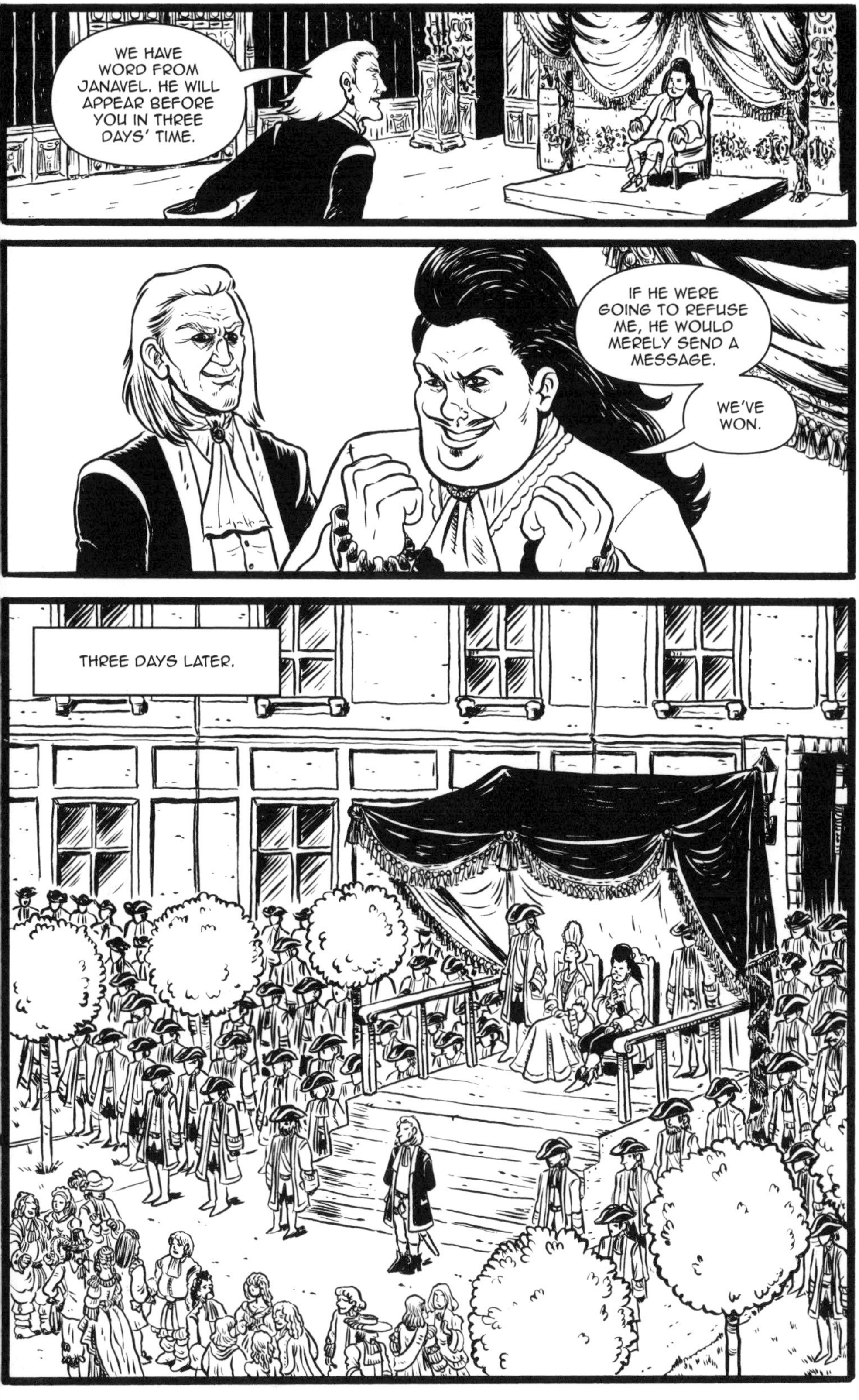
WE HAVE WORD FROM JANAVEL. HE WILL APPEAR BEFORE YOU IN THREE DAYS' TIME.
IF HE WERE GOING TO REFUSE ME, HE WOULD MERELY SEND A MESSAGE.
WE'VE WON.
THREE DAYS LATER.

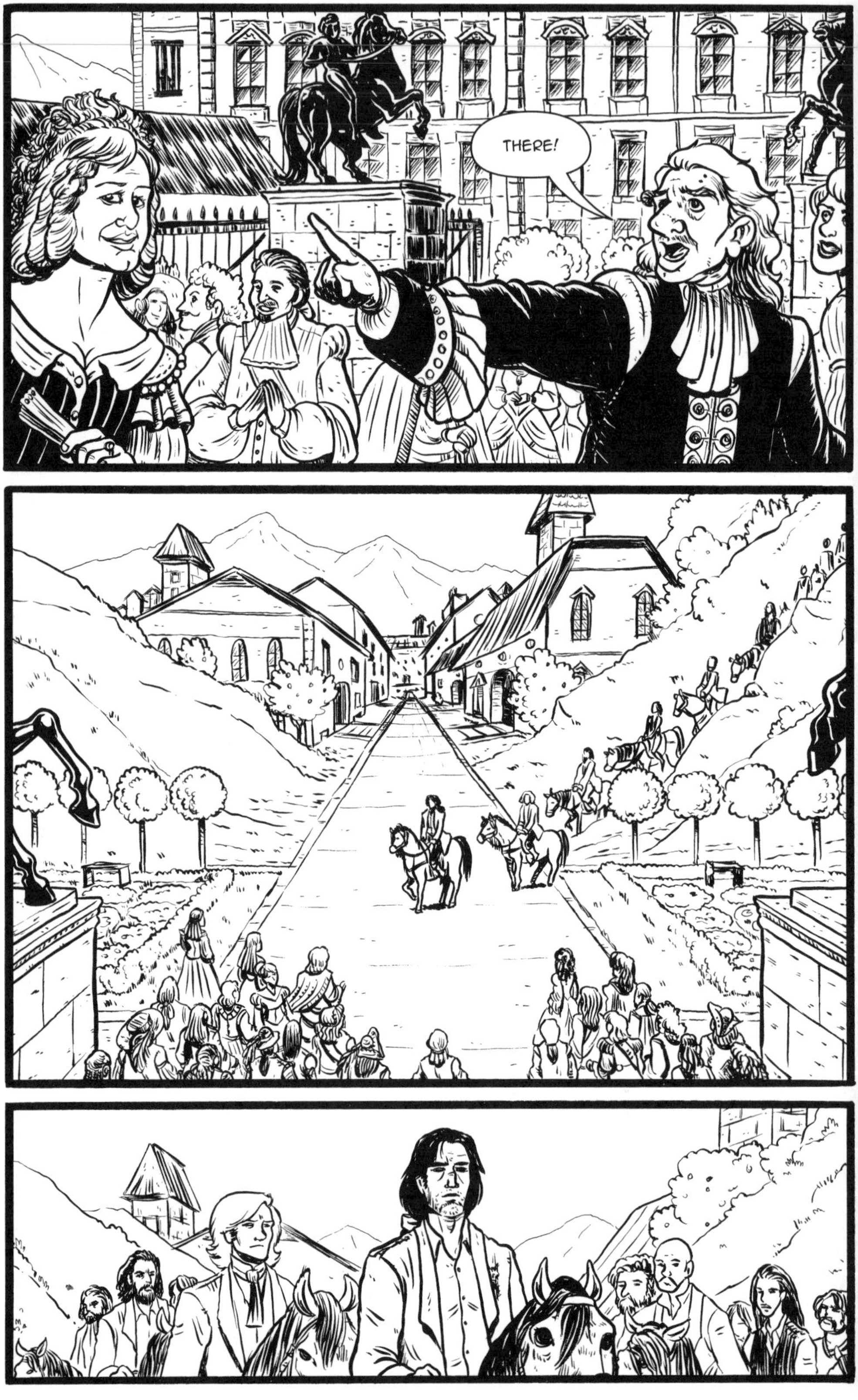
THERE!

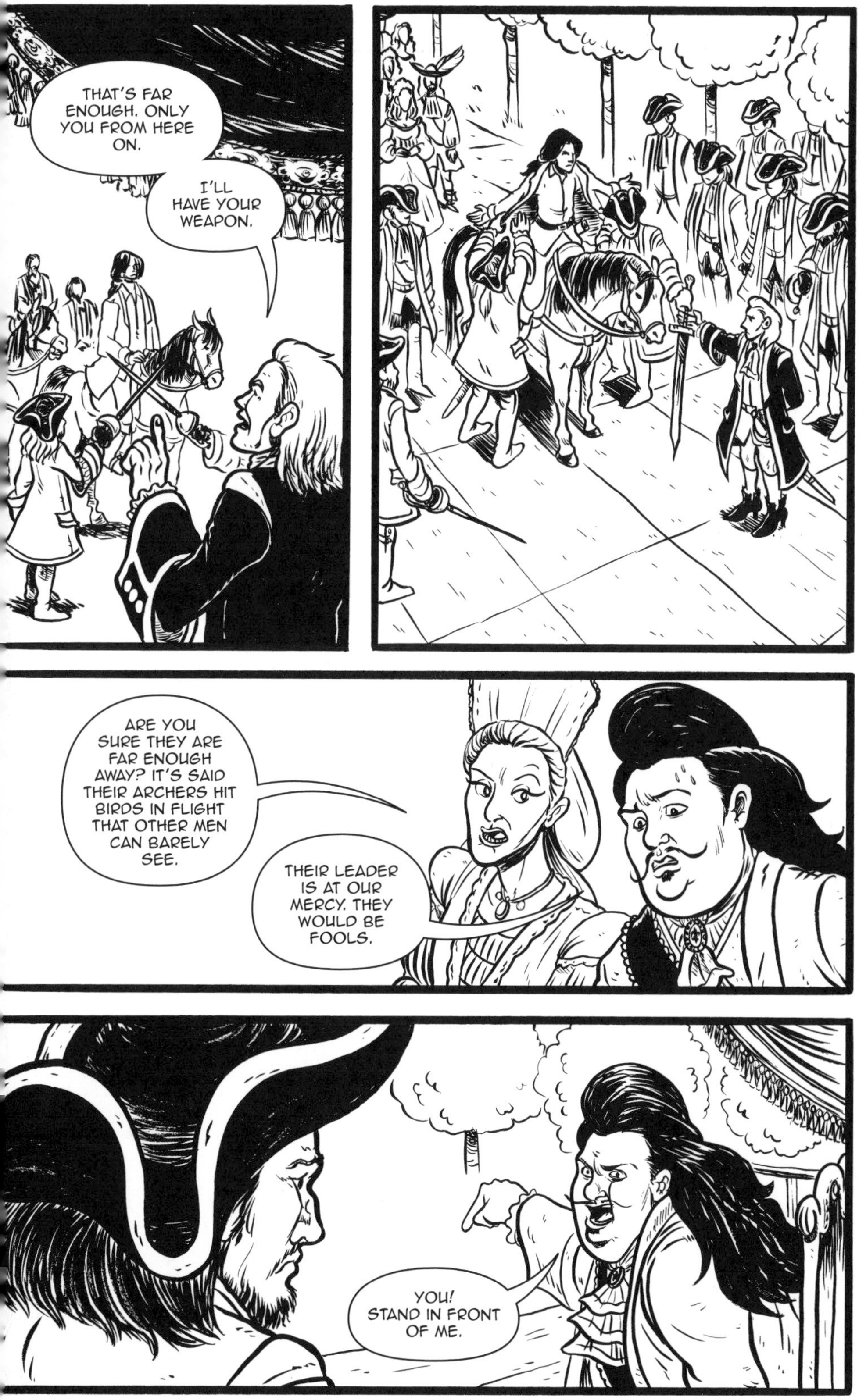
THAT'S FAR ENOUGH. ONLY YOU FROM HERE ON.
I'LL HAVE YOUR WEAPON.
ARE YOU SURE THEY ARE FAR ENOUGH AWAY? IT'S SAID THEIR ARCHERS HIT BIRDS IN FLIGHT THAT OTHER MEN CAN BARELY SEE.
THEIR LEADER IS AT OUR MERCY. THEY WOULD BE FOOLS.
YOU! STAND IN FRONT OF ME.

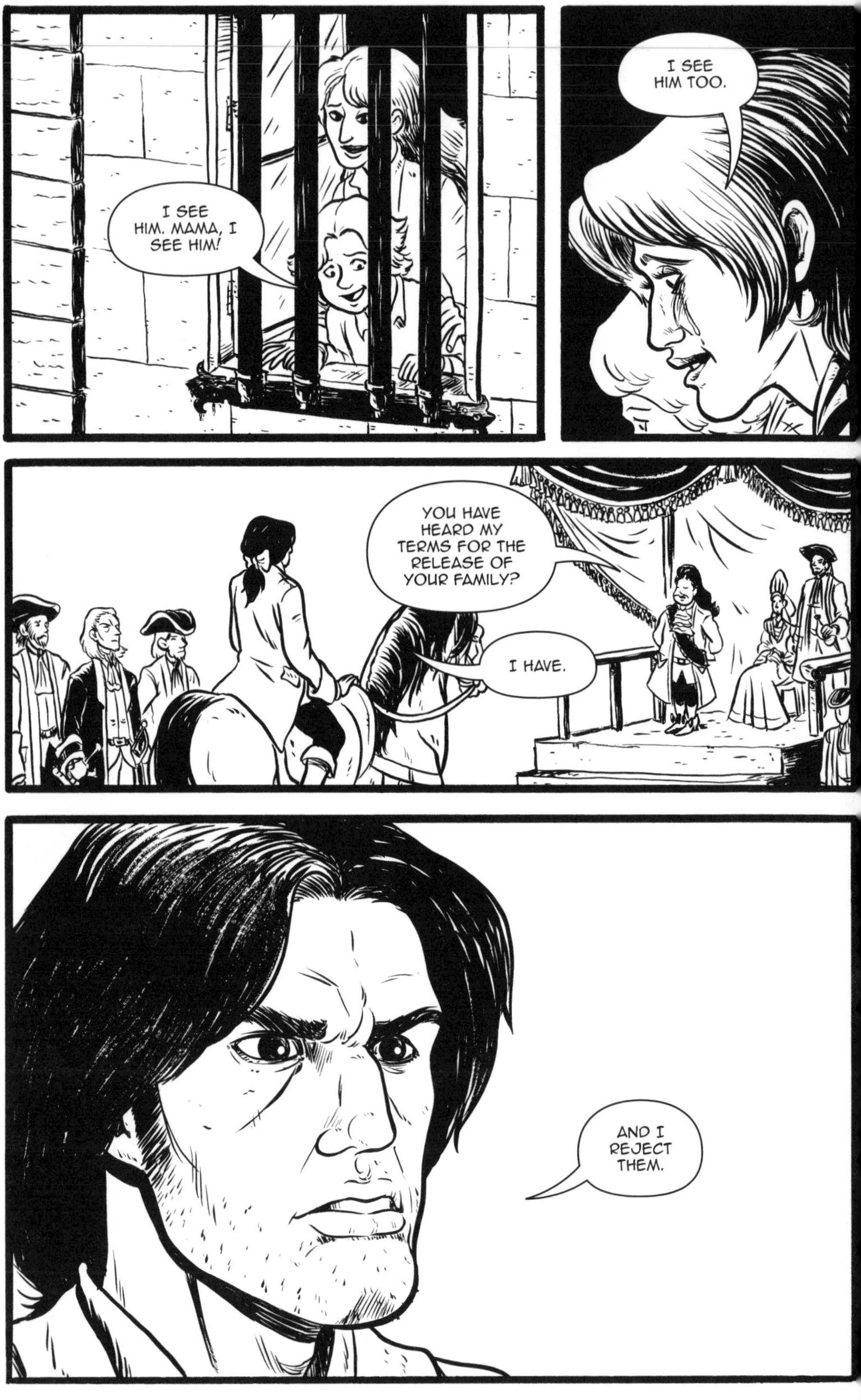
I SEE HIM. MAMA, I SEE HIM!
I SEE HIM TOO.
YOU HAVE HEARD MY TERMS FOR THE RELEASE OF YOUR FAMILY?
I HAVE.
AND I REJECT THEM.

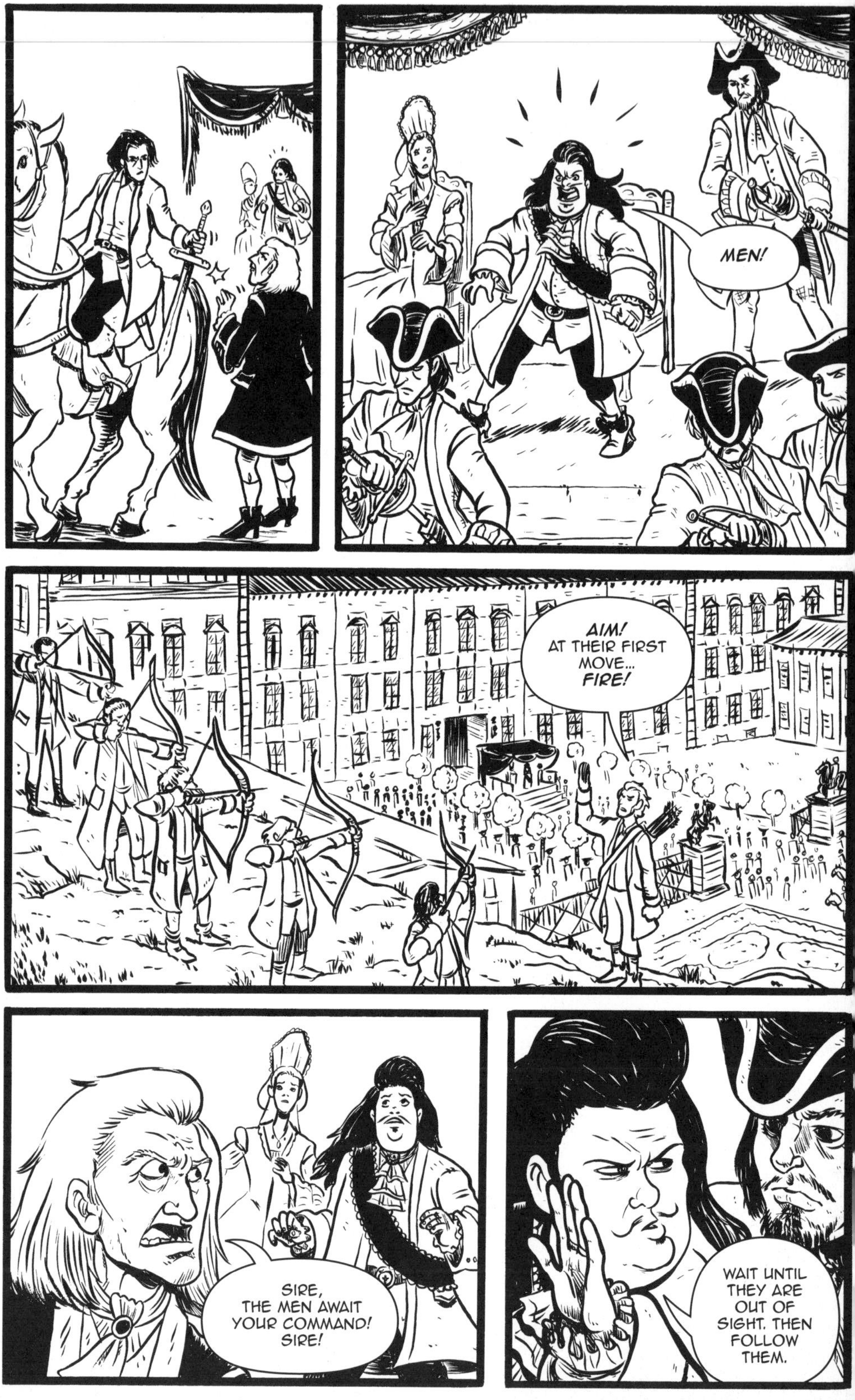
MEN!
AIM!
AT THEIR FIRST
MOVE...
FIRE!
SIRE,
THE MEN AWAIT
YOUR COMMAND!
SIRE!
WAIT UNTIL
THEY ARE
OUT OF
SIGHT. THEN
FOLLOW
THEM.

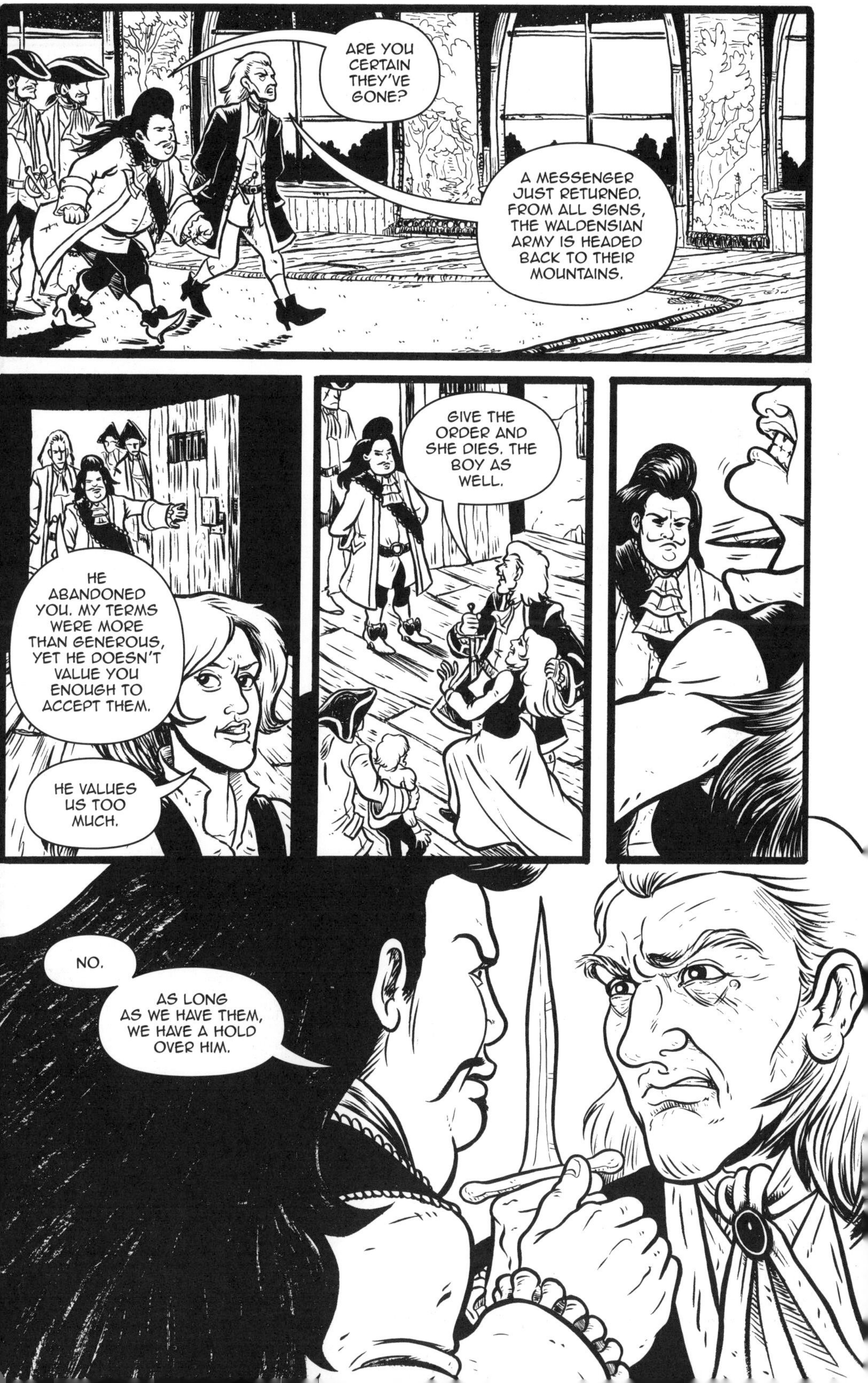
ARE YOU CERTAIN THEY'VE GONE?
A MESSENGER JUST RETURNED. FROM ALL SIGNS, THE WALDENSIAN ARMY IS HEADED BACK TO THEIR MOUNTAINS.
HE ABANDONED YOU. MY TERMS WERE MORE THAN GENEROUS, YET HE DOESN'T VALUE YOU ENOUGH TO ACCEPT THEM.
HE VALUES US TOO MUCH.
GIVE THE ORDER AND SHE DIES. THE BOY AS WELL.
NO.
AS LONG AS WE HAVE THEM, WE HAVE A HOLD OVER HIM.

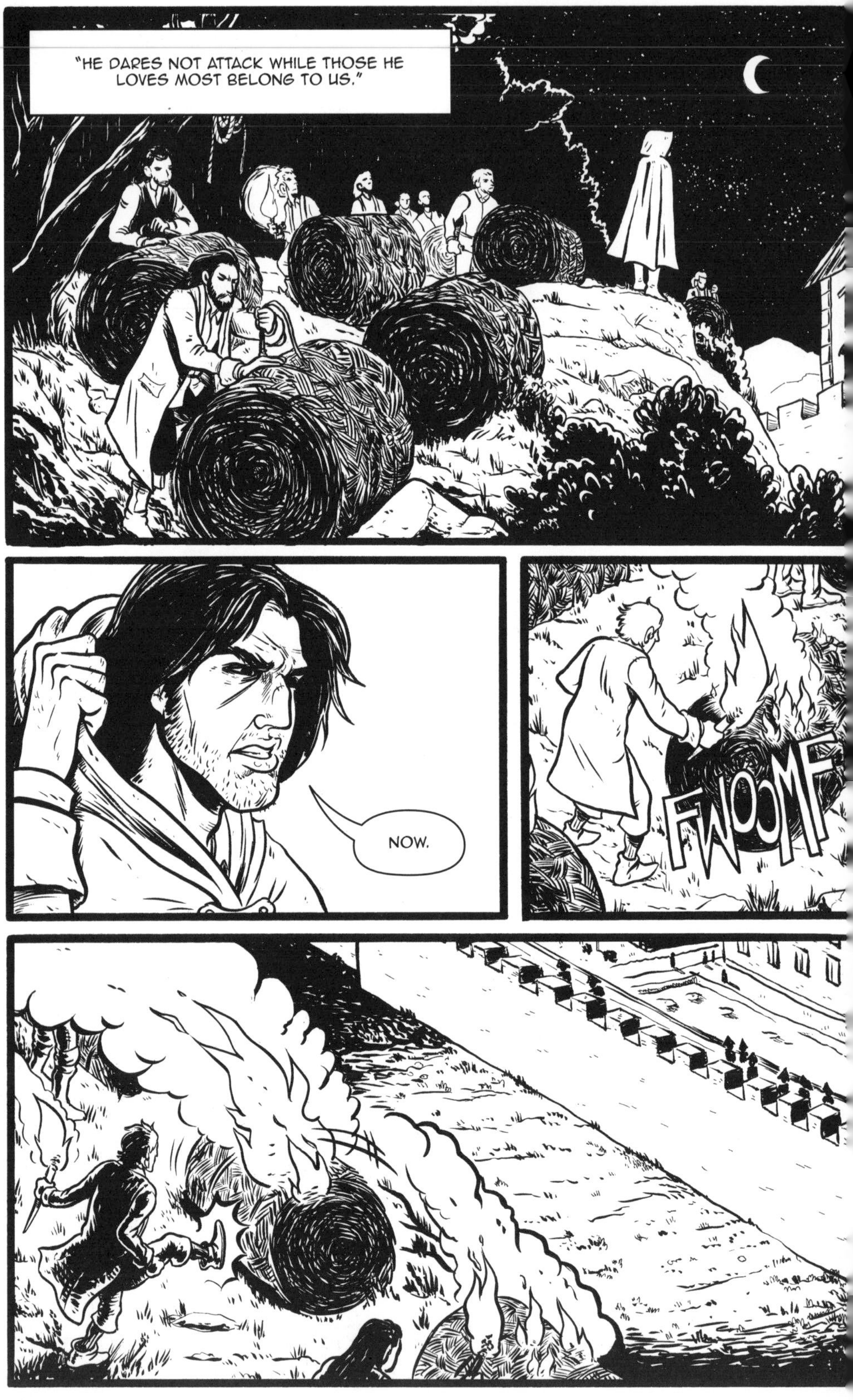
"HE DARES NOT ATTACK WHILE THOSE HE LOVES MOST BELONG TO US."
NOW.
FWOOMF

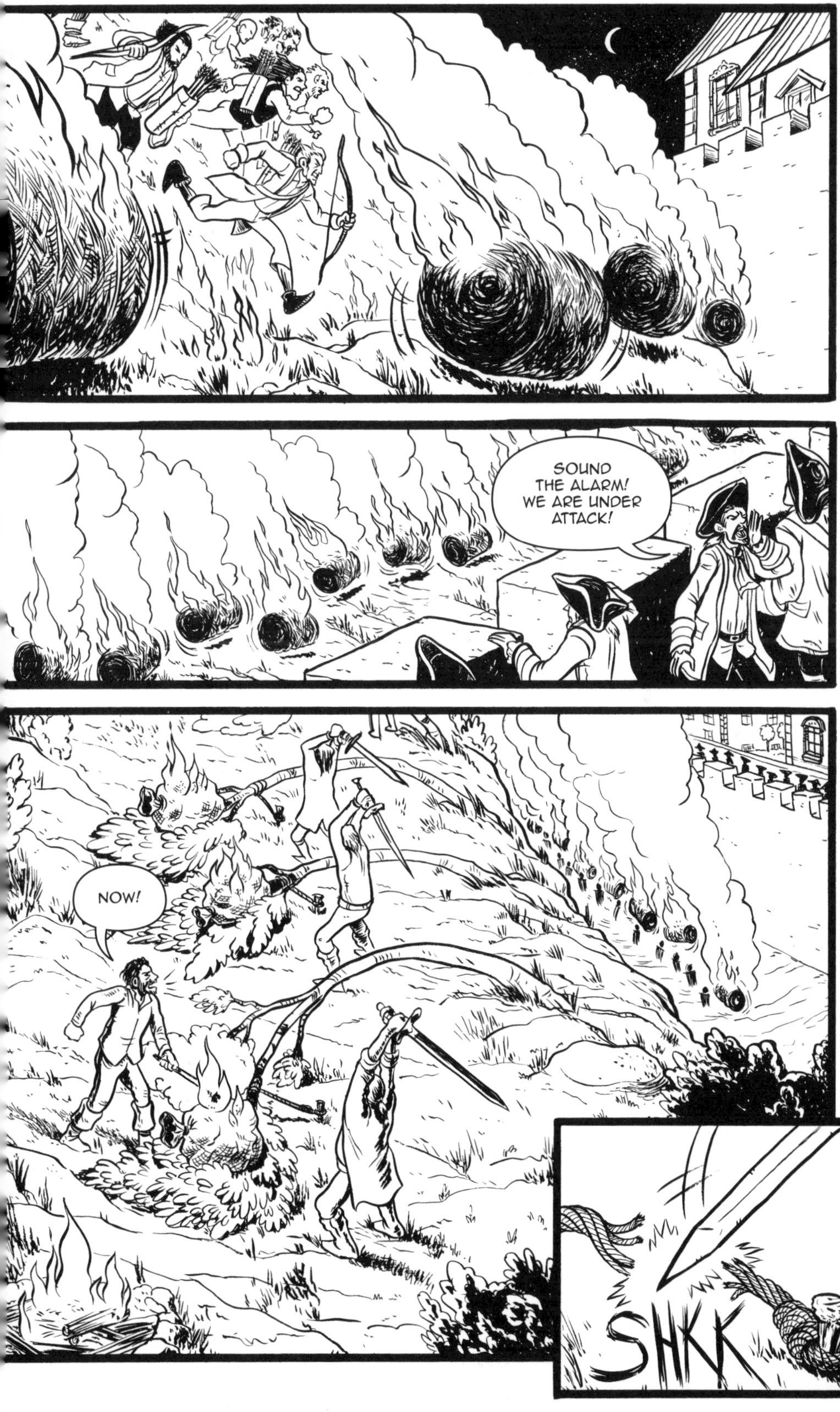
SOUND THE ALARM! WE ARE UNDER ATTACK!
NOW!
SHKK

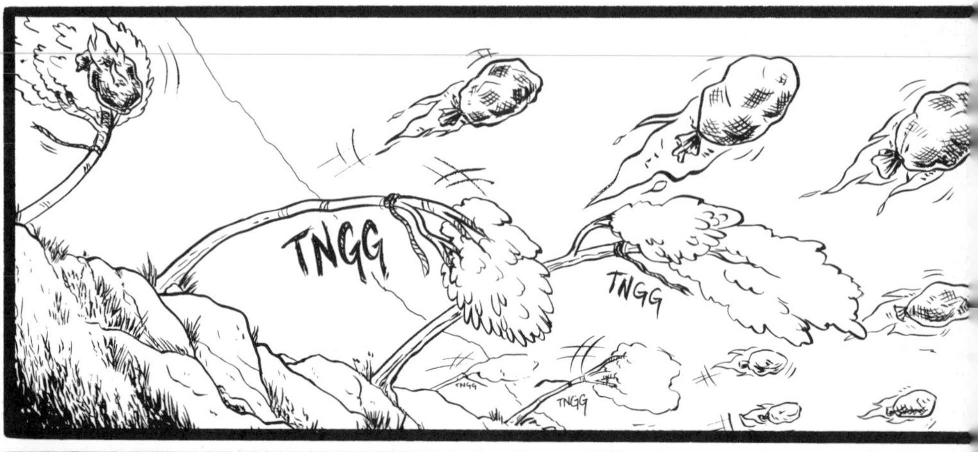
TNGG
TNGG
TNGG
TNGG

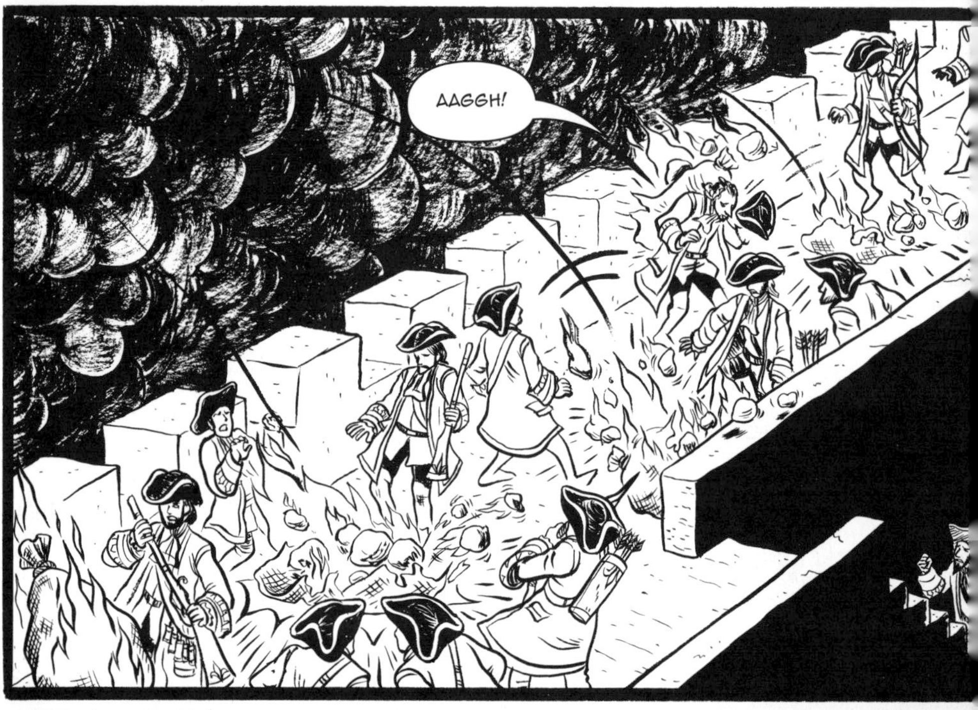
AAGGH!

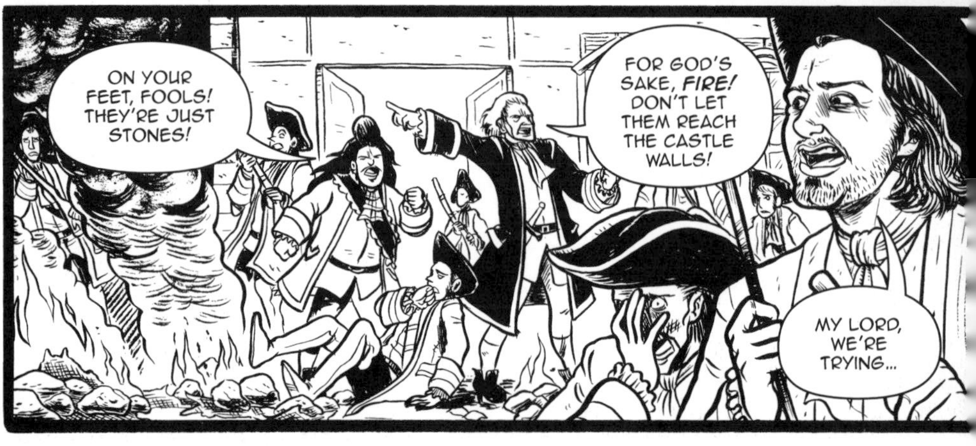
ON YOUR FEET, FOOLS! THEY'RE JUST STONES!
FOR GOD'S SAKE, *FIRE!* DON'T LET THEM REACH THE CASTLE WALLS!
MY LORD, WE'RE TRYING...

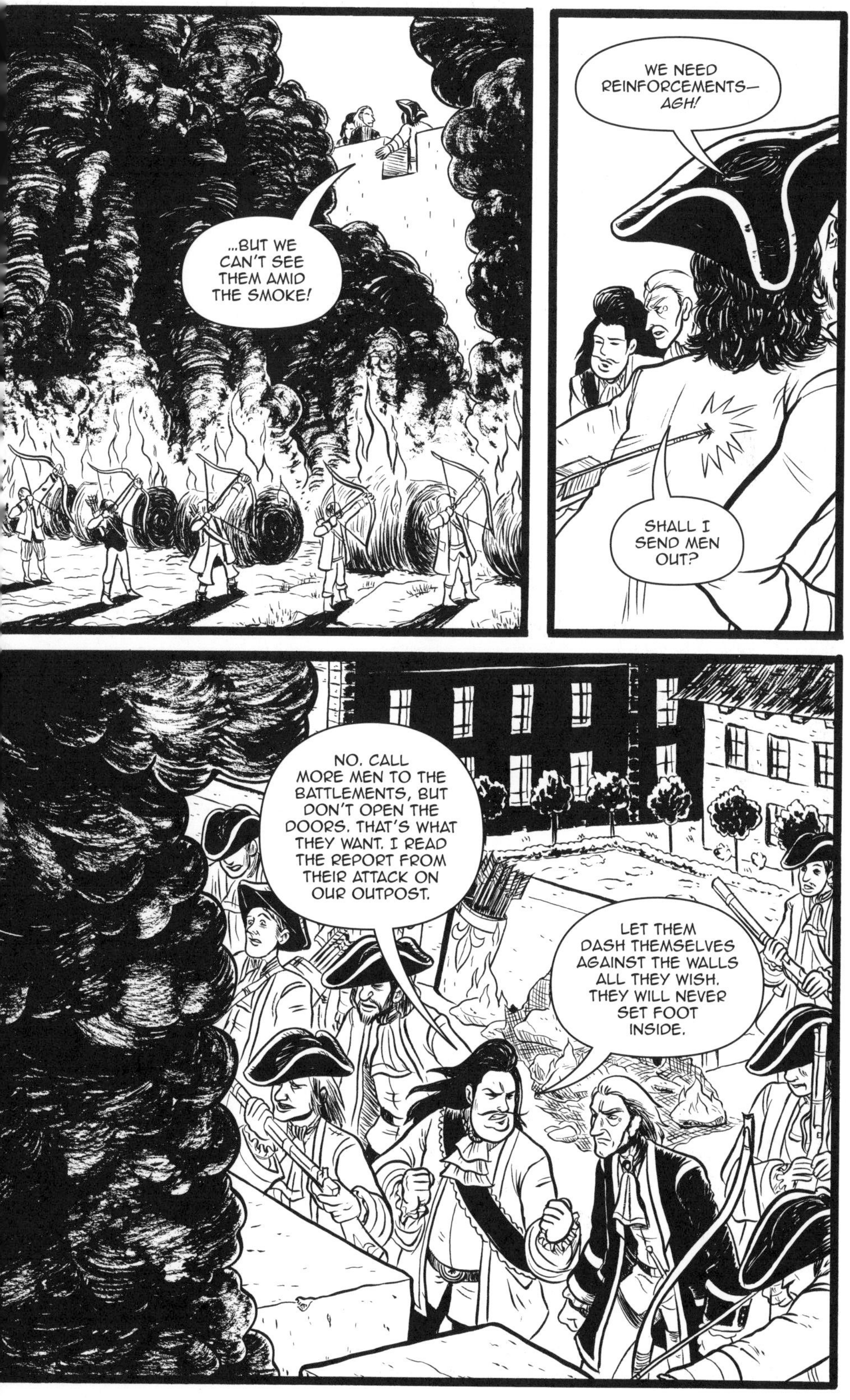
...BUT WE CAN'T SEE THEM AMID THE SMOKE!
WE NEED REINFORCEMENTS— AGH!
SHALL I SEND MEN OUT?
NO. CALL MORE MEN TO THE BATTLEMENTS, BUT DON'T OPEN THE DOORS. THAT'S WHAT THEY WANT. I READ THE REPORT FROM THEIR ATTACK ON OUR OUTPOST.
LET THEM DASH THEMSELVES AGAINST THE WALLS ALL THEY WISH. THEY WILL NEVER SET FOOT INSIDE.

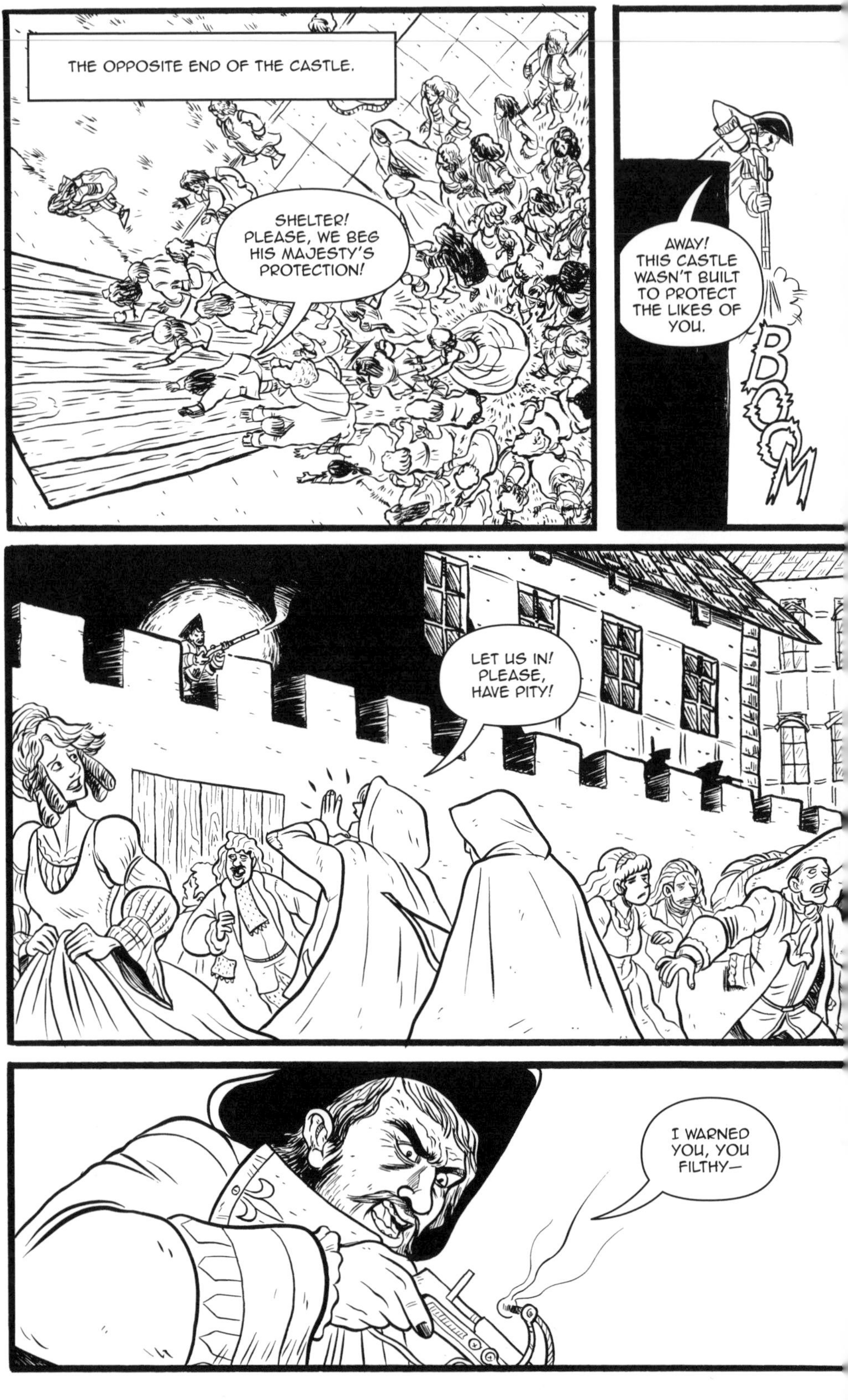
THE OPPOSITE END OF THE CASTLE.
SHELTER! PLEASE, WE BEG HIS MAJESTY'S PROTECTION!
AWAY! THIS CASTLE WASN'T BUILT TO PROTECT THE LIKES OF YOU.
BOOM
LET US IN! PLEASE, HAVE PITY!
I WARNED YOU, YOU FILTHY—

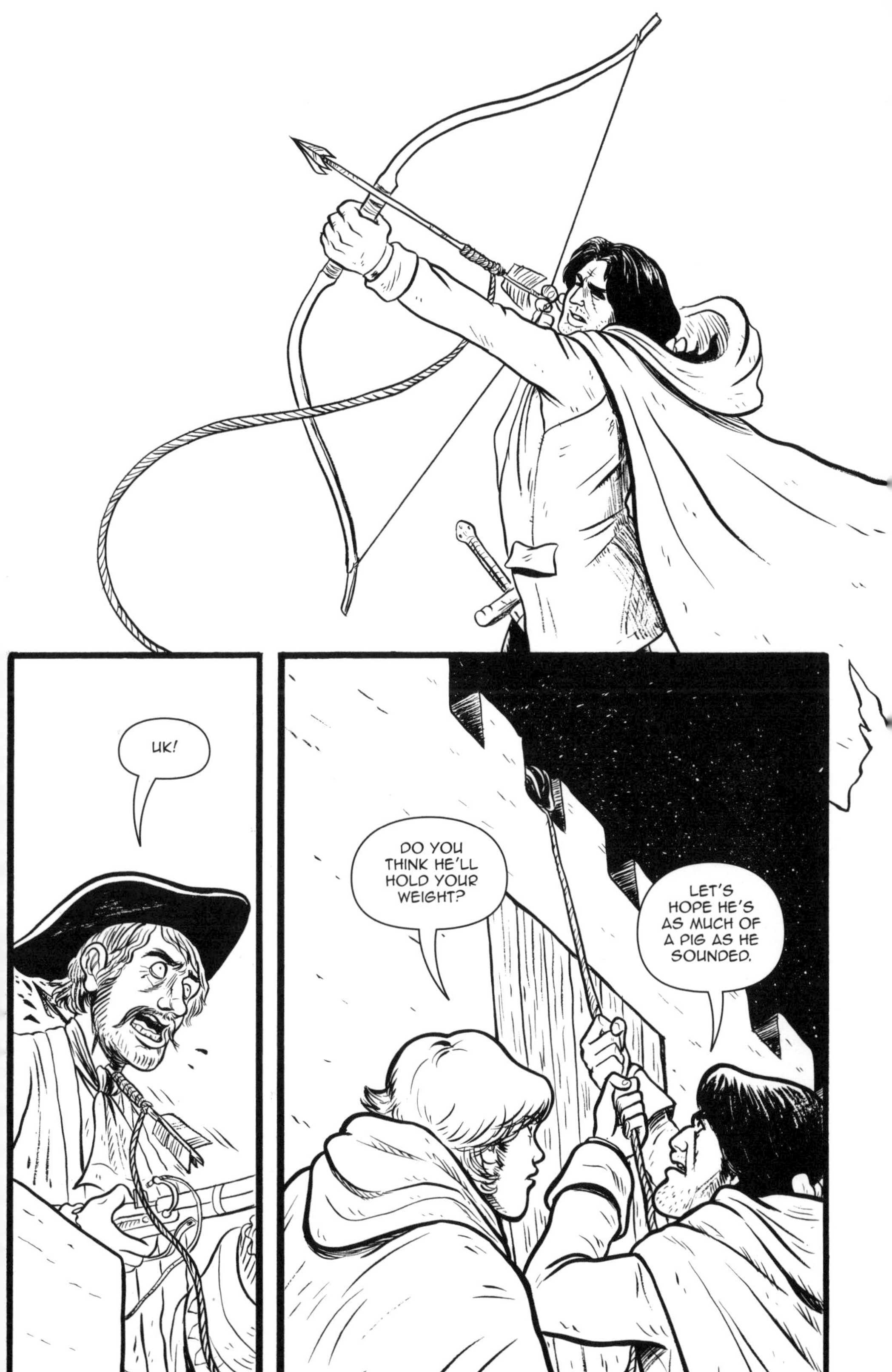
UK!
DO YOU THINK HE'LL HOLD YOUR WEIGHT?
LET'S HOPE HE'S AS MUCH OF A PIG AS HE SOUNDED.

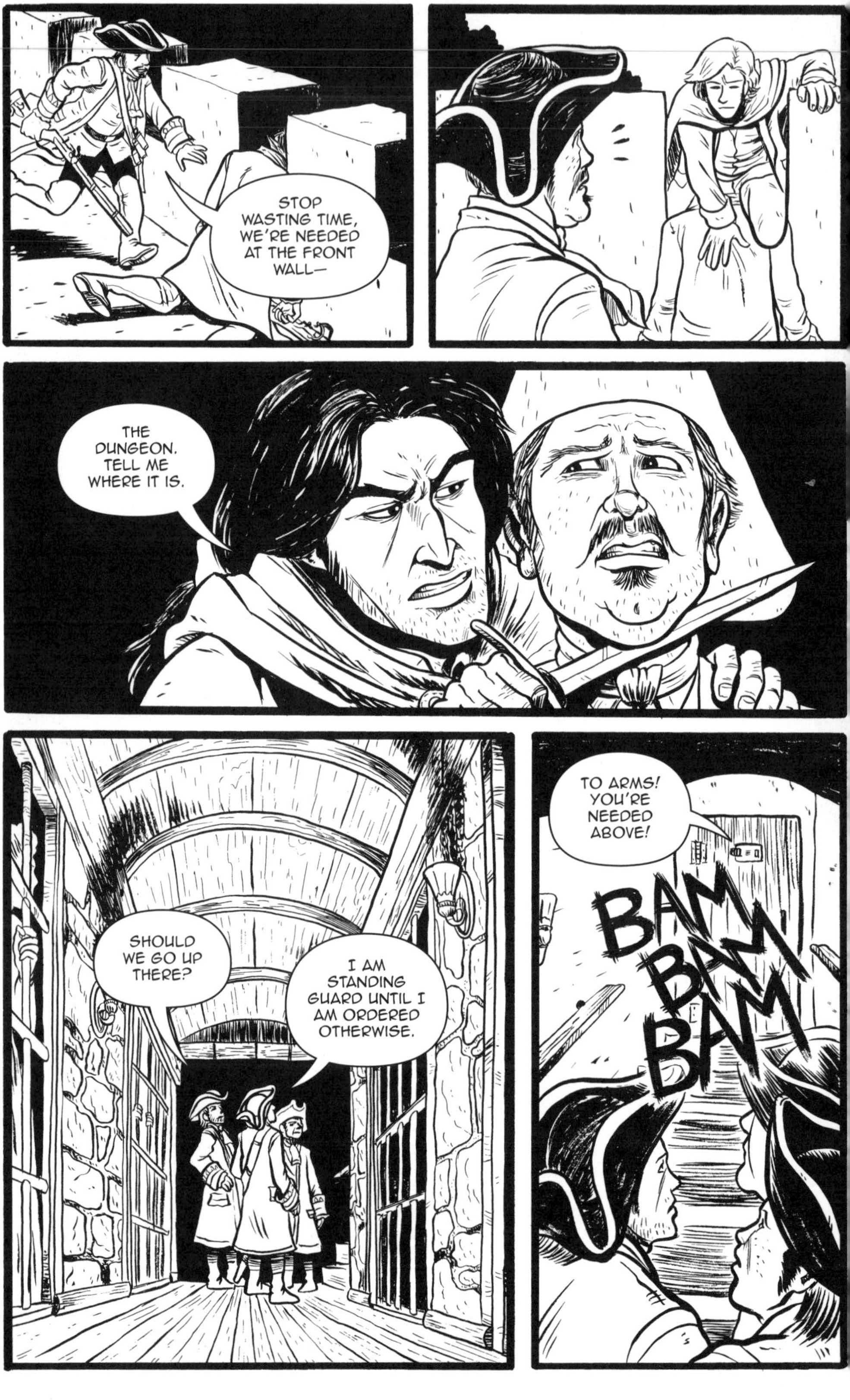
STOP WASTING TIME, WE'RE NEEDED AT THE FRONT WALL—
THE DUNGEON. TELL ME WHERE IT IS.
SHOULD WE GO UP THERE?
I AM STANDING GUARD UNTIL I AM ORDERED OTHERWISE.
TO ARMS! YOU'RE NEEDED ABOVE!
BAM BAM BAM

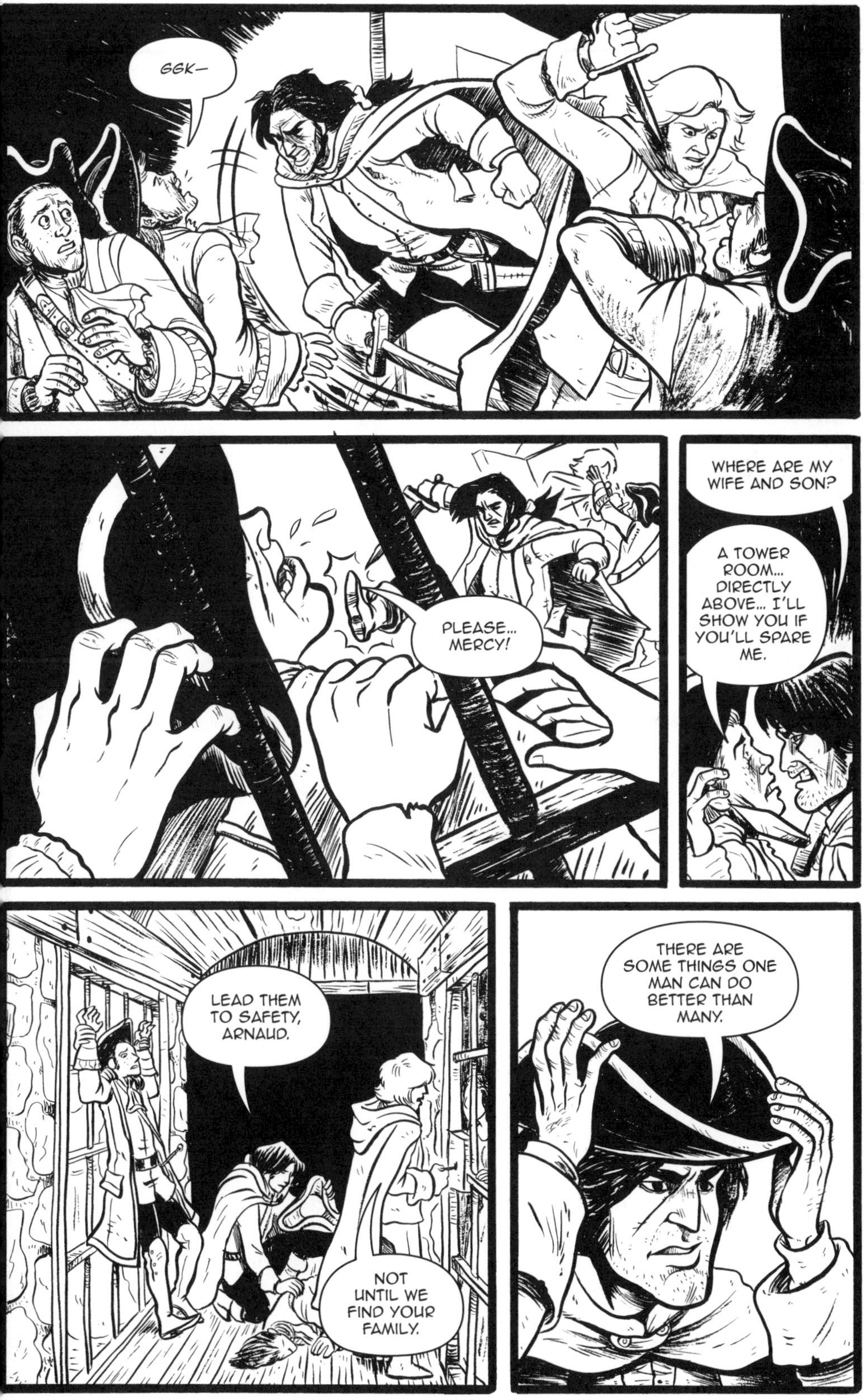
GGK—
PLEASE... MERCY!
WHERE ARE MY WIFE AND SON?
A TOWER ROOM... DIRECTLY ABOVE... I'LL SHOW YOU IF YOU'LL SPARE ME.
LEAD THEM TO SAFETY, ARNAUD.
NOT UNTIL WE FIND YOUR FAMILY.
THERE ARE SOME THINGS ONE MAN CAN DO BETTER THAN MANY.

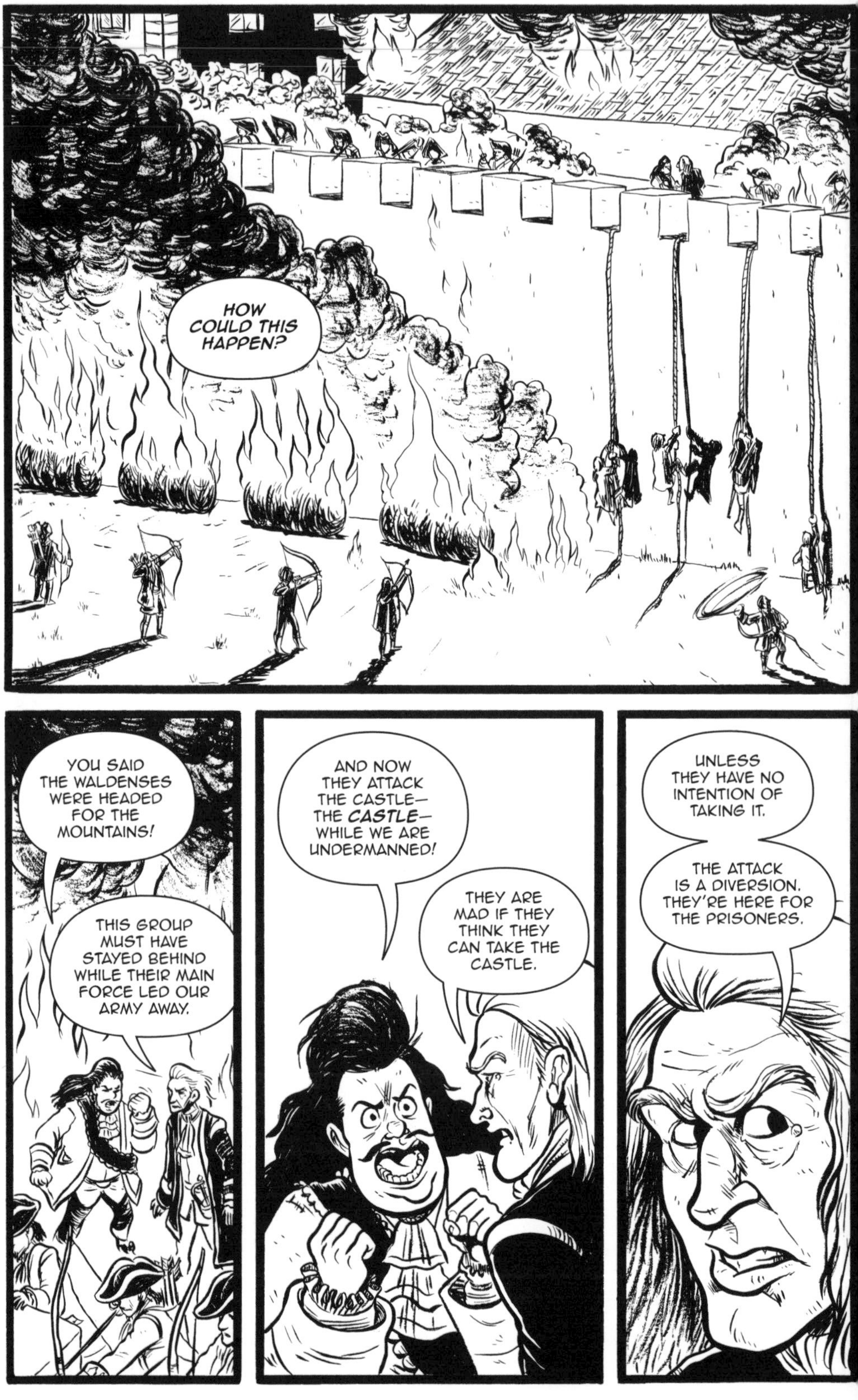
HOW COULD THIS HAPPEN?
YOU SAID THE WALDENSES WERE HEADED FOR THE MOUNTAINS!
THIS GROUP MUST HAVE STAYED BEHIND WHILE THEIR MAIN FORCE LED OUR ARMY AWAY.
AND NOW THEY ATTACK THE CASTLE— THE *CASTLE*— WHILE WE ARE UNDERMANNED!
THEY ARE MAD IF THEY THINK THEY CAN TAKE THE CASTLE.
UNLESS THEY HAVE NO INTENTION OF TAKING IT.
THE ATTACK IS A DIVERSION. THEY'RE HERE FOR THE PRISONERS.

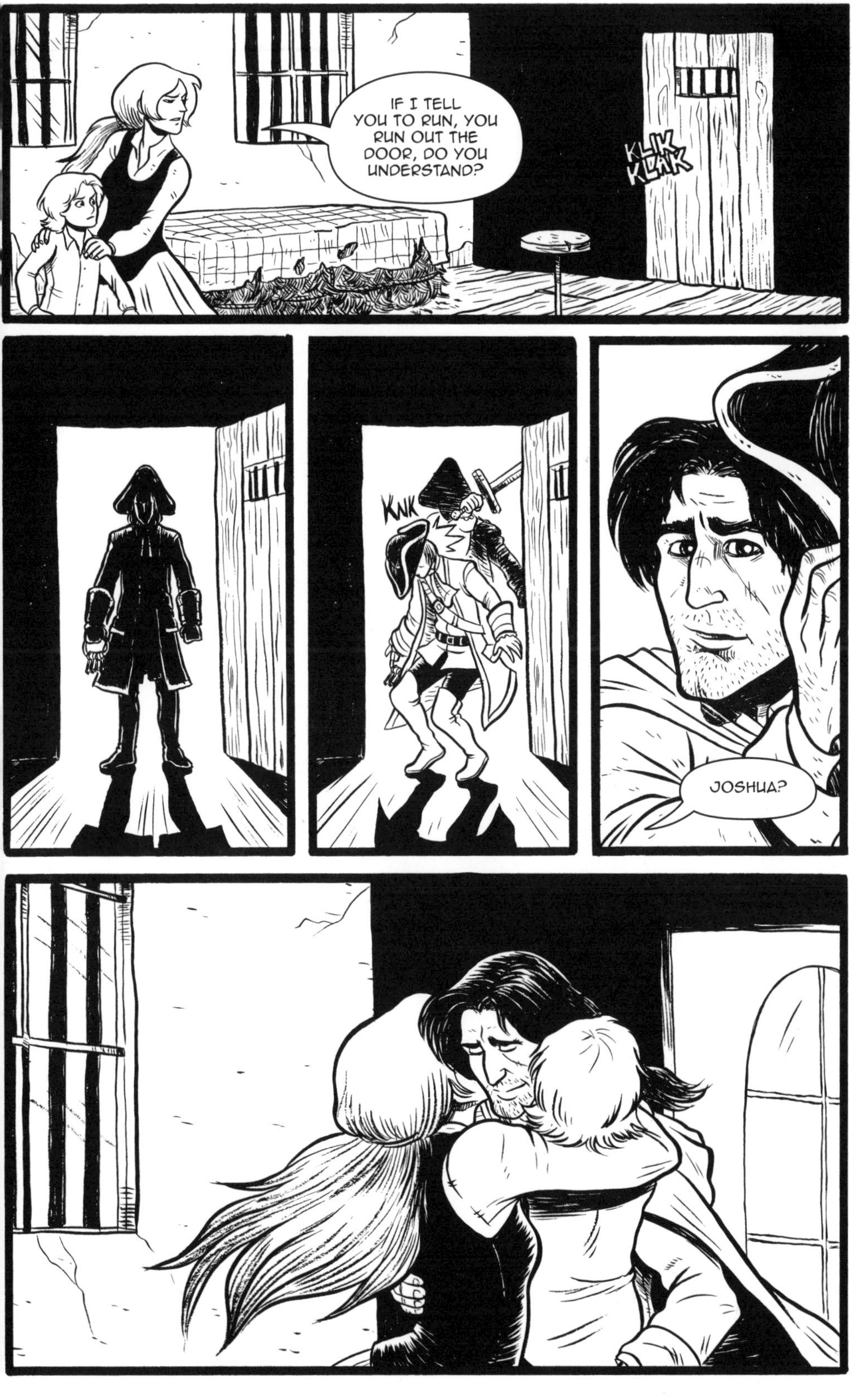
IF I TELL YOU TO RUN, YOU RUN OUT THE DOOR, DO YOU UNDERSTAND?
KLIK KLAK
KNK
JOSHUA?

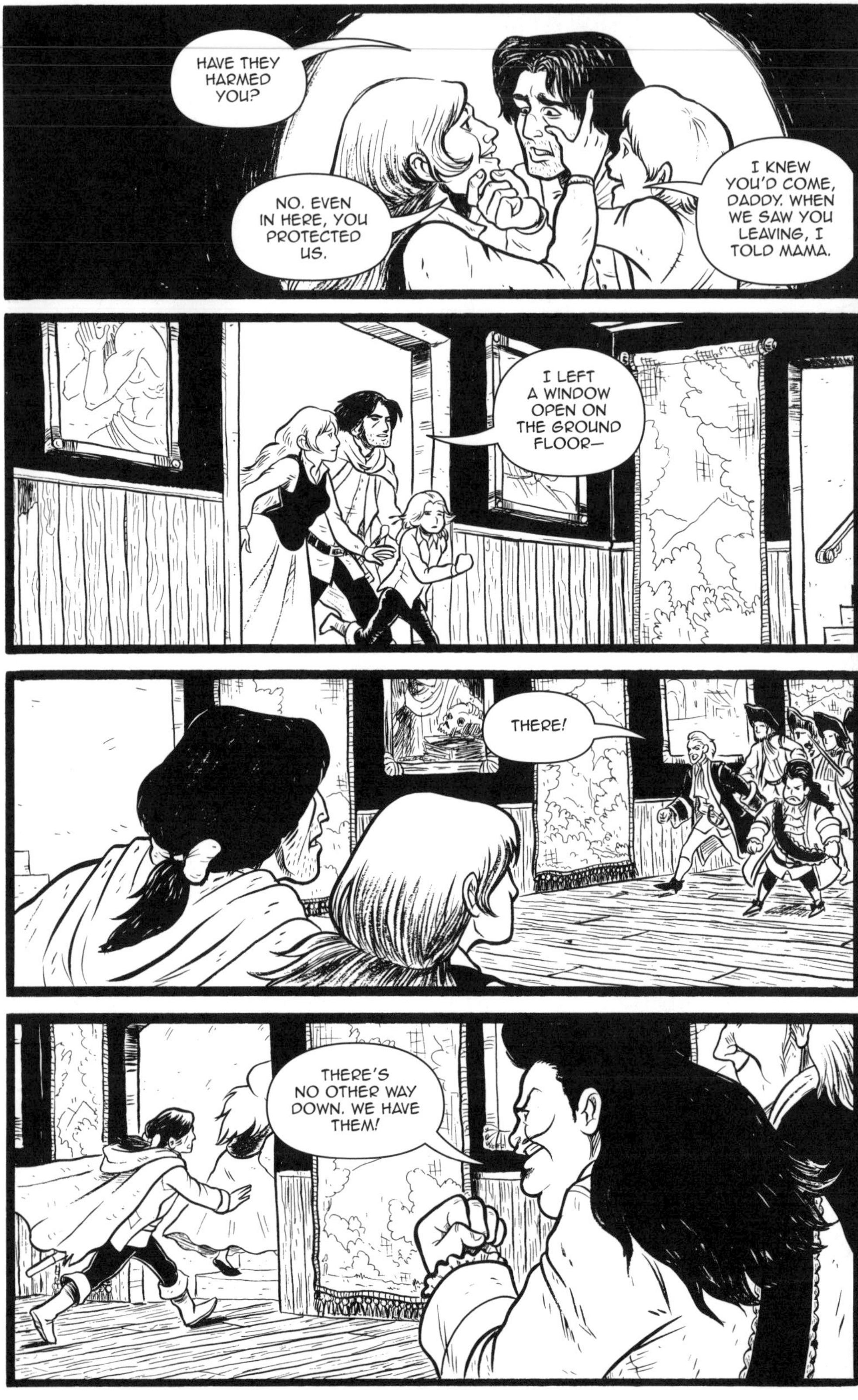
HAVE THEY HARMED YOU?
NO. EVEN IN HERE, YOU PROTECTED US.
I KNEW YOU'D COME, DADDY. WHEN WE SAW YOU LEAVING, I TOLD MAMA.
I LEFT A WINDOW OPEN ON THE GROUND FLOOR—
THERE!
THERE'S NO OTHER WAY DOWN. WE HAVE THEM!

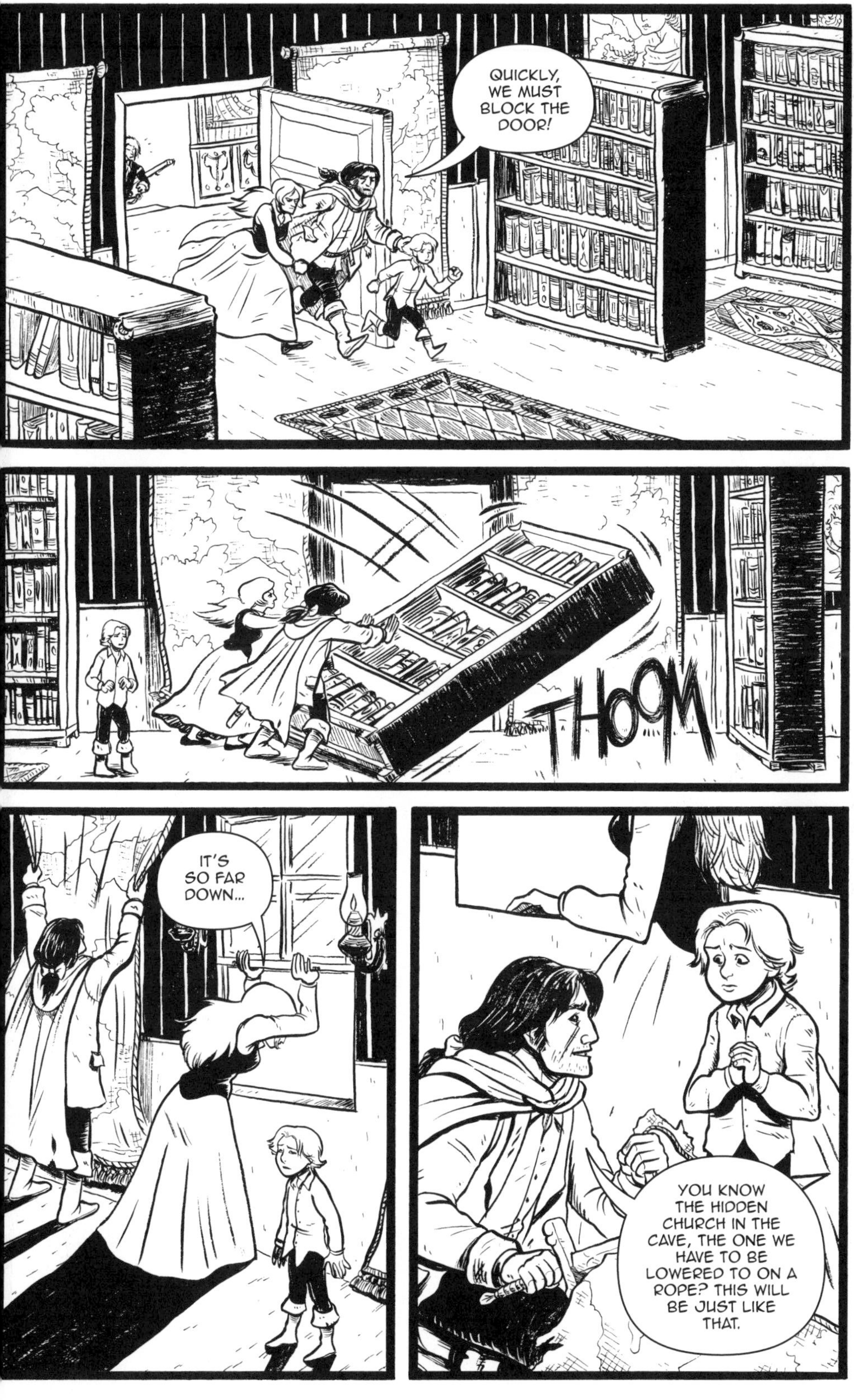
QUICKLY, WE MUST BLOCK THE DOOR!
THOOM
IT'S SO FAR DOWN...
YOU KNOW THE HIDDEN CHURCH IN THE CAVE, THE ONE WE HAVE TO BE LOWERED TO ON A ROPE? THIS WILL BE JUST LIKE THAT.

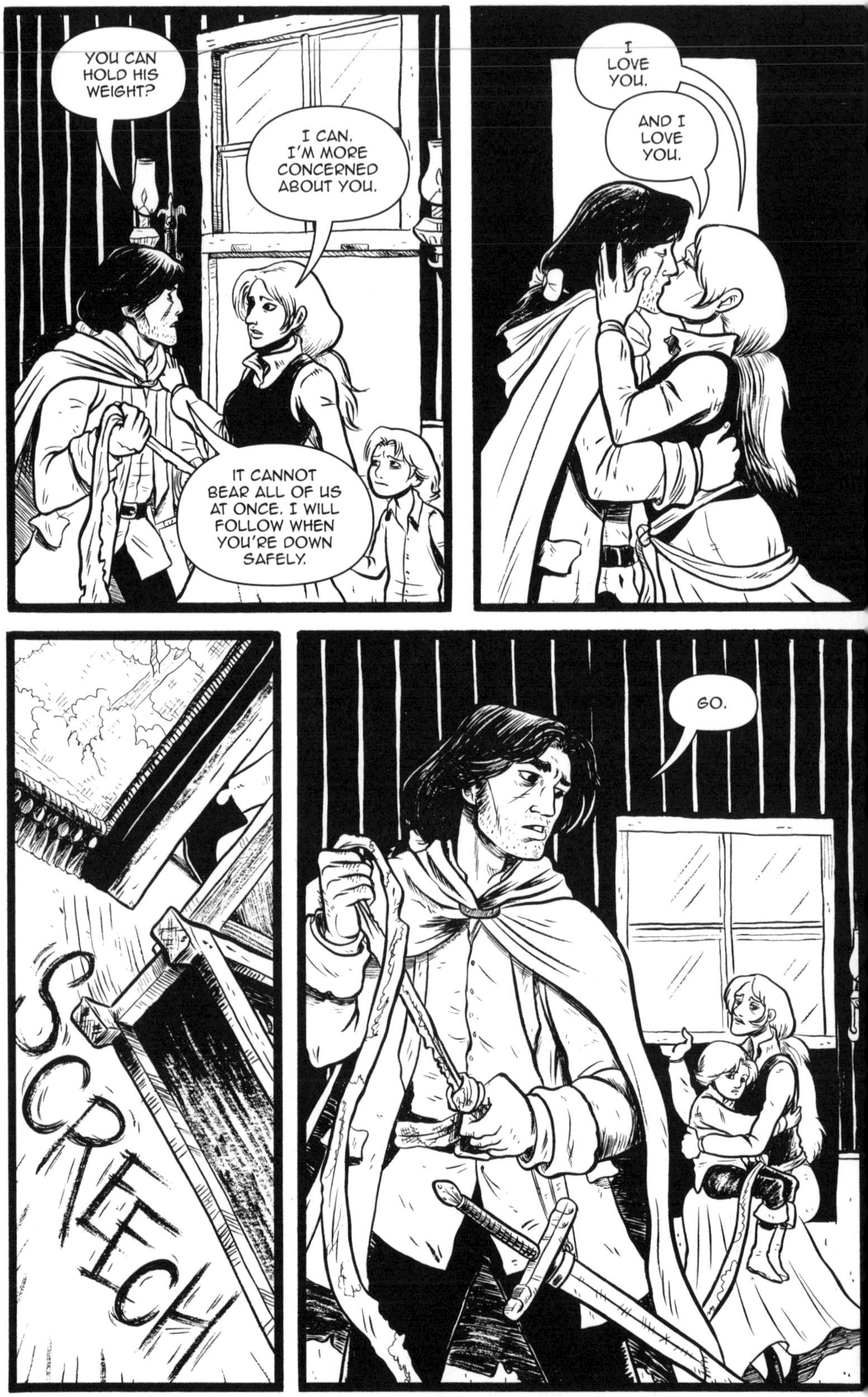
YOU CAN HOLD HIS WEIGHT?
I CAN. I'M MORE CONCERNED ABOUT YOU.
IT CANNOT BEAR ALL OF US AT ONCE. I WILL FOLLOW WHEN YOU'RE DOWN SAFELY.
I LOVE YOU.
AND I LOVE YOU.
SCREECH
GO.

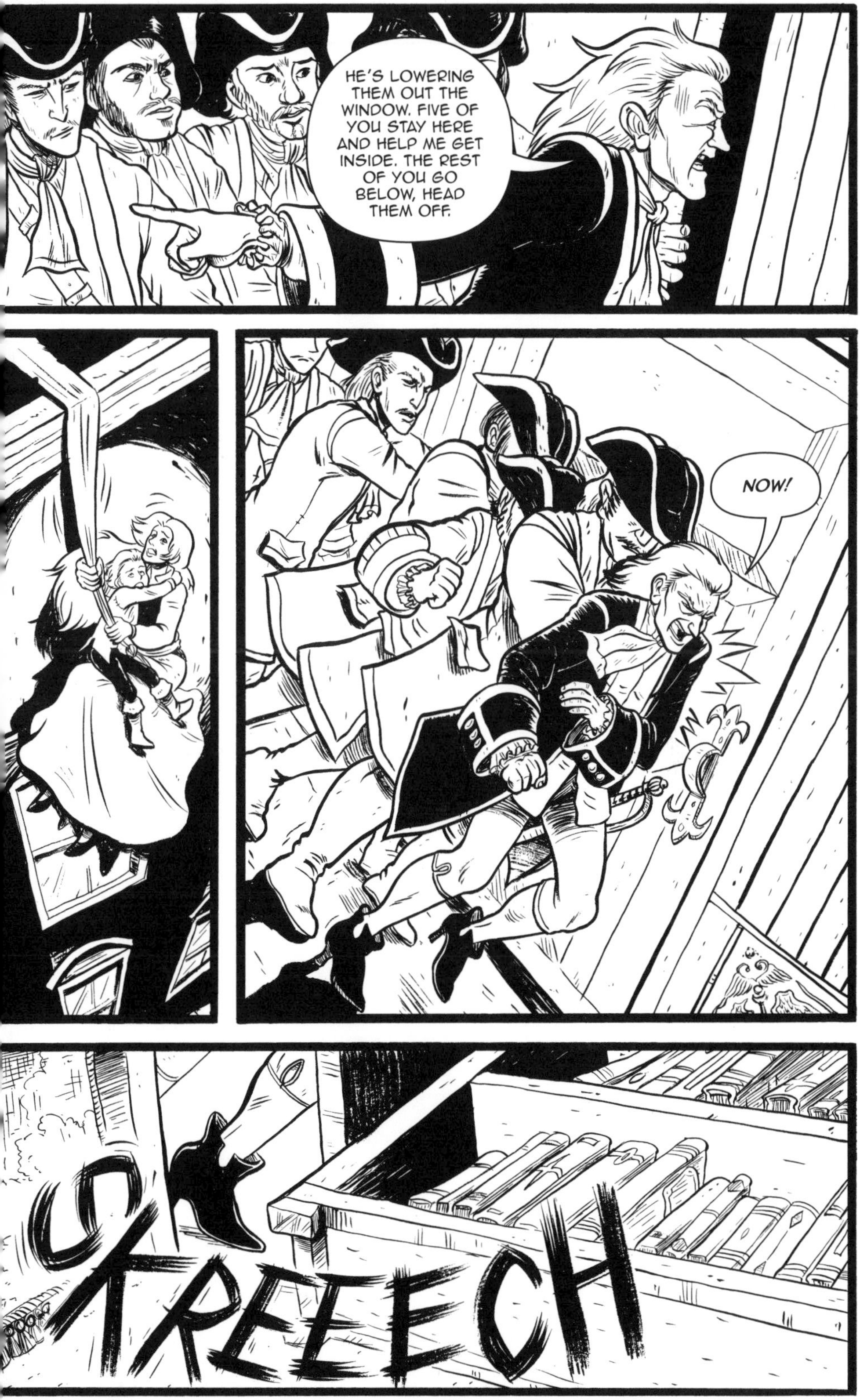
HE'S LOWERING THEM OUT THE WINDOW. FIVE OF YOU STAY HERE AND HELP ME GET INSIDE. THE REST OF YOU GO BELOW, HEAD THEM OFF.
NOW!
SKREEECH

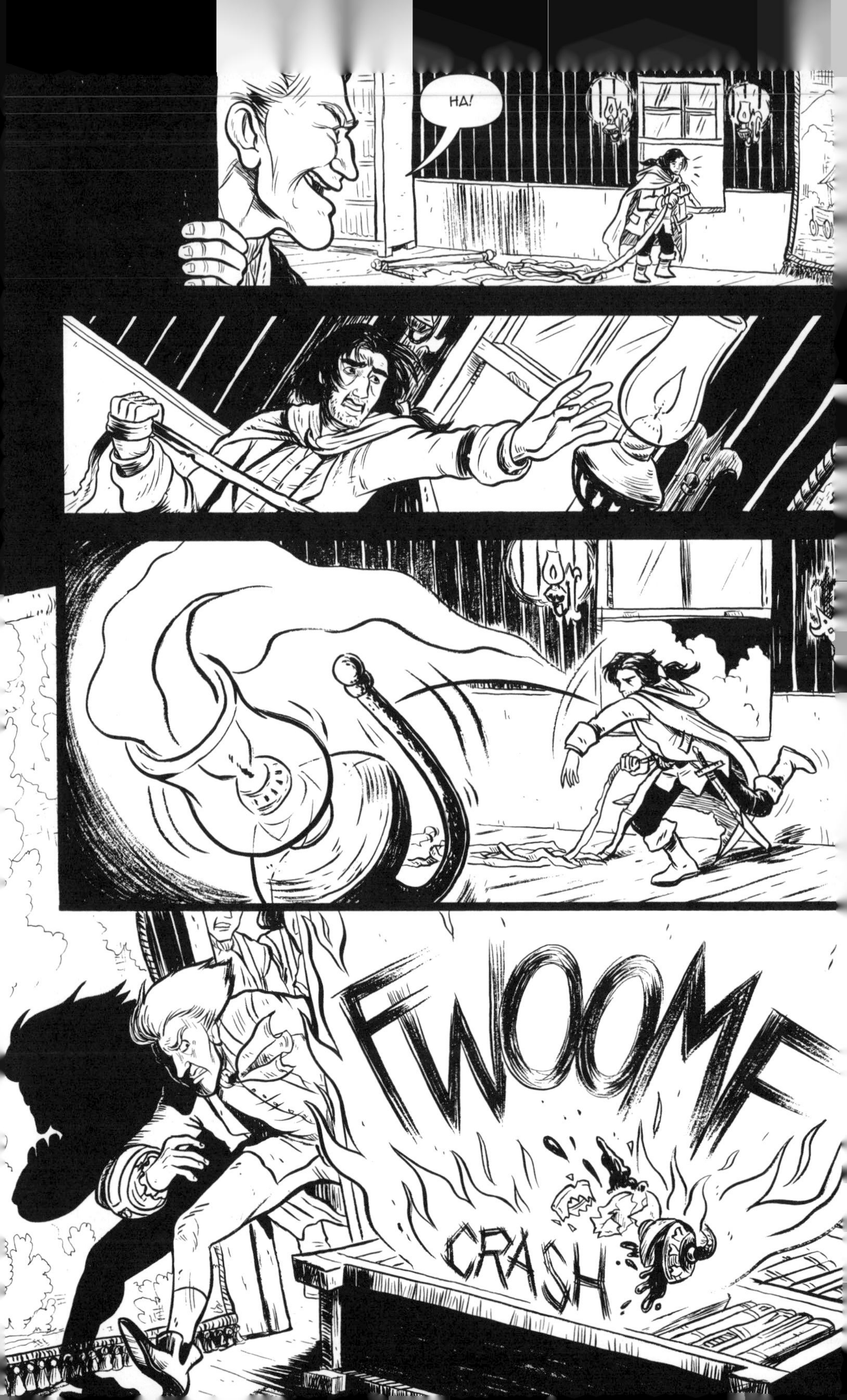
HA!
FWOOMF
CRASH

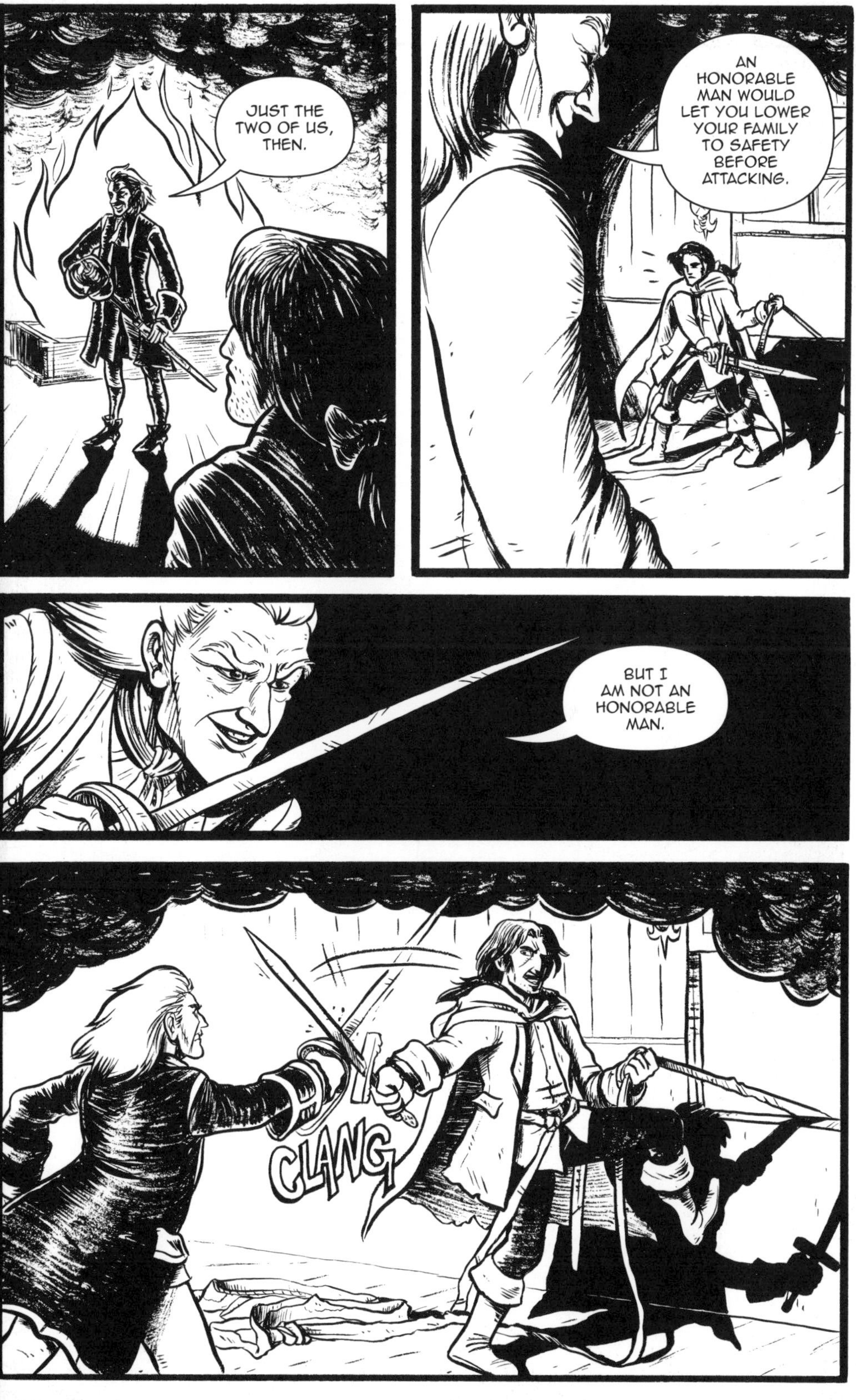
JUST THE TWO OF US, THEN.
AN HONORABLE MAN WOULD LET YOU LOWER YOUR FAMILY TO SAFETY BEFORE ATTACKING.
BUT I AM NOT AN HONORABLE MAN.
CLANG

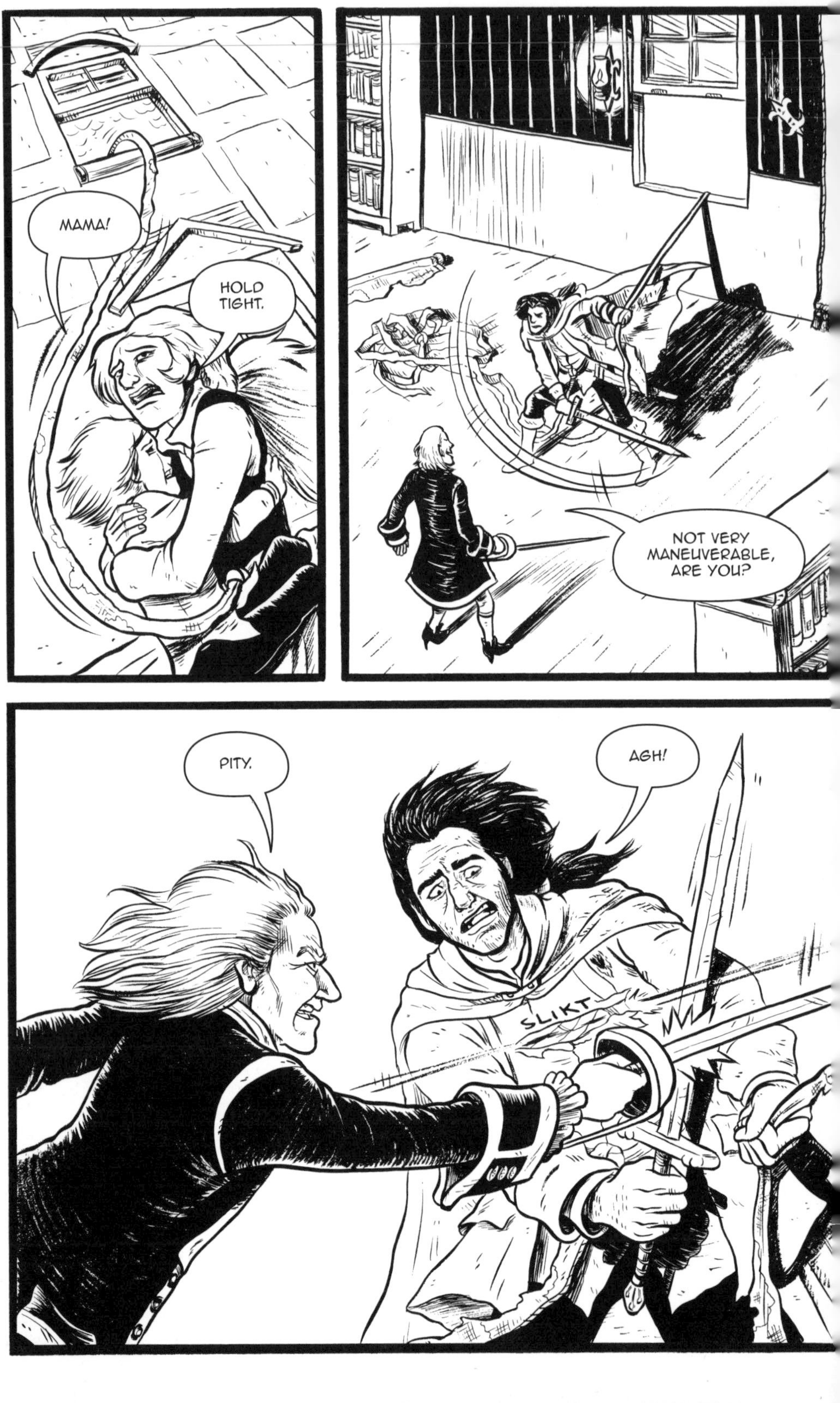
MAMA!
HOLD TIGHT.
NOT VERY MANEUVERABLE, ARE YOU?
PITY.
AGH!
SLIKT

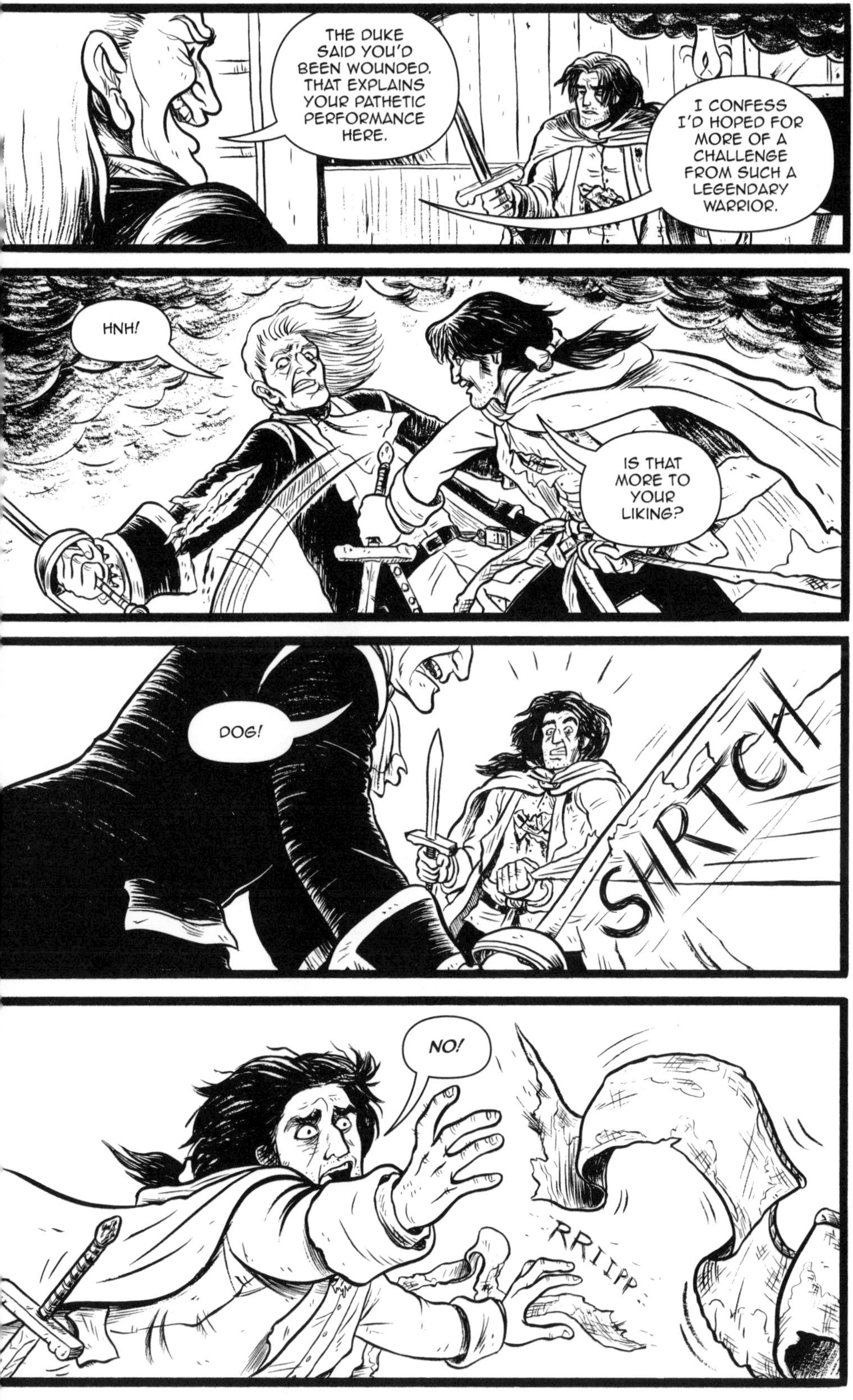
THE DUKE SAID YOU'D BEEN WOUNDED. THAT EXPLAINS YOUR PATHETIC PERFORMANCE HERE.
I CONFESS I'D HOPED FOR MORE OF A CHALLENGE FROM SUCH A LEGENDARY WARRIOR.
HNH!
IS THAT MORE TO YOUR LIKING?
DOG!
SHRTCH
NO!
RRIIPP

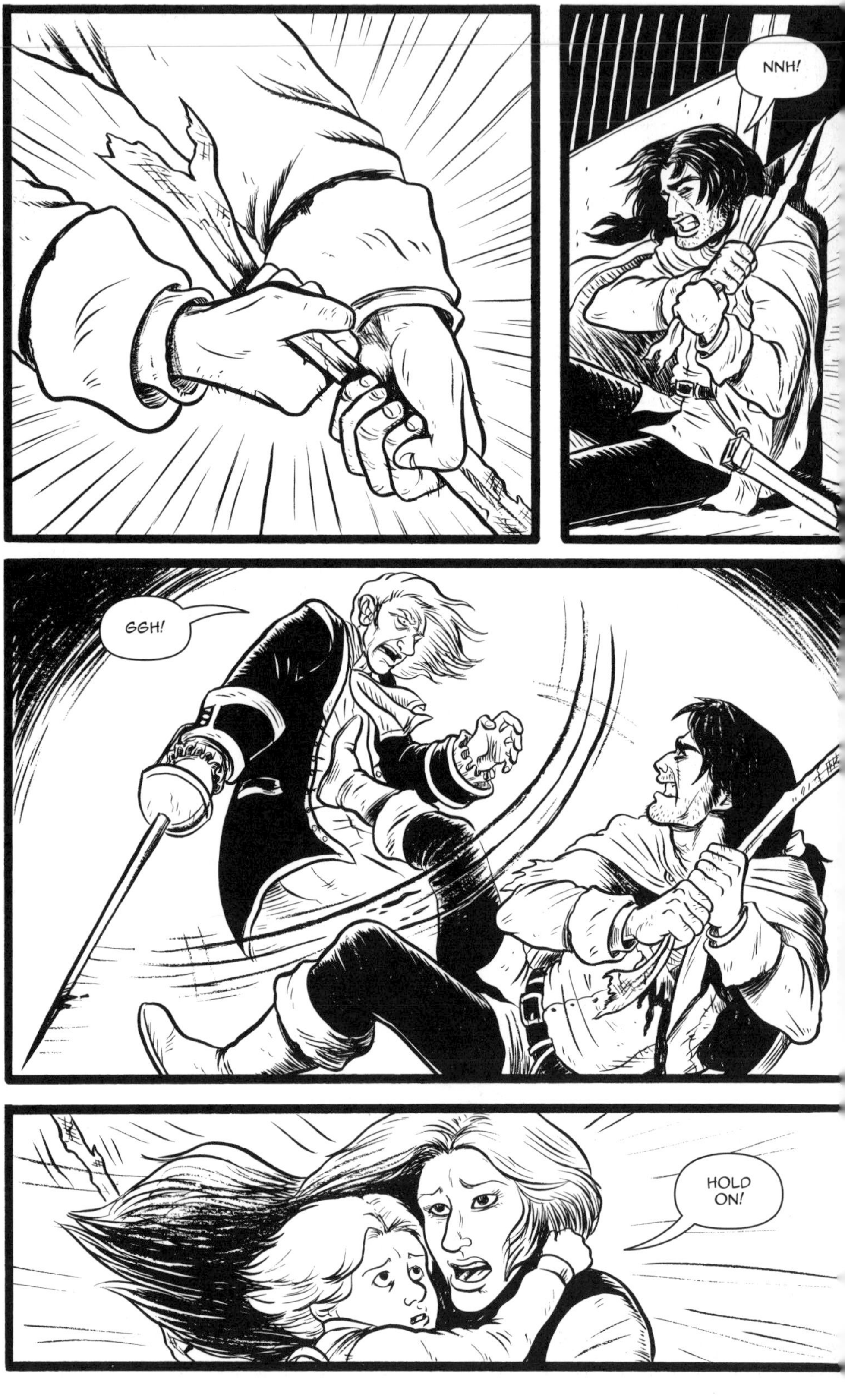
NNH!
GGH!
HOLD ON!

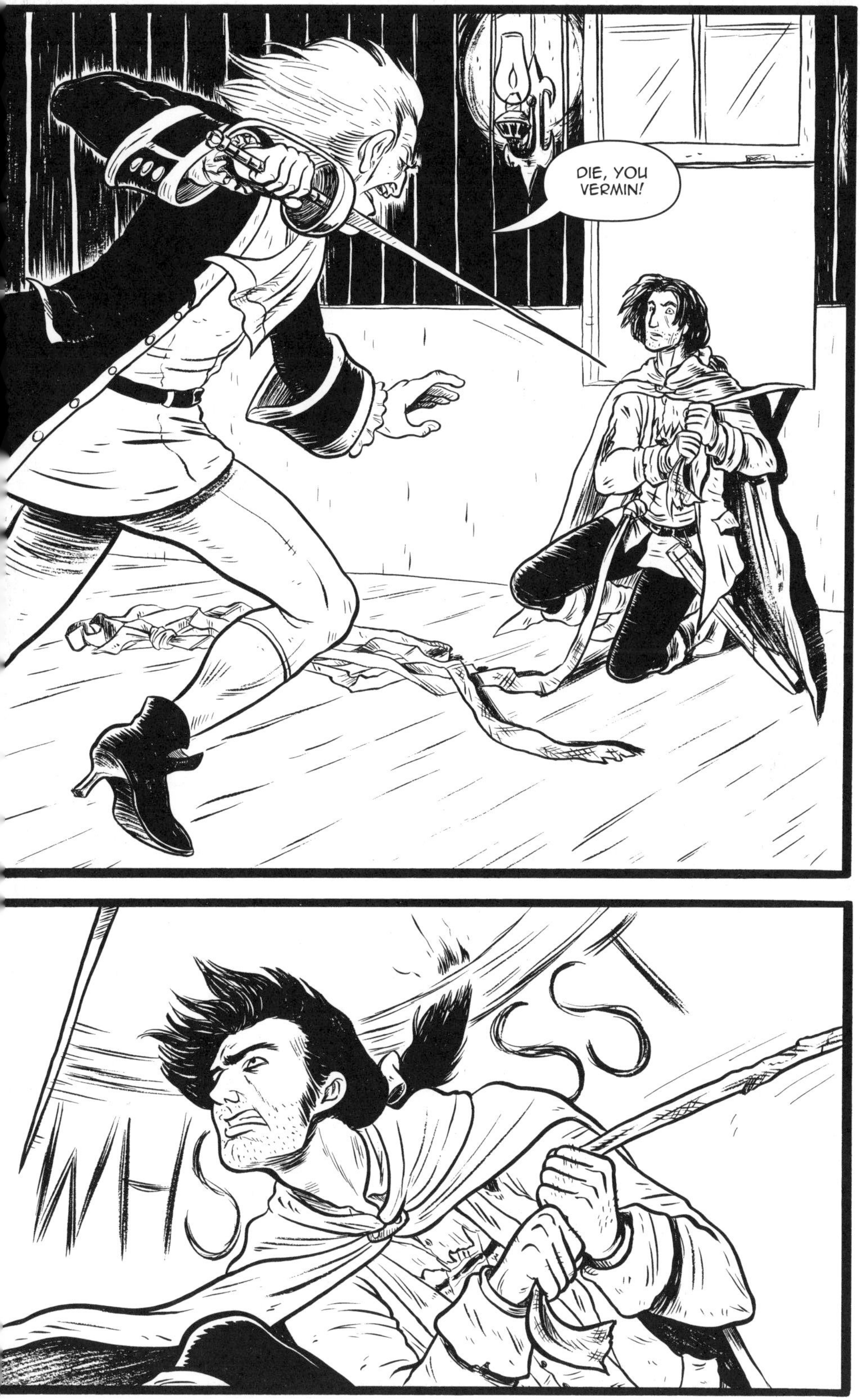
DIE, YOU VERMIN!
WHISSS

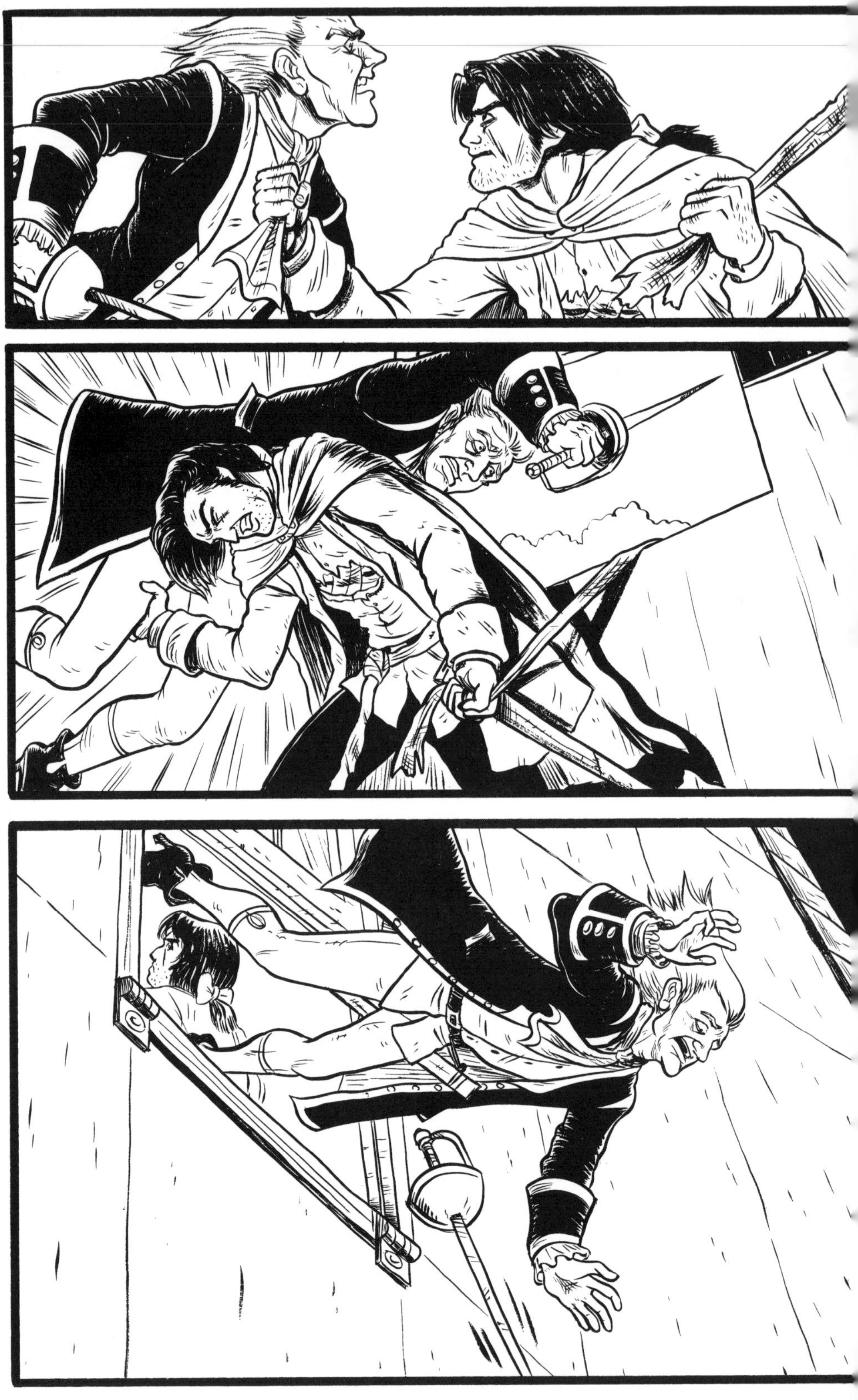

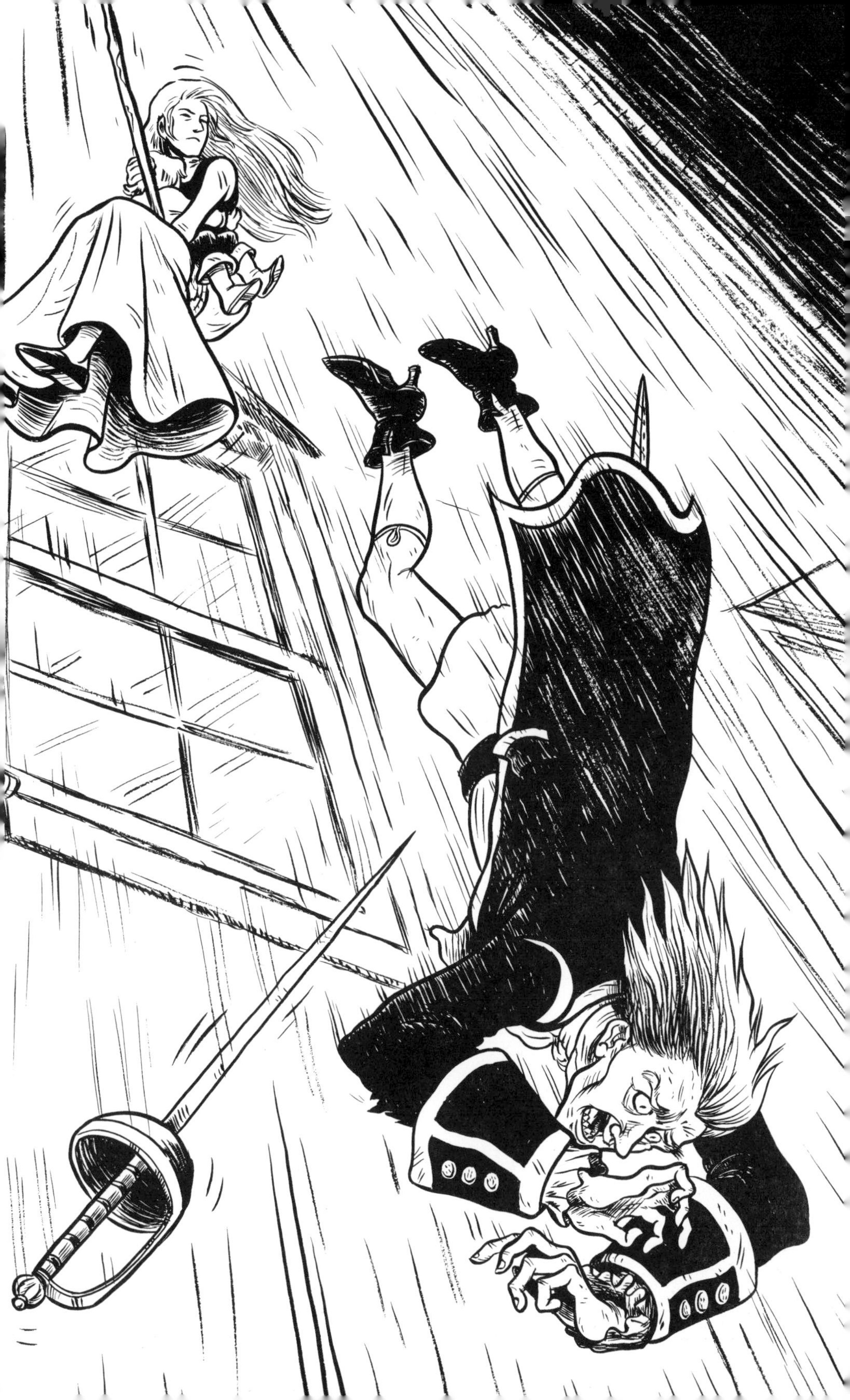

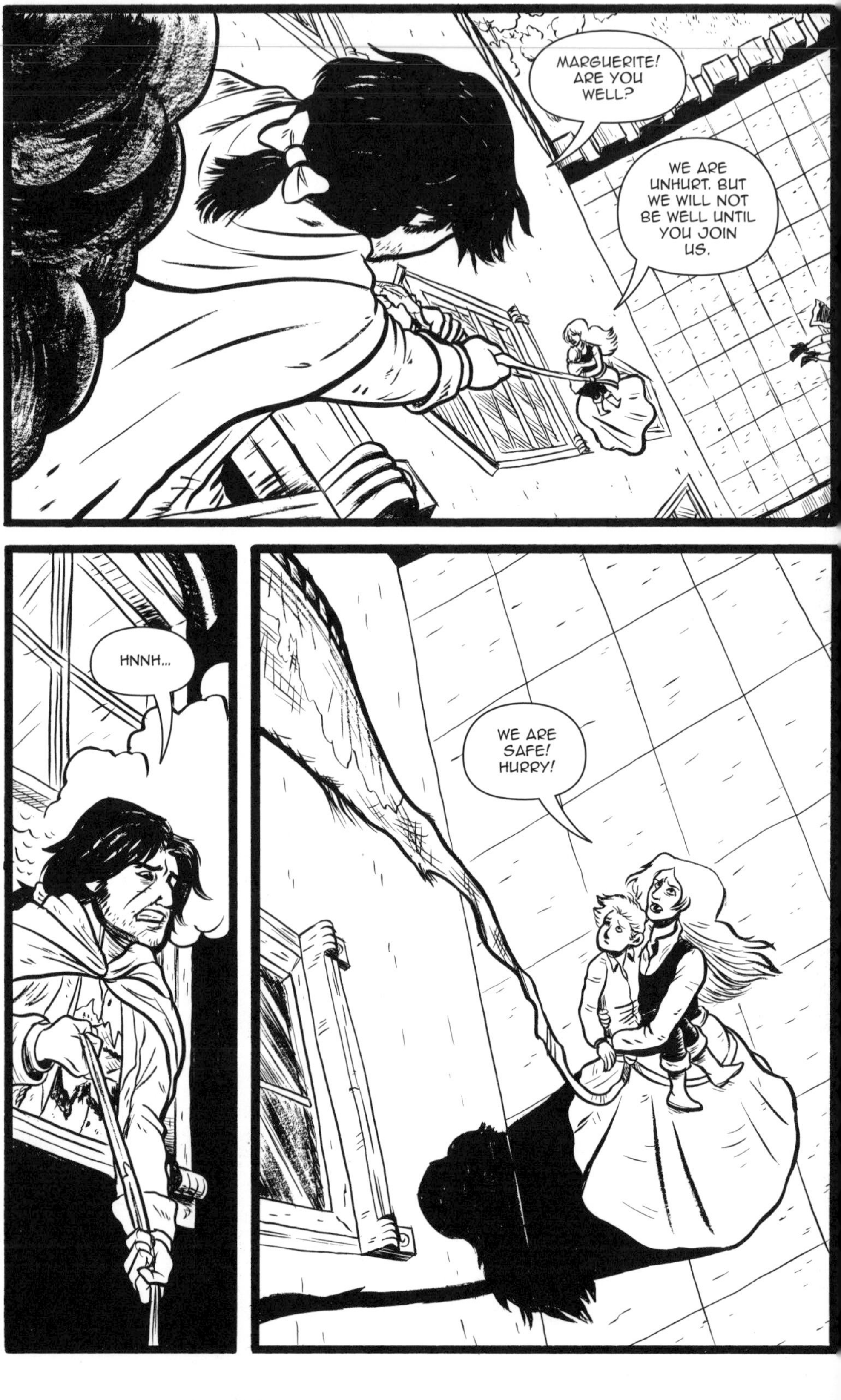
MARGUERITE! ARE YOU WELL?
WE ARE UNHURT. BUT WE WILL NOT BE WELL UNTIL YOU JOIN US.
HNNH...
WE ARE SAFE! HURRY!

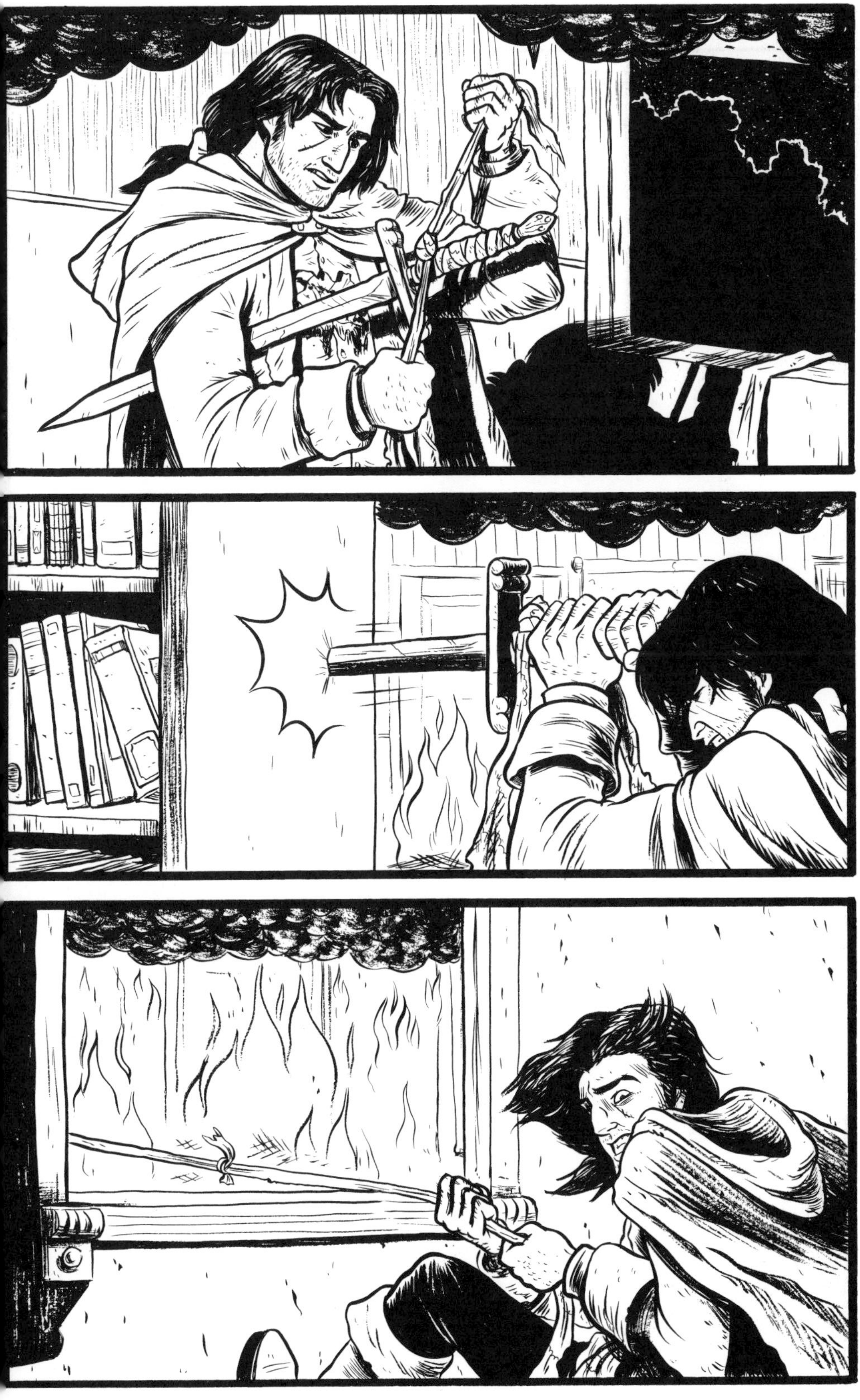

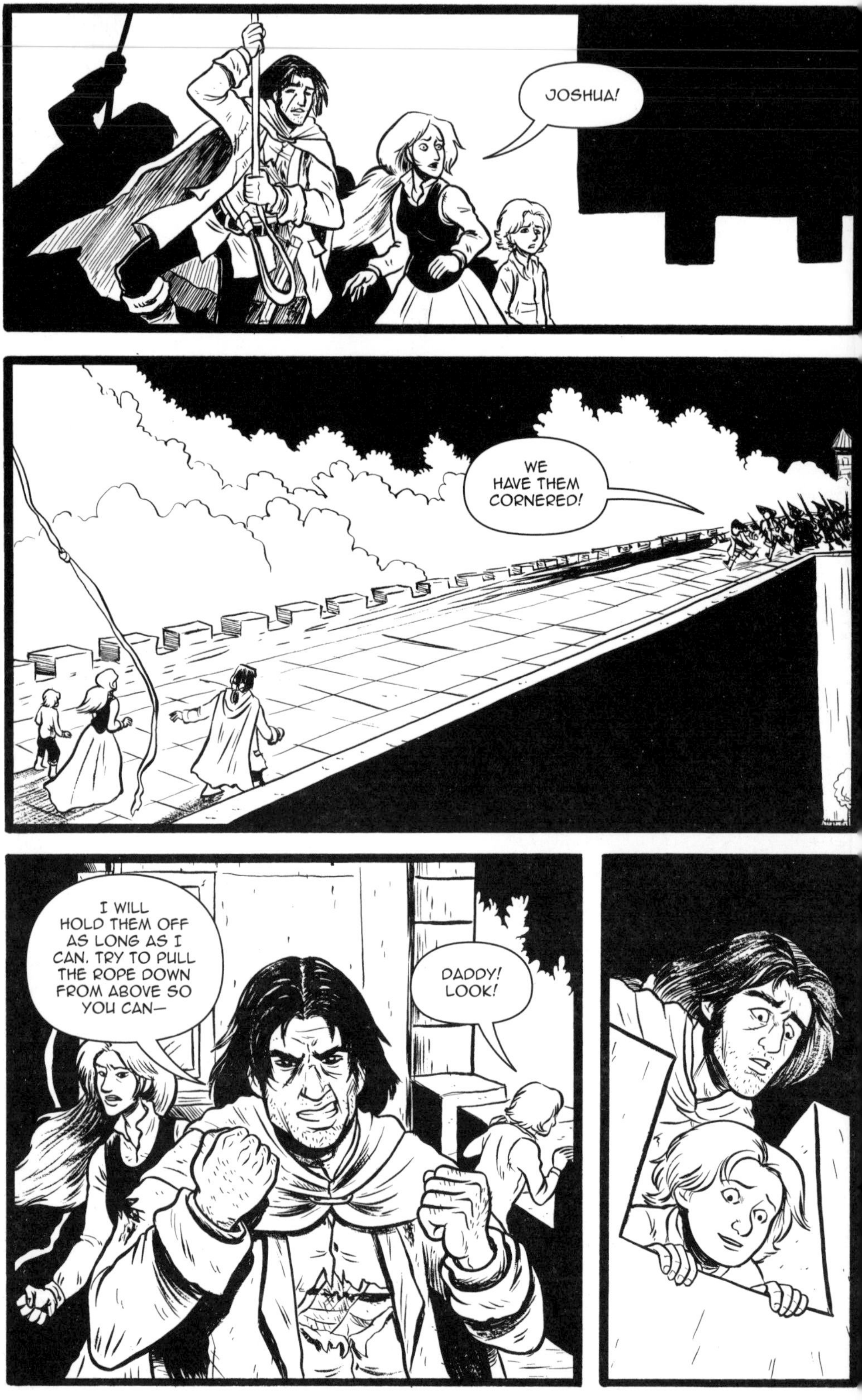
JOSHUA!
WE HAVE THEM CORNERED!
I WILL HOLD THEM OFF AS LONG AS I CAN. TRY TO PULL THE ROPE DOWN FROM ABOVE SO YOU CAN—
DADDY! LOOK!

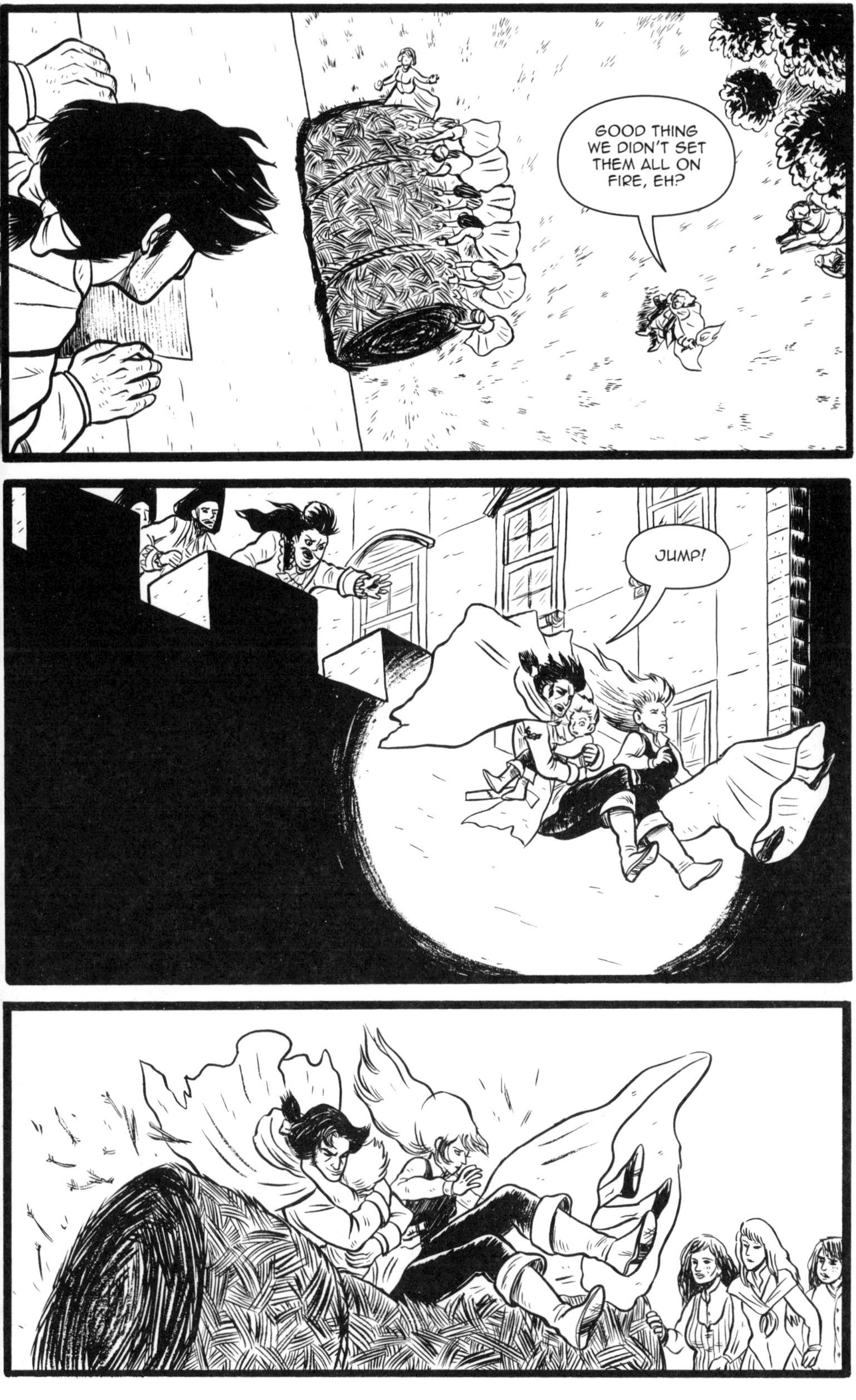
GOOD THING WE DIDN'T SET THEM ALL ON FIRE, EH?
JUMP!

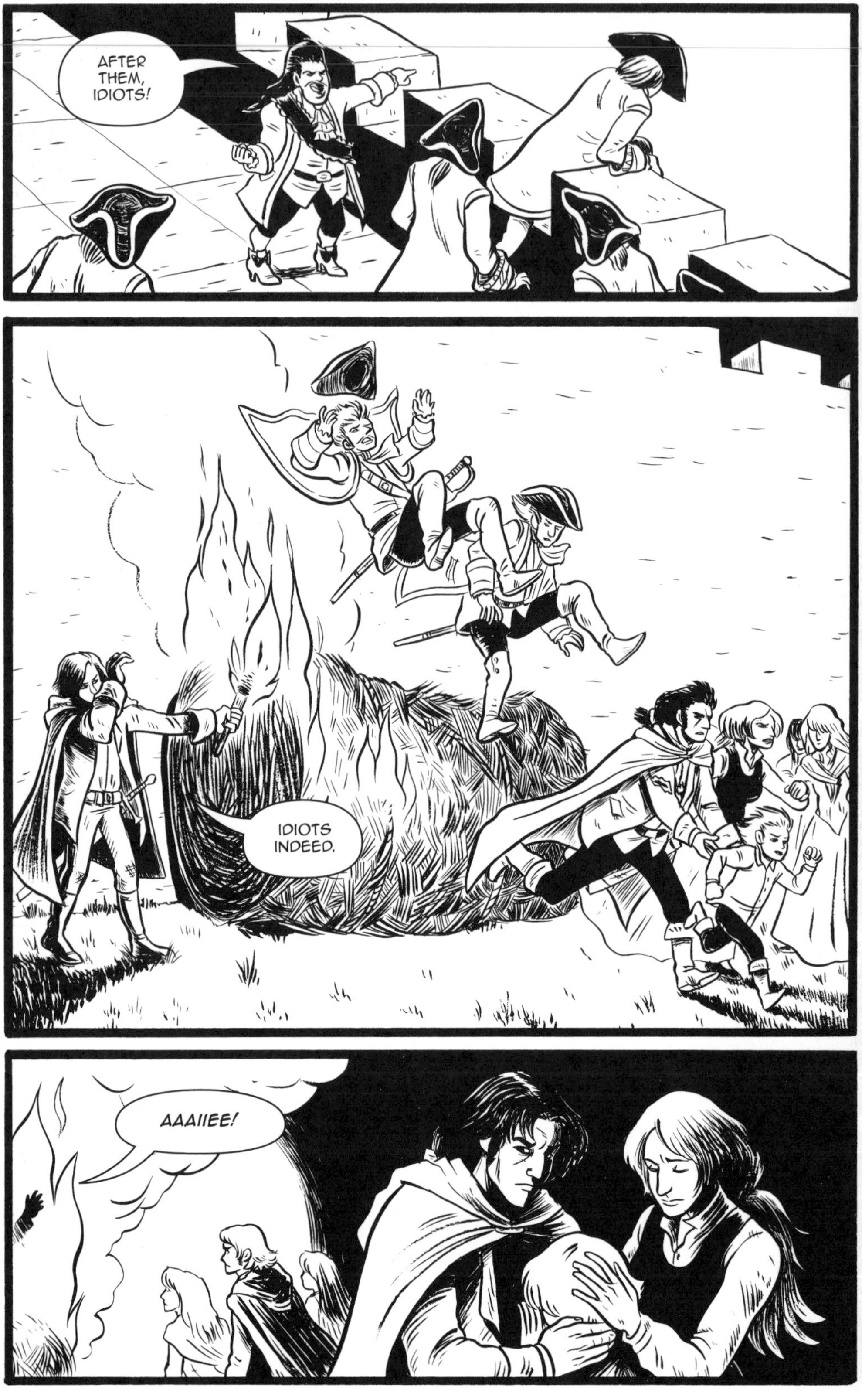
AFTER THEM, IDIOTS!
IDIOTS INDEED.
AAAIIEE!

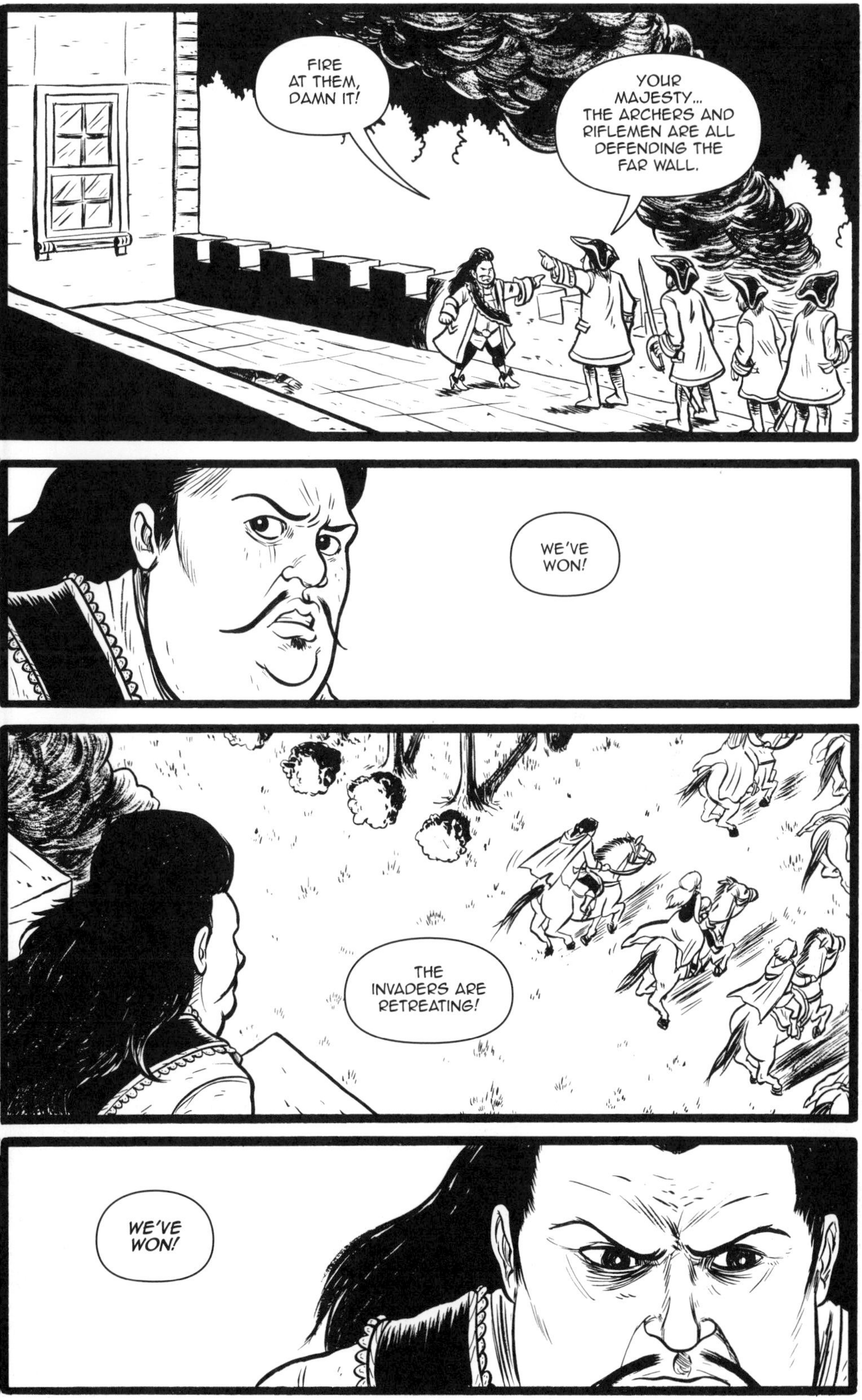
FIRE AT THEM, DAMN IT!
YOUR MAJESTY... THE ARCHERS AND RIFLEMEN ARE ALL DEFENDING THE FAR WALL.
WE'VE WON!
THE INVADERS ARE RETREATING!
WE'VE WON!

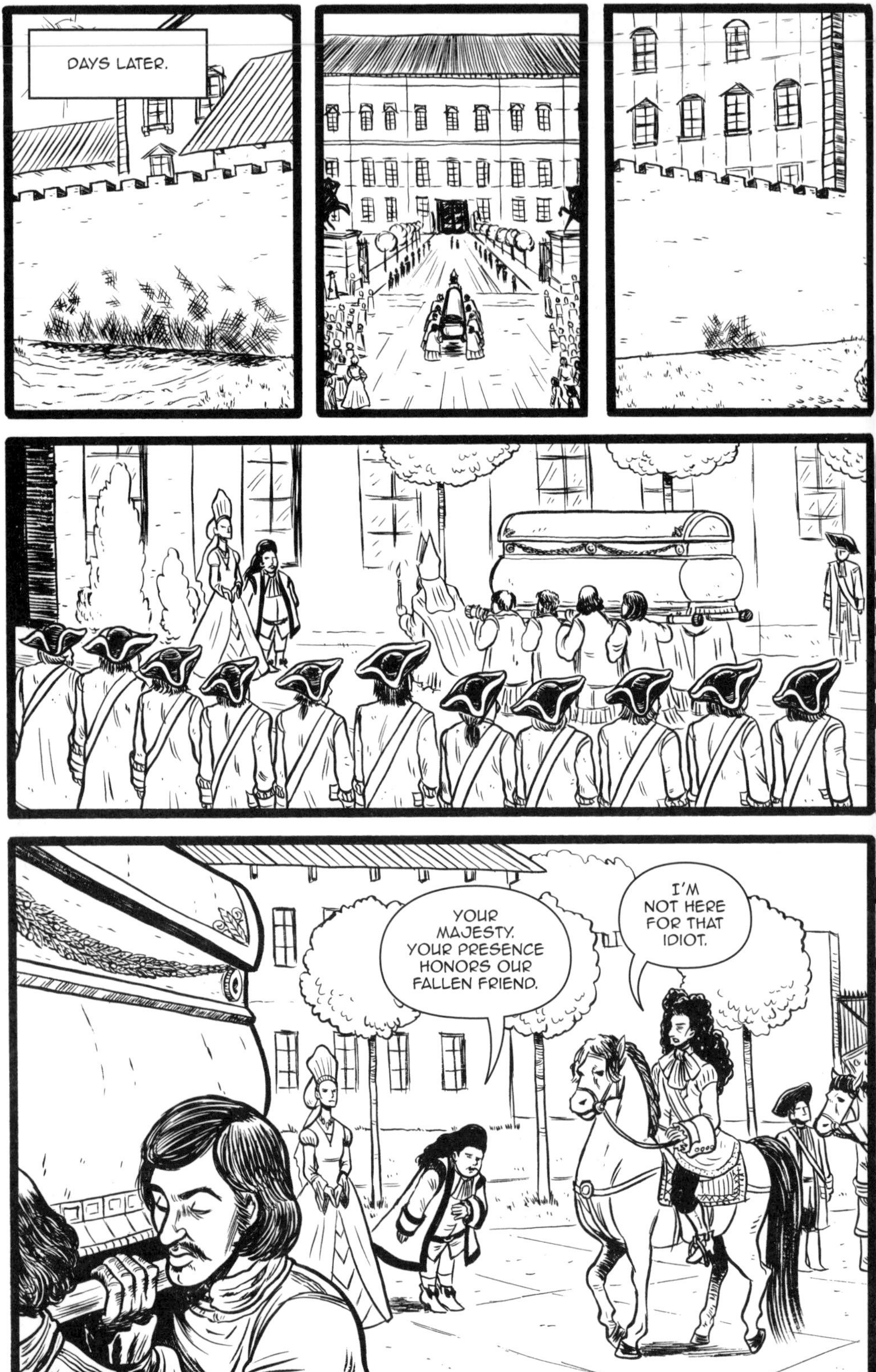
DAYS LATER.
YOUR MAJESTY. YOUR PRESENCE HONORS OUR FALLEN FRIEND.
I'M NOT HERE FOR THAT IDIOT.

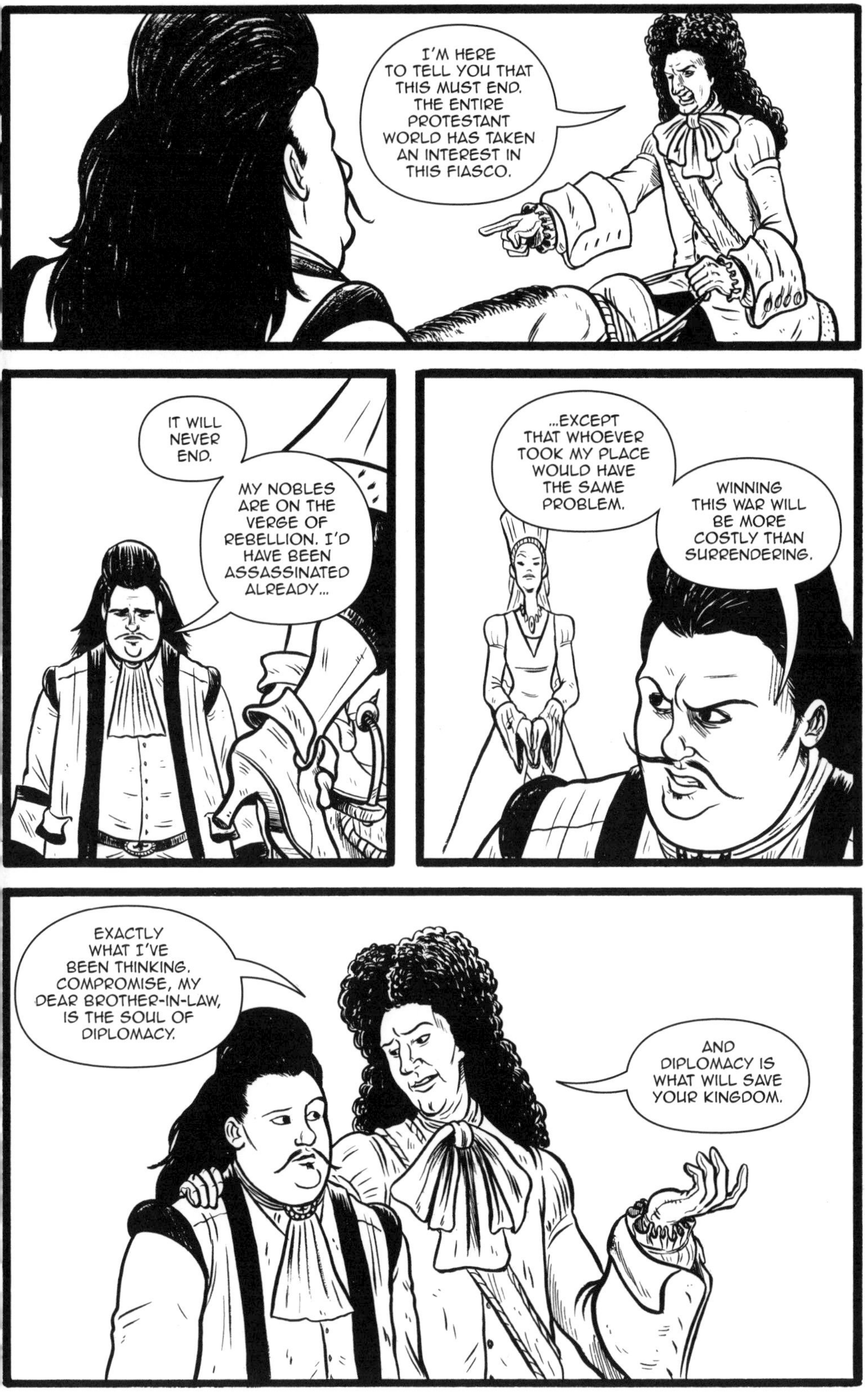
I'M HERE TO TELL YOU THAT THIS MUST END. THE ENTIRE PROTESTANT WORLD HAS TAKEN AN INTEREST IN THIS FIASCO.
IT WILL NEVER END.
MY NOBLES ARE ON THE VERGE OF REBELLION. I'D HAVE BEEN ASSASSINATED ALREADY...
...EXCEPT THAT WHOEVER TOOK MY PLACE WOULD HAVE THE SAME PROBLEM.
WINNING THIS WAR WILL BE MORE COSTLY THAN SURRENDERING.
EXACTLY WHAT I'VE BEEN THINKING. COMPROMISE, MY DEAR BROTHER-IN-LAW, IS THE SOUL OF DIPLOMACY.
AND DIPLOMACY IS WHAT WILL SAVE YOUR KINGDOM.

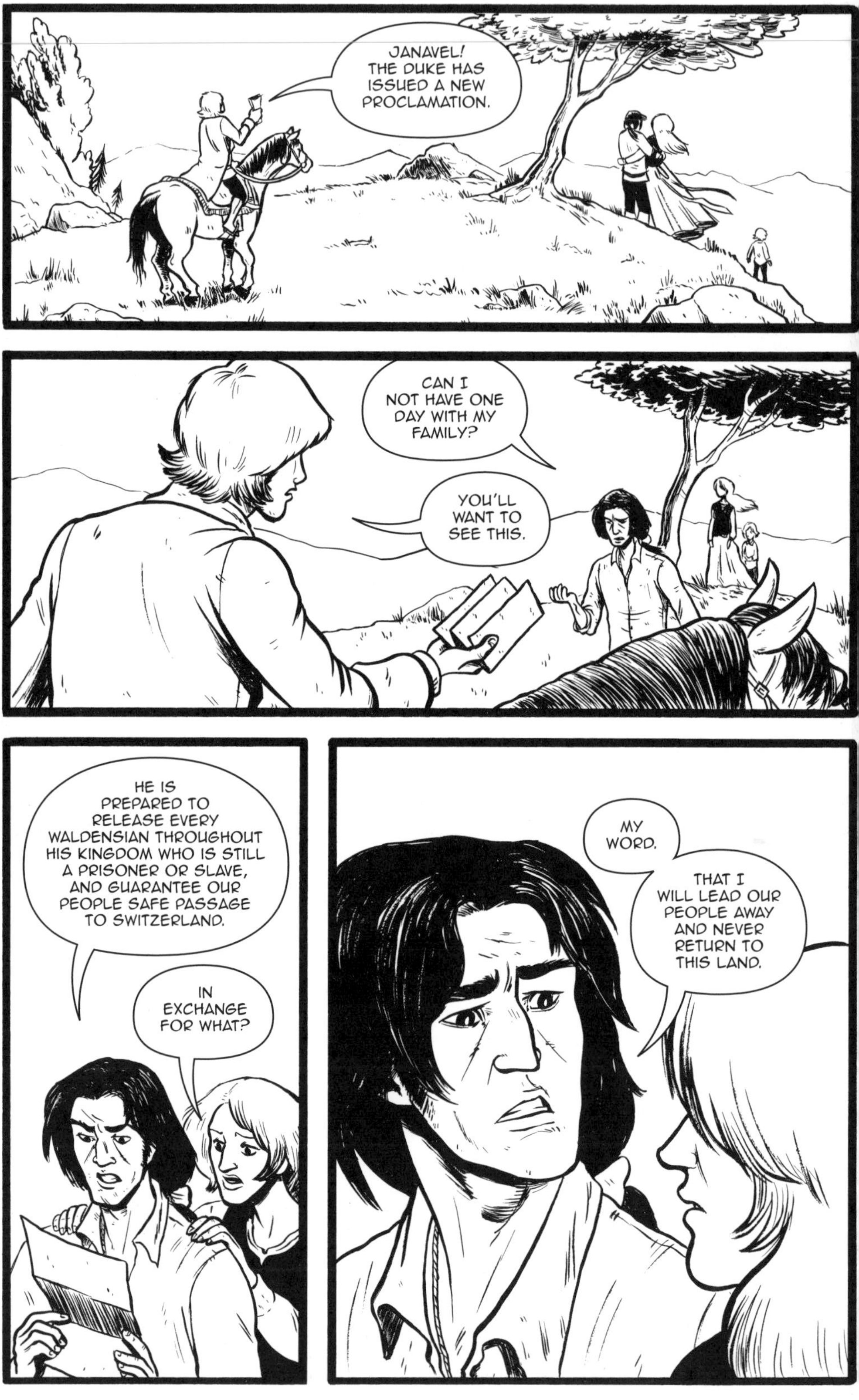
JANAVEL! THE DUKE HAS ISSUED A NEW PROCLAMATION.
CAN I NOT HAVE ONE DAY WITH MY FAMILY?
YOU'LL WANT TO SEE THIS.
HE IS PREPARED TO RELEASE EVERY WALDENSIAN THROUGHOUT HIS KINGDOM WHO IS STILL A PRISONER OR SLAVE, AND GUARANTEE OUR PEOPLE SAFE PASSAGE TO SWITZERLAND.
IN EXCHANGE FOR WHAT?
MY WORD.
THAT I WILL LEAD OUR PEOPLE AWAY AND NEVER RETURN TO THIS LAND.

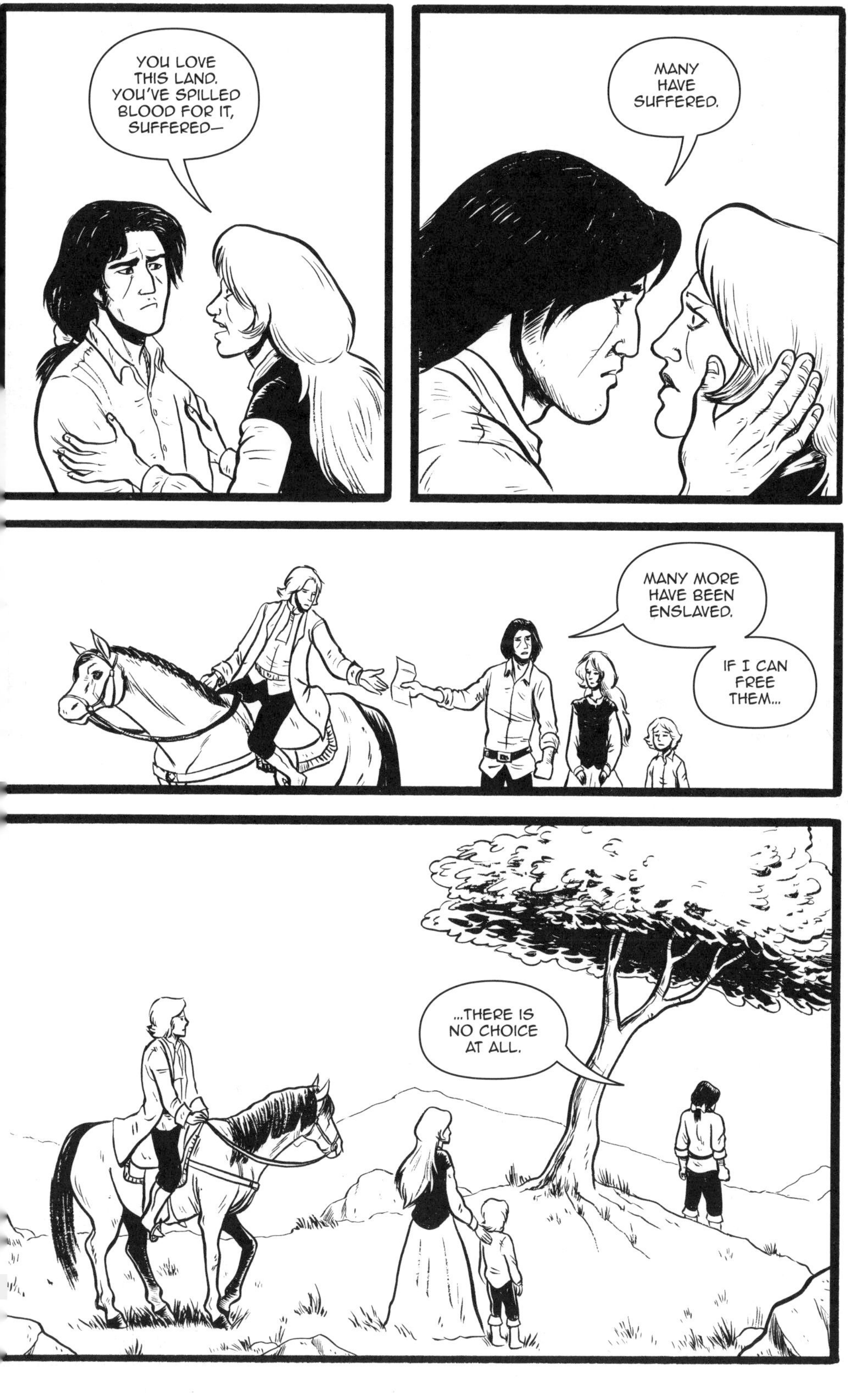
YOU LOVE THIS LAND. YOU'VE SPILLED BLOOD FOR IT, SUFFERED—
MANY HAVE SUFFERED.
MANY MORE HAVE BEEN ENSLAVED.
IF I CAN FREE THEM...
...THERE IS NO CHOICE AT ALL.

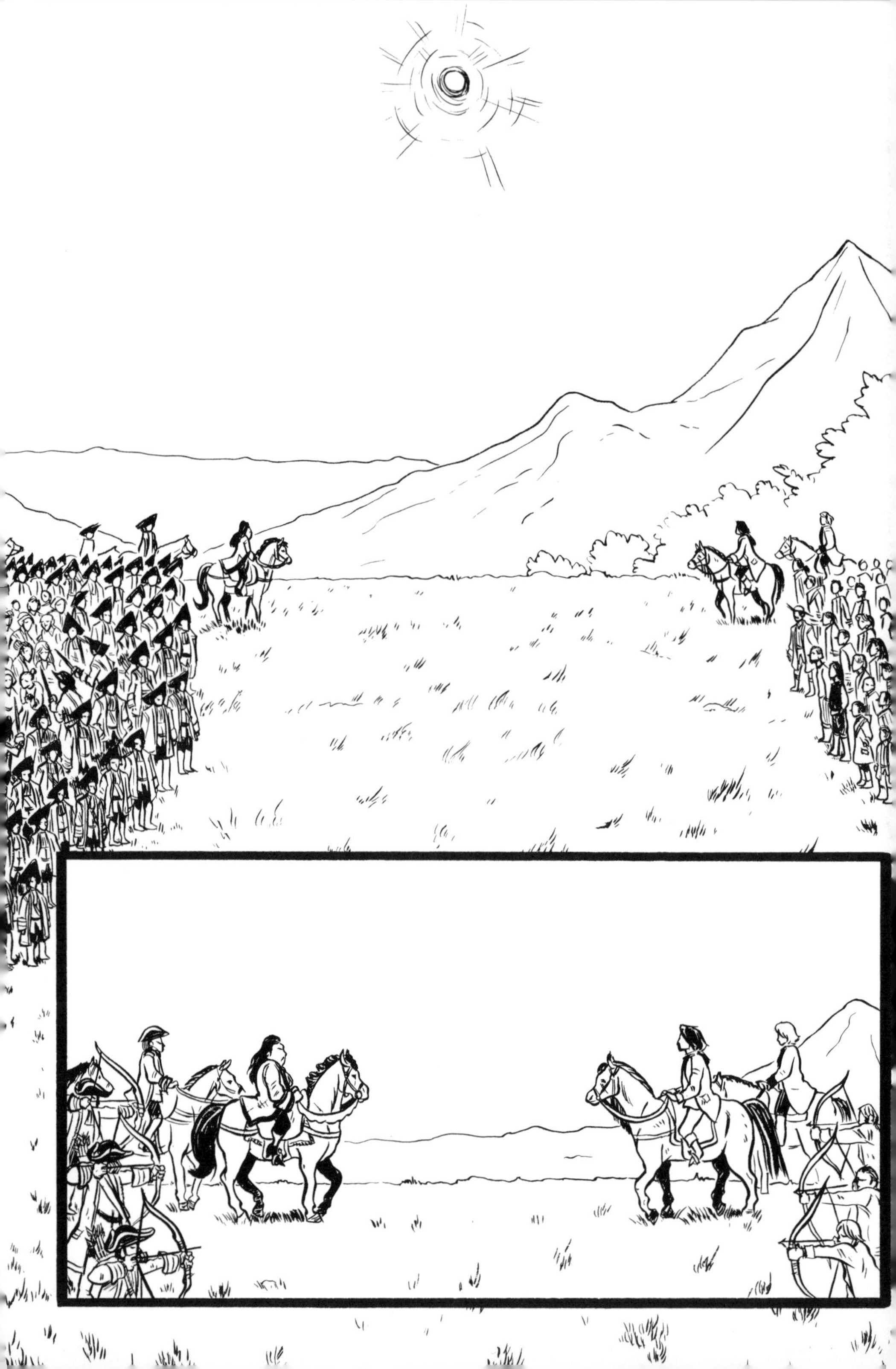

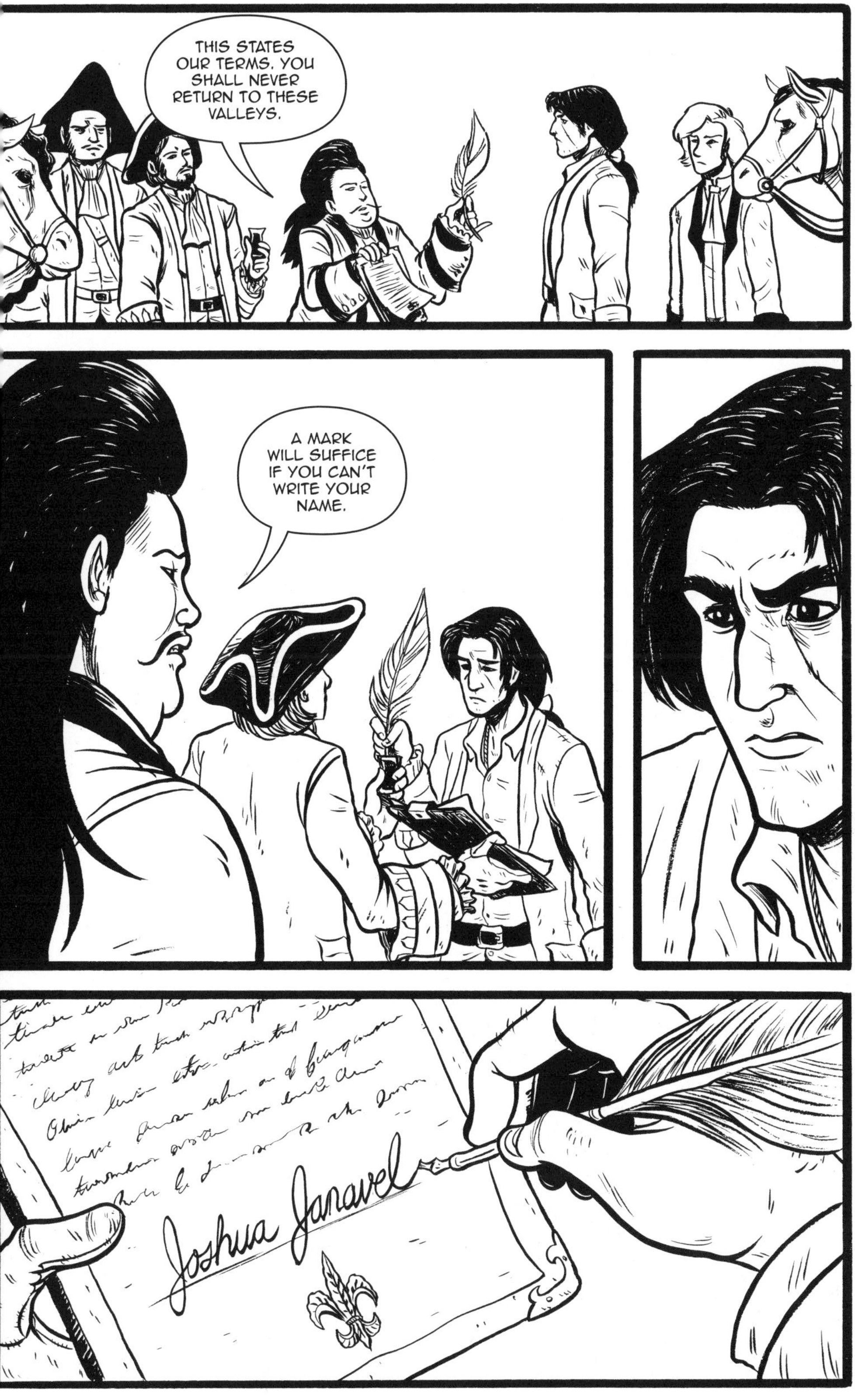
THIS STATES OUR TERMS. YOU SHALL NEVER RETURN TO THESE VALLEYS.
A MARK WILL SUFFICE IF YOU CAN'T WRITE YOUR NAME.
Joshua Janavel

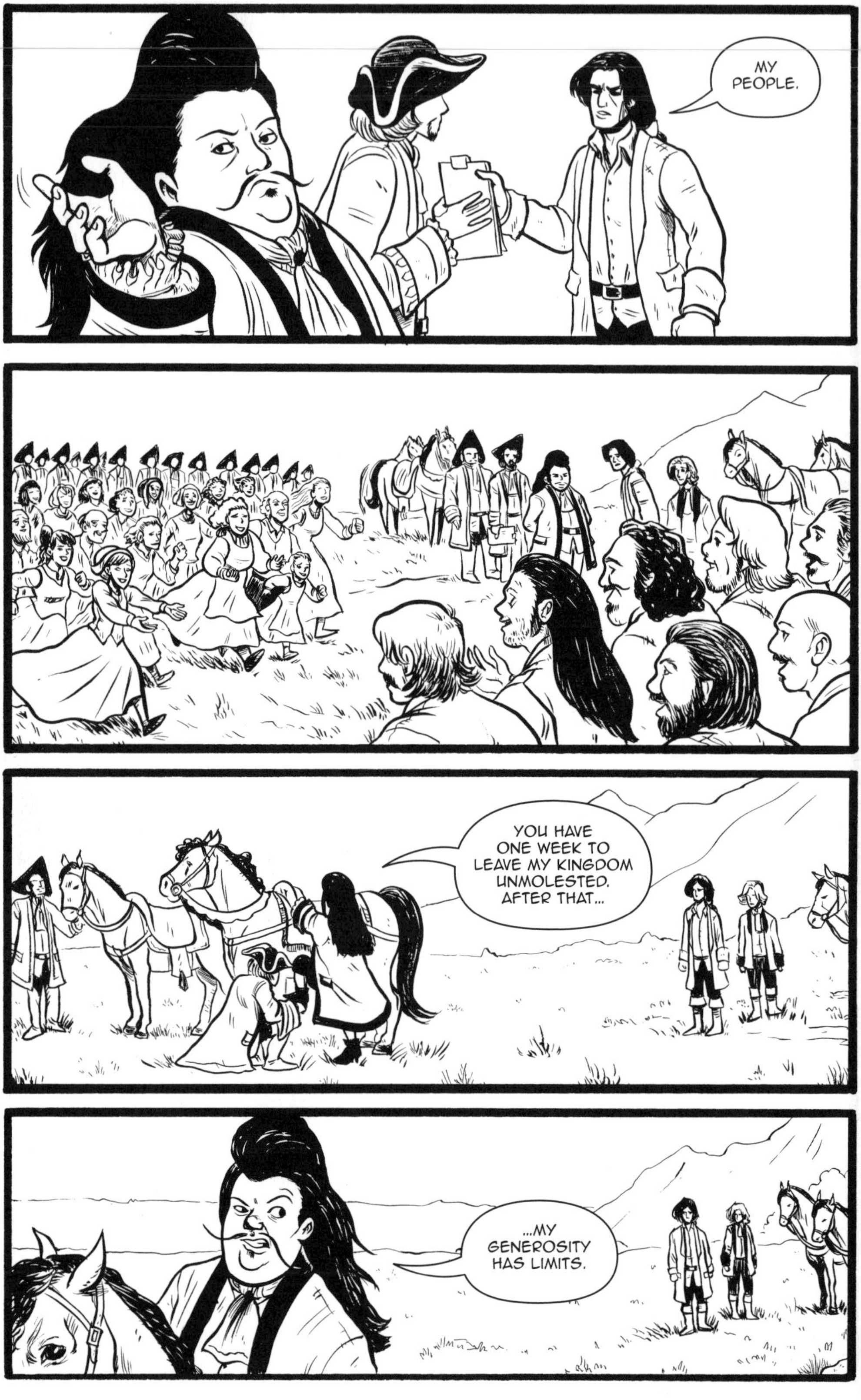
MY PEOPLE.
YOU HAVE ONE WEEK TO LEAVE MY KINGDOM UNMOLESTED. AFTER THAT...
...MY GENEROSITY HAS LIMITS.

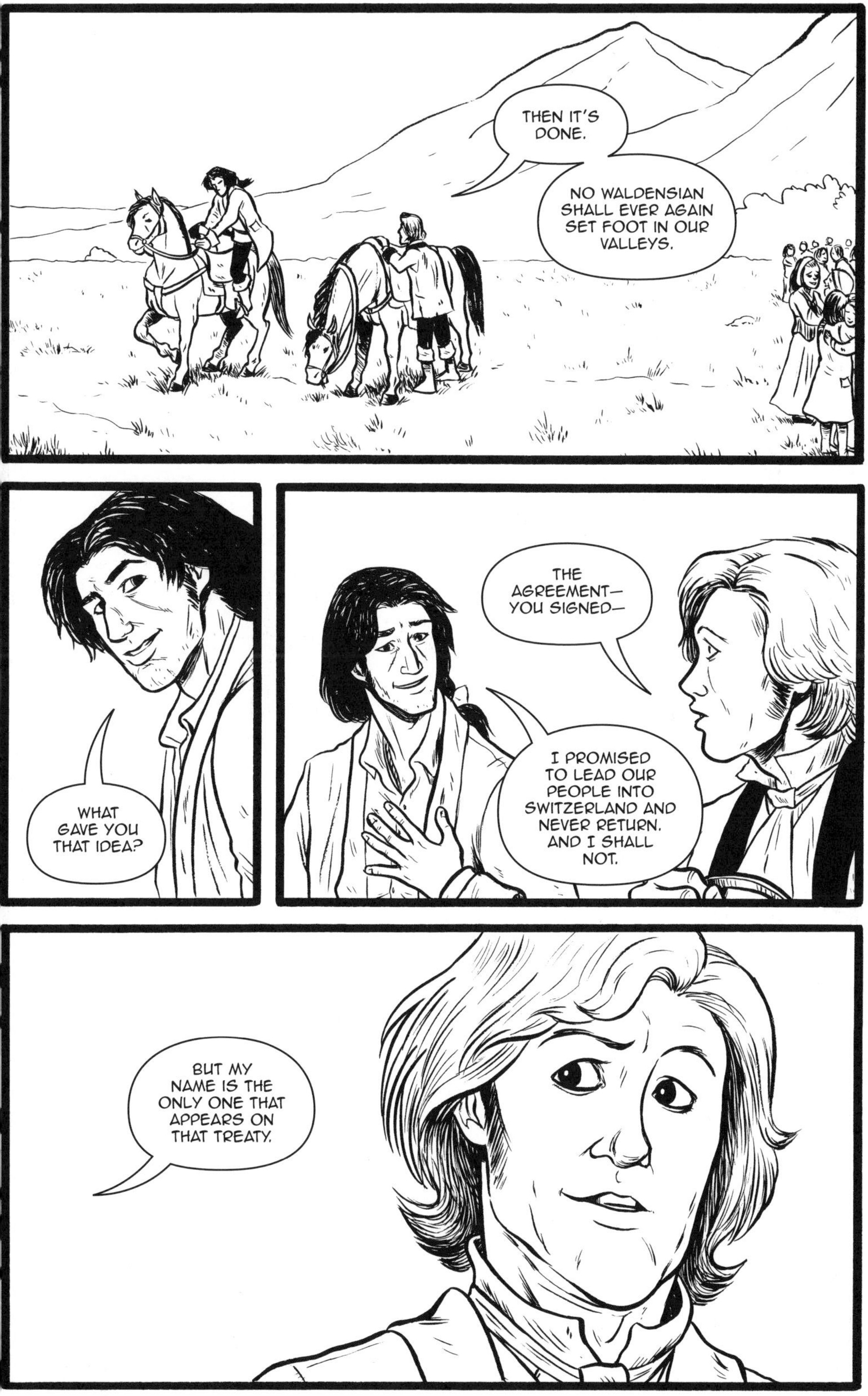
THEN IT'S DONE.
NO WALDENSIAN SHALL EVER AGAIN SET FOOT IN OUR VALLEYS.
WHAT GAVE YOU THAT IDEA?
THE AGREEMENT— YOU SIGNED—
I PROMISED TO LEAD OUR PEOPLE INTO SWITZERLAND AND NEVER RETURN. AND I SHALL NOT.
BUT MY NAME IS THE ONLY ONE THAT APPEARS ON THAT TREATY.

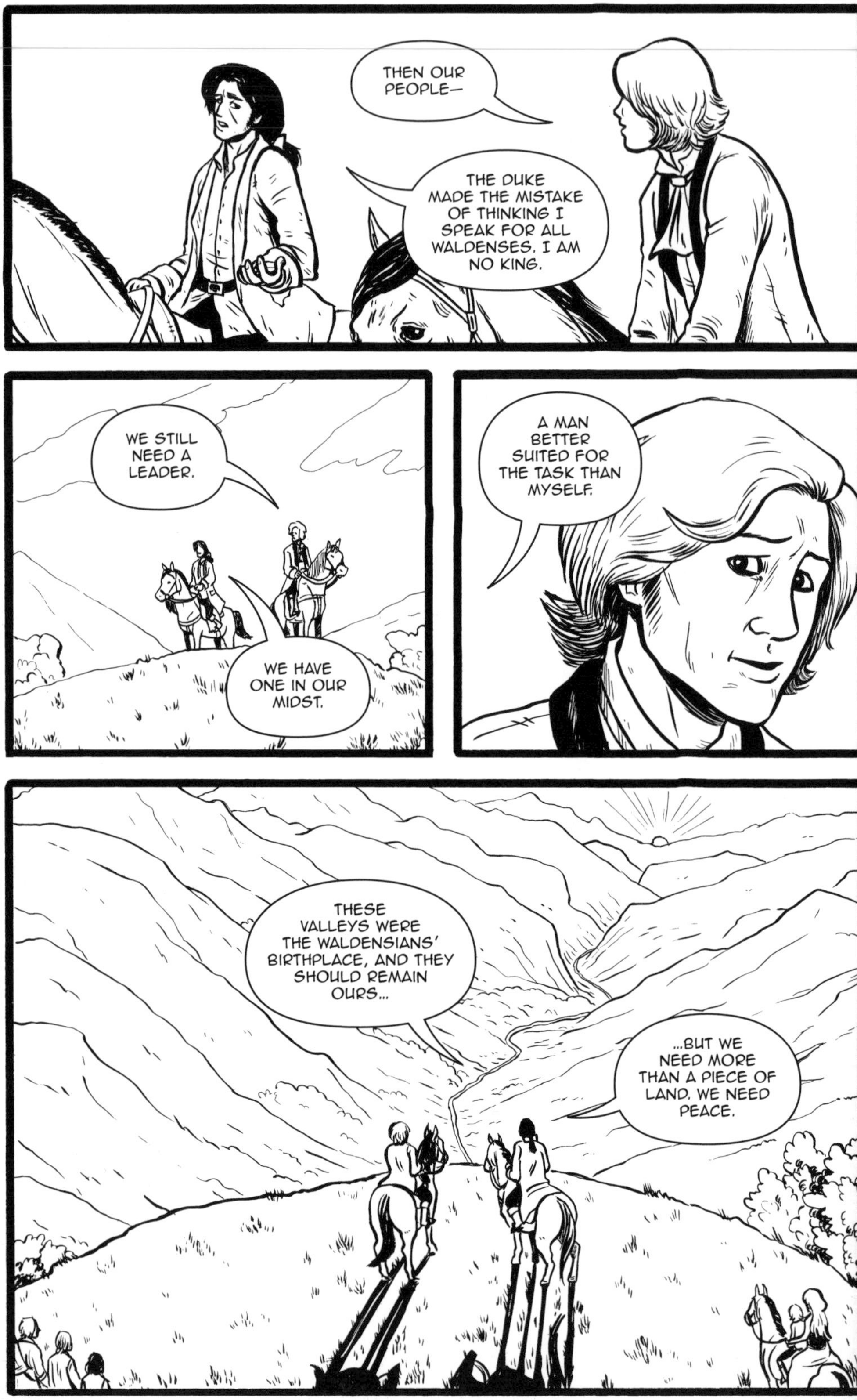
THEN OUR PEOPLE—
THE DUKE MADE THE MISTAKE OF THINKING I SPEAK FOR ALL WALDENSES. I AM NO KING.
WE STILL NEED A LEADER.
WE HAVE ONE IN OUR MIDST.
A MAN BETTER SUITED FOR THE TASK THAN MYSELF.
THESE VALLEYS WERE THE WALDENSIANS' BIRTHPLACE, AND THEY SHOULD REMAIN OURS...
...BUT WE NEED MORE THAN A PIECE OF LAND. WE NEED PEACE.

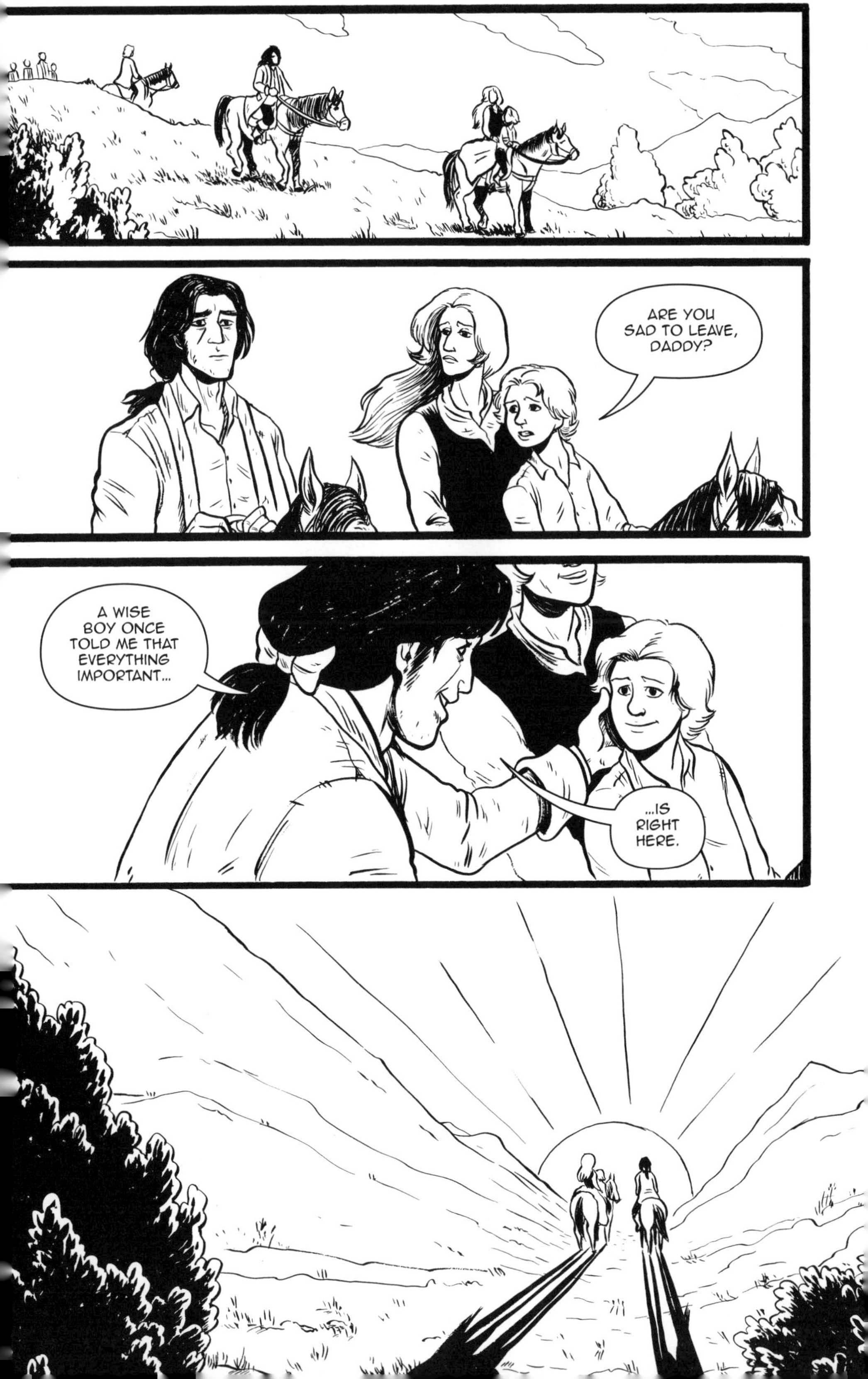
ARE YOU SAD TO LEAVE, DADDY?
A WISE BOY ONCE TOLD ME THAT EVERYTHING IMPORTANT...
...IS RIGHT HERE.

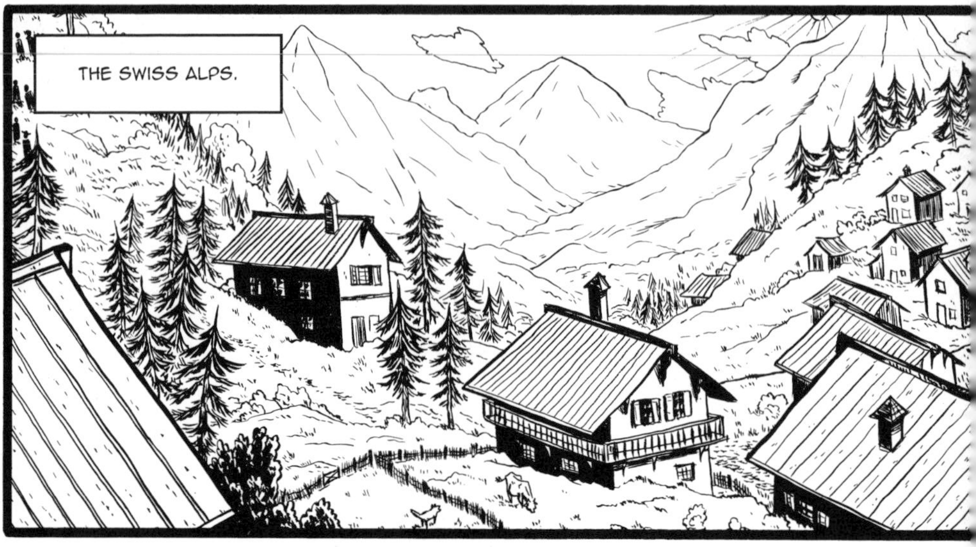
THE SWISS ALPS.

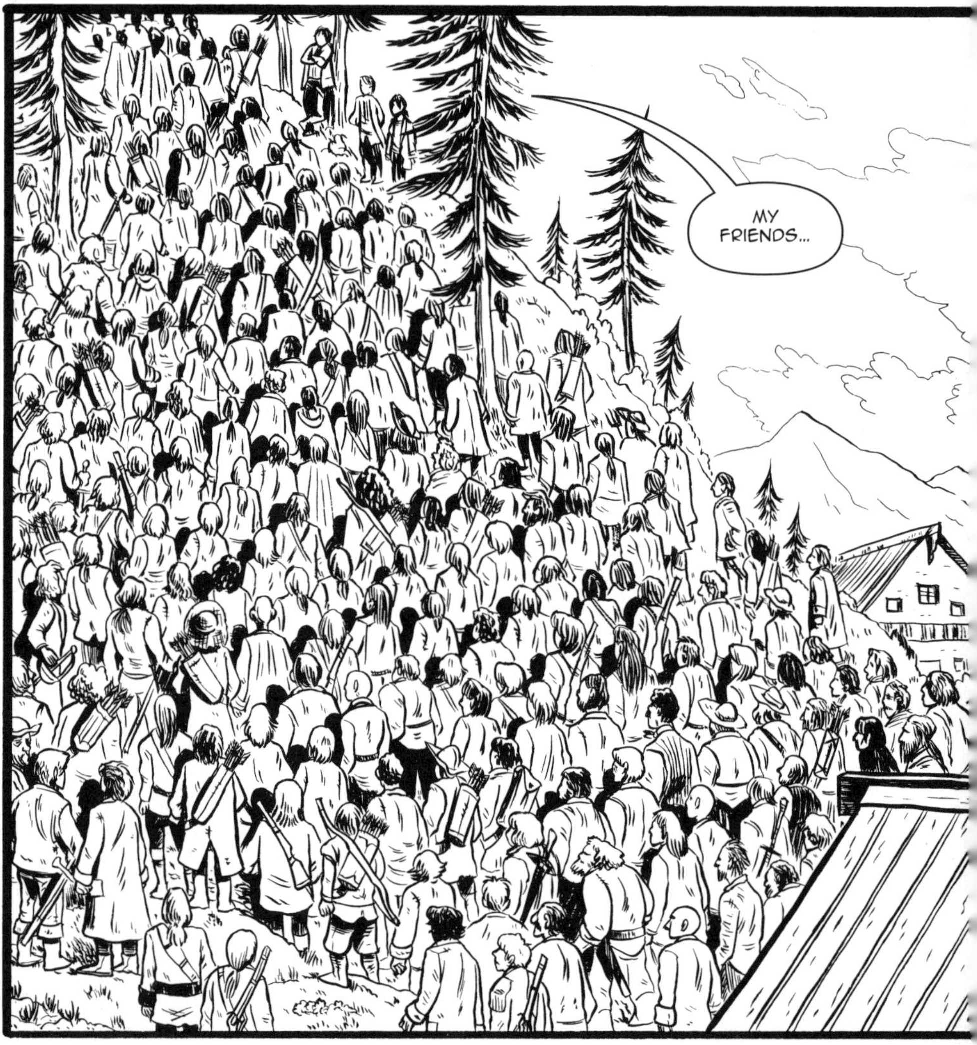
MY FRIENDS...

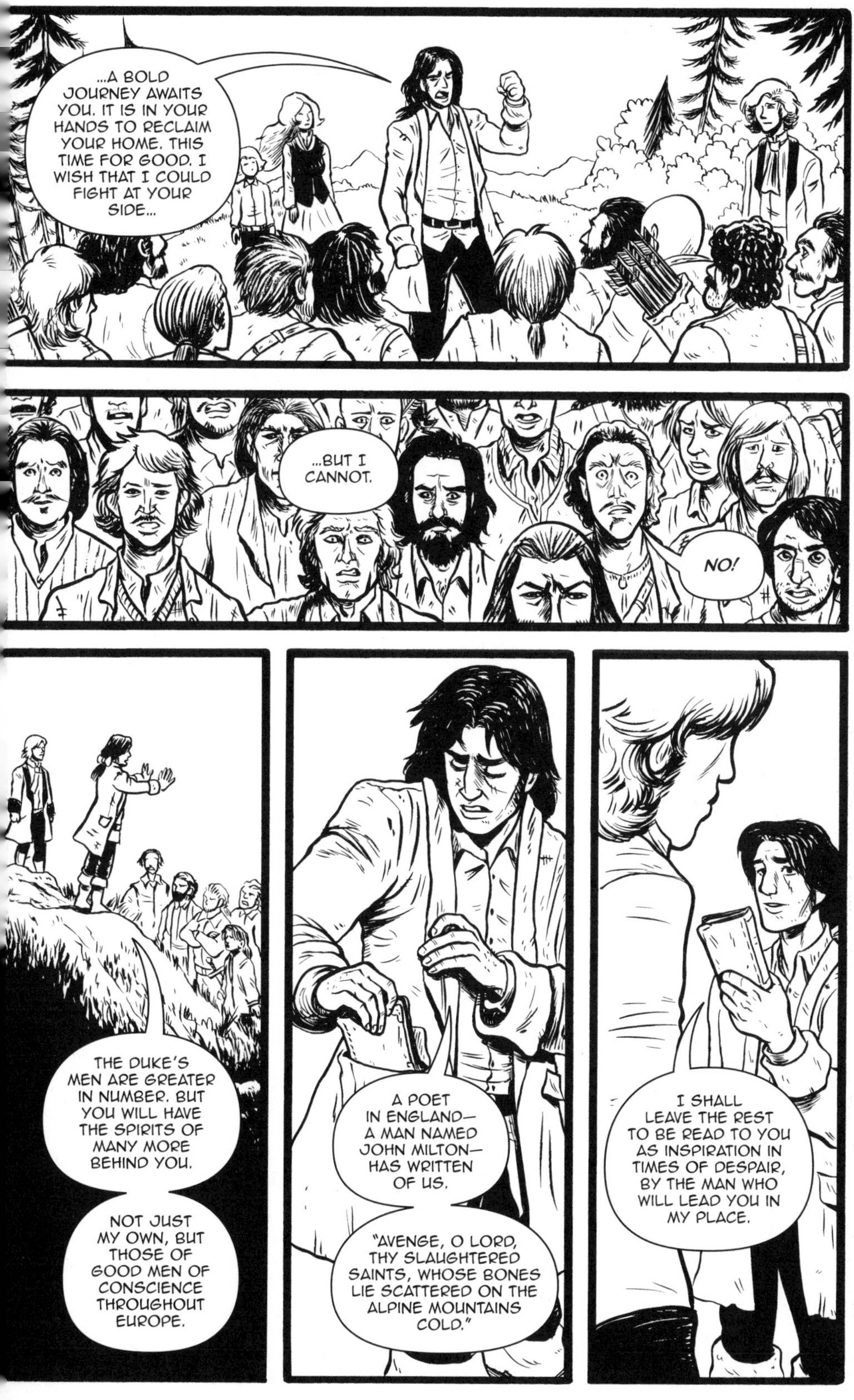
...A BOLD JOURNEY AWAITS YOU. IT IS IN YOUR HANDS TO RECLAIM YOUR HOME. THIS TIME FOR GOOD. I WISH THAT I COULD FIGHT AT YOUR SIDE...
...BUT I CANNOT.
NO!
THE DUKE'S MEN ARE GREATER IN NUMBER. BUT YOU WILL HAVE THE SPIRITS OF MANY MORE BEHIND YOU.
NOT JUST MY OWN, BUT THOSE OF GOOD MEN OF CONSCIENCE THROUGHOUT EUROPE.
A POET IN ENGLAND— A MAN NAMED JOHN MILTON— HAS WRITTEN OF US.
"AVENGE, O LORD, THY SLAUGHTERED SAINTS, WHOSE BONES LIE SCATTERED ON THE ALPINE MOUNTAINS COLD."
I SHALL LEAVE THE REST TO BE READ TO YOU AS INSPIRATION IN TIMES OF DESPAIR, BY THE MAN WHO WILL LEAD YOU IN MY PLACE.

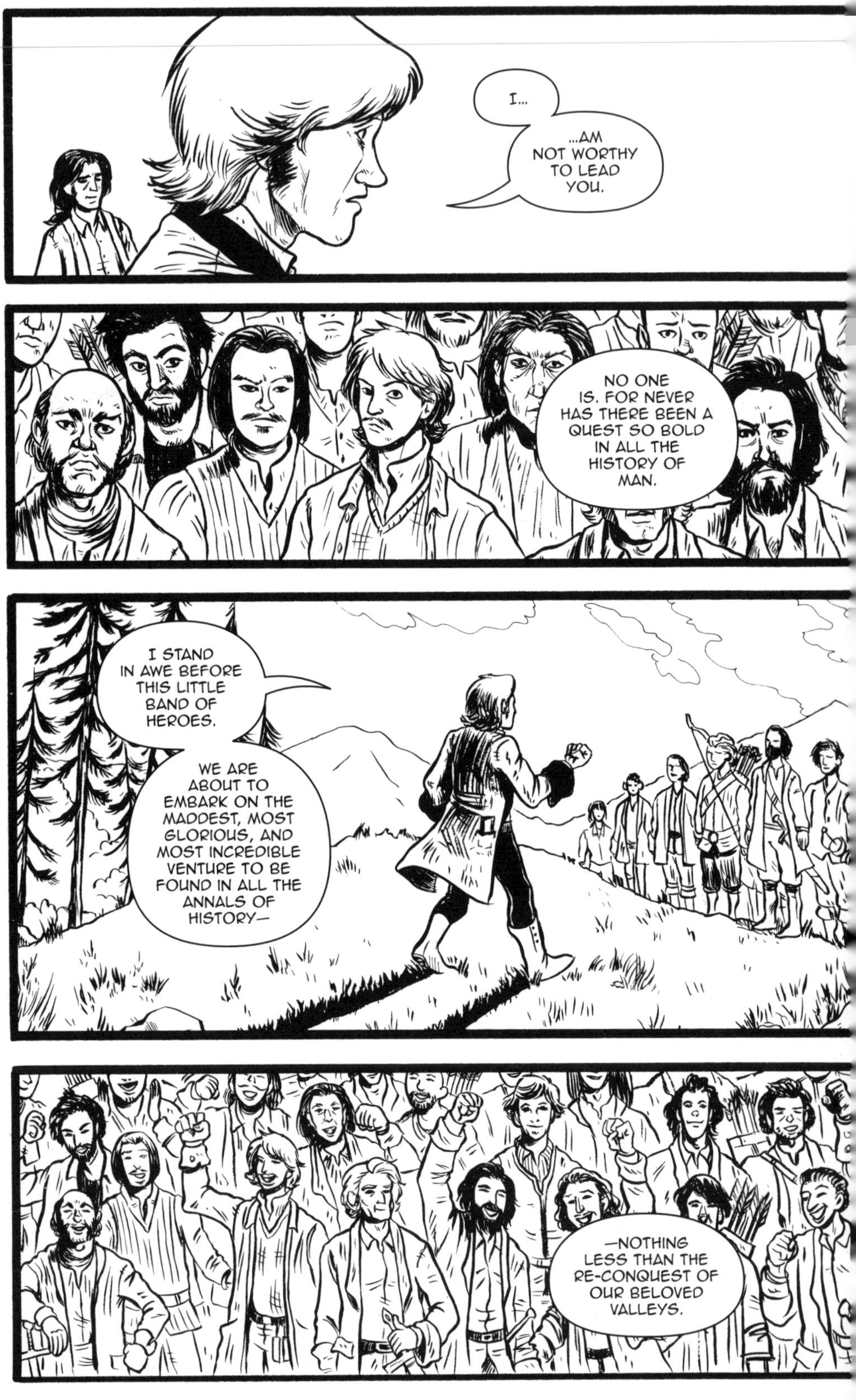
I...
...AM NOT WORTHY TO LEAD YOU.
NO ONE IS. FOR NEVER HAS THERE BEEN A QUEST SO BOLD IN ALL THE HISTORY OF MAN.
I STAND IN AWE BEFORE THIS LITTLE BAND OF HEROES.
WE ARE ABOUT TO EMBARK ON THE MADDEST, MOST GLORIOUS, AND MOST INCREDIBLE VENTURE TO BE FOUND IN ALL THE ANNALS OF HISTORY—
—NOTHING LESS THAN THE RE-CONQUEST OF OUR BELOVED VALLEYS.

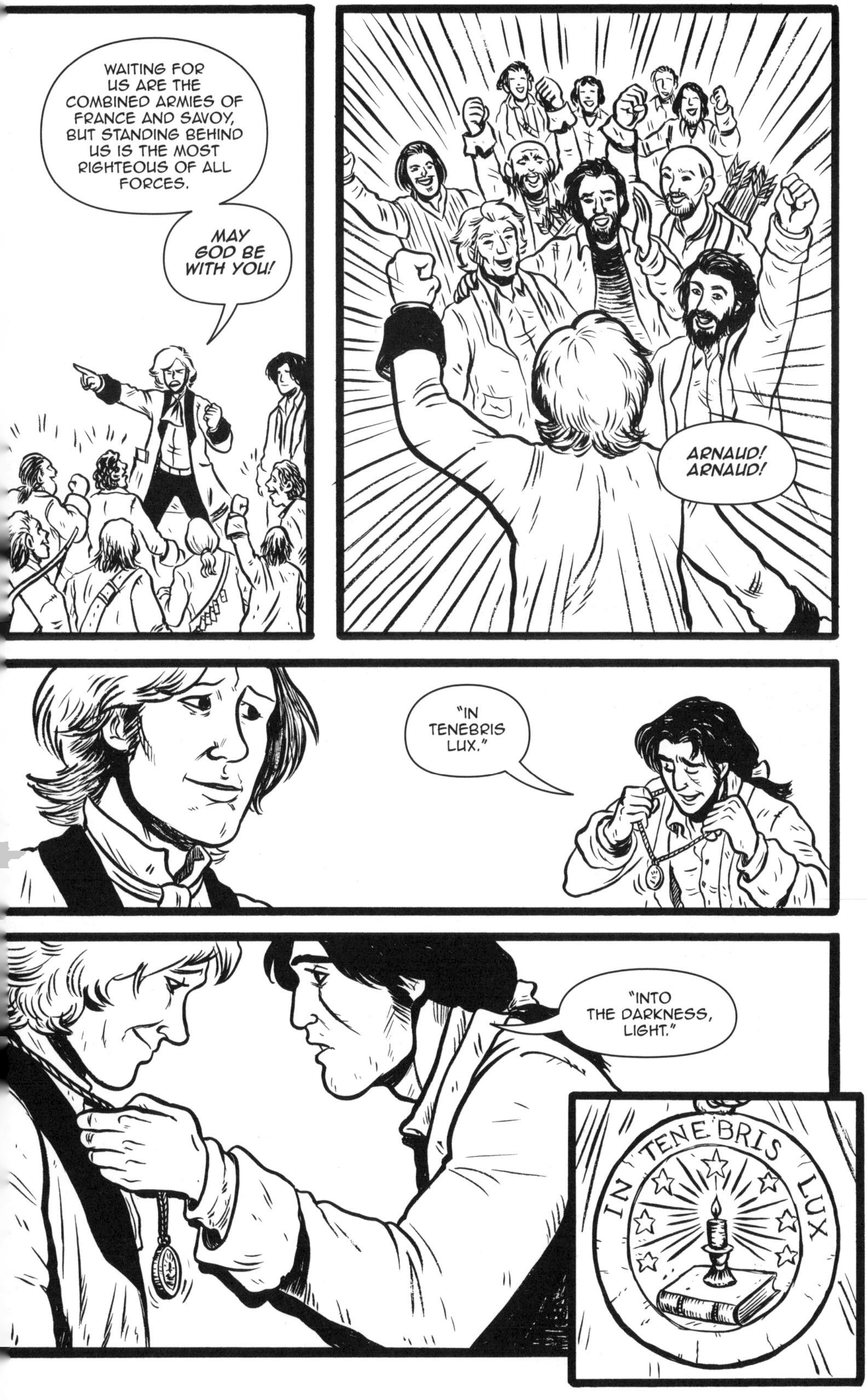

WAITING FOR US ARE THE COMBINED ARMIES OF FRANCE AND SAVOY, BUT STANDING BEHIND US IS THE MOST RIGHTEOUS OF ALL FORCES.
MAY GOD BE WITH YOU!
ARNAUD! ARNAUD!
"IN TENEBRIS LUX."
"INTO THE DARKNESS, LIGHT."
IN TENE BRIS LUX

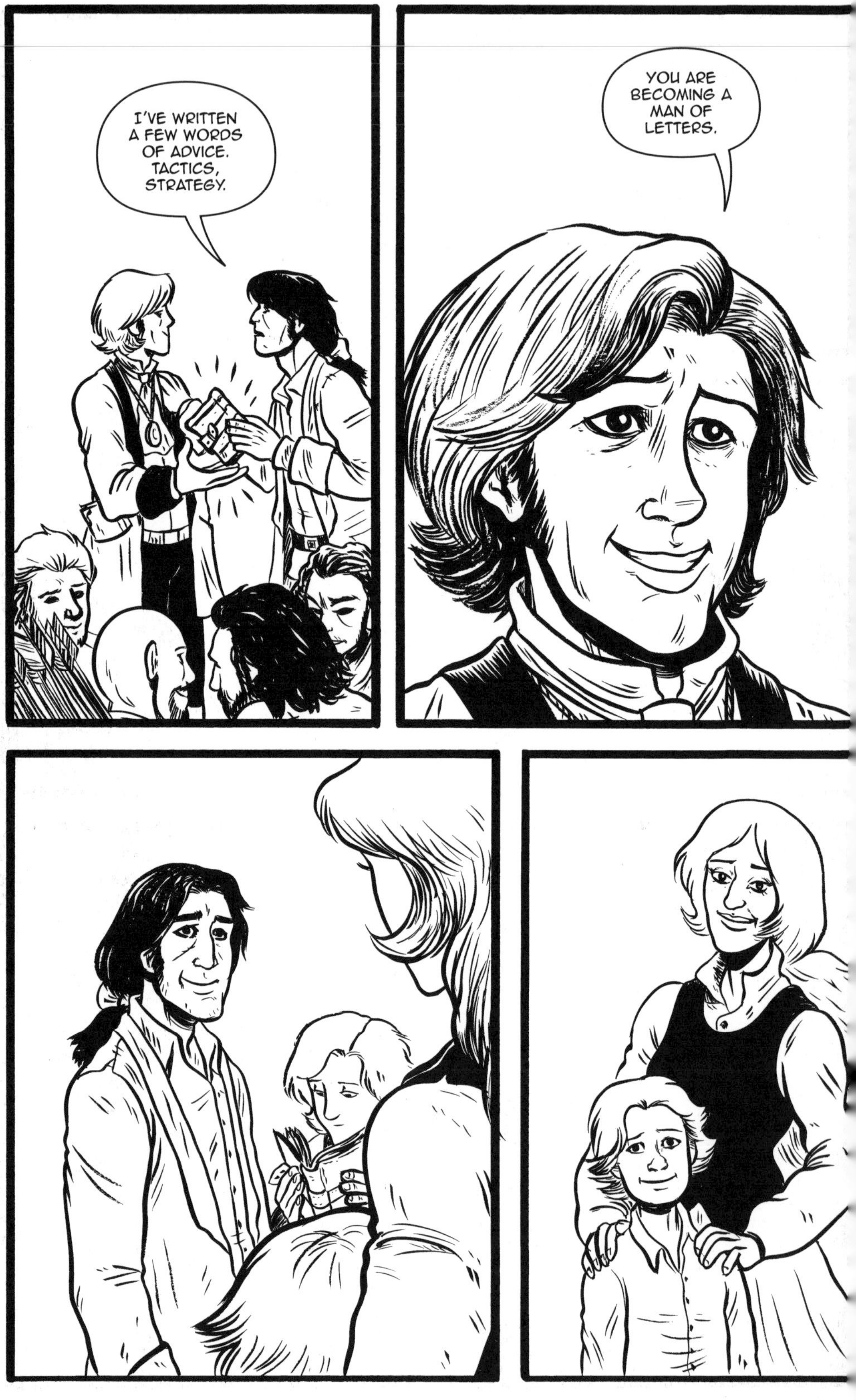
I'VE WRITTEN A FEW WORDS OF ADVICE. TACTICS, STRATEGY.
YOU ARE BECOMING A MAN OF LETTERS.

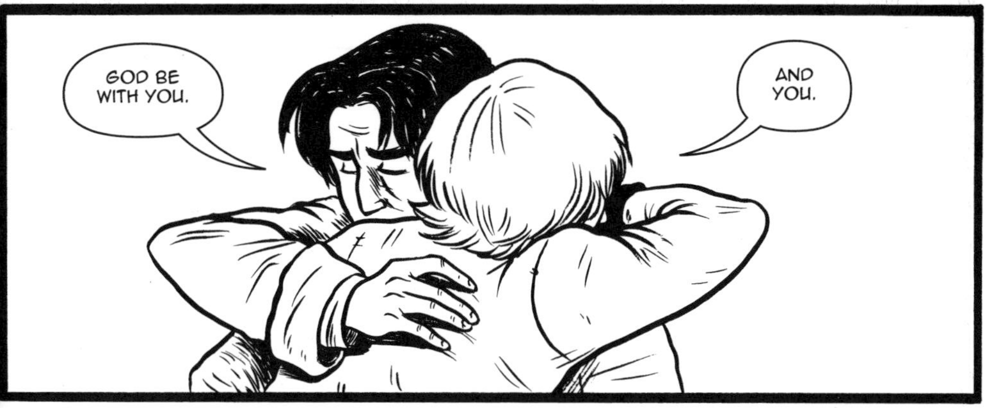
GOD BE WITH YOU.
AND YOU.

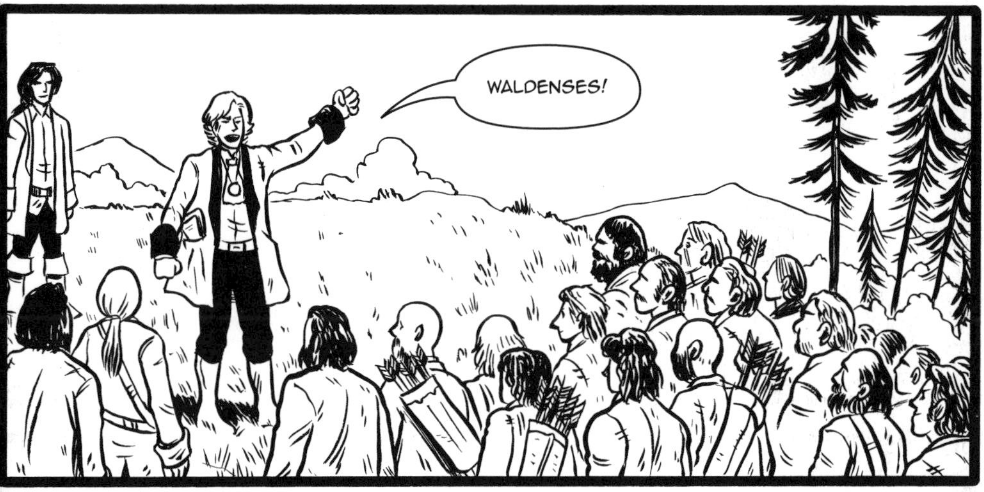
WALDENSES!

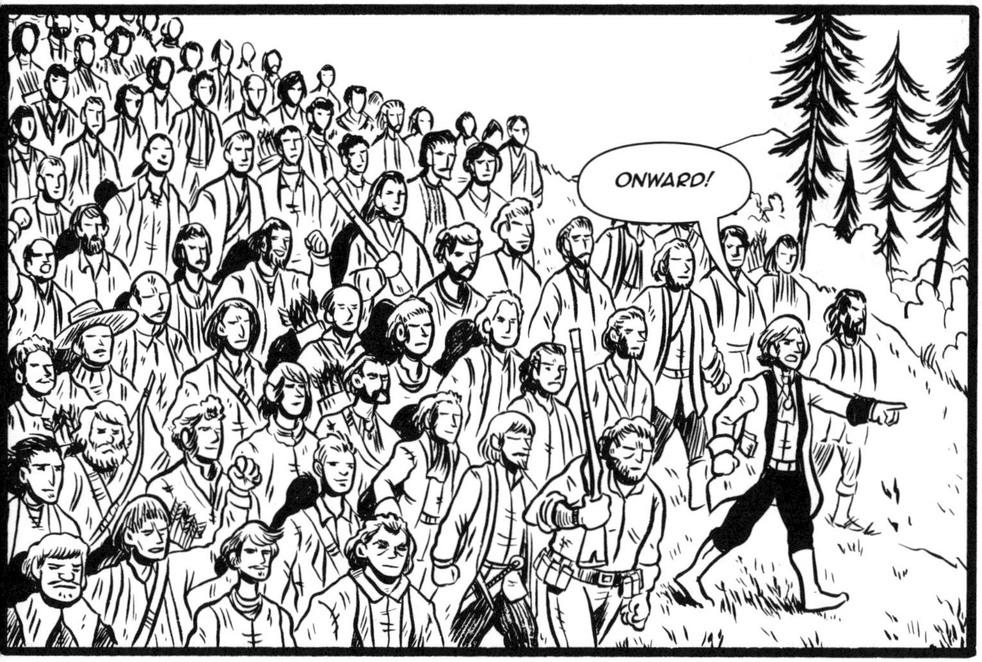
ONWARD!

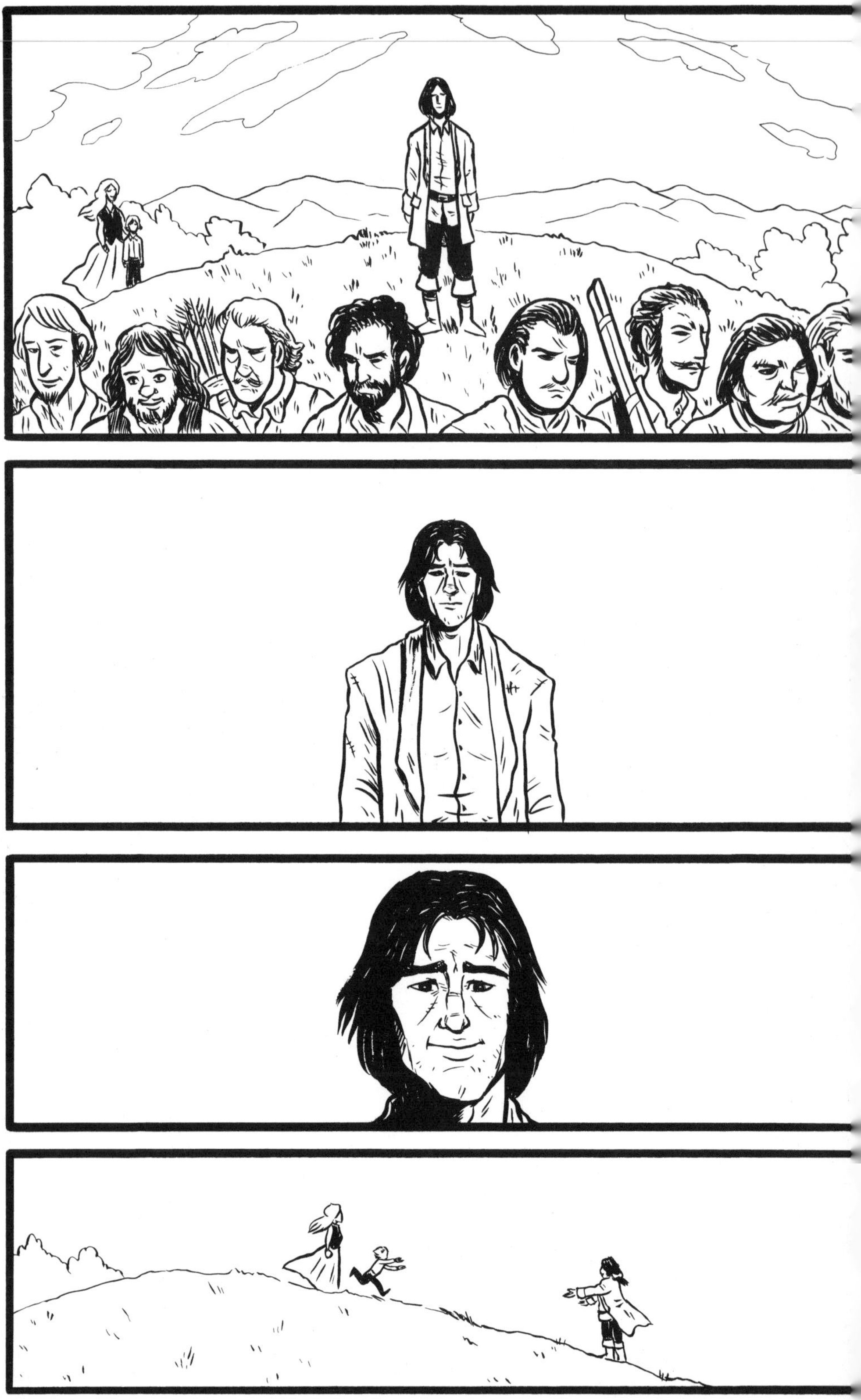

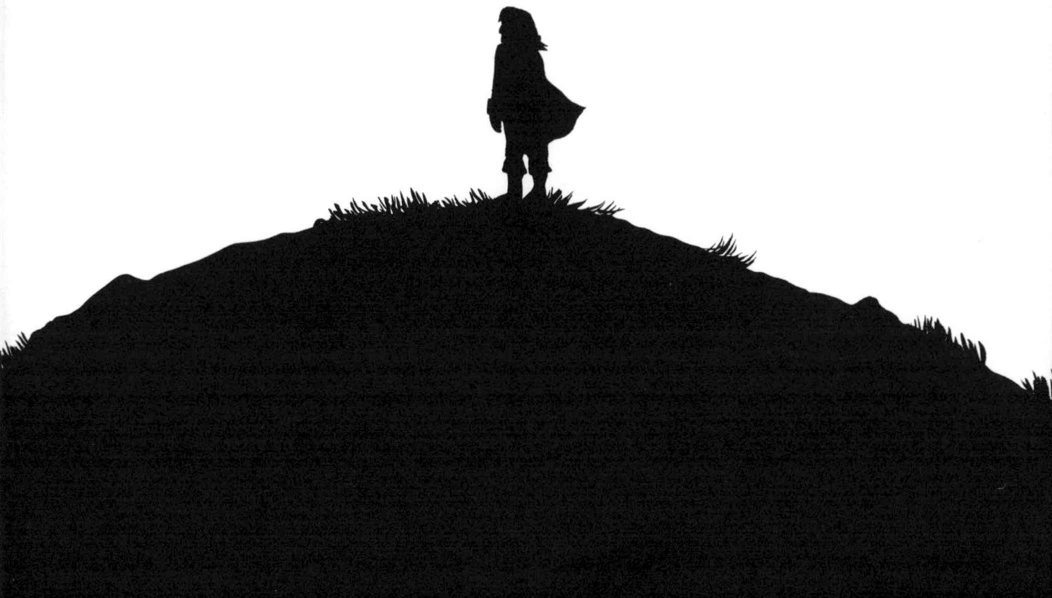

DURING THE GLORIOUS RETURN OF THE WALDENSES, HENRI ARNAUD AND 900 MEN TOOK BACK EVERY ONE OF THEIR VILLAGES. IN THE PROCESS, THEY DEFEATED SEVERAL THOUSAND ARMED TROOPS.

JOSHUA JANAVEL PLANNED THE ENTIRE ENDEAVOR, BUT HE NEVER AGAIN SAW HIS HOMELAND.

HIS BOOK OF MILITARY TACTICS INSPIRED MANY FUTURE GENERALS, INCLUDING NAPOLEON, WHO USED THESE STRATEGIES IN SOME OF HIS MOST SUCCESSFUL CAMPAIGNS.

THE WALDENSIAN UPRISING WAS THE FIRST CASE IN EUROPEAN HISTORY IN WHICH THE SUBJECTS OF A RULER REBELLED TO DEFEND THEIR RELIGIOUS FREEDOM. THESE ACTIONS INSPIRED THE PROTESTANT REFORMATION, THE FRENCH REVOLUTION AND THE AMERICAN REVOLUTION.

DURING WORLD WAR II, THE WALDENSES WERE OFFERED FULL CITIZENSHIP IF THEY WOULD JOIN THE AXIS FORCES. THEY REFUSED. SEEING SIMILARITIES BETWEEN THE PERSECUTION OF THE JEWS AND THEIR OWN STRUGGLES, THEY TOOK UP ARMS ONCE AGAIN AND BECAME LEADERS IN THE ITALIAN RESISTANCE.

MANY WALDENSIANS WERE KILLED IN ACTION. OTHERS WERE EXECUTED FOR HIDING JEWISH REFUGEES, OFTEN IN THE SAME PLACES THE WALDENSES THEMSELVES HAD HIDDEN FROM SOLDIERS CENTURIES BEFORE.

BUT THIS STRUGGLE WON THEM A FINAL FREEDOM.

IN 1948, FOR THE FIRST TIME IN HISTORY, AN ITALIAN CONSTITUTION STATED: "ALL RELIGIOUS CONFESSIONS ARE FREE BEFORE THE LAW."

THE END

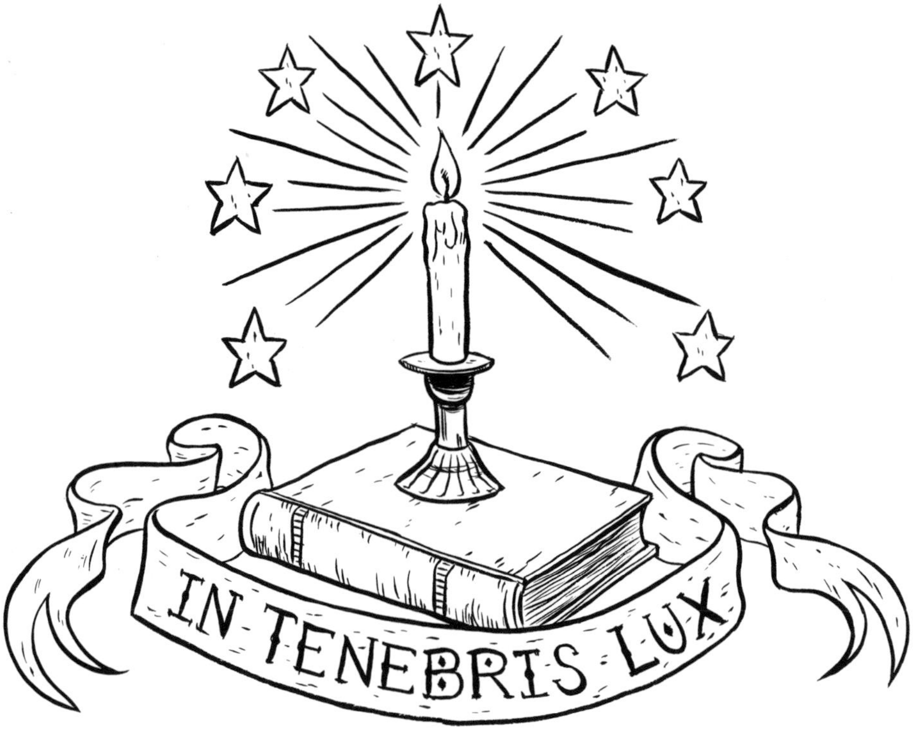
IN TENEBRIS LUX

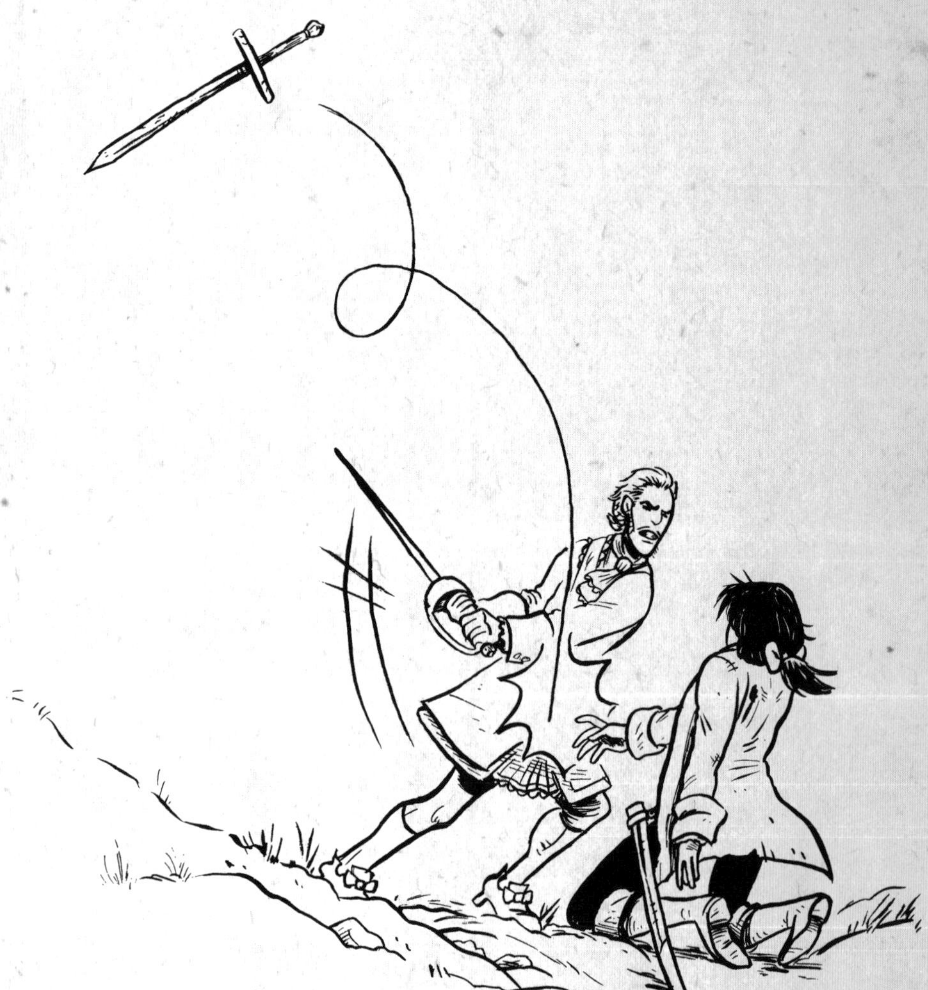

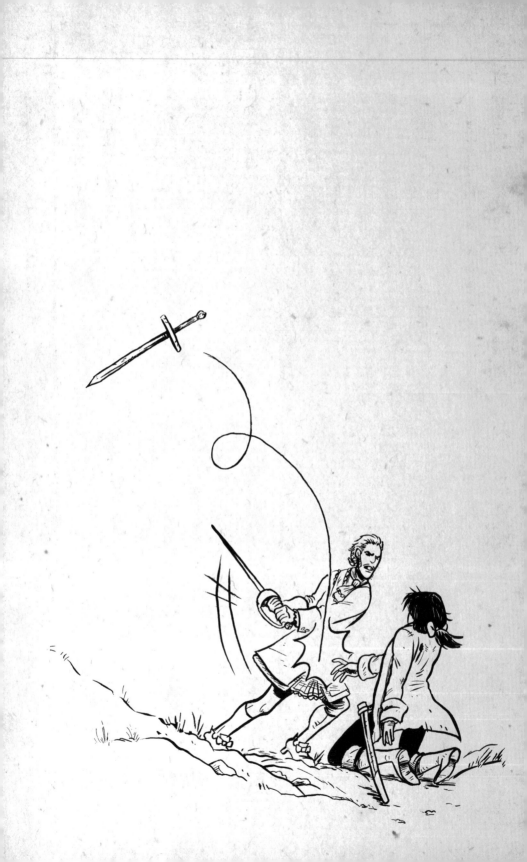

FURTHER READING

FOR THOSE INTERESTED IN FURTHER INFORMATION ABOUT THE
WALDENSIANS AND THEIR HISTORY, WE RECOMMEND THE FOLLOWING:

THE AMERICAN WALDENSIAN SOCIETY
www.waldensian.org

—

THE WALDENSIAN HERITAGE MUSEUM
208 Rodoret Street South
Valdese, NC 28690
828-879-2126
www.waldensianheritagemuseum.org

—

SONNET 18
"ON THE LATE MASSACRE IN PIEDMONT"
The John Milton Reading Room, Dartmouth University
www.dartmouth.edu/~milton/reading_room/sonnets/sonnet_18/text.shtml

FURTHER READING

THE WALDENSIAN DISSENT:
PERSECUTION AND SURVIVAL, C.1170-C.1570
Gabriel Audisio; Claire Davison, *translator*
Cambridge Medieval Textbooks
Cambridge: Cambridge University Press, 1999
ISBN: 0521559847

—

THE REFORMATION OF THE HERETICS:
THE WALDENSES OF THE ALPS, 1450-1560
Euan Cameron
Oxford: Clarendon Press, 1984
ISBN: 0198229305

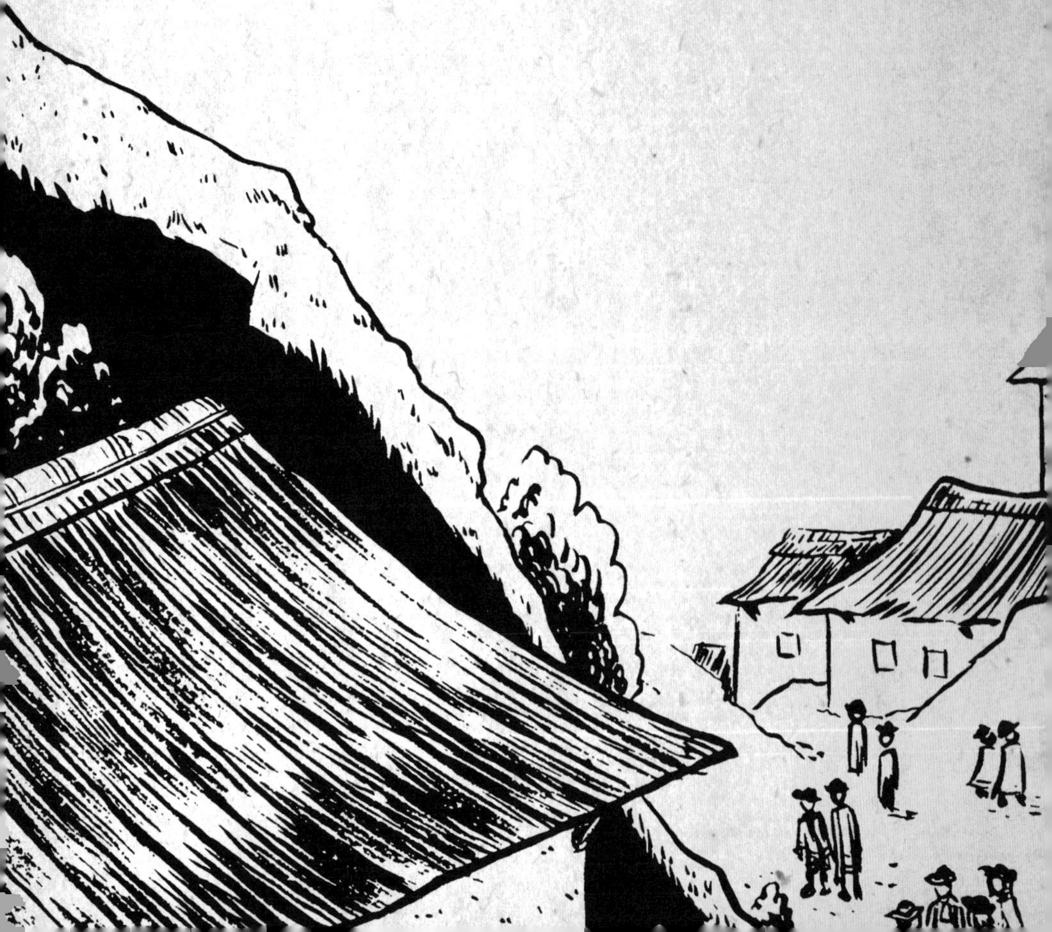

FURTHER READING

THE WALDENSIAN STORY
A Study in Faith, Intolerance and Survival
Prescot Stephens
Lewes: The Book Guild Ltd, 1998
ISBN: 1857762800

—

THE WALDENSES: REJECTIONS OF HOLY CHURCH IN MEDIEVAL EUROPE
Euan Cameron
Polity Press, 2000
ISBN: 0631224971

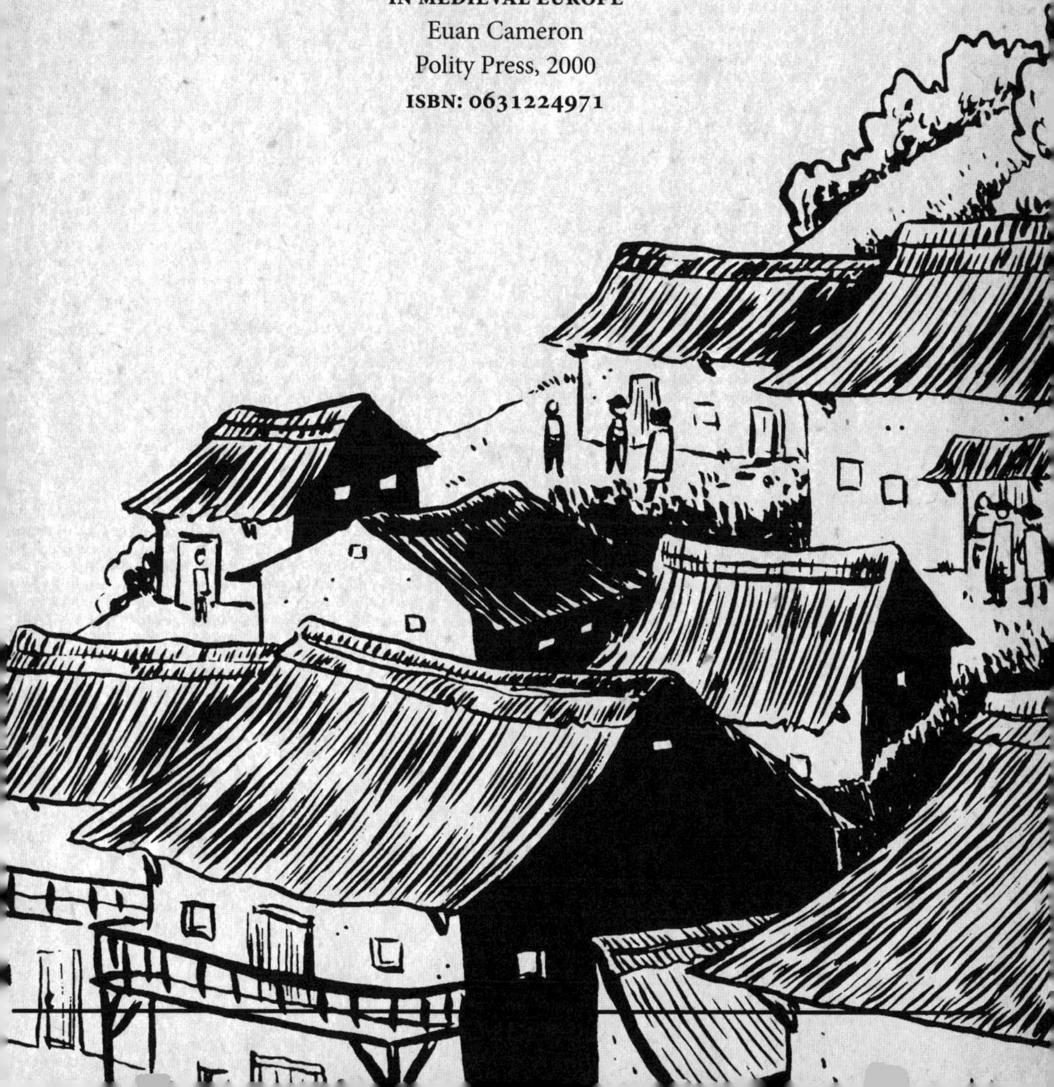

ABOUT THE AUTHORS

New York Times-bestselling writer **CHRISTOS GAGE** has numerous comic book credits, including *Buffy*, *Spider-Man*, and graphic novels *Area 10* and *Sunset*. He wrote and Associate Produced the Larry Clark film *Teenage Caveman* for HBO. Video game credits include *Captain America: Super Soldier*, *Iron Man 3* and *Captain America: The Winter Soldier*. He graduated Brown University and holds a Master's in screenwriting from the American Film Institute.

RUTH FLETCHER GAGE graduated Phi Beta Kappa from UNC Chapel Hill as an IBM/Awalt Scholar in Directing. She attended Oxford University and worked at the Goodman Theater with Tony, Pulitzer and Academy Award winning writers and directors like August Wilson and Steve Tesich. After working for Michael Mann and Jon Landau on *Last Of The Mohicans*, she earned a Master's from the American Film Institute, producing the Directing Workshop for Women and attaching Emmy Award winner Charles S. Dutton to her screenplay. As Development Executive at Thunderbird Pictures, she developed the indie *Klash* and sold *A Place For Us* with Dennis Hopper.

As a team, Ruth and Chris have written screenplays and teleplays for Universal, Sony and Warner Brothers, as well as actors George Clooney and Morgan Freeman; their credits include *The Breed* and *Paradox*. In television, where they've worked with award-winning actors Michael Emerson, Viola Davis and Vincent D'Onofrio, credits include *Numbers* and *Law & Order: SVU*, where Dick Wolf called their episode "Mercy" his favorite and "an incredible paradigm for where the show should be going." Most recently they were hired by Drew Goddard to join the inaugural writing staff of the Marvel/Netflix show *Daredevil*.

ABOUT THE AUTHORS

JACKIE LEWIS is an Atlanta-based comic book creator. She grew up on a steady diet of fantasy movies, dinosaur cartoons, and mutant comics, and nothing's really changed since then. A graduate of both Emory University and SCAD Atlanta, she first studied theater and then made the reasonable switch to comics in 2007. She somehow found a way to get paid for drawing stuff like monsters, cats, and hairy dudes (which is the dream, really). She gets really excited about hand-bound books, tattoos, and video games. Her previous Oni Press work includes *Play Ball* and a short from *Jam: Tales From the World of Roller Derby.*

—

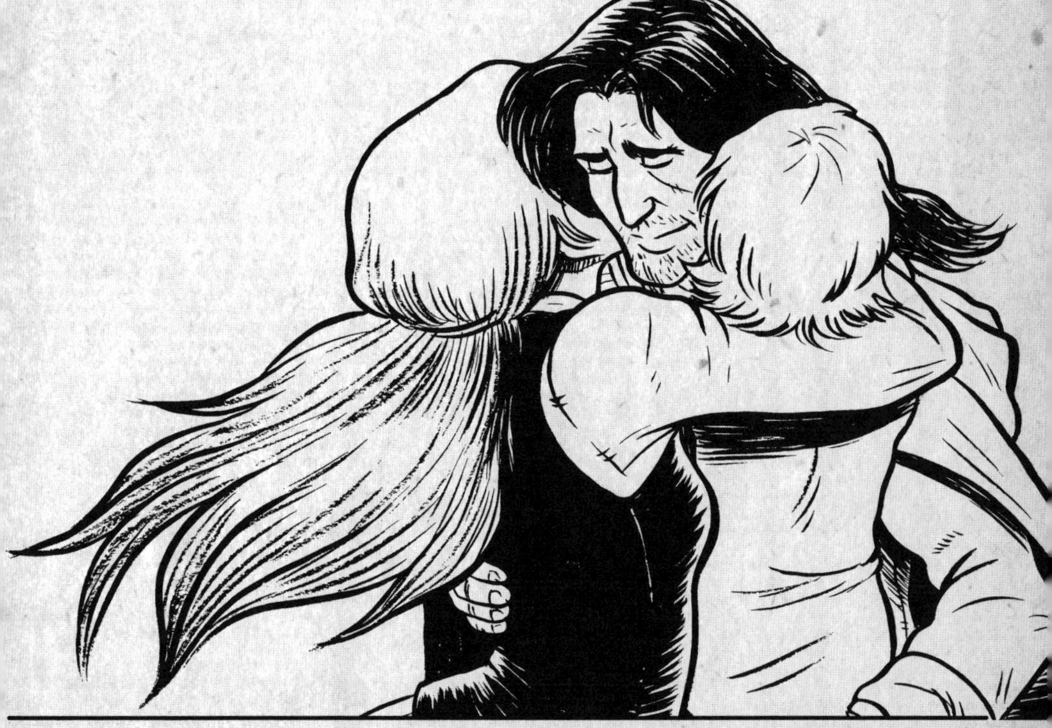

OTHER BOOKS FROM ONI PRESS

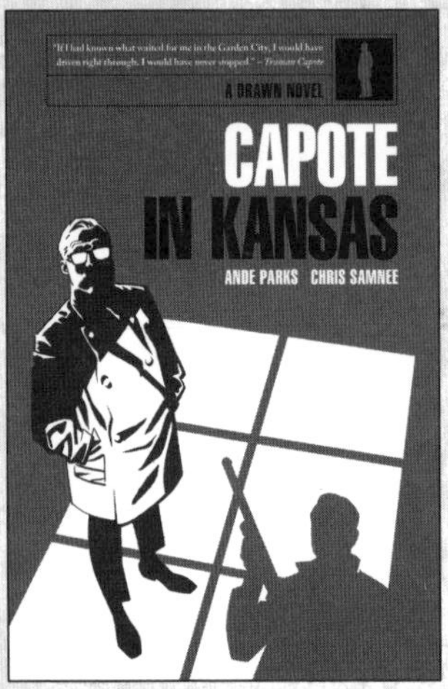
"If I had known what waited for me in the Garden City, I would have driven right through. I would have never stopped." – Truman Capote
A DRAWN NOVEL
CAPOTE IN KANSAS
ANDE PARKS CHRIS SAMNEE

CAPOTE IN KANSAS
By Ande Parks and Chris Samnee
160 pages, Hardcover, B&W
ISBN: 978-1-934964-87-3

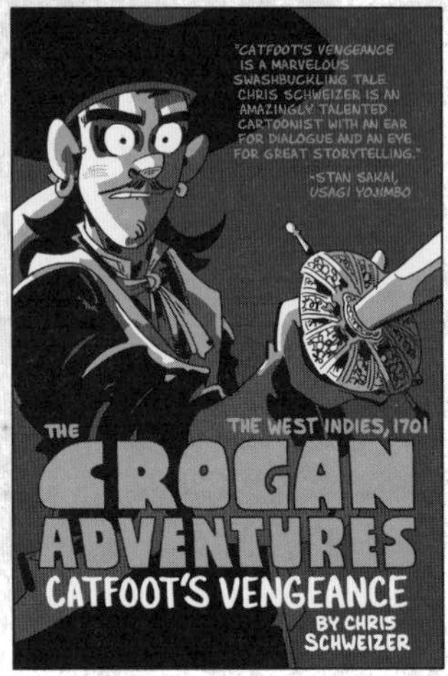
"CATFOOT'S VENGEANCE IS A MARVELOUS SWASHBUCKLING TALE. CHRIS SCHWEIZER IS AN AMAZINGLY TALENTED CARTOONIST WITH AN EAR FOR DIALOGUE AND AN EYE FOR GREAT STORYTELLING."
-STAN SAKAI, USAGI YOJIMBO
THE WEST INDIES, 1701
THE CROGAN ADVENTURES
CATFOOT'S VENGEANCE
BY CHRIS SCHWEIZER

THE CROGAN ADVENTURES: CATFOOT'S VENGEANCE
By Chris Schweizer
200 pages, Softcover, Color
ISBN: 978-1-62010-203-9

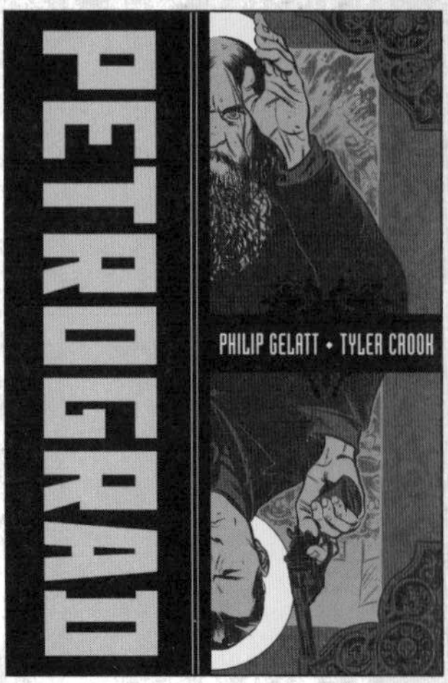
PETROGRAD
PHILIP GELATT • TYLER CROOK

PETROGRAD
By Philip Gelatt and Tyler Crook
264 pages, Hardcover, Two-olor
ISBN: 978-1-934964-44-6

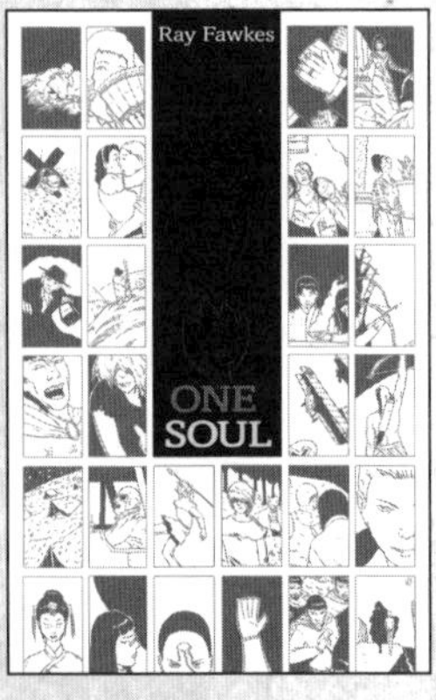
Ray Fawkes
ONE SOUL

ONE SOUL
By Ray Fawkes
176 pages, Hardcover, B&W
ISBN: 978-1-934964-66-8

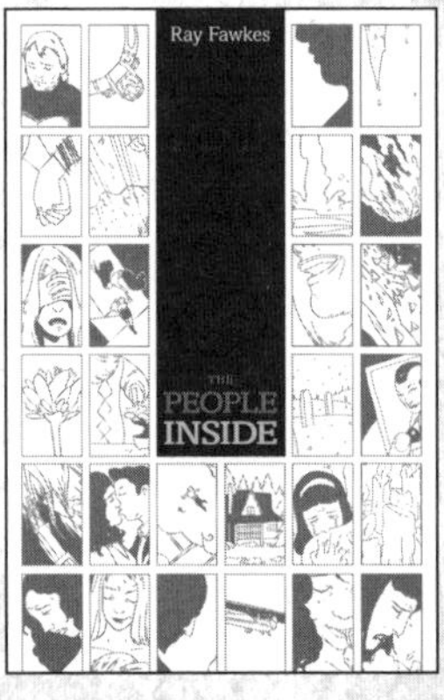
Ray Fawkes
THE PEOPLE INSIDE

THE PEOPLE INSIDE
By Ray Fawkes
144 pages, Hardcover, B&W
ISBN: 978-1-62010-168-1

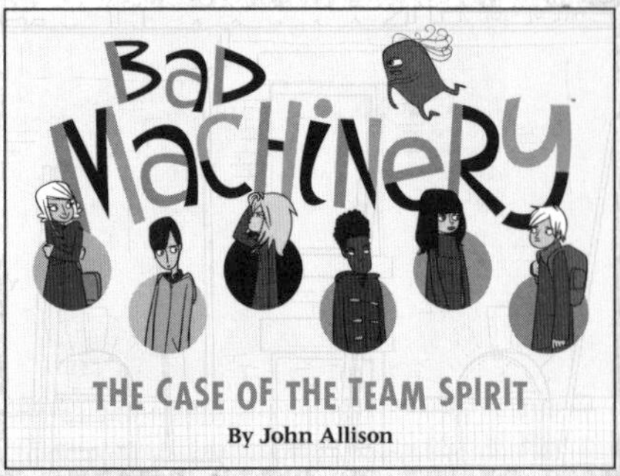
BAD MACHINERY
THE CASE OF THE TEAM SPIRIT
By John Allison

BAD MACHINERY, VOL. 1: THE CASE OF THE TEAM SPIRIT
By John Allison
136 pages, Softcover, Color
ISBN: 978-1-62010-084-4

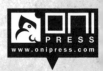

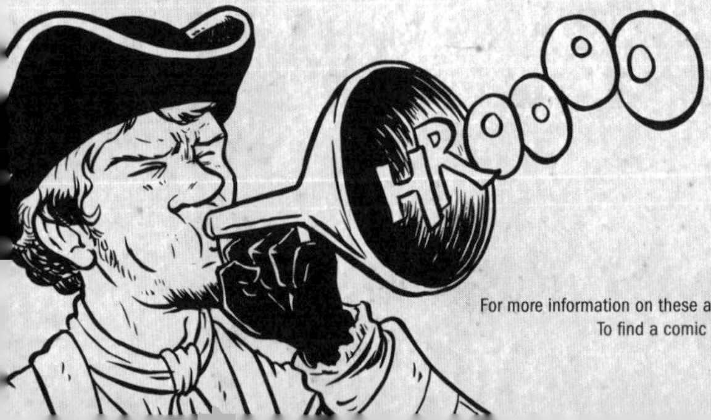
HROOOOO